## About the Writers

Cornelius J. Dyck, the editor of this volume, is director of the Institute of Mennonite Studies and Professor of Historical Theology at the Associated Mennonite Biblical Seminaries, Elkhart-Goshen, Indiana. The other writers are: John H. Yoder and J. C. Wenger of the Associated Seminaries faculty of Goshen-Elkhart; William Keeney of Bluffton College, Bluffton, Ohio; Walter Klaassen of Conrad Grebel College, Waterloo, Ontario; John S. Oyer of Goshen College and editor of *The Mennonite Quarterly Review;* Ernst Crous of Krefeld, Germany; Frank H. Epp of Winnipeg, Manitoba; and Frank C. Peters of Waterloo Lutheran University, Kitchener, Ontario.

## Forward Through the Ages

Forward through the ages, in unbroken line,
Move the faithful spirits, at the call divine;
Gifts in diff'ring measure, hearts of one accord,
Manifold the service, one the sure reward.

> Forward through the ages, in unbroken line,
> Move the faithful spirits, at the call divine.

Wider grows the kingdom, reign of love and light;
For it we must labor, till our faith is sight;
Prophets have proclaimed it, martyrs testified,
Poets sung its glory, heroes for it died.

Not alone we conquer, not alone we fall;
In each loss or triumph, lose or triumph all.
Bound by God's far purpose, in one living whole,
Move we on together, to the shining goal.

*–Frederick L. Hosmer, 1908*

## *Preface*

This is a history of Anabaptist-Mennonite life and thought from the sixteenth century to the present, written particularly for young adults. The progress of scholarly studies of Anabaptism during the past twenty-five years, and the growing unity among Mennonites around the world, seemed to call for a book which would describe in simple terms who the Mennonites are in relation to their sixteenth-century fathers, and in relation to each other. It is intended to introduce students, church study groups, and others to the basic historical and doctrinal developments through four centuries of Anabaptist and Mennonite efforts to be the faithful church.

The manuscript for this volume was prepared under the direction of the Institute of Mennonite Studies, in which the editor serves as director and John H. Yoder as associate director. The Institute is a research agency of the Associated Mennonite Biblical Seminaries of Elkhart and Goshen, Indiana. It is a pleasure to acknowledge here the generous help of Dr. John H. Yoder, who not only wrote chapters 2, 3, and 8, but critically read all of the others as well. Equally significant has been the help of the following: Dr. William Keeney of Bluffton College, Ohio, who wrote chapters 6, 7, and 19; Dr. Walter Klaassen of Conrad Grebel College, Waterloo, Ontario, who wrote chapters 5, 18, and part of 20; Dr. John Oyer of Goshen College, Goshen, Indiana, who wrote chapter 4; and Dr. J. C. Wenger of the Goshen College Biblical Seminary, who wrote chapters 11, 12, and 13. Each of these men also participated in the planning of the entire manuscript and in a critical reading of most of the chapters.

Appreciation is herewith also expressed to Dr. Ernst Crous of Krefeld, Germany, Dr. Frank H. Epp of Winnipeg, Manitoba, and Dr. Frank C. Peters of Kitchener, Ontario, for preparing rough drafts of chapters 9, 10, and 15 respectively. The writers generously allowed the editor to use his editorial privileges in the interest of achieving a relative uniformity of style. It is hoped, however, that the chapters still retain the unique approach and content organization of each writer. The editor was directly responsible for the writing of chapters

5

1, 14, 16, 17, most of 20, and 21. *The Mennonite Encyclopedia* has kindly granted permission for the use of the maps appearing on pages 74, 161, and 162. Mrs. Evelyn Habegger's patient and efficient secretarial work is here gratefully acknowledged.

C. J. D.

World Day of Prayer, 1966
Elkhart, Indiana

# Contents

## Maps and Charts

# Chapter 1

# THE CHURCH
# BEFORE THE REFORMATION

THE REFORMATION was a sixteenth-century move-ment in Europe to reform the church. Sometimes October 31, 1517, is given as the date of its beginning, since on that day Martin Luther posted ninety-five theses about the church for discussion in the Wittenberg university community, but other dates and occasions are also used. The events which triggered the Reformation were spiritual in origin, but combined with the political, social, and economic forces of that time to bring about radical changes in the life and thought of the western world. In some ways these changes marked the end of the Middle Ages and a beginning of the modern era.

At the center of these developments was a strong desire to reform the church. All through the Middle Ages the voices of councils, clergy, kings, and lay people had been crying for an end to the corruption and worldliness of the body of Christ. Those who saw greed as the biggest sin urged economic reforms, those who deplored the scandal of illiterate and often immoral clergy urged reform of the priesthood, and those who saw the pride and power of the papacy as the root of all evil called for more church councils to exercise control. By the year 1500, many proposals for reform had been heard, but there was little agreement among them about how and where these might be carried out. All, however, seemed to agree on one point–that reformation meant a return of the church to its original purity. The Reformation was a backward-looking movement. Somewhere along the way the church had fallen and needed to return to a virtue it had once possessed. The precise point of the fall in history might be debated, but the fact of the fall was doubted by very few. A brief review of the pre-Reformation life of the church will help us to understand more fully the dramatic events of the early sixteenth century and their influence upon us.

*Persecution:* Soon after Pentecost the church which Jesus Christ had founded suffered persecution. The baptism with water and by the Spirit was followed by the baptism of blood. Hated by the Jews and suspected by the Romans as "enemies of the human race" (Tacitus), the shape of the cross became the shape of the new life in Christ for His disciples:

They were stoned, they were sawn in two, they were killed with the sword; they went about in skins of sheep and goats, destitute, afflicted, ill-treated—of whom the world was not worthy—wandering over deserts and mountains, and in dens and caves of the earth (Hebrews 11:37, 38, RSV).

But "the blood of martyrs is seed" (Tertullian). By mid-second century the *Epistle to Diognetus* reminded the persecutors that they were fighting a losing battle: "Do you not see that the more of them are punished, the more do others increase? These things do not seem to come from a human power; they are a mighty act of God; they are proofs of His presence." Fifty years later Tertullian answered critics of the faith with the words, "We are but of yesterday, and we have filled everything you have—cities, tenements, forts, towns, exchanges, yes! and camps, tribes, palace, senate, forum." [1] The church was everywhere, from North Africa to Europe, and from Rome to Asia Minor and India; it was adapting to its environment, and it was being accepted by more and more of the people.

*Constantine:* A new era began for the church when Constantine became emperor of Rome early in the fourth century. The tables were suddenly turned: Christians were now the royal favorites while non-Christians were persecuted. Those who a few years before had suffered grievously under Diocletian, could now draw on state funds to build churches and to support ministers. Sunday was decreed a public day of rest and worship. As emperor, Constantine wrote well-meaning letters of instruction to the clergy, though he himself was not a baptized Christian, and enforced the discipline of the church with the power of the state. He called the clergy together at state expense to consider basic issues of the faith, and often chaired their meetings personally. Why he did all this is not clear. He had seen that the church could not easily be destroyed by persecution, he needed an appealing state religion to unify the empire, and he may himself have been attracted to the Christian faith. Whatever the reasons, from that time on church and state went hand in hand. Though they were to quarrel often in

10

the centuries to come, no one seriously questioned this *Constantinian synthesis* for over 1,000 years. A Christian society into which all persons were born as citizens, and baptized in infancy as Christians, seemed to be the fulfillment of God's plan for mankind. Nevertheless, it was this development which the Anabaptists of the sixteenth century were to identify as the fall of the church.

The church now faced the enormous task of making society Christian, and absorbing into its own life the masses of people who had become members without knowing it. This already hopeless undertaking was doomed to certain failure soon after it began, by the infiltration into the Roman Empire, and therefore into the church, of thousands upon thousands of Goths, Vandals, and other barbarian tribes from the North. By A.D. 500 all of Italy was under the rule of their king Theodoric (d. 526). Much of northern Europe was ruled by Clovis (d. 511), who became a Christian because, like Constantine, he believed that God had given him victory in battle. Soon vast masses of people in the church were little more than baptized heathens. Externally the church prospered. Some of the old glory of the disintegrating Roman Empire came to be associated with the papacy. As spiritual successors of the Apostle Peter, and political successors in Rome of the emperors who had moved to Constantinople, the bishops (popes) of Rome soon became the most powerful men in Europe. They had the most income, the largest armies, the best scholars, and the most influence since the people believed them to be the only authorized representatives of God on earth, following in the steps of St. Peter.

*A double standard:* There were those, of course, who protested against the worldliness of the church. Hermits arose to live in lonely and desert places, torturing their bodies to liberate the spirit for communion with God. Monks banded together to build monasteries in which they could escape the sin and temptation of a wicked world by giving themselves to endless prayer and fasting. But instead of calling all Christians to imitate the dedication of these men, the church made saints out of these few. Instead of leading to a general repentance, the lives of these few stimulated the developing double moral standard. By a system of spiritual bookkeeping the excess merit which these saints were assumed to possess was transferred to those who seemed unable to or did not want to live a godly life. Soon lay people were not expected to live on the same moral and spiritual level as saints or even clergy.

*Some tried to renew the church:* Reforms of a more general nature were actually attempted during the Middle Ages, and they did

11

make an impact here and there, but they also served to accent even more the deep-seated problems of the church. Among these reforms was, for example, the Rule of Benedict, which did much to improve the quality of life in the monasteries after the sixth century. Early in the seventh century Gregory the Great prepared new forms of worship, and sent missionaries to England, which led to a return missionary program from England to the continent under Boniface in the eighth century. In the ninth century King Charlemagne, with great zeal and rather limited ability, did what he could to revitalize the church. In the tenth century the monastic reforms of Cluny touched most of the monasteries of Europe, and in the eleventh priests were forbidden to marry, in order to prevent them from being a hereditary caste with inherited power and wealth. In the twelfth century the Franciscans, Dominicans, and other priestly orders arose to teach, preach, and serve among the people. And in the thirteenth century Innocent III convened a council to reform the church, while Thomas Aquinas hammered out a theological system which attempted to pull together all the traditions of the church into a meaningful faith. So impressive did all these developments seem even to later historians, that they called the thirteenth the greatest of all centuries, the century of faith.

Yet none of these reforms turned the church in a new direction, and the external power of the church over the world continued to increase. By the ninth century, for example, almost one-half of the land in Europe was under the control of the church, which therefore increasingly considered itself responsible for the total welfare of all men. It became ever more difficult for the church to limit itself to spiritual affairs while leaving secular things to the authorities of the state. By the twelfth century the authority of the church was almost universal, and little happened without its consent. Princes and statesmen, bankers and scholars were subject to its will. As the moon shines only by the reflected light of the sun, so the glory and power of the state is only a reflection of the greater glory and power of the church, it was said.

*The Crusades:* But the very success of the church became its undoing. Under an illusion of pious grandeur Pope Urban II launched the Crusades in 1096, to recover the Holy Land from the Turks; instead of fighting each other, let Christians fight against the enemies of God. The sword became the missionary instrument of the church. All who went to fight were assured of the full remission of the penalties for their sins, and tens of thousands went in repeated waves until the

12

thirteenth century. There was even a children's Crusade in 1212. The wealthy, and those who could not go, were able to buy indulgences granting the same remission as those who went received, a development which was to become the direct cause of Luther's protest in 1517. The Crusades brutalized the life of the church. By 1208 Innocent III could declare a Crusade in Europe itself, against the Cathari of France. When a Crusader asked how he might know the heretical Cathari from true believers, he was told to kill them all since the Lord would know His own and could sort them out when they knocked on the gates of heaven.

*Other problems of the church*: To the heritage of the Crusade was added the burden of rising nationalism, which brought grave financial problems for the church with it. The papacy went bankrupt. From its zenith in 1200, the prestige of the papacy fell to an all-time low in 1300. To the fiscal chaos was added the burden of division. For seventy-three years, from 1305 to 1378, the papal court was in a "Babylonian Captivity" at Avignon and at the mercy of the French kings. When it returned to Rome, there were suddenly two popes and then three popes excommunicating each other, all claiming to be the sole representative of Christ on earth. Though councils were convened and the schism finally healed in 1417, even the simpleminded were under no illusions about the spirituality of the church. The clergy were ill-trained and often greedy or simply hungry. The rich could purchase heaven itself, while the poor were consigned to purgatory or even hell because they could not pay the fees demanded by the church for its services. The sacramental system beginning with baptism and ending with extreme unction as last rite controlled the temporal and eternal destiny of every person. The people knew no access to God except through the creaking machinery of the church. And so the voices calling for reform grew ever stronger, and could not be silenced.

*Late medieval piety*: The voice of the common people was among those calling for reform. Late medieval piety clung frantically to the penance system. The plague, war, and superstition made everyone long for a guaranteed escape from hell. These the church offered in abundance indeed. Woodcuts were the Bible of the common man, but printed Bibles were also available and read. No fewer than twenty-five editions of the Gospels and epistles, twenty-two editions of the Psalms, and eighteen editions of the entire Bible were published in Germany before 1517. More popular were the relics of saints, and pilgrimages to shrines often assumed epidemic proportions. In 1509, Frederick the Wise had 5,005 relic items, of which the viewing of each gave one hundred days' remission from purgatory. A grand total reduction of 500,000 years of purgatory could be obtained at Wittenberg. At Halle over three million years could be secured. Among these relics were hay from the manger at Bethlehem, twigs from the burning bush of Moses, the thumb of St. Anne (mother of Mary), a part of the diaper of the baby Jesus, and a feather from the wing of the archangel Michael. Unending repetition of liturgical prayers was also a comfort and guarantee of safe passage to heaven. One sisterhood recorded 6,455 masses, 3,550 psalters, 200,000 rosary prayers, 200,000 Te Deums, 63,000 times 10,000 Our Fathers, and Ave Marias too numerous to count.

Particular reliance was placed upon the help of saints. Every ache and pain was believed to have a saint to guard against it–St. Vitus guarded against epilepsy, St. Denice against headache and rabies, St. Margaret against insanity–and so an unending host of helpers in need. None were called on more frequently than Mary, for whom veneration increased enormously in the twelfth and following centuries. Folk piety had to have a sinless Mary to intercede for them with the sinless Christ. Mary was considered the second Eve–as the disobedience of the first Eve had made the coming of Christ necessary, so the obedience of the second Eve (Mary) had made it possible. Miracles were no problem; they seemed to happen every day in the lives of the simple and God-fearing people. The line between fear of death and hell, miracle, and superstition was very thin. The devil and his seduction became a dominant theme in literature, art, and conversation. He was a real competitor with God for the soul of the miserable sinner. Some people, of course, did not care but many were afraid. They thought that the end of the world was near, and God seemed far away; they longed for a personal rather than an institutional church relationship to God.

*Preparing the Way*

The Reformation did not come unannounced, though the way in which it shook the very foundations of Europe was unexpected. The influence of the Crusades and of the Renaissance, the rise of nationalism and its inevitable clash with the international papal church, the corruption of the clergy and the church, the growing restlessness of the common people all became signs that a major storm was about to break out.

Not least among these signs were men and movements which helped to prepare the way for a spiritual breakthrough such as the Reformation was to bring. Consciously or unconsciously the reformers of the sixteenth century stood on the shoulders of these men and movements, achieving what they did because of them. We think, for example, of Francis of Assisi (d. 1226), who became a living reproach of the greed and wealth of the church, and who recaptured in his own life what it means to be a disciple of Christ. We think also of Girolamo Savonarola, the Billy Graham of the fifteenth century, who was hanged in Florence in 1498, because of his preaching. And there were many others!

Among these others were three men and two groups of men whose thought and work was particularly instrumental in preparing the way for the Reformation. The men were Peter Waldo, John Wyclif, and John Hus; the groups of men were the Mystics and the Humanists. Waldo, Wyclif, and Hus were men of deep conviction. They were also men of action. The Mystics and the Humanists were not reformers, but their spiritual and intellectual leadership prepared the way for the men of action and created the kind of climate in the minds of the people which made reform possible. We turn now to a brief discussion of these pioneers.

*Peter Waldo (d. ca. 1218):* In 1176, the song of a minstrel stirred a deep longing in the heart of Waldo, a rich merchant of Lyon, France. Upon asking a theologian for the best way to God, he was quoted Matthew 19:21: "If you would be perfect, go, sell what you possess and give to the poor, and you will have treasure in heaven; and come, follow me." A new life began for Waldo with this verse. He sold his property, resolving to be as poor as Jesus and the apostles had been. His wife and family received enough to support them. Then he began to study the New Testament, memorizing favorite passages, and reciting them to whoever would listen, together with his own interpretation of the passage. Within a year he was joined by others and the group eventually became known as Waldensians. They called themselves the *Poor in Spirit,* and asked the Third Lateran Council in 1179 for permission to preach as laymen. This was denied, but they felt compelled by God to continue nevertheless, and severe persecution followed for almost 700 years. Relative freedom was granted them in Italy only in 1848, where the largest groups came to live.

At the heart of the Waldensian reform movement was a love for the Scriptures, and a desire to put into practice in their own lives what they read in them. They studied the Bible together in small group meetings. In their writings the Word of God is called

. . . salvation for the soul of the poor, a tonic for the weak, food for the hungry, teaching for the true, comfort unto the chastened, the cessation of slander and the acquisition of virtue.

15

Even as they who are assailed by the enemy flee to a strong tower so do the assailed saints betake themselves to the Holy Scripture. There they find weapons against heresies, armor against the assaults of the devil, the assaults of the flesh, the glory of the world. [2]

Because they placed special emphasis on the New Testament and obedience to the words of Jesus recorded in Matthew 5, 6, and 7, they became known as the Sermon on the Mount people. And, because they were convinced that the Scriptures held the answer to the problems of men, they traveled all over Europe two by two, preaching, witnessing, and suffering for the sake of Christ. The neglect of the Scriptures in Roman Catholicism was to them a certain sign that the church had indeed fallen from the faith.

The Waldensians were not Protestants before the Reformation, but Christians who took the Word of God seriously. They rejected the mass, purgatory, and participation in warfare as unbiblical, but continued to practice infant baptism. They believed that every Christian, whether man or woman, was called to witness to his faith by living it and preaching it. So effective were they in this lay witnessing that long before the Reformation a Roman Catholic leader wrote, "one third of Christendom if not more has attended illicit Waldensian conventicles [meetings] and is at heart Waldensian." [3] Numerous attempts to link the Anabaptists historically with the Waldensians have failed, but through them the spiritual soil was being prepared for the events of the sixteenth century.

*John Wyclif (d. 1384):* A man who prepared the way for Martin Luther and other reformers much more than the Waldensians was John Wyclif, the "Morning Star of the Reformation." Wyclif was professor at Oxford University and became a reformer only in the last decade of his life. He had long believed that the church should be poor as were the apostles and that Christ had given it authority over spiritual matters only. It was when he met representatives of the pope at Bruges in 1374 that he gave up all hope of reform through councils and clergy.

On his return to England he called upon the king to take the initiative in reforming the church by force, if necessary. At the same time, however, he urged that the Scriptures be made available to all people as the only certain ground for reform; "Holy Scripture is the highest authority for every Christian and the standard of faith and of all human perfection." [4] Because his hope for reform rested with a recovery of the Word of God by the people, he trained men to memorize long passages and recite them as they traveled through the country. These "poor preachers" or "Lollards," as they were called, were really traveling evangelists in England.

In the meantime, Wyclif's own Biblical studies led him to reject the pope as necessary for the church. The church, he said, is made up of those whom God elects for salvation. He also rejected the papal interpretation of the Lord's Supper as being the actual flesh and blood of Christ, saying that the bread and wine are symbols or signs of the work and grace of Christ. He considered indulgences, which were taken to forgive sin, to be the work of the devil, and he taught that priests should marry. The work of the clergy is acceptable before God only, he said, if they themselves lead holy lives; those who did not should be removed from office by the state.

Because he had powerful protectors among the nobles, who wanted him to succeed for their own selfish interests, Wyclif died a natural death. Later, his bones were dug up, burned, and cast on the River Swift, often the practice with heretics. His books were also burned. Nevertheless, he, like the Waldensians, had pioneered in the recovery of the authority of the Scriptures over the life of the church. He had drawn attention to the corruption in the church and pointed to solutions. He was one of the greatest English preachers before the Reformation. Later, in 1572, a picture was published in Bohemia showing Wyclif striking a spark, Hus kindling the coals with it, and Luther holding up the flaming torch. A monument to the Reformation in Worms shows Luther surrounded by four men, Waldo, Wyclif, Hus, and Savonarola.

*John Hus (d. 1415):* The central events in the life of Hus are quickly told. As a professor at the university of Prague he became a major leader of the reform movement in Bohemia. In this he was guided by the writings of Wyclif, but he placed less reliance on the reforming ability of the state, and he developed a deeper understanding of the nature of the church. With Wyclif he urged the study of the Scriptures by the people and based his own arguments on them without rejecting tradition as strongly as Wyclif did.

His preaching and reform proposals were extremely popular. Because he attacked the papacy, the corruption of the clergy, and other problems of the church–especially the sale of indulgences–he lost the support of the bishops and of King Wenceslas. He went into hiding with friends in the country and continued his reform writing. It was during this period that he wrote his treatise on the church. The church, he said, is not where the pope is, but where two or three are gathered in the name of Christ. Similarly it is not the pope but the Holy Spirit who gives unity to the church. Nor does the pope have any power to include or exclude people from heaven; this power of the keys is held by the believing church under the guidance of the Holy Spirit and consists in preaching, witnessing, counseling, church discipline, and the Lord's Supper.

Because he was accused of heresy and rejected the authority of the pope, Hus repeatedly declared his desire to defend his views before a general council of the church. When such a council convened at Constance to end the schism in the church, and he was asked to appear before it, he went. Though his friends warned him of the dangers to his life, he said:

I confide altogether in my Saviour. I trust that He will accord me His Holy Spirit to fortify me in His truth, so that I may face with courage temptations, prison, and if necessary a cruel death. [5]

Emperor Sigismund issued a safe-conduct guarantee for him, but after his arrival in Constance he spent most of his time in prison. Instead of presenting his teachings to the council fathers, they put him on trial for his life as a heretic. Pope John 23, who was a wicked man and had reportedly been a pirate before his ordination, pressed for his condemnation. His fate was sealed. From his prison he wrote:

It is better to die well than to live ill. One should not flinch before the sentence of death. To finish the present life in grace is to go away from pain and misery. He who fears death loses the joy of life. Above all else truth triumphs. He conquers who dies, because no adversity can hurt the one over whom iniquity holds no sway. [6]

He was given one last chance to recant, which he refused. Then they put a paper crown on his head with three demons on it and the words, "We commit your soul to the devil," after which they took him outside of the city and burned him to ashes. The date was July 6, 1415.

So effectively had John Hus prepared the way for the Reformation that 105 years later Martin Luther said, "We are all Hussites without knowing it." In the intervening century, however, bloody Hussite wars devastated the land as his followers struggled for religious and political independence. A Crusade was eventually launched against them. Most of them finally made their peace with Roman Catholicism, but some continued separately as the Bohemian Brethren, known today as the Moravians.

*The Mystics:* Influencing the thought and work of these reformers, and of the entire Middle Ages, were the Mystics, men and women who cultivated an inner, personal religion and practiced the presence of God. The Mystic sought union with God. Personal, firsthand experience was for him the final authority in matters of faith. The church with its priests, sacraments, and traditions was not rejected; all of its rites and ceremonies could, in fact, help the Mystic along in his spiritual pilgrimage, but they were not really necessary. God could be known best, they believed, through self-denial, contemplation, and intuition. The master key to the knowledge of God was love.

There were almost as many kinds of mysticism in the Middle Ages as there were Mystics. In Bernard of Clairvaux (d. 1153), who has sometimes been called the father of western mysticism, we find a man of orthodox Catholic theology who could lose himself completely in the love of God, and who was still one of the most active church reformers of all time, giving himself completely to the service of others. Hugh (d. 1141) of St. Victor near Paris was much more intellectual by inclination, yet his mysticism is apparent, for example, in his description of the three levels of faith. On the lowest level the Christian believes what the church teaches because the church says it is true; on the second level he believes it because his reason tells him it makes sense; and on the highest level he believes it because he knows by inner experience what the church and reason have already told him to be true.

Very different from the ideas of either of these men were the visions of Joachim of Fiore (d. 1202) in Italy. Instead of relying on the Scriptures as had Waldo, and as Wyclif and Hus were to do, Joachim felt himself to be completely taught by the Holy Spirit, but he did use the books of Daniel and Revelation to support his interpretation of history. A new, third age lay ahead for the world, to be followed by the millennium in which the elect of God would be supreme. This crisis theology influenced many churchmen to count the days till the end of the world would come, even in the sixteenth century, graphically reaffirming the then common belief that the end of all things was at hand.

Of great importance in the development of Luther's thought were the German Mystics Master Eckhart (d. 1327) and John Tauler (d. 1361) as well as an anonymous book called *A German Theology*. Luther was not a Mystic, but the writings of these men and the *German Theology* mirrored the longing for God which he himself felt and which drove him unrelentingly to find a gracious God. These Mystics wanted to remain faithful members of the Roman Catholic Church, but the corruption within it shocked them. They wanted the church reformed and believed this could only come about through a deeper commitment to the inner voice and work of the Spirit. Their utter abandonment to the will of God is reflected in Luther's later willingness to face any threat regardless of the personal consequences for himself.

In the Netherlands mysticism was particularly at home among the Brethren of the Common Life, the most famous of whom was possibly Thomas a Kempis (d. 1471), author of *The Imitation of Christ*. In contrast to many earlier Mystics, the Brethren of the Common Life were serious and able students of the Bible. They tended to take its message quite literally and personally, as a result of which following in the footsteps of Jesus became their highest goal. This piety came to be known as the *devotio moderna* or new devotion, and did much to make Christ available to the common man in simple form. During the fifteenth century they established many schools which soon gained an excellent reputation for piety and learning. Both Erasmus and Luther studied under the Brethren, but neither seemed to enjoy the experience particularly. The influence of the schools was clearly evident, nevertheless, in the later work of both.

*The Humanists:* It is possible that humanism did more to prepare the way for the coming of the Reformation than any other single man or movement in the later Middle Ages. Humanism was the life and spirit of the Renaissance, which in turn was the fourteenth- and fifteenth-century recovery of the ancient culture of Greece and Rome. Humanism was this-worldly, called on people to shift their gaze from heaven to the earth around them, and rejected many of the irrational superstitions and customs of the age. It expressed itself in a flowering of the arts and sciences—the poetry of Dante (d. 1321) and Petrarch (d. 1374), the sculpture of Donatello (d. 1466), the architecture of Alberti (d. 1472), the painting of da Vinci (d. 1519) and Michelangelo (d. 1564), and a multitude of other creative masters. Humanism was inspired by a new spirit of freedom and inquiry which found ample moral and financial support in the papacy as the great patron of the arts. Unfortunately the same papacy strongly resisted similar change and progress in the life of the church, especially when it touched the prestige and finances of the pope.

The humanists north of the Alps generally had a stronger religious concern than those in Italy, giving themselves more to Biblical studies than to classical souces. As Christian humanists they were also concerned with the problems of the church, though they did not usually participate in action programs of reform; their tools were a pen, a critical intellect, satire, humor, and thorough scholarship. Humanist circles could be found in most of the major universities and cities, and everywhere they were respected, hated, feared, and loved. In these circles and throughout Europe, no one was more respected than Desiderius Erasmus (d. 1536), the "prince of the humanists." As a young man Luther almost worshiped Erasmus, writing to him, "Where is he in whom Erasmus does not control the inner thoughts, does not teach, does not rule . . . ?" but by 1524 he called him a babbler and a skeptic and felt he was undercutting the Reformation. And yet in some ways the old saying that Erasmus laid the egg which Luther hatched is right.

Erasmus and Luther had many things in common. Both deplored the corruption of the clergy and the papacy and the stranglehold which the sacraments had upon the people; both emphasized the central place Scripture should have in the life of the church; both taught the importance of Christ for the believer. Nevertheless, the two men were very different. Erasmus was scholarly and polite; Luther could be vulgar and dogmatic. Erasmus believed reform could come to the church without destroying its unity; Luther was a man of action ready to die for his faith. Erasmus was always ready to talk–he did not have martyrs' blood in his veins; Luther came to be a reformer because of his personal search for faith. Erasmus had more of a detached scholar's interest in Reformation issues. There were also basic differences in understanding the faith. Luther saw salvation primarily as grace, Erasmus primarily as ethics–imitating Christ. Luther held man to be a miserable sinner, while Erasmus, together with all humanists, stressed the fundamental goodness of man. Luther might be described as crying, "Back to the Bible," while Erasmus might have asked, "What is the Bible?"

In all of this Erasmus represented the best in humanism. The Reformation would not have been possible, it seems, without the humanists' recovery of the Scriptures and of Biblical scholarship. Their sharp pens goaded the church to act where the actions of the reformers often caused a reaction. The humanists added spiritual depth to the church by stressing the inward and personal dimension of faith, where the reformers were often forced to quarrel over doctrine or external church issues. Yet all of the major reformers had a humanist education and were scholars in their own right–Luther wrote much more than Erasmus, and during his university student days was known as "the learned philosopher"–but at a given point each of the reformers became deeply and personally involved in the life and problems of the church. How the humanists' vision of gradual reform through education, criticism, and patience would have worked out we will never know.

## The Lutheran Reformation

The Lutheran Reformation centered in Wittenberg, Germany, where Martin Luther was professor of theology at the university from 1512 until his death in 1546. His road to becoming a theologian, prophet, and reformer had been a stormy one because of his own inner struggles of faith. He had learned that man must love God and do good works in order to be saved, but he could not love God—he was terribly afraid of Him—and he was constantly seeing himself as a sinner. All the well-meant counsel of friends did not change this fear of God and this awareness of himself as a sinner. God was angry with him, he said, and would send him straight to hell if he should die.

In desperation he finally became a monk, as he later said, "against the wishes of my father, of my mother, of God, and of the devil." Surely he would find peace as a holy man and learn to love God. His doubts continued, however, though he fasted and prayed more than other monks. His studies led him deep into the Scriptures and he became a very effective and popular teacher at the university. It was while lecturing on the Book of Galatians and then Romans that the final breakthrough came for him. One day, while studying in his little tower room, he discovered the real meaning of the words of the Apostle Paul in Romans 1:17, "He who through faith is righteous shall live"; God is not angry with man, He loves him; not because of what man does for God, but because of what God does for man in Christ. Man is justified by faith in Christ, not by good works. After discovering this Luther could finally say, "Now I felt myself newborn and in Paradise. All the Holy Scriptures looked different to me. . . . This passage in Paul appeared to me as the gate of Paradise."

This experience of the grace of God was at the heart of Luther's zeal. He now became an extremely busy man, preaching, writing, counseling, and traveling. He was commanded to come to Rome to be tried for heresy, but he remembered the fate of Hus and did not go. Consequently he was excommunicated and later placed under the ban of the empire, meaning that anyone could kill him as a heretic, but he spoke the language of the people and they loved him. He defended his faith before Emperor Charles and had to flee for safety to Wartburg castle, where he translated the Greek New Testament into German because he wanted every German, including every simple plowboy, to be able to read the Bible. Later he translated the Old Testament also. After his return to Wittenberg under the protection of Duke Frederick the Wise, he sent teachers and ministers to the churches to help the clergy, who were poorly trained and knew little about the Gospel. He wrote catechisms for use in the churches and many hymns, including *A Mighty Fortress Is Our God.* Soon the Gospel was singing its way into the hearts of the people who had never sung in church before. He knew their spiritual needs and wanted to share the answer he had found with them.

Opposition to Luther's work did not come only from Rome. Among his own friends were those who disagreed with him, as we saw in Erasmus. Another critic was Andreas Carlstadt (d. 1541), a man who said many things close to what the Anabaptists were to say a few years later. He urged Luther to give more attention in his preaching to the importance of following Jesus in life, since many people took the Reformation emphasis on grace to mean that works were not important so long as they believed in Christ. He also rejected the swearing of oaths, and instead of the sacramental interpretation of the Lord's Supper, whereby the bread and wine were taken to have saving power in and of themselves, he began to celebrate the Lord's Supper as a memorial service of what Christ had done on the cross. He forbade others to call him doctor, saying that all are equal in the church of Christ. All of this greatly distressed Luther, but did not change his program.

Thomas Müntzer (d. 1525), whose reform demands went much further than those of Carlstadt, gave Luther a great deal of trouble. He had become a pastor at Luther's suggestion, and was an able speaker but easily carried away by his own ideas and eloquence. Soon these ideas and visions seemed to him to be direct inspirations of the Holy Spirit, and he began to rely more on them than on the Scriptures. When this brought him into conflict with the others, who were committed to the *sola scriptura* (Scripture alone) principle of the Reformation, he began holding meetings in homes. Persons from the lower classes of society felt particularly attracted to his messages about equality and freedom.

Among those attending the meetings were three men who came to be known as the Zwickau Prophets. Zwickau was the name of their hometown, and the prophet role was ascribed to them because they, like Müntzer, had moved from Bible study to spiritual visions which they freely shared with others. In 1521, in fact, they went to Wittenberg to show the Lutheran reformers that they must rely more on the Holy Spirit. Some of the Wittenberg men, including Carlstadt, were deeply impressed by them, but when Luther heard of their work he returned quickly from his hiding place in the Wartburg and sent them scurrying. Following this incident Müntzer was reported to have said that he would not trust Luther even if he had swallowed a dozen Bibles, to which Luther replied that he would not trust Müntzer either, even if he had swallowed the Holy Ghost feathers and all.

Gradually Müntzer succeeded in gaining a large following among the peasants, who saw in him a man who could help them gain relief from the oppression of the nobles. He organized many of them into an armed force, using a red cross and naked sword as banner emblem. Soon armed uprisings were occurring everywhere as the peasants took justice into their own hands. In doing this they thought they were simply helping to fulfill the divine plan for society as they had learned to understand it from the preaching of Luther and his helpers. A military showdown came on May 15, 1525, at Frankenhausen and thousands of peasants were killed by the well-armed nobles. Müntzer himself was captured, tortured, and executed several days later. In history these events have been known as the Peasant's Revolt.

Carlstadt, the Zwickau Prophets, and the Peasant's Revolt closed Luther's mind to the Anabaptists when they appeared in 1525. He lumped together as fanatics all those who felt that his Reformation had not gone far enough. One of his favorite terms for them was *Schwärmer,* meaning a beatnik kind of enthusiast, a person driven by impulses and emotions rather than by common sense. Perhaps it was this term which prompted Stanislas Orzechowski, in sixteenth-century Poland, to describe the Anabaptists as "people with bees in their bonnets." The Anabaptists actually rejoiced at the work Luther had done but called it a halfway Reformation. They did not find the Bible teaching his sacramental understanding of the Lord's Supper and baptism as having saving power, but they were particularly disappointed in his definition of the church as being wherever the Word of God was preached and the sacraments rightly administered. To them the church, according to the New Testament, should consist of believers only. These would voluntarily join the church, instead of being brought in through infant baptism, and by their free decision bind themselves to witness and to discipline as the body of Christ. While Luther had brought many changes and had, above all, restored the Gospel as grace, they felt that he had left unchanged the really basic problem of the church which had come when Constantine merged the church with the state.

It will be noted in the following chapter that Ulrich Zwingli also relied on the state to reform the church. Because of this the Anabaptists were finally forced to proceed in their own way. They agreed with the Protestant reformers at many points. Their intention was not to start a separate movement, but to complete what the others had left unfinished. The men and movements which prepared the way for the Reformation, therefore, also helped to prepare the way for Anabaptism. Anabaptism cannot really be understood without seeing its development in relation to these movements, as well as its relation to the day by day developments in the Reformation itself. The history of the universal church through the ages is also a part of the history of the Anabaptists.

*Notes*

1. *Apology,* 37:4.
2. Quoted in Leonard Verduin, *The Reformers and Their Stepchildren.* Grand Rapids: Wm. B. Eerdmans Publishing Co., 1964, p. 143 note 1.
3. Quoted in *ibid.,* p. 173.
4. Quoted in Matthew Spinka (ed.), *Advocates of Reform,* Vol. XIV, *The Library of Christian Classics.* Philadelphia: Westminster Press, 1953, p. 26.
5. Quoted in Elgin S. Moyer, *Great Leaders of the Christian Church.* Chicago: Moody Press, 1951, p. 296.
6. Quoted in Harry E. Fosdick, *Great Voices of the Reformation.* New York: Modern Library, 1952, p. 41.

## FOR FURTHER READING:

*The Mennonite Encyclopedia,* 4 vols.

Roland H. Bainton, *The Church of Our Fathers.* New York: Charles Scribners Sons, 1941.

Norman F. Langford, *Fire upon the Earth.* The Story of the Christian Church. Philadelphia: The Westminster Press, 1950.

Elgin S. Moyer, *Great Leaders of the Christian Church.* Chicago: Moody Press, 1951.

# Chapter 2

# *ANABAPTIST ORIGINS IN SWITZERLAND*

SOUTH GERMANY and Switzerland had no city which served as a center of the Reformation movement in the way Wittenberg served Lutheranism in the North. The major South German and Swiss cities were independent states with their own laws, commerce, and religious interests. Because of this the men who arose from among these people to renew the church, and whom history has called *reformers,* had differing emphases from region to region. In their own way each of these men led in the process of church reorganization, dealing with the authorities of the cities and Roman Catholic opposition as best they could.

With all these variations, however, the one man who was strongest and most respected among these first-generation reformers was Ulrich Zwingli (d. 1531), of Zurich. Zwingli first became known through his criticism of the system whereby an endless stream of Swiss youth was sent to the great military powers of Europe as mercenary soldiers. He was also a good friend of the famous humanist Erasmus. Zwingli was a popular preacher as well, as a result of which he left his small parish at Einsiedeln in January of 1519, to be installed in the prestigious church in Zurich itself. Here he startled his listeners by beginning to preach day after day directly from the Bible, beginning his sermon invariably at the place he had ended with in the Scripture reading the day before. As he did this, he became increasingly independent of and critical of the traditional practices of Roman Catholicism even as Luther was criticizing them, but he was not greatly influenced by Luther in this. His own studies and Biblical preaching led him to these new conclusions.

By the middle of 1522 it had become clear that Zwingli and others of like mind were coming to demand such radical renewal measures within the church that no bishop or other church authority would support them. How then should they go about reforming the church? The answer was given by Zwingli himself in November of that year, when he resigned as priest of the Roman Catholic Church and rejected its authority over him. Hereupon the Council of Two Hundred, which was the governing body of the city of Zurich, immediately reinstated him in his old position but under their authority. Formally speaking, it was this action of the government in calling a preacher which marked the beginning of the Swiss Reformation and of the state church.

Such action naturally brought criticism upon the council for having appointed a man whom the Roman Catholic Church considered a heretic. To clear themselves of this accusation and to give a formal justification to their action, the council called a disputation in January, 1523, to clarify the issues. According to the customs of the time a disputation was a formal debate carried on according to accepted standards, which included impartial chairmanship and record taking. The theses which Zwingli was willing to defend were published ahead of time, and invitations were sent to all concerned, including the great Catholic universities and the Bishop of Constance, in whose diocese Zurich belonged. Zwingli's intention was to show that these theses were according to the Word of God, but no real debate developed since Johannes Faber, sent to represent the bishop, denied that the politically constituted council of Zurich was authorized to serve as umpire in theological matters. Therefore, since no one had shown the Zwinglian proposals to be contrary to the Word of God, the council reconfirmed his appointment and instructed him to continue to preach nothing but the Gospel truth.

Both of these actions--the hiring of Zwingli in November, and his formal reaffirmation by the council in January-were conservative decisions in their intention; they simply allowed him to continue his preaching. And yet they were of revolutionary importance since they represented a declaration of independence from the control of the Roman hierarchy and a seizing of the right to name ministers by the local political authority.

### The State Resists Reform

As Zwingli's preaching and the consequent process of reformation went on, the council found it increasingly difficult to accept all the

27

demands arising from this rediscovery of the Gospel. Thus, for example, the peasants in the country surrounding Zurich asked to be relieved from paying the taxes with tithes which burdened them, since Zwingli had preached that the taking of interest was contrary to the Bible. The council would hear nothing of this, however, and ordered them to continue paying to the city and the monasteries as usual.

In late summer of 1523 Zwingli began to spell out more clearly how the traditional Roman Catholic mass might be replaced with an evangelical communion service. To demonstrate the rightness of his teaching that the mass is not a sacrifice but a commemoration, and to cast light on the further radical demand of some of his disciples that all paintings and statues should be removed from the churches, a second disputation was held October 27-29. But the council feared the consequences of doing away with the mass. This would not only seem sacrilegious to the other cantons in the Swiss Confederacy but would jeopardize Zurich's political and economic relationship to them as well. Thus it became clear that the council was in no hurry to permit external changes in religious practices, even though the theology of the Lord's Supper had been clearly stated by Zwingli and accepted as valid by the people and the council.

In December Zwingli finally decided to go ahead himself in his own congregation with a Biblical celebration of the Lord's Supper in both kinds, i.e., with the cup no longer reserved only for the priest. In a memorandum to the council he announced his intention to celebrate such a Lord's Supper on Christmas Day, 1523, adding that the preachers would "stand condemned as liars before the Word of God" if they did not go through with this. But the council refused to agree. Zwingli was obliged to submit a second statement nine days later in which the threat to go ahead with his own Protestant communion service was withdrawn, and the decision was again left in the hands of the council. Thereupon the council decreed that there would be no change at all in the mass at that time. Zwingli accepted this indefinite delay rather than jeopardize his working relationship with the council.

### The Dissatisfied Minority

Because of these delays and compromises a feeling of dissatisfaction began to arise within the circle of Zwingli's most devoted disciples. They had been as dissatisfied as he with the council's decision about tithes and taxes in June, 1523, and more outspoken about it. They had been critical of certain remainders of Roman Catholic practice in the draft of a new reformed liturgy which Zwingli had published in August. They had objected to the continued wearing of robes by the clergy, believing that this supported the idea that the mass was a sacrifice, and they had objected to the use of prescribed songs and prayers other than the Lord's Prayer in the liturgy. Zwingli had accepted these criticisms, changing his proposals at some points and defending others; the fellowship among them remained open.

After the discussion of the mass in the October debate, however, these disciples were much less willing than Zwingli to see the council left with the responsibility of determining how the reformation was to be carried out. The record of the debate reports:

Conrad Grebel rose and thought that the priests should be given instructions, since they were all present, as to what should be done about the Mass; [the disputation] would be in vain, if something were not done about the Mass. . . .

Zwingli: My Lords [the Council] will decide how to proceed henceforth with the Mass.

Simon Stumpf: Master Ulrich: You have no authority to place the decision in the hands of My Lords, for the decision is already made; the Spirit of God decides.

Zwingli: That is right. I shall likewise preach and act against it if they decide otherwise. I do not place the decision in their hands. Nor shall I pass judgment on the Word of God. . . . This convocation did not have the purpose of deciding for or against the Word of God, but to ascertain from Scripture whether the Mass is a sacrifice or not. Hereafter they will deliberate as to the way in which that may be done most appropriately and without disturbance.

Simon Stumpf was a priest in the country town of Höngg, and one of Zwingli's devoted followers. Conrad Grebel was the scion of an upper-class Zurich family, who had spent his youth aimlessly in the universities of Vienna and Paris until Zwingli had led him to a strong, personal commitment to the cause of the Gospel. The exchange quoted above marks the first sign of their doubts about whether the state would be an adequate tool for reforming the church, but they accepted Zwingli's explanations for the time being.

With Zwingli's December compromise on the mass, however, these disciples realized that they were really in opposition to Zwingli who agreed that the Reformation should go no faster than the state was willing to put it into effect. Looking back on the October disputation with the perspective of later developments, Grebel was now able to say that the essential compromise had already been made then: "The Word was overthrown, trampled upon, and enslaved by its most learned heralds." In mock debating style Grebel set forth the thesis: "Whoever thinks, believes, or says that Zwingli is performing his duties as a shepherd, thinks, believes, and speaks impiously." From this point on Grebel and his friends became increasingly distrustful of the council as a source of initiative in the purifying of the church. [1]

*Growing Disagreement*

Little is known about the group of disappointed disciples of Zwingli from December, 1523, to the fall of 1524. We know neither how many there were nor what they did. Only two known developments are certain to have fallen within this period—the idea of a basic change in the political organization of Zurich, and a growing conviction against the practice of infant baptism.

*Political reorganization:* In considering the halfheartedness of the council and Zwingli's unwillingness to move ahead without its support, these disciples concluded that the best way might be to get a sympathetic council elected. Conrad Grebel and Felix Manz seem to have proposed to Zwingli that the friends of the Reformation might constitute something like a political party. They were confident that if Zwingli were to challenge the population of Zurich publicly to take sides for or against the Word of God as he was preaching it, the majority would be on his side. This majority could then elect a properly disposed city council and the Reformation would again move forward with state approval. This proposal met Zwingli halfway. It did not ask him to act against the state, nor did it say that the state would have no business carrying out the Reformation as long as it acted according to the Word of God. Yet by making the membership of such a "Reformation Party" voluntary, this proposal would in effect have created an independent religious institution and would, therefore, have begun to break the bond between church and state.

Zwingli had two objections to this proposal. On the one hand, he was still confident that the council could be trusted to move ahead responsibly, though slowly, with the Reformation program. A more basic reason was his growing fear of the divisive social effects of asking individuals within society to make their own decisions. The result might be Roman Catholic worship in one part of Zurich and Protestant worship in another, thus destroying the unity of the city and with it of the church. This, in turn, would dishonor God by casting doubt upon His sovereignty and upon the clarity of His revealed will.

*Baptism of infants:* In the early days of the Reformation Martin

30

Luther and Ulrich Zwingli, together with many of their lesser colleagues, could not avoid challenging the Roman Catholic practice of infant baptism. As a sacrament with its own effectiveness regardless of the attitude of the infant, this practice was believed to purify the child from the stain of original sin, making salvation certain in case of early death and predisposing him toward a mature Christian life. The Reformation principles challenged this understanding from both sides. From the perspective of the individual the reformers defined faith as a personal response of trusting obedience and repentance. It must be genuine and personal to meet the conditions for salvation. They insisted that no church ceremony (sacraments) could have saving value.

In looking back on these events from our own times we need to remember that when questions were raised about the rightness of baptizing infants it was not clear in anyone's mind what else could be done in its place. One might have suggested that baptism be postponed until the child was three or four years of age and could have some consciousness of what was happening to him, and could remember it. Or one might have suggested that parents should at least cease these baptisms following immediately upon the birth of a child, while waiting for light about what to do in its place. It was, in any case, not the only logical implication in anyone's mind that those who had been baptized in infancy—which meant everyone in Europe at that time except Jews—should be *rebaptized* as adult believers.

It was reported early in 1524 that two Zurich priests, Wilhelm Reublin and Johannes Brotli, were preaching against infant baptism and refusing to baptize infants born in their parishes. They had not asked the city council, but had simply preached and acted according to their own convictions, a sign that Zwingli's disciples were growing spiritually independent of their leader. It is significant that they were doing this in the villages of Witikon and Zollikon around Zurich, rather than in the city itself, indicating the relative freedom of the country folk from the authority of the city government though they were politically subject to it. By the same token the city council found it difficult to assert its will in these country regions, and the actions of these priests continued to be a source of agitation through the summer.

### Autumn 1524

The first real explanation of their thinking behind the rejection of infant baptism, and the first sign of them as a self-conscious group of persons rejecting Zwingli's leadership, is found in three letters written by Conrad Grebel and his friends in September of 1524.

Having abandoned their hope that Zwingli himself could be won to a restored initiative in leading the Reformation, they wrote to three major Protestant leaders—Martin Luther, Andreas Carlstadt, and Thomas Müntzer. Both Carlstadt and Müntzer were themselves in the process of separating from the Lutheran movement because of frustration with its progress. Only the letter to Müntzer has been preserved, probably because no one was found to carry it to him. Luther and Carlstadt received theirs but no further relationship resulted.

The primary concern expressed in the letter to Müntzer is for recognizing the Word of God as the only authority in matters of church reformation, in contrast to Zwingli's caution and "forbearance." They had read some of Müntzer's writings criticizing unreal faith and superficial religious practices and had come to believe they would find an ally in him. At the same time they clearly rejected the position which they had just heard that he held, that physical violence could be used to further the cause of the reformation or in the interest of social justice for the peasants. Consequently their letter stated that

. . . the Gospel and its adherents are not to be protected by the sword, neither are they thus to protect themselves. . . . True Christian believers are sheep among wolves, sheep for the slaughter; they must be baptized in anguish and affliction, tribulation, persecution, suffering, and death; they must be tried with fire, and must reach the fatherland of eternal rest, not by killing their bodily, but by mortifying their spiritual enemies. Neither do they use worldly sword or war, since all killing has ceased with them . . . .[2]

In addition, they made two points on baptism—that it means the entrance of the believer into membership and into the discipline of the Christian congregation and that it reflects the personal experience and commitment of the believer:

We understand that even an adult is not to be baptized without Christ's rule of binding and loosing. The Scripture describes baptism for us thus, that it signifies that by faith and the blood of Christ sins have been washed away for him who is baptized, changes his mind, and believes before and after; that it signifies that a man is dead and ought to be dead to sin and walks in newness of life and spirit, and that he shall certainly be saved if, according to this meaning, he lives his faith by inner baptism; so that the water does not confirm or increase faith, as the scholars at Wittenberg say, and [does not ] give comfort [nor ] is it the final refuge on the death bed. Also baptism does not save. . . .

By "Christ's rule of binding and loosing" they meant the instructions of Jesus in Matthew 18:15-18, according to which Christians are responsible to one another for counsel, admonition, and forgiveness. Baptism thus also meant committing oneself to give and receive counsel, which a child cannot do. The further meaning of baptism as a symbolism of washing seemed meaningful to them only if the spiritual reality to which it points is there. Apart from this, they held, water cannot purify, reassure, or save.

## A Breakthrough

By December, 1524, agitation around the question of infant baptism had become a problem which would lead to social difficulties if left unchecked. The city council, therefore, instructed Zwingli to meet once a week with all those who rejected infant baptism until the matter could be resolved. After two meetings on successive Tuesday evenings in December the talks were broken off by Zwingli because "it would be dangerous," i.e., because he feared discussion with those who did not respect his spiritual authority would only make matters worse. When the discussions were thus broken off, Felix Manz submitted to the council a document in which he asked the members of the council themselves, as a group of Christian leaders, to renew the conversation since Zwingli himself was impossible to work with. The council responded by calling for a public meeting on January 17, but the announcements calling that meeting already showed that there was no intention to deal with the matter as an open question:

As some are mistakenly saying that young children should not be baptized until they come to maturity, our lords, the mayor and the small and the Great Council of the city of Zurich announce that all . . . should appear next Tuesday. . . . [3]

Consequently the outcome of this pseudo-disputation was never in doubt. The council ruled that children should continue to be baptized and that any parents who persisted in refusal should be expelled from Zurich lands. This decision of January 18, 1525, meant that force would now be used in persecuting religious minorities in this area.

The small circle of seekers for a more faithful Reformation had no more time now for further careful study. Baptism had not been their first concern, and it was not the central one, but it was the point at which the line had been drawn by Zwingli. They had one week to choose between compliance and exile. Under the pressure of this choice before them they met in the home of Felix Manz, near Zwingli's church, on the evening of January 21 to consider what they ought to do. What then happened is reported as follows:

. . . they had been meeting until anxiety arose and penetrated their hearts. They began to bow the knee before the highest God in Heaven, calling on Him as the One who knows what is in men's hearts, praying that He would grant them to do His divine Will and that He would show them mercy; for flesh and blood and human imagination did not drive them. They well knew what they would have to suffer and endure because of it.

After prayer Georg Cajacob stood up and begged Conrad Grebel for God's sake to baptize him with true Christian baptism upon his faith and confession. And because he was kneeling with such a request and desire Conrad baptized him, because there was no minister ordained to take such an action. When that had happened the others in the same way desired of Georg that he baptize them, which he did at their request. Thus in the great fear of God they committed one another to the Name of the Lord and installed one another in the ministry of the Gospel, began to teach and to keep the faith. Thereby began separation from the world and from its evil works. [4]

It may be that this report is the oldest existing Anabaptist historical document. Three conclusions about the significance of this event emerge as we study it. First, that the action taken that evening was spontaneous, working both anxiety and a readiness to face suffering, under the deeply felt pressure of the presence of the Holy Spirit. There had been no advance calculation to the end that "the way to make the break would be to baptize adults," and no strategic weighing of whether this was "the right time to make the break." Second, we note that the group was respectful of the place of regular church authorities, Georg Cajacob (later known as Blaurock) acting only exceptionally in the absence of a more authorized person. [5] Third, the significance of this act lay not so much in the proper practice of baptism itself, as in the creation of a new, visible church body distinct from the established church controlled by the state, as was true of the all-inclusive establishment of medieval Catholicism. That the intention of the newly formed group was to establish a different form of church body is seen from the phrase "thereby began separation from the world."

It must be remembered that both Zwingli and Luther were still celebrating the mass at this time. They had begun to explain what a Protestant church order and practice would be like but had made no substantial changes in worship and written no new confessions of faith. Thus this prayer meeting and the events of January 21 under the cloud of threatened persecution mark not only the beginning of Anabaptism but of Protestantism as a visible reality. Here arose the first Protestant church.

*Notes*

1. The story of these earliest beginnings is told more fully by Fritz Blanke in *Brothers in Christ* (Scottdale, 1961), and by John H. Yoder in "The Turning Point in the Zwinglian Reformation," *Mennonite Quarterly Review*, XXXII (April, 1958), pp. 128-40.

2. "Letters to Thomas Müntzer by Conrad Grebel and Friends" in *Spiritual and Anabaptist Writers*, Vol. XXV of *The Library of Christian Classics*, edited by George H. Williams and Angel M. Mergal. Philadelphia: Westminster Press, 1957, pp. 73-85.

3. No. 22, page 33 in *Quellen zur Geschichte der Täufer in der Schweiz*. Vol. I, *Zürich*. Edited by Leonhard von Muralt and Walter Schmid. Zurich: S. Hirzel Verlag, 1952.

4. Quoted in Harold S. Bender, *The Life and Letters of Conrad Grebel*. Goshen, Indiana: Mennonite Historical Society, 1950, p. 137 in translation from Rudolf Wolkan (ed.) *Geschicht-Buch der Hutterischen Brüder*. Wien: Carl Fromme, 1923, p. 35.

5. It should be noted that the reference to "no ordained minister" shows a low, rather than high view of "sacramental" ordination. The group included at least three men with prior Roman Catholic priestly ordination: Blaurock, Wilhelm Reublin, and Johannes Brötli. Thus the phrase really means that since there were as yet no restored congregations, there was no individual with congregational authorization to baptize.

## FOR FURTHER READING:

*The Mennonite Encyclopedia,* 4 vols.

*Mennonite Life* 2 (January, 1947), pp. 6, 7.

William R. Estep, *The Anabaptist Story.* Nashville: The Broadman Press, 1963.

Fritz Blanke, *Brothers in Christ,* Scottdale: Herald Press, 1961.

*Chapter 3*

# PERSECUTION AND CONSOLIDATION

THE JANUARY 21 MEETING which led to the first baptism had already taken place under the threat of persecution. The members of this group were soon called Anabaptists or *re-baptizers,* though they themselves preferred simply to be called *brethren.* Instead of trying to resist the decree of the council against them, the Brethren now made plans for the sharing of their newfound convictions with others. The first church meeting was a missionary meeting. Each of those who had to leave the city of Zurich returned to some place where he was known and could expect people to listen to him. For some, especially the tradesmen, this meant going northeast to St. Gall, northwest to Basel, or southwest to Bern––cities in which the stirrings of the Reformation had already begun to be felt. For others it meant taking refuge in rural areas where the repressive measures of the city government would be enforced less stringently. Thus John Brötli and Wilhelm Reublin went northward into the area between Zurich, Waldshut, and Schaffhausen, while others went eastward into Appenzell, and west into the area ruled jointly by Zurich and Bern and, therefore, not rigidly controlled by either. In the course of the spring and summer of 1525 small groups of sympathizers had been established in most of these places.

### *Hubmaier at Waldshut*

Situated on the north side of the Rhine, just twenty miles from Zurich, the small town of Waldshut was an Austrian possession under the rule of the still solidly Catholic Holy Roman Empire. Its nearness

36

to Schaffhausen and Zurich, however, had nevertheless brought it into close contact with religious developments in the Swiss cities. This contact was increased significantly by the arrival of Balthasar Hubmaier in Waldshut in 1521. As a south German priest and doctor of theology he was well known for his popular preaching in Regensburg and his service at the University of Ingolstadt. While he showed no special sympathies for the young Reformation movement upon his arrival, he soon became a close friend and collaborator of Ulrich Zwingli in Zurich. By 1523 his sympathies for the Reformation cause were so outspoken that Waldshut itself became suspect in the eyes of the Austrian government.

Though he considered Zwingli both his friend and colleague, Hubmaier was less his disciple and intellectually more independent than were the younger men in Zurich. Nevertheless, he shared Zwingli's low opinion of infant baptism in 1523-24, and his concern for a pure church order according to the Bible. He was left out of the late 1524 discussions in Zurich which led to the January 18, 1525, decision of the council and the baptismal meeting of the Brethren, but considered himself a friend of Zwingli's while, at the same time, rejecting infant baptism. In the spring of 1525 Wilhelm Reublin, while preaching in the countryside east of Waldshut, also began to convince some members of Hubmaier's church in the city itself, several receiving baptism. In the Easter season, Hubmaier and most of the members of his congregation were baptized upon their profession of faith. This was the first time that an organized church joined the Anabaptist cause, with the government tolerating the action for the time being.

In December Waldshut was seized by the Austrian forces and recatholicized. Hubmaier had to flee, but in the months since Easter he had produced a flood of literature on baptism and the church. Most of his pamphlets, however, were not printed until later. The first and most complete statement of early Anabaptism on the question of baptism, called *On the Christian Baptism of Believers,* was written by Hubmaier during this period after Zwingli had refused to answer his letter inviting the reformer to a debate with Hubmaier on the subject. It is an analysis of the major Biblical texts on baptism as taught and practiced by John the Baptist, by Christ, and by the apostles. He concluded that everywhere baptism followed only after some kind of preaching or instruction, and after faith in the message heard had been expressed. The book does not deal with rebaptism, since he considered the infant baptism of the Roman Catholic Church not to be baptism by Biblical standards. The simplicity, clear Biblical basis, and blunt statement of the case make this 68-page booklet a classic. In later writings Hubmaier further elaborated his conviction, drawing upon statements from church fathers and theologians of all ages to support his position. He answered the anti-Anabaptist writings of Zwingli and Oecolampad, and drafted orders of worship in keeping with his vision of the committed, disciplined church of believers.

### The Brethren in St. Gall

In these early days the cause of the Reformation in St. Gall was carried by two laymen: the weaver John Kessler, and the humanist scholar and medical doctor Joachim von Watt. Both of these men, though not theologians but self-educated in matters of faith, led in Bible studies and encouraged renewal in the absence of strong clerical leadership. Late in 1523 their movement was strengthened with the coming of Lorenz Hochrütiner who had been banished from Zurich under the charge of having removed images from churches. The Bible reading movement in St. Gall had experienced tension even before they heard of the first baptisms in Zurich. Whereas Watt and Kessler favored a slow evolution within the church, Hochrütiner and Wolfgang Uolimann were calling for a more radical rejection of all traditions, even refusing to use the church building which had been offered to them for Bible reading meetings by the city authorities.

It was, therefore, no surprise that a division took place in St. Gall when news of the Zurich baptisms reached the Bible reading group. For a time it seemed that the more aggressive Anabaptist party was the stronger, it had weighty friends, if not actual baptized members, on the city council. On Palm Sunday, 1525, Conrad Grebel himself was present when a group of persons numbering perhaps two hundred publicly paraded down to the Sitter River for a mass baptism.

The movement was even more successful in some of the rural areas surrounding St. Gall, especially in the small canton of Appenzell, where the villages had a high degree of autonomy. Here it could happen that a whole village, being both a political and ecclesiastical unit at the same time, might vote to expel a Roman Catholic priest or even a Zwinglian preacher, and replace him with an Anabaptist. There was certainly an element of political and economic interest involved in this development. Since Anabaptism was opposed to the legal requirement of the tithe and to the support of ministers through compulsory taxation, there were those who saw in the movement the possibility of economic relief and even revolutionary social effects favoring the peasants even though this was not the motivation of the Anabaptist leaders themselves.

It was also for this reason that the developing sympathy for Anabaptism in St. Gall and Appenzell called forth such a strong reaction from the authorities. Hans Kern, the most active leader in the villages, was seized at night by the troops of the bishop of St. Gall and taken to Lucerne where he was executed. After a public debate the council of St. Gall imposed a fine on those who persisted in their Anabaptist commitment. The effect of these measures was that those whose enthusiasm had been superficial quickly returned to the official church, while the convictions of those who really were committed to the movement became stronger. For decades the Anabaptists of St. Gall were marked by an especially radical emphasis. It is reported that some of them refused to use medicine when the city was struck by a plague in 1530. They were also stricter about Christian simplicity of dress and about nonresistance than were other Anabaptists. Still others, especially among those who had first belonged to the movement and then withdrawn from it under pressure, seem to have justified various kinds of misbehavior on religious grounds; either claiming that the true believer was free from the law, or that they had received special visions and revelations.

*Suffering Comes to the Brethren*

We have seen that persecution began even before the first baptisms since the threat of banishment was announced January 18, 1525. The first imprisonment of Anabaptists in Zurich was in early February. Prisons, fines, and sometimes torture were standard procedure for prisoners. Release from prison came only when the prisoner would promise to forsake the Anabaptist meetings. By March, 1526, life imprisonment sentences were being imposed. Wherever Anabaptism became known similar measures were initiated.

The first death penalties were inflicted on Anabaptists by the governments of Roman Catholic cantons, who executed them simply as Protestants, rather than specifically as Anabaptists. Thus Hippolytus (popularly called Bolt) Eberle, who had apparently joined the Brethren at St. Gall in April or May, 1525, was executed just a few weeks later in his home canton of Schwyz. He is also known as the first Protestant martyr, since the authorities of the canton did not distinguish between Protestant and Anabaptist heresy. The first death penalty at the hands of a Protestant government was the drowning of Felix Manz in the Limmat River in Zurich on January 5, 1527.

The official grounds for these extreme measures included more than the simple offense of baptizing, being baptized, or attending Anabaptist meetings. The authorities held that the real reason for execution was either sedition, i.e., a refusal to obey the governmental injunction not to baptize, or perjury, i.e., returning to Anabaptism after having promised to forsake it. Thus a religious offense was transformed into a civil one.

By early 1527 the Zurich Anabaptist movement was severely threatened with disintegration. Of the original leadership circle, Conrad Grebel had died of illness, and Felix Manz had been executed. Georg Blaurock had escaped execution only because he was not a citizen of Zurich, and was not able to return. Other leaders were widely scattered, facing dangers and problems for which they were not prepared with ready answers. Under the mounting pressure of persecution the movement was threatened on two sides from within. On the one hand was a widening circle of those who were sympathetic with the Anabaptist message, especially its criticism of the abuses in the established churches, but who excused themselves from the high cost of full and open identification with the movement. Perhaps this caution was covered with an argument to the effect that true faith is spiritual and not bound by outward forms. Thus they could give inner assent to Anabaptist teaching without suffering for it. On the other side were those whom the pressure of persecution and religious enthusiasm could push into emotional moral excesses in the name of special revelation or heroic faithfulness. This latter group later came to be known as *Schwärmer* or fanatics.

### Consolidation

It was in response to these needs that a group of Anabaptist leaders met in the village of Schleitheim late in February of 1527. We cannot tell how the meeting was called nor how long it continued. Tradition tells us that Michael Sattler was the author of its conclusions. Georg Blaurock could have been there. But little as we know of the organization and attendance, it is still no exaggeration to say that it was this meeting, and the conclusions which it reached, which fixed the identity and saved the life of the young movement.

This was not a representative meeting to which delegates came each to vote for the position of his supporters, and whose conclusions represented a minimum to which they could all agree without changing their minds. The men who gathered at Schleitheim came together in disagreement and confusion, testifying later that during the meeting the Holy Spirit had led them to agreement and common convictions. [1]

> We announce to all who love God, that we have been brought to unity
> . . . and (God alone be praised and glorified) without any brother's
> contradiction, fully satisfied. Herein we have sensed the unity of the
> Father and of our common Christ with us in their Spirit. For the Lord
> is a God of peace and not of quarreling.

The first result of this coming to a common conviction was the
recognition that the Anabaptists were not in spiritual unity with those
who had a different understanding of "spiritual liberty." To some at
that time "spiritual liberty" meant the freedom of fanaticism and
licentiousness, to others the freedom of the conformists to continue in
the state church with its sacraments, civil oaths, and the wearing of
arms. In their meeting at Schleitheim the Brethren rejected both of
these alternatives:

> Some false brethren have introduced great scandal among us, in that
> some have turned away from faith, thinking to exercise the freedom of
> the Spirit and of Christ. But they have fallen short of the truth and have
> been given over (to their condemnation) to the vanity and the liberty of
> the flesh, thinking that faith and love can do and permit everything and
> nothing will be harmful or damnable because they are believers.

> Take note, members of God in Christ Jesus, that faith in the heavenly
> Father through Jesus Christ does not take such shape. . . .

In the first three articles substantial agreement was recorded
on the meaning of church membership, being defined in their
understanding of baptism, the ban, and the Lord's Supper. *Baptism*
is only for those who

> have learned repentance and amendment of life, and truly believe that
> their sins are removed by Christ, and who wish to walk in the resurrection
> of Jesus Christ and be buried with Him in death so as to rise with Him,
> and who themselves desire and ask it of us with this understanding.

Obviously no child could "walk in the resurrection," but only
those who had counted the cost, and these themselves had to take the
initiative in asking for baptism. Baptism was a covenant not only
with God, but also with the congregation, whereby the members
pledged to help each other in the life of obedience through admonition
and, if necessary, the *ban*. The *Lord's Supper* was to be a celebration only of those who were in full unity with the fellowship:
"Whoever has not been called by one God to one faith, to one baptism, to one Spirit, to one body, with all the children of God's church
cannot be made one bread with them. . . ."

The fourth article defined the principle of separation from the world of darkness and unbelief in specific terms appropriate to the situation:

Whatever is not united with our God and Christ, is none other than the abomination which we must avoid. This means all papist and antipapist works and worship, assemblies, churchgoing, taverns, unbelieving guarantees and commitments, and other things of the kind, which the world honors, but are done squarely counter to the command of God.

The fifth article provided for local church leadership more clearly than had been done before by stating that "The shepherd in the church of God shall be someone according to the rule of Paul, who has a completely good testimony among those outside the faith." The faithful are encouraged to support the shepherd according to his need, and if he is taken from them, either through persecution or through being sent on a missionary assignment, he is to be replaced immediately: "Should this shepherd be driven away or taken home to the Lord through the Cross, that very hour another shall be ordained in his place. . . ."

In the last two articles of agreement to emerge from their meeting, the relation of a Christian to the state is dealt with through a discussion of "the sword" and the swearing of oaths. Both articles are longer than the preceding five and enter into considerable detail of argument. The special emphasis given to these themes likely indicates both that they were subjects concerning which Anabaptists were especially criticized and threatened by the official churches, and that they were issues concerning which it was less clear to some of the members what position they should really take and how to explain it. The argument is based on a radical simplicity in following the words and example of Jesus, but this simplicity does not avoid the challenge of detailed argument with the opposing positions. It became clear that those who belong to Christ can neither resort to violence to achieve their objectives, nor swear by the name of God to confirm their own good intentions.

The Schleitheim meeting saved the Anabaptist movement in at least two ways. The very fact that this meeting took place successfully and was able to define the position against both conformists and fanatics made of Anabaptism an organized body able to meet its problems and survive instead of degenerating into a mere flurry of radical enthusiasm. On the level of doctrine, the position defined here was simple, Biblical, complete, and consistent enough that a simple Christian could understand it, testify to it, and suffer for it. The seven articles of agreement are sometimes referred to as the *Schleitheim Confession of Faith* (1527), the first such confession among the Anabaptists. It is closer to the intention of those who were present, however, to call it a *brotherly understanding* as they themselves did.

As indicated earlier, it is believed that Michael Sattler was the primary drafter of this statement of the faith. Soon after the meeting he was arrested together with thirteen other Anabaptists, and subjected to a merciless interrogation and tortured. When he was given the possibility of hiring an attorney to aid in his defense, he declined on the ground that this was not a legal matter but simply a defense of the faith which he, as a believer, must always be ready and willing to do himself. Nine charges were filed against him, including the charge that he intended to overthrow both the Roman Catholic Church and the civil order. Because of his great popularity with the people, a heavy guard had to be set around his prison to prevent a revolt in his behalf. On the day of execution his tongue was cut out, he was torn seven times with red-hot irons, and eventually burned. His wife was drowned a few days later. Heinrich Hug, the chronicler of these events, concluded his account with the words, "It was a miserable affair, they died for their conviction."

*Notes*
1. The quotations of the Schleitheim meeting are taken from the complete translation prepared by John C. Wenger, *The Doctrines of the Mennonites.* Scottdale: Mennonite Publishing House, 1950, pp. 69-74.

*FOR FURTHER READING:*

*The Mennonite Encyclopedia,* 4 vols.

J. C. Wenger, *Even unto Death.* Richmond: John Knox Press, 1961.

Harold S. Bender, *Conrad Grebel.* Goshen: Mennonite Historical Society, 1950.

**Chapter 4**

## CENTRAL GERMAN AND
## MORAVIAN ANABAPTISM

THE PEOPLE of Europe were excited beyond their own capacity for self-control by the burning issues of the Reformation. Anabaptism was born and bred in that atmosphere, and shared in it. As Anabaptist ideas spread among the German- and Dutch-speaking people of Europe, they were developed by a variety of leaders and took a variety of forms. Anabaptism was not one united movement. It now becomes our task to examine several of the new leaders who arrived on the scene somewhat independent of each other and added their own characteristic touch to the work of the Spirit in the lives of the people of Europe.

### *Hans Denk*

One of the most kindly spirits among the early Anabaptist leaders was Hans Denk (d. 1527). Born in Bavaria and educated at the University of Ingolstadt, he applied his humanist training to the work of editing and proofreading in two of the better presses in Basel. Here he became a friend of the reformer Johannes Oecolampadius. Here too he must have absorbed some of the fresh Reformation teaching. Upon the recommendation of Oecolampadius, the city of Nurnberg engaged Denk as principal of its St. Sebald school in September of 1523.

Nurnberg witnessed its share of religious controversy during the course of the next year, and Denk became thoroughly involved in it. Both Müntzer and Carlstadt, who were becoming increasingly dissatisfied with the Lutheran Reformation, visited the town and left pamphlets to be printed there. The Lutheran pastor, who was trying to introduce the Reformation gradually, was disturbed by the growing radicalism. At his urging the city council asked three suspect artists to appear before it in defense of their view of the Lord's Supper. It was believed that they denied the official church teaching of the real, physical presence of the body and blood of Christ in the bread and wine of the Supper. In January, 1525, Denk himself was called before the city council because he had associated with one of the artists, and the town fathers were especially eager to make certain that the schoolmaster did not dabble in heresy. In a series of meetings throughout the month Denk's views on a variety of religious topics were examined by the council. It seemed to the town fathers that Denk was hedging in his responses to their questions and unwilling to give a clear and direct answer. Their suspicions seemed confirmed in his reply to their question about the Lord's Supper. While not denying directly the physical presence of Christ in the bread and wine, he stressed that the primary question was really whether the man who ate the bread and drank the wine had a living, personal faith. This answer was obviously not satisfactory and on January 21, 1525—the day on which the first baptism occurred in Zurich—Denk was banished from the city for life, threatened with death if he came within ten miles of the city limits. His property was confiscated, the council said, to provide for his wife and children.

Denk spent most of the year 1525 wandering around Germany. He may have been in Mühlhausen with Müntzer, and he visited with the Swiss Brethren and the Zwinglians in St. Gall. In the autumn of the year he turned his steps to Augsburg where he was able to secure a teaching position again. Within a year, however, the Lutheran pastor there began to attack Denk's religious views and, being unable to reach agreement with him in a series of meetings, Denk abruptly left town in November, 1526. During his Augsburg residence he had been persuaded by Balthasar Hubmaier to accept believer's baptism. There is no evidence that he formed an Anabaptist congregation, but he was undoubtedly responsible for the development of interest in Anabaptism on the part of many. A congregation was established in Augsburg after he left. Among his Augsburg activities was also the baptism of that most vigorous of Anabaptist missioners, Hans Hut.

From Augsburg Denk went to Strassburg, a city with more religious freedom than existed elsewhere, and one in which a number of Anabaptists found refuge from persecutions. Within a month, however, he was deeply involved in religious arguments, not only with Capito and Bucer, the leaders of the Reformation there, but also with Michael Sattler. On Christmas Day, 1526, he left Strassburg to wander down the Rhine, discussing his faith with the local Lutheran pastors in the towns to which he came and, when possible, speaking to the people also. He even tried to convert some Jews, but without success. By February, 1527, he was in Worms, where he joined Ludwig Hätzer in producing the first German translation of the Old Testament prophets. At the same time he was so busy discussing his faith with others that the leaders of the Reformation in both Strassburg and Basel became alarmed. Consequently the Elector of the Palatinate took firm measures against the Worms radicals, and Denk was on the march again.

In August of 1527 he returned to Augsburg where the Anabaptist congregation had meanwhile become established. Here he met with Hans Hut, whom he had baptized earlier, and possibly several others in religious discussion. This meeting has sometimes been called the *Martyrs' Synod* because some of its members met their death soon afterward. Discussion apparently centered around the role of the "last times" in the evangelistic preaching of the Anabaptists. Hut agreed not to give undue emphasis in his missionary preaching to the early return of Christ in the Second Coming and to the Last Judgment, both truths in which he believed devoutly. In September Denk was in Ulm, and from there he went to Basel. He was weary beyond measure with the life of a fugitive, and wrote to the Basel reformer Oecolampadius begging for permission to settle in that city. Oecolampadius wanted some form of written word from Denk that would indicate a renunciation of his Anabaptist views, and Denk provided a statement of belief which Oecolampadius published two years later. But it was not a recantation, as the reformer claimed it to be. Denk had not changed his basic position. He had been pained by the sharpness of disagreement between the major reformers and the Anabaptists and wanted to find some way of reconciliation. He remained in Basel until his death from the plague in November.

In his faith, Denk was influenced by medieval mysticism, which he got in part from the anonymous book known as the *German Theology* and in part from Müntzer and Carlstadt. Because of this he believed that God reveals Himself to the inner man in a reflective, nonrational way, as well as in the Scriptures. He disliked the Lutheran reliance on Scripture alone as revelation because Scripture by itself, unaided by the Spirit, could lead a man into a dead legalism.

The reader of Scripture, Denk believed, needs the presence of that same Spirit who inspired its authors in order to make Scripture come to life. It is likely that this was also the reason for his disagreement with the Swiss Anabaptists. Denk was primarily interested in the inner life, life in the Spirit.

Denk also was overwhelmed by the love of God. He praised this love of God so much, wrote a critic in 1525, that he seemed to suggest that all men, even the devil himself, would eventually be saved. Whether he actually taught that the love of God would save all men, regardless of their sin and unbelief, cannot be determined from his writings, but it is clear that the love of God forms the very core of his faith.

He was attracted to Anabaptism by the emphasis on discipleship, on right living. "No one may truly know Christ," he said, "except one follows Him in life." He deplored the absence of moral improvement in the lives of most of the new Protestants. This emphasis on moral living led him to join Anabaptism through believer's baptism, but he had difficulty fitting himself into their church life. Dogmatic statements and emphasis upon minor details of the faith distressed him. Hence he was a man born in the wrong century, for the early sixteenth century could not tolerate dissent and delighted in dogmatic statements of a most binding and restrictive sort. Because he could not bring himself to agree with statements of dogma, he was accused by the reformers, and one suspects also by the Anabaptists, of hedging, of never committing himself. They harried him out of sight.

### Hans Hut

Of all the traveling missioners who visited south Germany and Austria, Hans Hut stands out because of his wide influence. Hut was born and raised in southern Thuringia. For a time he served as sexton in the village of Bibra but soon developed a trade in books to supplement his income as a bookbinder. The pursuit of this trade took him to many parts of Germany, where he became familiar with Lutheran doctrine and promoted it after a fashion through the sale of tracts and pamphlets. But he also encountered more radical ideas. At his trial in 1527 he said that he had first heard attacks against the practice of infant baptism from three men whom he met in his travels. Stirred by this encounter, he studied the Scriptures on the issue and even consulted the Lutheran theologians during one of his trips to Wittenberg, but he remained dissatisfied with the practice. Indeed, he refused to have his newborn child baptized, sometime early in 1524. When the lords of Bibra heard of this they ordered a public debate, the result of which was that those who did not accept infant baptism would have to leave the region.

This event was a turning point in Hut's life. Leaving Bibra with his wife and five children, he began a life of wandering which ended only with his capture and death in Augsburg in 1527. He appeared at the Battle of Frankenhausen which crushed the Peasant's Revolt, in 1525, after having heard some of Müntzer's sermons to the peasants. Though he was captured first by the peasants and then by the lords, he was released unharmed. Müntzer perished in the battle, but his vision of the imminent return of the Lord made a profound impression on Hut. For over a year he wandered about Germany, preaching on baptism, the Lord's Supper, and the end times until he came to Augsburg in May, 1526. Here Hans Denk and a friend talked to him about the earnest Christian lives of those who had received believer's baptism. After lengthy persuasion, he accepted baptism himself at the hands of Denk on May 26.

For the remainder of his short life Hut went from village to town in Franconia, Bavaria, Austria, and Moravia, preaching and baptizing. On coming to a town he would begin speaking in any available place with the words, "Go into all the world and preach the Gospel to the whole creation. He who believes and is baptized will be saved [Mk. 16 ] and this is the baptism—to endure anxiety, want, sorrow, and all tribulations in patience." He preached wherever people were—in isolated farmhouses, or in forests, or in homes of workers in the towns. His fiery sermons made an appeal in part because they conveyed his own burning conviction of the imminent destruction of Europe at the hands of the Turks. His critics said he was actually preaching revolution, but he denied this at his trial. He won many to the Anabaptist movement; one historian has declared that he won more converts during the two years of his ministry than all of the other Anabaptist missioners together.

Hut was captured in Augsburg in August, 1527, tried, tortured severely, and killed accidentally in his cell. Some claimed that he tried to escape by lighting a fire in his cell intending to call it to the attention of the guards and grab their keys, but that he became asphyxiated in the process. His son declared that a lighted candle, placed by his pallet of straw by the guards when they brought him back unconscious from torture, ignited the straw and killed him. In any event his corpse was carried to the judgment hall and tied to the executioner's cart. The dead body was sentenced to death by burning, and was recommitted to the flames on December 7.

Hut's teaching had several characteristic features which set it off from that of the Swiss Brethren. In the first place, he was much more fascinated with Christ's Second Coming than they were. He was reported to have specified the exact time of Christ's visitation to be during Pentecost of 1528. Some even said he had counseled his listeners to prepare to destroy the godless after a dramatic battle in which the Turks would crush the flower of European chivalry near Nürnberg. Hut denied these charges, and we have seen that Denk helped him to modify his emphasis on the Second Coming when they met in Augsburg in 1526. It is necessary to point out that Hut was not the only preacher of Reformation times who stressed the Second Coming of Christ. Many devout people in those days believed that God was about to bring an end to human history with a decisive act of His own.

A second distinctive feature of Hut's teaching, as found especially in the writings and court testimonies of some of his followers, was his mysticism. This mysticism, which he learned from Müntzer, is found in an emphasis on personal suffering as the mark of the Christian who truly follows Christ. The Christian must suffer as Christ suffered, and this suffering becomes, in part, a means whereby the Christian is saved from the hell of this world. It is to the last part that the Swiss Brethren would have objected. No Anabaptist denied the fact of suffering for the true Christian, but some would deny that suffering played a role in salvation. By suffering, moreover, Hut did not mean only physical suffering but also mental anguish over sin and separation from God.

A third distinctive feature of Hut's teaching was the emphasis on sharing of material goods. There ran through his messages, at least as his listeners interpreted them, a note of rebuke to the owner of material goods who did not share these goods in the freest manner with his brethren. He made this sharing of goods more central than some Anabaptists did.

### Central German Anabaptism

Anabaptism in Central Germany began with the evangelizing work of Hut. Hut preached and baptized in his native Thuringia in 1526, but he also founded a congregation in the city of Königsberg. When the authorities discovered this movement, some of the new members were executed in February, 1527, while others managed to escape with Hut to Austria and beyond. Some also fled north, so

49

that despite persecution a flourishing movement arose within three years in both Saxony and Hesse. The most vigorous Anabaptist congregation, which furnished leadership and inspiration to the movement elsewhere and thus became a center, was in the small village of Sorga, a few miles east of the town of Hersfeld. Here Melchior Rink was the acknowledged leader and inspiration of the movement.

Rink appears as a humanist schoolteacher and sometime chaplain at Hersfeld in 1523. Having developed an interest in Reformation teachings together with a colleague, they began preaching them openly, including a denunciation of the sins of the local Franciscan monks. For this they were compelled to leave Hersfeld, but Rink found a pastorate south of Eisenach. Here he came under the influence of Müntzer and, like Hut, followed him into the Peasant's War in 1525, emerging unscathed in body but changed in spirit. He fled south to the Palatinate, where he met Denk and came under his influence. By 1528 he was back in the neighborhood of Hersfeld, attacking infant baptism in his sermons and winning converts to the Anabaptist cause. Hearing of his activities Landgrave Philip of Hesse summoned him to give an account for preaching the Anabaptist doctrines which had been expressly forbidden by law. In his usual tolerant manner Philip gave Rink three choices: to renounce his views publicly; to leave the area, or to submit to a theological examination by the theological faculty of the University of Marburg. Rink chose the latter and was, as expected, found guilty but refused to go into exile as commanded. Consequently he was arrested in 1529 and imprisoned for two years, released in 1531, rearrested in November of that year, and finally sentenced to life imprisonment. He died in prison near the scene of his labors, sometime in the 1540's.

Others succeeded Rink as leaders in Central Germany, including Fritz Erbe, whose imprisonment for sixteen years became a symbol of Lutheran persecution and Anabaptist patience in suffering. No one, however, had the same fiery zeal for believer's baptism that Rink had shown and by the 1540's continuing persecution, flight, and recantations led to a sharp decline in the movement in this area.

To the west of Rink's center at Sorga, within the heart of Landgrave Philip's land Hesse, a flourishing movement of Anabaptists was to be found in the 1530's. Able leaders came up the Rhine from the north and courageous missioners from the Moravian Anabaptists, who came to be called Hutterites, visited them. When persecution became too severe some, in turn, went to Moravia. Philip preferred exile to execution as punishment for the Anabaptists, arguing that if all heretics were to be killed he would need to include Jews and Catholics also. Most of the contemporary princes in Germany thought him far too mild in his treatment of the Anabaptists, and the movement in Hesse was indeed vigorous. When a group of them, perhaps as many as twelve, were jailed at one place for well over a year, they were able to make a hole in the wall large enough to escape, but most of them remained in order not to alarm the authorities. Those who were at large did not flee, but continued their evangelizing, one of them converting and baptizing thirty persons while he was supposedly in jail.

But for all their zeal, the Hessian Anabaptist leaders finally gave up and returned to the state (Lutheran) church. In 1538 Philip arranged for a debate between four of them and Martin Bucer, the reformer of Strassburg. Bucer persuaded them that the evil of separation from the one body of Christ, the true church, was greater than the evil of immoral living among the people in the state church. But they had made their point that the Christian must lead a clean and pure life. As a result of this encounter the state church in Hesse decided to excommunicate those people who did not live morally as Christians should, a victory of sorts for the former Anabaptists.

### The Hutterian Brethren

Anabaptism spread from Switzerland and Bavaria into the Austrian lands and the Tirol. Late in 1527 Leonhard Schiemer and Hans Schlaffer were spreading Anabaptist doctrine in the Inn Valley, where Schiemer was caught and executed in January, 1528. Both missioners reflected the teachings and evangelical zeal of Hans Hut, by whom they had been baptized and instructed. These men and others worked from Rattenberg and Schwaz east into Upper and Lower Austria, and south into the Tirol. Blaurock of the Zurich circle baptized converts and established congregations south of the Brenner Pass in the Tirol. It was in this region that he was finally caught, tortured, and burned at the stake in September, 1529. Other Anabaptist leaders were Georg Zaunring and eventually Jacob Hutter.

The Austrian authorities were especially harsh in their treatment of Anabaptists. Within the old Austrian holdings the Archduke Ferdinand held a firmer control over his feudal noble-vassals than in the Tirol. But in all regions he struck with relentless fury at the heretics, issuing mandates to the local authorities to ferret out and punish the Anabaptists. He appointed special officials to judge those who were caught. He organized bands of *Täuferjäger,* Anabaptist hunters, whose task it was to find them among the people. The punishment was always the same: death. Even the Anabaptist who recanted under torture was to be killed, though the form of his execution was the more merciful beheading rather than the crueler burning.

It was this severity of persecution that gave rise to a flow of refugees into Moravia, which became a promised land for the Anabaptists in the early decades of the movement. Moravia also came under the political control of Ferdinand, in 1526, but the Moravian nobles had a tradition of relative freedom from control by their political overlord and they were not inclined to look with favor on Ferdinand's attempts to bring them under his control on the Anabaptist question or on any other issue. Ferdinand was able to enforce his will in Anabaptist matters in Moravia only very slowly, and for a period of several decades it therefore became a haven second to none in Europe for the persecuted flocks. Austrian refugees fleeing to Moravia made up a large share of the Hutterite communities after the early 1530's.

Hubmaier was one of these refugees who welcomed the relative peace and quiet of the Moravian lands. After his unhappy experiences with Zwingli and the other Zurichers, he was only too happy to settle down in Nicolsburg, where we find him early in the summer of 1526. There the lords of Liechtenstein, particularly Leonhard, gave protection to the Anabaptists. Nicolsburg had a Lutheran congregation among its German-speaking people and Hubmaier set himself to the task of converting it into an Anabaptist one, with the aid of the refugees. Most of the Anabaptists tried by the courts in Tirol in 1528 and 1529 indicated that they either had been baptized in Nicolsburg or had lived there for some period of time. By late spring of 1527 Nicolsburg was a major center, boasting perhaps as many as 12,000 Anabaptists.

At this juncture the fiery evangelist Hans Hut entered the town. Even before his coming the Anabaptists had grown restless with conflicting opinions on several major issues including the Christian's attitude toward the use of force in political affairs. Hut helped to bring the issues to a head. One of the most pressing issues was that of the war tax, brought on by the somewhat feverish preparations of the Austrian political leaders and some Germans to fight the Turks: should a Christian pay war tax? Hubmaier had always sided with the major reformers on letting the state regulate religious affairs. Consequently he was interested in winning political leaders to his cause in whose lands he and his fellow Anabaptists could find refuge. When those political rulers faced the necessity of levying a war tax it naturally had to be paid. Hut was far less willing than Hubmaier to support political rulers in any shape or form, but especially when they asked for money to outfit their armies against the Turks. Hut believed that the Turks were being used by God to destroy the political rulers of Europe. Of course the Christian could not pay war tax!

There were other issues in this Nicolsburg Disputation of May, 1527. Hut challenged Hubmaier's interpretation of the role of even the Christian magistrate in the work of the Lord in view of Christ's imminent return. Hut joined the band, made up largely of refugees, who insisted on a radical sharing of material goods in the form of a Christian communism. No one owned private property in their group. On the other hand, Hubmaier with his noble backing felt the lords of Liechtenstein were generous enough in providing a place of refuge for the Anabaptists without going to the extreme of renouncing title to all their lands and property, when those lords became Anabaptists. But the central issue, disputed the most hotly, was nonresistance. Hut's nonresistance seemed dangerously irresponsible, in view of the Turkish threat; Leonhard von Liechtenstein thought so at any rate and imprisoned him. A friend helped him to escape. But the remaining Anabaptists were hopelessly divided into those who came to be called the *Schwertler* (sword-bearers) and the *Stäbler* (staff-bearers).

Neither of the two opponents lived long after the debate. Hut was caught in Augsburg in August and died the following December. Hubmaier was arrested a few months after the debate, and his noble protectors proved either unwilling or unable to defend him. Archduke Ferdinand of Austria had been elected Margrave of Moravia in October, 1526, after the former Margrave, Louis of Hungary, had been killed in the war against the Turks at Mohacs. Ferdinand was as determined to repress the Anabaptists in his newly acquired territory as he was in his hereditary Austrian lands. He demanded the life of Hubmaier, against whom he had an old grudge: Hubmaier had been one of the leaders of the revolt of Waldshut against the Austrian overlord. The circumstances of Hubmaier's capture are not known. For the last several months in 1527 until March, 1528, Hubmaier was held prisoner in Vienna and Kreuzenstein castle. He went through a series of trials or examinations, with the customary use of torture. He also carried on a lengthy conversation with at least one Catholic theologian, an old university colleague and friend, Johannes Faber.

Hubmaier could give more ground to a Catholic than most Anabaptists could, on such issues as the authority of the state and the place of works within salvation, but he could not reach agreement with Faber on believer's baptism and on the nature of the Lord's Supper. He decided, therefore, to write an account of his faith to be presented to Ferdinand in an attempt to gain mercy from the archduke and composed his *Rechenschaft seines Glaubens,* but mercy was not granted. He was condemned to death both for heresy and for treason and burned at the stake on March 10, 1528, before a large crowd of people. The executioner rubbed gunpower into his hair and beard as an act of mercy: it would explode and bring quick death. His wife, who faithfully urged him to keep up his courage, was drowned a few days later.

With the death of their spiritual leader the *Schwertler* group faded away. Not so the *Stäbler.* Before the Nicolsburg Disputation a number of them had withdrawn from fellowship with the former. Now, in the spring of 1528, Leonhard of Liechtenstein felt he could no longer tolerate religious differences among them and ordered those *Stäbler* who had broken fellowship with the others, to leave. Approximately two hundred adults prepared to leave with their families. Outside of Nicolsburg they spread a coat on the ground and "everyone willingly laid his fortune down without compulsion or urging for the support of the needy." [1] They spent three weeks traveling to Austerlitz, where the lords of Kaunitz took them in and gave them a place to live and work. Under their leaders Jacob Widemann and Philip Weber, they increased in number through the addition of refugees.

The years from 1529 to the coming of Jacob Hutter in 1533 were, nevertheless, difficult for this Austerlitz group. Frequent tensions arose because they had not yet developed a thoroughgoing Christian community of goods. The initial action at Nicolsburg had been aimed primarily at meeting an immediate need on the part of those who had nothing at all, but there had also been in it the eschatological urging spirit of Hans Hut. He had received a vision of dramatic events to occur in the spring of 1528 and some *Stäbler* consequently believed it useless to own any property after that time of Christ's return. While their first sharing had been to meet a specific need, they soon moved to sharing both the things they consumed and the work of production as a community. Eventually they were to move to where the community owned everything and gave each person his task to perform as also his food, clothing, and housing.

In the fully developed idea of community of goods, from the mid-

1530's to the present, the single most important factor was that of love for the brother. The Hutterites, as they were to be called, considered their expression of Christian love to be the only true one. There could be no Christian love among Christian brethren who did not renounce all of their private possessions and commit them wholly to the community of brethren; indeed, failure to join with the brethren in community of goods called into question, in the Hutterite mind, the reality of the individual's salvation. Their great leader of the mid-seventeenth century, Andreas Ehrenpreis, wrote: "If Christian love to the neighbor cannot achieve as much as community in things temporal, in assistance and counsel, then the blood of Christ does not cleanse a man from his sins."[2] The Hutterites also used an argument derived from the practice of the Lord's Supper. Just as the grain of wheat and the single grape each lost its own identity completely in the loaf of bread and the wine, so also each brother must completely dissolve himself within the larger unity of the brotherhood; indeed, without this complete disappearance of the individual, no unity that was uniquely Christian was possible at all. The Hutterites cut at the natural selfishness of the human being and demanded of each member a yieldedness of self, a surrender, which they called *Gelassenheit*. No true discipleship, following after Christ, was possible without it.

The problems which had arisen from a lack of experience in communal living were eventually solved under the vigorous leadership of Jacob Hutter. Hutter, which means hat-maker, came from the Tirol in 1529 to investigate the Moravian lands as a possible place of refuge for his fellow Anabaptists. Both he and a co-worker were favorably impressed by what they saw in Moravia, and soon sent group after group of Tirolean Anabaptists to that haven. Hutter himself remained in the Tirol to continue his evangelical work, but he was appealed to by the Brethren in Moravia on several occasions to settle differences of opinion among them. The original Austerlitz group that practiced community of goods separated by 1530 from some of the unhappy ones moving to Auspitz. When Hutter returned to Moravia in 1530 to determine where the blame for this split lay, he found the Austerlitz leaders to be most at fault. In 1533 Hutter came to Auspitz where continued frictions among leaders and mismanagement of the community resources compelled him to remain for two years. By 1535 the community's affairs were competently managed through his vigorous leadership, but several of the former leaders, dissatisfied with his decisions and probably jealous of his popularity with the majority of the members, left Auspitz for other regions. In that year all of the Anabaptists in Moravia faced renewed persecution under the prodding of Archduke Ferdinand of Austria. The communities centering at Auspitz, which had grown larger through the addition of countless refugees from the Tirol and elsewhere, were broken up; their inhabitants were reduced to wandering about under the open skies, and finally to settling in smaller groups on those estates whose lords were willing to wink at Ferdinand's commands. But in the meantime the brotherhood had insisted that Hutter leave them because the civil authorities placed such a high priority on the capture of this leader. He returned to the Tirol in the hopes that persecution would have declined there, but within a few months he and his wife were surprised at night in the home of a friend. Tried in December, he was publicly burned at the stake on February 25, 1536. The measure of his influence on the Brethren in Moravia is evidenced by their referring to themselves henceforth as the *Hutterische Brüder,* from which we derive the English name Hutterian Brethren.

After Hutter's departure the Brethren were led by a succession of very able men, including Hans Amon, Peter Ridemann, Peter Walpot, and Klaus Braidl. The communities thrived, for precisely when the Anabaptists elsewhere in Europe faced fresh and vigorous efforts of the Catholic Counter-Reformation, efforts aimed at complete suppression, the Brethren in Moravia were permitted a remarkable degree of freedom. From approximately 1555 to 1595 the Brethren flourished; they referred to a part of this period as their "Golden Period." They sent out a succession of missioners to many parts of Europe; most of these paid for their activities with their lives, but they did so with the courage that was in itself a most attractive feature of Anabaptism, helping to win converts. The Brethren added to their number, through converts and through an almost constant stream of refugees from other parts of Europe. New colonies were founded, both in Moravia and beyond the eastern borders into Slovakia, then a part of Hungary. Perhaps they had as many as one hundred communities, with between 20,000 and 30,000 members. This was also a period of vigorous literary activity. Braitmichel began the *Geschicht-Buch* (Chronicle) which his successors carried on down to 1665. The Brethren were careful to keep records of letters to and from the brotherhood and of tracts written by and against them. Their organizational skills, developed to the highest degree by the demands of the community life which they practiced, were apparent in the fact that they could organize original materials into a historical account far in advance of their own times.

What was the organizational pattern of their colonies? The entire brotherhood was under the direction of one bishop. (*Vorsteher*). Each colony *(Bruderhof)*, then, had one or more preachers *(Diener des Wortes)* and several men who managed the economic affairs, including the farming *(Diener der Notdurft)*. Each colony consisted of a series of whitewashed houses grouped around a central courtyard. Here the members, numbering usually several hundred, lived and performed their various tasks, bound less by family ties than by ties of the entire colony. The continuous performance of the same kinds of tasks by the members developed in them an efficiency of operation that turned their colonies into establishments so economically successful that neighboring peasants complained of unfair competition. "It was like a big clockwork, where one wheel drives the other one, promotes, helps, and makes the whole clock function." Or "it is like a beehive where all the busy bees work together to a common end, the one doing this, the other that, not for their own need but for the good of all." [3]

Their very efficiency led to tales among the neighboring outsiders about their enormous wealth. Later monetary fines imposed on them by the civil authorities indicate that they were wealthy enough, but persecution and the rigor of their self-imposed discipline kept them from an economic and spiritual laxity which such comparative wealth often produces.

In the course of time the Brethren wrote a large number of rules and regulations, governing how they lived together and how they practiced certain crafts. The most famous of these was formulated in 1651 during the rule of Andreas Ehrenpreis; this *Gemeinde-Ordnungen* is still in use today. The Brethren excelled in the exercise of certain crafts: the making of ceramics, cutlery, carriages, certain kinds of beds, and clocks. Medicinal skills were developed to such an extent that Hutterite physicians and surgeons were sometimes called to the courts of nobles to practice their arts. Any income which a visiting brother gained from his outside employment was to be turned over to the community. Even the occasional coin found on the roadside was to go into this treasury.

Family life was not emphasized in the colony. The children left their parents for the·communal nursery-kindergarten at the age of two or three. Here they were under the care of women attendants who devoted all their time to the supervision and training of the children. They were taught a proper cleanliness, how to pray, and how to conduct themselves. From the kindergarten they passed to the elementary school, arranged in what we could call a boarding-school fashion. Children from outside the colony, including some from the families of nobles, were accepted and trained in the Hutterite elementary schools. The quality of the education was high, as evidenced by the later writings of the schools' graduates. Penmanship and spelling were excellent, and knowledge of the Bible together with certain elements of logic used in debate was very high.

By the time the young adult reached his early twenties, he became a candidate for baptism. The ceremony itself was performed after he had undergone a period of instruction; it was based on the candidate's solemn promise to be faithful to God and to the brother-hood. Also while in the early twenties the young people married. Romance was not the basis for choice of marriage partners. The elders brought together all the unmarried people of both sexes and suggested two or three possible males to each girl, one of whom she had to choose. [4] The wedding ceremony followed the assembly by a few days, allowing no time for courtship. Marriage was viewed as one of several human relations which God had commanded humans to enter. The Christian did so, as the Hutterites had it, reluctantly and with no thought for his own pleasure. Marriage was entered into because the Lord had commanded His children to marry in order to multiply.

The relative peace of the "Golden Period" came to an end late in the 1590's and in the first decade of the seventeenth century. It was inevitable that persecution would break out against people whom most Europeans thought of as heretical. Cardinal Franz von Dietrich-stein led the renewed persecution while, at the same time, keeping Balthasar Goller, a Hutterite physician, in his employ until the latter's death in 1619. A campaign of vilification was pressed against them by the Austrian government in the hope of winning popular support for further suppressive measures. In this campaign they were aided by two priests who knew them well and by two former Hutterites who were urged to show their orthodoxy by denouncing their former brethren. The comparative wealth of the Hutterite communities came under frequent attack, and financial demands for help against the Turks were pressed upon them. In 1605 the Turks plundered the Hutterite colonies and carried off not only material goods but also women and children. One Hutterite wandered in Turkish lands for three years trying to locate and ransom some of his fellow believers, but he had little success and died in the attempt. The events of the

Turkish War from 1593 to 1606, and the persecution of their own Austrian government shook these Moravian communities to the core. The Thirty Years' War (1618-48) was another calamity which struck them. With the Roman Catholic forces victorious in the early part of the war, pressure against the Hutterites became even more severe. In 1622 they were forced to retreat to their colonies in Slovakia, then under the rule of Hungary, with the loss of their land, buildings, and most of their possessions. With these migrations and the loss of spiritual leadership much of the earlier life went out of them. They lost the precision and orderliness of their group life and their self-discipline; the forces of disorder were too powerful for the moment. But in this hour of need another leader of exceptional ability arose to guide them: Andreas Ehrenpreis, who ruled as bishop from 1639 to his death in 1662. Ehrenpreis' greatest contributions were a fresh ordering of the organizational pattern and the direction of a spiritual renewal among them. During this period also began the practice of recording sermons that were preached which, together with the *Gemeinde-Ordnungen* of 1651, are much used today by the Hutterites in Canada and the United States.

After the death of Ehrenpreis a new decline set in. Late in the seventeenth century they abandoned their earlier form of communal living in favor of forms which gave a larger role to private property and initiative. They appealed to the Dutch Mennonites for financial help on several occasions and apparently received some. The internal decay and loss of discipline were too great, however, and in the eighteenth century most of the Hutterites surrendered to the arguments of the Catholic Jesuits coupled with the threat of force by the Austrian government. One of their colonies, far to the southeast in Transylvania, revived in spirit and in numbers by Lutherans who accepted the Hutterite position in the 1750's, decided to migrate eastward into the Ukraine in 1767. A few families from Slovakia followed them in 1782-83 under the leadership of Jacob Walter, but the remaining colonies in these regions turned Roman Catholic.

Despite the internal decay among the Hutterites, the Jesuits did not have an easy time converting them. Many tactics were used to this end. They sent the spiritual leaders among the males to monasteries, where most of them finally gave in. Catholic services were held in the colonies, and the remaining brothers and sisters were compelled by force to attend. Children were taken from the colonies and brought up by dedicated Catholics. For a time in the 1750's and 1760's the Hutterites became nominal Catholics, but met secretly to practice their old faith. By the late eighteenth century it appears that their resistance was completely overcome. They were given the nickname *Habaner* by the peasants, and their decendants still occupied some of the old Slovakian colonies at least until World War II. But the distinctive religious tradition and practice was lost in these regions; it was carried to the Ukraine, and from there again to Canada and the United States in the 1870's.

*Notes*
1. *Mennonite Encyclopedia,* I, p. 193, quoting from Wolkan, 63.
2. *Sendbrief,* 1652, in *Mennonite Encyclopedia,* I, p. 660.
3. *Chronicle,* in Robert Friedmann, *Hutterite Studies.* Goshen, Indiana: Mennonite Historical Society, 1961, p. 79.
4. One source turns it the other way: the young man chose from among two or three girls suggested to him by the elders. These meetings took place once or twice a year. This practice continued, with greater or lesser degrees of conformity to it, until the middle of the nineteenth century when the Hutterites finally permitted the young people greater freedom in the choice of a mate.

## FOR FURTHER READING:

*The Mennonite Encyclopedia,* 4 vols.

*Mennonite Life* 15 (July, 1960), pp. 109-11.

John Oyer, *Lutheran Reformers Against the Anabaptists.* The Hague: Martinus Nijhoff, 1964.

F. L. Weis, *The Life, Teachings and Works of Johannes Denck.* Strassburg, 1924.

John Horsch, *The Hutterian Brethren.* Goshen, Indiana: Mennonite Historical Society, 1931.

Peter Rideman, *Account of Our Religion, Doctrine and Faith.* Rifton, N.Y.: Plough Publishing House, 1950.

Victor Peters, *All Things Common, The Hutterian Way of Life.* Minneapolis: University of Minnesota Press, 1965.

Robert Friedmann, *Hutterite Studies.* Goshen: Mennonite Historical Society, 1961.

An excellent film on Hutterite life is available for use from the Historical Library, Goshen College, Goshen, Indiana, or from the Canadian Film Board.

John A. Hostetler, *Hutterite Life.* Scottdale: Herald Press, 1965.

# Chapter 5

## PILGRAM MARPECK AND
## SOUTH GERMAN ANABAPTISM

THE RECORDS of the ancient imperial city of Strassburg on the Rhine reveal that on September 19, 1528, an Austrian civil engineer by the name of Pilgram Marpeck became a citizen of that city. He had come to Strassburg because his life was in danger in his ancestral home of Rattenberg, located in the beautiful valley of the Inn River in Austria. The events of his life leading up to September, 1528, can be reconstructed from the sixteenth-century records of Rattenberg and neighboring cities, as well as from some comments Marpeck himself made several years later.

The date of his birth is not known, and the only fragment of information we have about his early life is that, as he himself tells us, he was raised by God-fearing parents in the Roman Catholic faith. To judge from his later social prominence and technical ability he must have enjoyed a good education, most likely in the Rattenberg Latin School. In the year 1520 he became a member of the miner's guild of Rattenberg and was occupied with transporting copper ore from the mines to the city of Kitzbühel, some miles to the east of Rattenberg. Several years later his name appears on the roster of the city council of Rattenberg. As a trusted civic official he was appointed to the post of mining magistrate which involved legal jurisdiction over the extensive mining operations in the lower Inn Valley. His salary was 65 pounds with a three-pound allowance for the proper dress on official occasions.

Marpeck was moderately wealthy. He was able to make a large loan to the city in 1525, and he is known to have owned several houses. He and his wife undertook to pay for the education of three orphan children, which reflects that he was a man of means as well as a man with a sense of social responsibility. Because of his wealth and social standing Marpeck moved freely in the circles of the nobility, an example of which was his lifelong friendship with Countess Helene von Freyberg, whose castle was near Kitzbühel.

Life apparently flowed along pleasantly for the Marpecks for several years after 1525. They were wealthy. Pilgram was a member of the inner council of the city, business was thriving, and it appeared that the Marpeck tradition of social standing and responsibility would be perpetuated. But it was not to be. The next entry in the Rattenberg records announces that Pilgram Marpeck had been dismissed from his office as mining magistrate but without stating a reason. It was most likely because, as a public official, he refused to aid in the detection and capture of Anabaptists. The date is January 28, 1528. Sometime during the next eight months he left his wealth, home, and station, never to return. His property, valued at 3,500 guilders, was confiscated by the city.

What was it that made a fugitive of so solid and respected a citizen as Pilgram Marpeck? Only something more compelling than wealth, position, and social prominence could have brought about such a change. Although all direct evidence is lacking, the reason was clearly that Marpeck had become an Anabaptist. That meant that he had promised obedience to Jesus Christ even though it demanded the sacrifice of all he had, including life itself. It was dangerous to be an Anabaptist in Austria in 1528, as we have seen in the preceding chapter. On August 20, 1527, Ferdinand I of Austria had issued a mandate against all "sectarians and heretics." He would tolerate no beliefs within his domain that were contrary to those held by the church of Rome. Everywhere Anabaptists were caught and imprisoned and many executed. We know that an Anabaptist congregation existed in Rattenberg late in 1527, because on November 25 Leonhard Schiemer was arrested after being bishop of the congregation for only one day. He was beheaded on January 14, 1528. Another notable Anabaptist preacher by the name of Hans Schlaffer was caught near Rattenberg on December 5, 1527, and executed on February 4, 1528. Marpeck must have known of these two martyrs and particularly the letters Schiemer wrote to the Rattenberg congregation during his imprisonment. If Marpeck was an Anabaptist at the time, he would have been a member of that congregation.

It is likely that Marpeck and his family were among the many

Anabaptist refugees who left their homes for places of safety, for to remain meant almost certain death. This was especially true after April 1, 1528, when an even harsher mandate was issued by Ferdinand against the Anabaptists. The Marpecks decided upon Strassburg as their destination. That city had a reputation for tolerance toward Anabaptists and was one of the few such places in all of Europe.

## Strassburg

Strassburg was an unusually important city in the Europe of the sixteenth century. It was the link between the Netherlands and Italy, between Paris and Vienna, and its location on the junction of two important routes of commerce contributed much to its prosperity in the sixteenth century. But along those same highways came men with ideas, traveling voluntarily in search of a better hearing or forced to flee by persecution. The range and diversity of the ideas held by people who either traveled through or settled down in Strassburg is truly astonishing.

But Strassburg was not only a popular and exciting place for overnight stops on the way to some other place. Like a magnet it drew people who, because of some point of view usually connected with Christian belief, were unwanted elsewhere. As a result of political revolts in the thirteenth and fourteenth centuries the city had become independent of its ruler who, as was so often the case, was both prince and bishop at the same time. A democratic form of government was developed with a complicated system of councils and elected officials representing the two main social groups, the nobility and the commoners. The main center of power lay with the twenty guilds, which were unions of craftsmen.

Wherever the bishops of the church of Rome were in full control they dealt decisively with any dissenters. For many centuries church law had insisted on the death penalty for denial of any church doctrine or for rebaptism. But in Strassburg the bishop had little power and could therefore not significantly interfere in religious matters. Strassburg's tolerant attitude to difference of opinion and moderation in punishing offenders had a long tradition. "He who would be hanged anywhere is simply driven from Strassburg by flogging," was a saying of the day.

When the Reformation began and its main ideas flooded the countries of Europe in the form of pamphlets and tracts, Strassburg was quickly in the middle of things. Because of its reputation for toleration it became a center for printing and distribution of all kinds of Reformation literature. Naturally the citizens did not remain un-affected by what was happening. The insistence of Martin Luther that a person is acceptable to God only through faith and never through the works prescribed by the church of Rome found welcome ears in a city that had already in its own way challenged the big church. When Luther's ninety-five theses arrived in Strassburg in 1518, copies were nailed to the doors of every church and parsonage in the city.

In the same year Matthew Zell came to Strassburg to serve as pastor of the cathedral parish. He was won for the Reformation and began soon after to express his newly won convictions. By 1523 he supported the use of German instead of Latin in church worship and rejected the Roman practice of giving only the bread to the people at communion. When he was denied the use of the cathedral pulpit by the authorities of the Roman church, the powerful guilds came to his aid and built for him a wooden platform from which he preached to congregations numbering as many as 3,000 people. Support was so strongly on the side of reform that the government of Strassburg issued a mandate at the end of 1523 authorizing evangelical preaching. When Zell was excommunicated in 1524 for having married, the government kept him in office. By August, 1524, the city authorities took over the responsibility for nominating, installing, and paying the pastors of the seven churches in the city in a manner similar to that of Zürich under Zwingli. In May, 1523, Martin Bucer arrived in the city and, because of his talent for leadership and his energy, soon became the chief reformer of Strassburg. We shall hear more of him later in the chapter.

Anabaptists began coming to Strassburg early in 1526 although Balthasar Hubmaier had his book on baptism published there in July, 1525. Among the first to arrive were Michael Sattler and Wilhelm Reublin, both belonging to the Swiss Brethren. In November, 1526, Hans Denk arrived from Augsburg and had a public debate with the Strassburg ministers. Denk was ordered out of the city, as we have seen, and the council decreed that no more public debates between the ministers and dissenters should be held without the express per-mission of the council. Several more prominent Anabaptists as well as other sorts of Reformation dissenters came to Strassburg in 1526-27.

Matthew Zell exhibited a truly Christian spirit toward the Anabap-tists and completely rejected the notion that anyone should be persecuted for his faith. He regarded most of the Anabaptists as true Christians who ought to be commended, not coerced. He publicly stated that he was not in agreement with the oppressive measures proposed by Bucer and city officials. Wolfgang Capito, another of the Strassburg reformers, although he found himself drawn to the Anabaptists, especially to Michael Sattler, and although he held some views in common with them, nevertheless agreed that those Anabaptists who stubbornly insisted on their schismatic views were to be punished. It was due mainly to Zell and Capito that Strassburg was the "City of Hope" for the persecuted Anabaptists. Martin Bucer, the chief reformer, also had friendly feelings for Anabaptists at the beginning, due chiefly to his friendship with Michael Sattler, but when the Anabaptists insisted on forming their own brotherhood, his attitude toward them became one of total opposition. Although he strongly advocated that Anabaptists be turned from their beliefs by persuasion, he did not hesitate to use violence if they showed no inclination to change. On July 27, 1527, a severe mandate was issued prohibiting all citizens from giving assistance and shelter to Anabaptists. It was put into effect immediately, but the tradition of tolerance in Strassburg made it impossible to win the struggle with the Anabaptists. Even with the expulsion in 1534 of Leopold Scharnschlager, a strong leader and associate of Pilgram Marpeck, organized congregational life continued, although not as strongly as before. The tradition of tolerance made possible Anabaptist conferences in Strassburg in the years 1554, 1556, 1557, 1568, 1592, and 1607.

## Marpeck and Anabaptism

After that digression into the history of the city of Strassburg and its attitude toward the Anabaptists we return now to the story of Pilgram Marpeck. It is clear that he came to Strassburg in order to join and work in the Anabaptist brotherhood, for a notation from October 22, 1528, read: ". . . Pilgram Marpeck from Rattenberg in the Inn Valley, a citizen, with his wife, in whose house the meetings of the Anabaptists took place. . . ." He seems also to have gained immediate employment in the city, perhaps as a member of the gardener's guild. Apparently it was not long before his engineering talents were discovered, for he was soon employed by the city as engineer.

Across the Rhine to the east of Strassburg lies the Black Forest, presently a favorite haunt of tourists. In 1528 as today it contained vast stands of silver fir on the higher elevations of the mountains and beech, birch, and oak lower down in the valleys. But the forests were at least fifteen to twenty miles from Strassburg and the transport of logs over mountainous roads a laborious, slow, and inefficient affair. It was to solve this economic problem that Marpeck was hired by the city.

His task was to bring the timber from the mountains into Strassburg by water. The Kinzig River divides the Black Forest into its northern and southern sections and flows into the Rhine near Strassburg. This river had been used for generations to float logs into Strassburg, but its usefulness for this purpose was limited to the springtime when it ran high from thawing snow up in the mountains. Marpeck's assignment was certainly to make possible the use of the river at least for the duration of the summer and autumn. This he accomplished by constructing a system of dams, behind which water was conserved in the spring. When the timbers were ready to float, a gate in the dam was opened, releasing enough water to float the logs down. In addition to the dams he also constructed a series of special spillways primarily to bypass rock obstructions and rapids of which there are many on the Kinzig. He did similar work on the Murg River further to the north and also on several small streams flowing into the Rhine from the Vosges Mountains to the west. This engineering accomplishment added much to the economic welfare of Strassburg, and it was undoubtedly his usefulness to the city which made possible his stay there even though he was known as an Anabaptist leader from the beginning. Evidently his work had lasting significance, for generations later the timber brought down from the Black Forest was still known as "Pilgram-wood."

Martin Bucer and Wolfgang Capito were the most influential Protestant leaders in Strassburg while Marpeck lived there. Capito regarded him highly and seems to have been chiefly responsible for his extended stay. It was Bucer who was determined to get rid of Marpeck. He was prompted in his attitude primarily by Marpeck's public and penetrating criticism of church affairs in Strassburg for which Bucer bore the main responsibility. Nor is it altogether surprising that he should have resented and feared Marpeck, for Marpeck was a strong and forthright leader. His theological writings reveal a man of high intelligence, especially when we remember that he was a layman with no formal theological training. Although his writings tend to be wordy and repetitious, they reveal the mind of a man who had struggled effectively with some of the basic religious questions of his day. Evidently he had read much and listened carefully. Even though the Strassburg clergy found his presence highly disturbing, they gave him the testimony that "he had many splendid gifts from

66

God and in many respects manifested a vigorous good zeal" and Bucer himself agreed that, although he was a "stiff-necked heretic," he and his wife exhibited a "fine, blameless behavior." [2]

But Marpeck was not content quietly to be the leader of the Anabaptist church in Strassburg. He felt compelled to speak to other Christians about his understanding of the Christian faith, and since Bucer and his fellow ministers were so influential in the city he spoke to them. In fact, during a discussion with Bucer in December of 1531 he said that the opportunity for such discussion with other Christians was the reason for his coming to Strassburg. This conviction about the necessity to witness to his fellow Christians, however, finally led to his expulsion from the city.

He was known as an Anabaptist leader from the beginning of his stay in Strassburg, but because of his professional skill he had been left unmolested. By 1531, however, Bucer began to get impatient, for Marpeck was influencing not only the common people but also some of higher standing. Bucer's letters to his friends revealed more and more that he could no longer tolerate his presence. Late in 1531 he therefore managed to have him arrested and put in prison, but his success was of short duration, for Marpeck was released unconditionally, in part upon Capito's intercession, and likely in part because the city needed his professional services.

This experience did not discourage Marpeck. In fact, it seems to have prompted his next step which was a request to the council for a public debate with the ministers. He evidently felt that a public hearing would aid the true understanding of the Christian faith. The council, however, remembering the pubic debate with Hans Denk five years earlier, denied the request, and instead arranged for a private discussion between Marpeck and Bucer before the council and other city officials. The public was excluded, very likely because the council feared that the simple logic of the Anabaptist leader would turn the public against the established order in the city. Capito had left Strassburg for an extended vacation on the insistence of Bucer. Thus the stage was set for the contest. Actually it was no contest because it was like a baseball game in which the manager of one of the ball clubs is the umpire. Under such conditions the outcome was predictable. The council decided on December 18 that unless Marpeck abandoned his opinions and his efforts to "overthrow infant baptism" he be banished from the city. He was also warned that if he returned, his reception would be such that he would soon wish he had stayed away.

Marpeck responded calmly and without anger or excitement to this shattering announcement. He said that he could make no promise never to return since God might lead him back. He also requested four weeks of grace so that he could settle the sale of his property and some financial matters relating to his employment with the city. During this time he wrote a long confession of faith which fills about thirty-five printed pages. To this Bucer wrote an equally long reply, point by point. These documents, as well as the minutes of the debate of December 9, clearly reveal the two main points of difference between Christians of the Anabaptist and Reformed faiths in Strassburg in 1531: baptism and the relationship of the church to the civic government.

It is not enough simply to state their positions on these matters, for there were reasons for their convictions. We must try to understand why Bucer defended infant baptism and why Marpeck rejected it; why Bucer felt compelled to persecute the Anabaptists and why Marpeck made a plea for religious freedom. This can perhaps be done best by examining how these men understood and interpreted the Bible. Both of them believed that the Bible was the Christian's authority in the church and in private life, but in their interpretation of Scripture they ended up at opposite poles on some basic questions.

## The Interpretation of Scripture

We begin with Bucer because his interpretation of Scripture and the position derived from it was accepted as the official view of the city of Strassburg. This was the interpretation Marpeck criticized and against which we must see and understand Marpeck's own interpretation. Bucer believed that the Old and New Testaments formed an indivisible unity, with the Old Testament having practically the same authority for the Christian as the New. God made a covenant with Abraham in which He graciously and freely pledged Himself to be the God of Abraham's descendants. This same covenant extended through both Old and New Testaments and on into the present day. Since the coming of Jesus men have better understood that covenant, they understand better what God has done and what He wants them to do, but the original covenant has in no basic way been changed or canceled out by His coming.

This understanding of the Bible led to a number of important consequences in Bucer's thinking. First, baptism in the Christian Church was regarded as the equivalent of circumcision in the Hebrew community. As circumcision was the sign of the covenant, that is, a visible proof that a person was included in the covenant, so baptism was also the sign of the same covenant. It is the sign that God is gracious and merciful, and desires to be gracious to this particular child. Faith is not connected with baptism, for both man's sin and man's salvation begin before there is any faith. Each child is a sinner, having inherited evil from Adam, and since therefore he needs God's grace and forgiveness, he must also have the sign of baptism.

The second consequence of Bucer's understanding of the Bible was that although not all the people in the city of Strassburg were obedient followers of Christ, yet they must all be in the church even as all the Hebrews were included in the covenant in the Old Testament. That would be like saying that everyone belongs to the ball team whether he observes the rules or not. God, said Bucer, was the only one who could decide who was a Christian and who was not; man cannot make such decisions. In fact, Bucer held to the idea of special election which really means that God has in His mysterious wisdom appointed some persons to salvation and some to damnation. No one knows what God's choice is with respect to any person. Thus man cannot decide who belongs to the church because even a thoroughly evil person may be elected to salvation. To say therefore that such a person may not be in the church is to put oneself in the place of God.

A third consequence had to do with the relationship of the church and the civil government which in Strassburg was the city council. Bucer held that God has two kinds of servants. The first preach the Word of God and tell people what is right and what is wrong like the prophets and priests in the Old Testament. The second, like the Old Testament kings, are responsible for seeing that everyone does what is right and punish those who do not. This meant that all who opposed the work of the ministers whether by evil living or by contradicting their ideas would be punished. An example of how this worked was the petition of Bucer and his fellow ministers to the council in December of 1531 to punish those who contradicted and despised their teachings. There can be little doubt that Marpeck was among those aimed at. Bucer insisted that it was a Christian's responsibility to bear the sword of a magistrate since only the Christian knew what God wanted men to do. He also believed in the support of the council for the sake of those who did not have a sufficiently strong will to do what was right; such weak persons would be helped to do the right by the threat of force. Church and government were thus thoroughly intermixed, and there was some confusion about the responsibility of each. The outcome of such an arrangement was often that the decisions in the life of the church were governed by political and social considerations rather than by the Bible.

The fourth consequence of Bucer's understanding of the Bible was that since Christians had a fuller understanding of God's will than the Old Testament Hebrews, most of the rules and regulations of the Old Testament were no longer binding. The Hebrews needed such external observances as sacrifice and food laws because of their lack of understanding, but in the Christian Church only faith and love are required. For the situation in Strassburg this meant simply that there was no definite order in church life. Everyone was assumed to be a member of the church regardless of what he did or whether he wanted to be in the church or not.

We now turn to Marpeck's understanding of the Bible and his views of baptism and the relationship of the church to the civic government that flowed from it. The Old and New Testaments formed a unity for him, but of a different kind than the unity which Bucer found. Marpeck said that Old and New Testaments stand to each other in a relationship of promise and fulfillment, just as today, for example, the pledge of marriage in the engagement and the marriage itself are inseparable, but still quite clearly distinguishable. One is introductory to the other. When Jesus came, the old order was replaced by a new one. The old is no longer authoritative because the new covenant in Christ is of a different nature than the old covenant made with Abraham. The same gracious God gave both covenants, but the old covenant was characterized by a complex system of rules and regulations because, although people wanted to do God's will, they neither clearly understood it nor did they have the strength to do it. It was, said Marpeck, a covenant of slavery. The new covenant, however, is characterized by freedom. No system of regulations is necessary because the people that accept it both know God's will and are free and able to do it because God gives them the strength. Briefly then Marpeck held that under the old covenant men were forced to do right and under the new they are free to do right. From this view followed four important consequences.

First, he believed that God wants all persons to obey Him freely, without compulsion, and that it is possible for each person to obey God if he so chooses. This means that Marpeck completely rejected Bucer's doctrine of election; God wants every person to be saved.

Because he rejected the doctrine of election he also rejected infant baptism, since an infant cannot freely choose to obey God. Actually infant baptism compels a person to be in the church without giving that person any choice in the matter. Furthermore, before any person can freely obey God, he must repent of his sins and believe that God loves him and wants his obedience, but infants can neither repent nor believe. Furthermore, we need not worry about the welfare of innocent babies. They have no sin until they are able to distinguish between good and evil, and since they are not sinners they need no redemption; God has already accepted them because Jesus said, "Let the children come to me, for theirs is the kingdom of heaven." Even the child of Christian parents, once he becomes responsible, has no advantage before God and it should not be assumed that he is or will be a Christian. He too must repent and believe in order to be saved.

The second consequence was that Marpeck regarded the New Testament as the final authority for the Christian life in the church. He agreed with Bucer that faith and love were all-important, but he went on to say that only the person who is unconditionally obedient to Christ has true faith and true love. Since in the New Testament baptism clearly follows faith, it must be so today; only those who have faith may be baptized. Jesus commanded His followers to love their enemies. That allows for no exceptions and means that Christians may not participate in war.

Thirdly, since the New Testament is the Christian's final authority, it cancels out the Old Testament wherever the two do not agree. Bucer appealed to the Old Testament union of church and state, but for Marpeck that was a slavish system. Since freedom is characteristic of the New Testament, freedom in matters of faith must be taken seriously, and this would inevitably mean the clear separation of church and world. To Marpeck not only God's gracious favor but also man's free response mattered. The church is the society only of those who freely choose to be obedient to Christ. Joining the church is therefore not merely the acceptance of God's grace but also a willingness to live in obedience to it. It is not doing a person a favor to regard him as a member of the church if he does not want to be obedient to Christ of his own free will. Bucer rejected this reasoning because it would inevitably lead to the formation of a new church.

The fourth and final consequence of Marpeck's view of the Scriptures was that he rejected the idea of two servants in the church, the preacher and the magistrate, as held by Bucer. The preacher is in the church to be sure because he tells about God's love and grace and offers it to people, but the magistrate does not function within the church because there only Christ rules over the spirits of men. The magistrate is appointed by God to restrain evil among those persons who have no desire to obey Christ. In practice this meant the rejection of all coercion in matters of faith. No magistrate has the authority even to judge in such matters, much less to force people to accept such judgments. Since God wants a free response from all men, compelling people to believe that of which they are not convinced interferes with God's order. This even applies to children of Christian parents who cannot simply be told what to believe; it applies also to persons who believe otherwise than those in power. To use the magistrate to punish dissenters or blasphemers is to admit that the Word of Christ is not able to do what it is said to be capable of, to convert evil men. It is simply contrary to God's order and the Spirit of Christ to persecute anyone for his faith or for having no faith at all. Those who do not want to believe should be left alone; they should not be expected to live as Christians when they have no power to do so. Not only did Marpeck state these convictions in his confession, he also appealed directly to the city council to let liberty of conscience and religious freedom prevail in Strassburg.

Marpeck's confession convinced neither Bucer nor the council that he was right and he finally left Strassburg in February, 1532. For the next decade we know practically nothing of the life of Marpeck. He evidently continued as an important leader among the Anabaptists of Germany, Switzerland, and Moravia, apparently traveling a great deal and writing letters to churches and individuals.

### An Invisible Church?

In 1542 he suddenly emerged again with the publication of a little book on baptism, which was in fact a careful revision of a work by some Anabaptist preachers from North Germany. Marpeck's purpose in publishing it was that it might help to unite and strengthen the Anabaptist brotherhood. While certainly performing this function, the little book caught the attention of another dissenter, Caspar Schwenckfeld, who lived not far from Augsburg. He was not an Anabaptist but what one might call an "invisiblist." He believed that what is truly real in life is invisible and that therefore all concern about such visible matters as baptism and the Lord's Supper was idolatry because it prevented people from being concerned for what was truly important. Since Marpeck had argued for the importance of right observance of baptism and the Lord's Supper in the church, Schwenckfeld regarded the book as an attack on himself. He replied with a book of his own charging the Anabaptists with completely misunderstanding the Bible and the Christian faith.

The position represented by Schwenckfeld proved a great temptation for the persecuted Anabaptists. Why not, some of them seriously asked, abandon baptism and the Lord's Supper since they are not important anyway? Why not become an "invisible" church so that we will not be persecuted anymore? These questions had already been asked in 1531 in Strassburg while Marpeck was there and he had in that year written two little books against this view. Now he and some of his co-workers took up the task of replying to Schwenckfeld's criticism in a work of about 800 pages. The basic question was again the interpretation of the Bible and especially the matter of the relationship of the New to the Old Testament. There is no need to discuss this argument in detail because it was almost identical to Marpeck's argument with Bucer which we described earlier.

In 1544 Marpeck gained employment with the city of Augsburg as an engineer and did work similar to that which he had done at Strassburg. Although efforts were made to prosecute him he remained in his position until his death in 1556.

Throughout his time as an Anabaptist leader and elder he was deeply concerned for the unity of the Anabaptist fellowship. This concern is clearly reflected in the fourteen remaining letters from his hand addressed to Anabaptists at Strassburg, in Switzerland, in Moravia, and in Germany. He writes about the unity of the church; warns some that although the Christian is free in Christ, he is not free to live a life of sin; criticizes others for judging each other too harshly. He urges members separated by misunderstanding to be reconciled, writes very practically about the place of the minister in the congregation, and deals with a variety of other matters.

Pilgram Marpeck was the most notable German Anabaptist leader and theologian. He contributed a great deal to the clarification of the Anabaptist interpretation of the Christian faith. Even today he inspires us with his passion for unity among believers in Christ.

*FOR FURTHER READING:*

*The Mennonite Encyclopedia,* 4 vols.

C. Henry Smith, *The Story of the Mennonites.* Third revised edition. Newton, Kansas: Mennonite Publication Office, 1950.

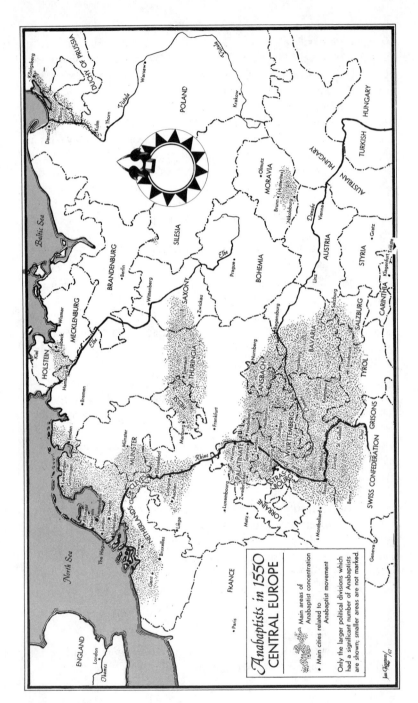

Anabaptists in 1550
CENTRAL EUROPE

Main areas of
Anabaptist concentration

• Main cities related to
Anabaptist movement

Only the larger political divisions which
had a significant number of Anabaptists
are shown; smaller areas are not marked.

Jan Gleysteen '67

*Chapter 6*

# ANABAPTISM IN THE NETHERLANDS

THE HEADWATERS of the Rhine are in Switzerland, but the river flows through Germany into the Netherlands, where it divides into several branches as it reaches the sea. The Anabaptist movement also had its headwaters in Switzerland and, like the Rhine, divided into several streams as it passed through Germany and down to the Netherlands, but Anabaptism flowed in ideas rather than water and through people rather than through hills and valleys.

Ideas are powerful. In a changing society they can be creatively good or tragic. Some people use well the power of new ideas; others channel them to bad ends; still others fear them and try to dam them up and hold them back. The history of the birth of the Anabaptist movement in the Netherlands, from where its people came to be known as Mennonites, is about the flow of new ideas into a society ready for change. This history has in it abuse, opposition, but also creative use of the new ideas.

*Melchior Hoffman*

Melchior Hoffman was the man through whom Anabaptism came to the Netherlands. He was a gifted but uneducated leader, a tanner or furrier by training. Born in Swabia in southern Germany in 1493, he first came to attention as a self-taught Lutheran preacher active in Sweden and the small countries on the east shore of the Baltic. When he was driven from this area, he went to Holstein in northern Germany and to Denmark, but after experiencing opposition there also, he went to Emden and then up the Rhine to Strassburg.

Hoffman moved from one idea to another almost as easily as he moved from one place to another. While at first an evangelist for the Lutherans, he later moved closer to Zwingli, and then to the more radical Carlstadt, both of whom differed from Luther in their understanding of the Lord's Supper and other doctrines. Nevertheless his own originality and Bible study, especially the books of Daniel and The Revelation of John, led him to develop his own views. In Strassburg he first met the Anabaptists and absorbed many of their ideas into his own thinking, but added other ideas of his own. In the Netherlands this mixture was to separate, creating in the process one of the darkest moments in Anabaptist history.

In 1530 Hoffman left Strassburg to return to Emden, soon after having become an Anabaptist. Here he found a ready response among people already inclined to reform and about three hundred were baptized. From Emden he also sent lay preachers into the Netherlands and later traveled there himself. In the meantime his continuing interest in prophecy led him to more extreme ideas, among which was a radical emphasis upon the nearness of Christ's return to set up His kingdom on earth. The prophecies of Leonard and Ursula Jost, Barbara Rebstock, and other visionaries led him to believe that Strassburg would be the spiritual Jerusalem, and that he himself was Elijah chosen to proclaim the coming event to all people. Finding his way back to Strassburg, he acted on his faith in these prophecies by having himself imprisoned. This was to be a necessary precondition to the coming of the kingdom. Obbe Philips, whom we will meet again later, said of these events:

Thus, through the mediation of this prophecy, Melchior removed to Strasbourg and there began to preach and to teach here and there in the houses of the burghers. Then to be brief, the authorities sent their servants to take him prisoner. When Melchior saw that he was going to prison, he thanked God that the hour had come and threw his hat from his head and took a knife and cut off his hose [the trousers and stockings were one garment] at the ankle, threw his shoes away and extended his hand with the fingers to heaven and swore by the living God who lives there from eternity to eternity that he would take no food and enjoy no drink other than bread and water until the time that he could point out with his hand and outstretched fingers the One who had sent him. And with this he went willingly, cheerfully, and well comforted to prison. [1]

He remained in prison until his death some ten years later. The prophecies he had believed in so fervently remained unfulfilled, but his influence on other leaders in the Netherlands was of great importance for the future of the movement.

Among the apostles whom Hoffman had sent into the Netherlands from Emden were Sicke Freerks, a tailor and for that reason
sometimes called Snijder, who went to Leeuwarden, and Jan Volkerts-
zoon Tripmaker, who went to Amsterdam. As a people with a long
history of freedom, but now suffering under the oppressive rule of
Spain, the Dutch were ready to listen to the words of these men. The
Spanish king, who was also Holy Roman Emperor, ruled with a heavy
hand. Because of this and because of the new winds of social change
sweeping across Europe, the people were restless and disturbed. They
resented the armies which were constantly moving across the land; a
series of floods had destroyed property and killed both livestock and
people. The plague also troubled them. In Leiden it was reportedly
so bad that people said, "Oh, dear Lord, do not pass us by with
the gift of the hot sickness, for we would rather die than live any
longer." Disaster and adversity were believed to be signs of the anger
of God.

There was also dissatisfaction among the people with the poor
state of the medieval church. They knew of the Brethren of the
Common Life, who had brought reforms and provided schools where
a better religious life was taught. With the coming of printing more
people could get Bibles. As many as thirty printings of different
translations of the Bible as a whole or in part appeared in less
than ten years before 1530. The Sacramentarians too had offered
growing opposition to the Roman Catholic interpretation of the Lord's
Supper by rejecting the doctrine of the physical presence of the body
and blood of Christ in the bread and wine. Already in 1527, three
years before the Anabaptists came, the Sacramentarian widow Weynken
of Monnickendam was arrested for heresy on this issue. When she
was asked, "What do you hold concerning the sacrament?" she answered, "I hold your sacrament to be bread and flour, and if you hold
it as God, I say that it is your devil." She was burned at the stake.

With the coming of the Hoffmanite apostles to the Netherlands
these yearnings and frustrations found new hope of fulfillment in the
teachings of Anabaptism. Not all of the responses were encouraging,
however. When Hoffman was imprisoned in 1533, a baker from Haarlem named Jan Matthijs claimed the leadership in Amsterdam,
sending twelve apostles out in pairs to convert the people. One
pair visited Leeuwarden late that year where they succeeded in
winning and baptizing Obbe and Dirk Philips, two brothers who

were to become key figures in the early history of the movement. Other apostles reached the city of Münster in northern Germany and began the countdown leading to the tragedy which was to overtake the city.

Upon their arrival in Münster these apostles of Jan Matthijs found several preachers who were in close agreement with them and ready to have them remain there. This they quickly reported to Matthijs, who moved to the city early in 1534, eager to see the fulfillment of the Hoffmanite prophecy. But whereas Hoffman had claimed Strassburg to be the site of the New Jerusalem, Matthijs used a new prophecy to change the location to his own Münster. Far more important was the change to violence; whereas Hoffman had been peaceful and urged his followers to wait for God to set up the kingdom, Matthijs taught that the faithful were to prepare for the coming of the kingdom by making a place for it by force of arms. As a result, everyone was soon forced to receive baptism and join the movement, or leave the city. Military preparations were quickly made for the great battle which would usher in the kingdom.

In alarm over these developments the Bishop of Münster, who did not live in the city, gathered an army with some support from the German princes, and laid siege to the supposed New Jerusalem. Believing himself to have received special divine protection, Jan Matthijs selected a small band of soldiers and attempted to break through the lines, but he was killed and his body dumped before the city gate. Leadership now passed to another Jan--Jan van Leiden, whose ideas were even more extreme than those of Matthijs. He proclaimed himself the new King David and ruled with an iron hand. Polygamy was introduced on the basis of the examples from the Old Testament, and other devious practices were decreed. The small group that survived suffered grievously from hunger and disease before the city finally fell to the bishop's troops on June 24, 1535.

The Münsterite movement had aroused the hopes of many among the common people in northwestern Germany and the Netherlands. Now they were not only disappointed at its failure, but even more at the bad name it gave to Anabaptists everywhere. Because of Münster they were all now labeled as visionaries and revolutionaries. It was one of those times in history when persecution drove people to extreme action, and extreme action convinced the persecutors that they were right and justified even more severe measures against them.

## The Peaceful Anabaptists

Not all of those who became Anabaptists in the Netherlands followed the Münsterites, nor even the more moderate and peaceful views of Hoffman. With Obbe and Dirk Philips, whom we have already referred to, Anabaptism followed another course even under severe persecution, and in Dirk the Dutch movement was eventually to have one of its major spokesmen and theologians as also churchman.

Obbe and Dirk Philips were sons of a priest in Leeuwarden. Their education was probably better than the average of the day. Obbe was both a surgeon and barber as was customary at the time. Dirk was associated with the Franciscans and may have had training in theology. They were both baptized by apostles of Jan Matthijs in December-January of 1533-34 and Obbe was immediately ordained as elder. This authorized him to ordain other leaders in addition to carrying other church responsibilities.

Obbe did not accept the revolutionary teachings of Jan Matthijs and soon gathered about himself a group of potential leaders concerned for a more faithful study and use of the Scriptures. The use of force was rejected by them as were the prophecies which had led to the armed attempts of Münster. But Obbe's spiritual pilgrimage was not yet at an end. Though he worked diligently to restore order after the Münster tragedy, he became increasingly disillusioned with Anabaptism as a movement which had originally spawned Münster and now, in reaction, seemed to be becoming increasingly rigid and legalistic in its demands. Because of this he pulled back from the movement in 1539-40, having earlier, however, ordained his brother Dirk as well as David Joris and Menno Simons as leaders. It is probable that he became a spiritualist who practiced an inward religion without openly joining any church. We know very little about him after his withdrawal, except that he lived in Rostock along the north German coast and died in 1568. A confession which he wrote to explain why he left the Anabaptists is the only writing we have from his hand.

Dirk worked faithfully with Obbe in opposing the revolutionary Münsterites. As his writings became known among the Anabaptists, they strengthened and encouraged the progress of the peaceful group. He might, in fact, have taken Obbe's place as leader had it not been for another who had risen in the group, Menno Simons. We now turn our attention to him as the most important leader in the first generation of Dutch Anabaptism.

79

Menno Simons became an Anabaptist more than ten years after the first baptism in Zurich on January 21, 1525, and about six years after the apostles of Melchior Hoffman began preaching in the Netherlands. He was born in Witmarsum, a small village in the northern Dutch province of Friesland where his parents lived, most likely as farmers. We know that he studied for the priesthood and was ordained by the Bishop of Utrecht in 1524, but he knew only a little Greek and no Hebrew. His first assignment was as the second of three priests in Pingjum, a mile west of his hometown.

In his later recollections of these early years as a village priest, he tells how he spent his time in "playing cards, drinking, and in diversions as, alas, is the fashion and usage of such useless people." He did not engage in serious immoral activities but wasted away his time in careless living. Already in his first year as priest, however, he began to be troubled about the Roman Catholic doctrine of the physical presence of the flesh and blood of Christ in the bread and wine of the mass. It is likely that he had been influenced by the Sacramentarians, of whom there were many in the Netherlands. Since he could not rid himself of these doubts even through prayer and confession, he decided to turn to the Scriptures in his further search. In taking this step, he writes, he was influenced by Luther. This study of the Scriptures convinced him that the church was wrong in its teaching that Christ was physically present in the Lord's Supper. The study also quickly earned him the reputation of being an evangelical preacher.

Soon he began to doubt in another area. To his amazement he heard that Sicke Freerks (Snijder), the apostle who had been sent by Hoffman, had been beheaded in nearby Leeuwarden for having himself rebaptized. This time Menno turned to the Scriptures immediately but was unable to find support for the practice of infant baptism in them. Thereupon he studied the writings of the reformers Luther, Bucer, and Bullinger, but while they defended infant baptism, he again did not find their arguments supported by Scripture. Yet despite these doubts he remained in the priesthood. He was, in fact, promoted to become priest in his hometown of Witmarsum. It was there that his reputation as an evangelical preacher increased, for he had much occasion to refute the Münsterite doctrine which was making inroads among his people. He conferred with the Münsterite leaders, and though he respected their zeal and sincerity, he was certain they were in error and tried publicly to correct these errors through his preaching.

The decisive moment came for Menno in one of the tragic events; connected with Münster. A band of about three hundred rallied to support Münster and took over a monastery called the Old Cloister near Witmarsum. They were besieged, captured, and many of them were killed in battle or executed. It is believed that one of them, named Peter Simons, was Menno's brother. This event, in any case, moved Menno to action. While he agreed with these men at many points, he deplored their misguided zeal. They were like sheep without a shepherd, while he remained in comfort and ease, even building his reputation by opposing them. And so, after much inward struggle, and with the typical deliberateness of his Frisian people, he broke with the past. In a public statement on January 30, 1536, he told of his new commitment to the cause of Christ, and then went into hiding with the help of the peaceful Anabaptists with whom he was most in agreement. The next year was spent in study of the Scriptures and in writing. It is, no doubt, during this period that he worked out the fuller meaning of the position to which he had come and on which he stood committed until his death twenty-five years later. At the end of this year of preparation, he was visited by a delegation of six to eight men who asked him to become leader and elder of their people. After hesitating because of the serious implications of this call to lead a persecuted group, he finally consented to serve and was ordained by Obbe Philips, who had also baptized him earlier.

### Neither Traditionalist nor Fanatic

In 1539-40, two or three years after Menno Simons' ordination, Obbe Philips withdrew from the movement, as we have seen. He had grown weary of the struggle against Roman Catholic traditionalism on the one hand, and the fanatical extremism of Münster on the other. Whereas the former seemed to be guided more by tradition than by the Scriptures, the latter seemed to read every Biblical text in the light of their own visions and expectations. In between were the Lutherans and Calvinists who wanted reform but kept many of the traditions of the Roman Catholic past, and disagreed sharply with the Anabaptists on numerous issues.

To lead the fledgling Anabaptist group through this spiritual wilderness became the lot of Menno Simons; to sift truth from half-truth, oppose error with clear teaching, encourage the persecuted, correct the misguided and build the young church while himself being hunted as a heretic was to be his life. In this time of struggle during the 1540's and 1550's he had many helpers, especially Dirk Philips, but it was Menno's leadership which saved the Dutch Anabaptist movement from fanaticism and possible disintegration. Because of this, those who belonged to the movement were soon known as *Mennists,* or *Mennonists,* and eventually as *Mennonites.*

In a way the most difficult part of the struggle during these years was not that against Roman Catholic persecution, nor against the revolutionary ideas of the fanatics on the other hand. The struggle was most intense against the Lutherans, Calvinists, and even the brethren among his own following with whom Menno had much in common. With these it was much more difficult to know where, when, and how to take a stand. The Mennonites agreed with the Lutherans and Calvinists on the major points of Reformation doctrine, especially on justification by faith and the authority of the Scriptures, but drew different implications from these doctrines. For the Mennonites, justification by faith meant that only persons old enough to have a conscious faith and make decisions for themselves could be baptized; only those whose life showed the results of faith were to be gathered into the church.

In contrast to this the Lutherans and Calvinists (Reformed) still held to the idea that a society which does not have a common religion is dangerous. They pointed to the Münsterites as evidence of the danger when people are free to choose membership in any church group, or free to refuse altogether. Menno engaged in personal and written debate with the leaders of these state churches in the decade following 1540, and many of the writings we have from his hand today reflect the issues of that period.

The first major meeting was with John a Lasco at Emden in 1544, followed by two lengthy written statements from Menno. The second debate was with Martin Micron, pastor of the Reformed Church in London. When Queen Mary restored Catholicism as the official religion after the reforms of Henry VIII and Edward VI, the Calvinists had to leave England. They arrived off the coast of north Germany near Wismar in the winter of 1553. The Mennonites, who were themselves refugees in hiding, helped the group when their boat was frozen in the ice and no one else would accept them.

At the insistence of the Reformed leaders a series of meetings was held between them and the Mennonites in February, 1554. Micron, who had meanwhile located at Emden, was brought in to participate. Contrary to their understanding, he then published an account of these meetings, forcing Menno to release his interpretation also and publicly answering the charges Micron made against him. Micron answered Menno and with that both the personal and written debate was closed, but the authorities had meanwhile become aroused and Menno had to flee from the region.

Another exchange came with Gellius Faber, who inclined toward the Lutherans, but cooperated with the Reformed John a Lasco in Emden. He had participated in the debate against Menno in 1544, and in 1552 wrote a booklet against the Anabaptists which Menno felt to be so unfair that he had to reply. This answer, which is simply entitled *Reply to Gellius Faber,* contains an account of Menno's conversion as well as a discussion of his call to the ministry. Beyond this it is particularly helpful for understanding how the Mennonites differed from the Reformed and the Lutherans on baptism, the Lord's Supper, church discipline, the nature of the church, and the incarnation of Christ.

These debates made it clear that the Mennonites differed with the state churches on two basic issues: the nature of the Christian life, and the nature of the church. On the first they stressed the importance of the new birth and discipleship. Only persons who were repentant and knew by experience the grace of God should be baptized and join the church. Evidence of the new birth was to be seen in the serious attempt to live as disciples who had committed themselves fully to Christ as Lord. Vital signs of this discipleship were love and non-resistance. On the nature of the church they insisted that it must be a voluntary gathering of believers. Church members were to be bound together only by their loyalty to Christ and their love for each other. Their life as disciples would separate them from the world and the ban served as instrument of love to warn and chasten the erring among them. The use of the sword or other instruments of the state to enforce the will of the church, was rejected as contrary to the example and teachings of Christ and the apostles.

### Batenburgers, Jorists, and Adam Pastor

To the opposition and persecution of these state churches and of Roman Catholicism was added the pressure of the fanatics who were not only eroding Menno's work among his own people, but bringing disrepute to the entire movement. Most active among these were the Batenburgers, Jorists, and Adam Pastor. Among these the first were the most corrupt, but fortunately, short-lived. They tried to carry on the violent tradition of Münster, robbing and plundering churches, and seeking to kill all who could not be converted. They adopted the practices of polygamy and community of goods as they had been practiced at Münster. Their influence did not last much beyond 1544, but their evil deeds caused great difficulties for the peaceful Anabaptists who were believed to be of the same type.

The Jorists were the followers of David Joris, a gifted and persuasive man who had also been ordained by Obbe Philips. It was Joris who had tried unsuccessfully to gather the scattered remnants after the fall of Münster. His controversy with Menno arose when he began to place increasing emphasis on spirit and prophecy while, at the same time, accusing Menno of living according to the dead letter of the Scripture. Menno felt the authority of the Bible was supreme and wrote very strongly against Joris who would "dare to put your dreams, your fantasies, enthusiasms, rhetorical figures, and other magic illusions ahead of the wisdom of the Holy Spirit, through which the prophetic and apostolic Scriptures have been given." [3] Joris felt that three time periods or dispensations in the history of man had been revealed: the age of the Father with David in the Old Testament, the age of the Son with Jesus Christ in the New Testament, and the age of the Spirit with himself (Joris) as the David of his age.

Because Joris believed that the inner, spiritual life was all that mattered for Christians, he could pretend to be Reformed or Roman Catholic and so escape persecution. After 1544 he, therefore, moved to Basel, Switzerland, under the assumed name of Jan van Brugge, and identified himself as a Reformed merchant who had fled from Belgium. He lived as a respectable citizen and honored churchman while, at the same time, carrying on secret correspondence with his followers in the Netherlands and writing little books for their instruction. After his death on August 25, 1556, a family quarrel led to the discovery of his real identity to the chagrin of his children who had married into respectable families of high Basel society. Because he had been a heretic his body was dug up and burned along with his books. His followers in the Netherlands maintained themselves into the seventeenth century.

The third group to trouble Menno were followers of Adam Pastor, a German priest whose original name had been Roelof Martens, and who had joined the Anabaptists in 1533. As co-worker with the other leaders, Menno ordained him as elder soon after 1542, and he participated in the debates with the Jorists at Lübeck in 1546, as well as in the conferences at Emden and Goch in 1547. Soon, however, it appeared that Pastor did not really believe in the Trinity, having intellectual problems with the incarnation and deity of Christ. He was consequently banned from the church by Menno and Dirk in 1547. In 1552 Menno met with him again to discuss the deity of Christ, but he could not win him back. Menno held firmly to the Scriptures as authority, while Pastor tended to put logic and reason above the Scriptures. Pastor was one of the best educated and most intelligent men among the Mennonites, but Menno and his followers believed that reason must be tested and judged by Scripture, not Scripture by reason. A group of "Adamites" continued for some time after Pastor's death in the 1560's.

Thus against both the traditionalists and the fanatics, Menno and Dirk held steadfastly to the Bible as final authority in faith and life. The use of prophecy, the inner word of the Spirit, visions, or reason all had to be checked against the Bible. It was clear to Menno and Dirk also that the Bible had to be understood from the teachings and example of Jesus to begin with.

And so Menno Simons labored after Obbe left them, to gather and defend the flock, but he did this against great odds. For most of this period he was a hunted man with a price on his head. In 1536 he married Gertrude, about whom we unfortunately know very little. Nine years later he wrote that he "could not find in all the country a 'cabin or hut' in which my poor wife and our little children could be put up in safety for a year or two." Tjaard Renicx of Kimswerd, a little village not far from Pingjum in Friesland, was executed in January, 1539, for having given shelter to Menno. Only one of Menno's two daughters and a son outlived him. His wife, son, and one daughter must have died from the rigors of refugee life. Menno himself was a cripple in later years, but we do not know how he became that way.

Despite these handicaps Menno traveled from Amsterdam to Danzig and perhaps further east along the Baltic seacoast. He was courageous in meeting his foes, tender in his sympathies to those in the church. He wrote devotional materials as well as treatises in the heat of controversy. He made mistakes, was not always consistent in his writings, and often felt deeply the burden of his calling, but his judgments were generally sound, as is evidenced by the wide acceptance of his leadership and writings.

### Witness Through Suffering

The leadership of men like Menno Simons and Dirk Philips

was needed for the founding of the church, but thousands of others demonstrated a heroic faith that was just as vital. They were soldiers of the cross who fought with spiritual weapons only. Menno wrote one of his best pamphlets on *The Cross of the Saints*. The meaning of the cross became very real to many of his followers in the Netherlands.

Church and state had been so closely linked in the medieval period that the state considered it a part of its duty to enforce the accepted belief of the established state church. If the church declared someone a heretic, he was considered dangerous to the state and removed from society. Anabaptists were considered heretics, and this name given to them by their opponents was chosen to point to an ancient heresy. In the Roman Empire anyone who was baptized a second time was put to death. These views continued to prevail in the sixteenth century, especially also in the Netherlands, which were under the despotic rule of Spain. Charles V had been more tolerant of Luther in Germany because he needed the military and political support of the German princes, but he was determined to stamp out the Reformation in the Netherlands. Since the Anabaptists were the major Reformation party there until 1560 when the Calvinists gained in strength, they suffered severely. Studies of the number of martyrs in Belgium and the Netherlands have shown that no less than 1,500 Anabaptists were killed, possibly as many as 2,500 from the early days of the movement to the death of the last martyr in 1574.

Typical of the spirit of the martyrs is that of Dirk Willems. He was pursued by a company of Anabaptist hunters when he escaped from prison in the midst of winter. He fled across the thin covering of ice on a river and seemed to have made good his escape when, looking back, he saw one of his pursuers break through the ice and cry for help. Dirk immediately turned back and managed to rescue him, but on orders of the burgomaster on the other side of the river, the man he saved arrested him on the spot. He was burned at the stake on May 16, 1569, paying for this deed of mercy with his life.

The treatment of prisoners was extremely cruel. They were broken on a torture device known as the rack to make them disclose the names of others, especially leaders. For those who remained steadfast, burning at the stake was the usual execution. Sometimes they were first strangled; sometimes a small sack of gunpowder was hung around their neck as an act of mercy since the quick fire and the smoke hastened the end. Those men who renounced the

Anabaptist faith were given the mercy of death by beheading, while the women were drowned, but some women were also buried alive, and some women as well as men were hanged. An account of three brethren and a sister taken in 1536 tells of the steadfastness of most of the martyrs:

They were then placed upon the rack, though contrary to their privilege, for they were mere citizens; however, they would not apostatize, though they were tortured so that the blood ran down their feet; but they trusted in and cried to God alone. After being tortured, they were brought up above again, where they comforted each other with the Word of God. I Thessalonians 4:18.

Finally, on the fourth of September, they were sentenced to death. They were brought bound upon the scaffold, yet came forth boldly and humbly, as lambs of Christ, and finally knelt down, saying with Stephen: "Lord Jesus, receive our spirits into Thy hands." Acts 7:59. They were all then speedily beheaded, their bodies burned, and their heads placed upon stakes. Thus they offered up their sacrifices. [4]

Persecution made believers learn to know their own faith early and well. Thomas van Imbroich, a printer's helper in Cologne, was put in prison in 1557. Two letters written to his wife have been preserved in the *Martyrs Mirror*. We also have a confession of faith from him which shows deep thought and conviction. In one of the letters to his wife and the brethren he wrote,

Yea, if the Lord should count me worthy to testify with my blood to His name, how greatly would I thank Him, for I hope not only to bear these bonds with patience, but also to die for Christ's sake, that I may finish my course with joy; for I would rather be with the Lord, than live again in this abominable, wicked world; however, His divine will be done. Amen. [5]

Thomas did testify with his death, dying on March 5, 1558, at the age of twenty-five. So powerful was the Anabaptist witness at the time of execution, that they were increasingly carried on in secret, or the martyrs were gagged. Since some of them managed to free their tongues, however, a clamp was henceforth placed over their tongue and the tip burned so that it would not slip back through the vise.

Not everyone wanted to execute the Anabaptists. Joris Wippe was mayor of Meenen in Flanders but moved to Dordrecht when he became an Anabaptist. Friends and officials warned him to flee but he refused. Consequently he was caught, tried, and ordered to be executed, but the man who was to carry out the order wept because Wippe had fed his wife and children in a time of need. Finally another man

87

was ordered to carry out the sentence.

The letters and testimonies of these martyrs are among the finest writings. Many have been collected and published in the *Martyrs Mirror*. They show that these believers looked upon their death by martyrdom as a seal of faith. God would not call them to such a fate if they were not with it to be given the grace to endure. So they gave thanks that they could witness to the truth in this way. Furthermore, they believed their sufferings to be a test that led to eternal life. They followed the way of the cross to final victory, believing fully that as they shared in the passion of Christ, they would also share in the joy of His final victory.

*Notes*
1. Williams and Mergal, *Spiritual and Anabaptist Writers*, pp. 209, 210.
2. T. J. van Braght, *Martyrs Mirror*. Scottdale: Mennonite Publishing House, 1951, p. 422.
3. J. C. Wenger (ed.), *The Complete Writings of Menno Simons*. Scottdale: Mennonite Publishing House, 1956, p. 1019.
4. *Martyrs Mirror*, p. 445.
5. *Martyrs Mirror*, p. 579.

*FOR FURTHER READING:*

*The Mennonite Encyclopedia*, 4 vols.

*Christian Living* (February, 1954), pp. 30, 31; (February, 1956), pp. 8, 9; (January, 1961), pp. 8-10.

*Mennonite Life* 7 (July, 1952), pp. 120-22; 16 (January, 1961), pp. 3-10, 21-38.

Henry E. Dosker, *The Dutch Anabaptists*. Boston: The Judson Press, 1921.

C. J. Dyck, *A Legacy of Faith*. Newton: Faith and Life Press, 1962.

J. C. Wenger, *Even unto Death*. Richmond: John Knox Press, 1961.

H. S. Bender and John Horsch, *Menno Simons' Life and Writings*. Scottdale: Mennonite Publishing House, 1936.

Franklin H. Littell, *A Tribute to Menno Simons*. Scottdale: Mennonite Publishing House, 1961.

**Chapter 7**


## ANABAPTIST-MENNONITES IN
## NORTHERN EUROPE, 1550-1650


MENNO was a Frisian from the northern part of the
Netherlands, but his labors were not restricted to that area. Indeed,
most of his ministry as an Anabaptist was carried on outside of the
Netherlands. His travels covered the territory where permanent
churches were founded. It even seems that where the persecution was
too intense or the group too small for a visit from Menno, there
no permanent congregations came to exist.

The distinctions between countries were not nearly as sharp in
sixteenth-century Europe as they are now, and movement across
national borders was much easier. Only in late sixteenth century did
the Dutch Mennonites become clearly defined as a brotherhood, and
even then congregations in northwestern Germany and as far away
as Danzig had close ties with the Dutch congregations. Still we can
look at the geographic spread by areas within the whole of northern
Europe to understand the size and growth of the movement to mid-
seventeenth century. In this chapter we will look first at Flanders,
a province in northwestern Belgium, then move across the channel to
England and on to northern Germany, as well as east to the Vistula
Delta in what is now Poland. To conclude we will return to look
more closely at the original center in the Netherlands.

### Anabaptism in Belgium

The origins of Anabaptism in Belgium are very similar to those
in the Netherlands. There too people had become weary with the
medieval religious life and were ready for new ideas. The apostles

of Melchior Hoffman also came to these areas and found a willing audience. Though their preaching was not confined to Flanders, the main impact of their message was felt in that area.

From 1530 to 1550 the major reform party in this area was Anabaptist. The first martyrs in 1523 had been Lutheran, but Lutheranism never gained a mass following. Likewise Calvinism had little influence before 1544 but increased in significance after 1550 with its greatest influence after 1560 during the war of independence from Spain. Later it was also driven out of Belgium but still constitutes the largest Protestant body in the Netherlands.

Anabaptism spread through the efforts of merchants and weavers who could move about with greater ease than many others. Persecution arose almost immediately with mandates being issued against them on October 10, 1535, January 24, 1539, and December 14, 1541. These mandates led to the death of many, but also to the flight of many more who followed the trade routes from Antwerp and other commercial centers. Flemish refugees are found very early in England and as far east as Danzig, where Flemish ships traveled for trade with the north German cities of the Hanseatic League.

The records show Anabaptists to have been very active, but the intense persecution prevented any one person from assuming prolonged leadership among them. The Flanders story, therefore, is primarily one of many faithful lay persons building, spreading, and upholding the church. We know, for example, of Jan Claeszen who in 1544 reported that he had 600 copies of the writings of Menno Simons printed in Antwerp. Not infrequently the witness of the death of the faithful was as effective as their living witness. The movement recorded steady growth from 1550 to 1576.

Some leadership help did come to these groups from the Netherlands. Gillis van Aken, a colleague of Menno and Dirk, worked here until his arrest in 1555. His story has a sad ending. Though he recanted at the threat of death, his weakness only changed the form of execution from burning to beheading. At his execution on July 10, 1557, he reportedly said, "It is too much to lose both body and soul at the same time." The great missionary Leonard Bouwens also labored here. His diary records over 10,000 baptisms which he performed, giving the exact date and place of each. Of these, 592 seem to have been in the area which is now Belgium. So far as we know this constitutes a record for the entire Anabaptist movement for any one man. A letter from Menno Simons to Bouwens' wife has been preserved, in which he encourages her not to worry about the safety of her husband who is secure in the care of God Himself. She had apparently asked for a less dangerous assignment for him closer to home.

The period from 1576 to 1586 was one of relative freedom for Anabaptism. The tug of war between Calvinists seeking independence and Catholics loyal to Spain left the authorities little time for persecution of others, though neither group was actually willing to see Anabaptism flourish at all. But persecution began again in 1586 with the Spanish and, therefore, Roman Catholic victory over Calvinism in Belgium. With renewed pressure upon them, and the attraction of greater freedom in the Dutch provinces to the north, a gradual exodus of Anabaptists came under way again. Some moved to the larger cities in Belgium in order to hide better, but eventually even these were forced to flee. By 1640 there were few Anabaptists left in Belgium, martyrdom and emigration having decimated their ranks. Thus a promising start ended with little more than a trace of its life remaining in the homeland.

### Anabaptists in England

To trace the Anabaptist movement in England is difficult but interesting. It is difficult because no separate church group can be identified as a direct result of Anabaptist efforts and because most of the records we now have come from those who opposed and persecuted them. It is interesting, however, because England differed considerably from the Germanic lands where most of the Anabaptists were, and because at least three major denominations show signs of influence from Anabaptism: the Congregationalists, the Baptists, and the Quakers.

As early as 1535-36 twenty-five Dutch Anabaptists were arrested and brought to trial in England. Anabaptist writings were known there even earlier. Most of these early refugees came to escape the wrath following the tragedy of Münster as, for example, Jan Matthijs of Middelburg (not to be confused with the Jan Matthijs who was at Münster). England was more tolerant later under Edward VI (1547-53) than under Henry VIII who preceded him and Mary who followed. Under Edward efforts at persuasion and some imprisonment constituted the extent of opposition to Anabaptism, as a result of which they soon worked more openly than before. Their greatest strength was in London and along the eastern coast where the refugees from Flanders landed first. The textile trade made it easy to move across the channel since it was a growing industry in England and continental weavers were much in demand.

Persecution increased under Mary (1553-58), but it is difficult to distinguish the Anabaptist martyrs from other Protestant martyrs, of whom there were many. It is significant, however, to note that the largest number of martyrs came from the areas where Anabaptism had been strongest. With Alva's "reign of terror" in Belgium from 1567 to 1573, thousands more sought safety in England where Elizabeth was now queen. She issued an edict against them in 1560, and another in 1568, while also appointing a church commission to hunt out and bring to trial all Anabaptists in the land. The *Martyrs Mirror* has a long account of the arrest and persecution of Anabaptists in London in 1575. [1]

After 1580 a new era began for Anabaptists in England. Increased tolerance was won when other groups separated from the state church and began to organize themselves. Some of their central ideas are the same as, or similar to, those distinctive of Anabaptism, including the separation of church and state, the baptism of adult believers only, and the freedom of the local congregation from outside control. Again the leading centers for these groups were in those places where Anabaptists had been numerous earlier. A number of these new groups had close relations with the Dutch Mennonites, and some even migrated to the Netherlands in search of greater freedom. An example of this is in the case of John Smyth, who came to the Netherlands with his group in 1608. Two congregations were organized, one in Amsterdam under Smyth and another under John Robinson in Leiden. Of these congregations it has been said: "To the Smyth congregation, which accepted adult baptism as a result of contact with Dutch Mennonites, the General Baptists owe their origin. . . . A number of members from Robinson's church were among the Pilgrim Fathers when they sailed for the new world in 1620." [2] Anabaptist doctrine is reflected most clearly in the Quakers, who arose in 1644. George Fox and other Quakers traveled extensively among the Mennonites in the Netherlands and Germany in the seventeenth century.

In summary, it may be said that Anabaptism did not become a permanent church group in England, nor was their number ever very large. Their beliefs and practices, however, did influence the history of the Protestant church in England. The Anabaptist name was lost, but other groups accepted some of the principal points which were causing the Mennonites to remain separate in Germany, Switzerland, France, and the Netherlands at that time.

In the previous chapter we told how Melchior Hoffman preached and baptized in Emden, in the province of East Friesland. The tolerance of the rulers, together with its crucial geographic location, made Emden a crossroads of northwestern Europe. Menno Simons spent much of his time from 1536 to 1544 in this area. Emden was, consequently, the site of several historic meetings of Mennonites. In 1547 Menno met there with six of his colleagues for a major discussion on the incarnation, infant baptism, and on avoidance, that is, whether a husband or wife should avoid his/her partner when the other partner was under discipline by the congregation. Usually such meetings included seven elders who had charge of the work in different areas. On January 17, 1568, the Waterlander Mennonites met at Emden and agreed on twenty-one points as a basis for working together. Still later, from February 25 to May 17, 1578, the Flemish Mennonites debated fourteen points of doctrine with the Reformed representatives in 124 sessions in Emden!

Mennonites could also be found in the late 1530's south of Emden along the lower Rhine, near the present Dutch border, but severe persecution destroyed the settlements eventually. Menno Simons worked there after 1544 for a time under the tolerance of Hermann von Wied, Archbishop of Cologne, but when a radical Roman Catholic replaced the archbishop, all Reformation progress ceased in the area. Thomas van Imbroich, whom we met in the previous chapter, and others tried to continue the work.

Late in the sixteenth century Mennonites found refuge again in this area in the city of Krefeld. Here the history of the Mennonites has been tied closely with the history of the city itself to the present day. They contributed decisively to the economic, social, and cultural growth of the city, making it an important textile center. The Krefeld congregation was the only one in this area to survive later.

East from Emden, along the north German coast lies Schleswig-Holstein, where Mennonite refugees early settled on the estates of sympathetic noblemen. They knew the Mennonites to be sober and industrious people. The land was marshy, and as Dutchmen these refugees knew about dikes and the recovery of such land for farming. For these reasons they were not only tolerated but even received protection from the noblemen, who would warn them of hostile parties and other dangers. Congregations were founded near Hamburg and Lübeck, and eventually in Altona near Hamburg, where they are still strong today. Here they were legally tolerated after 1601 upon an annual payment of one Thaler tax for each Mennonite householder. By 1605 it is reported that 130 families lived in Altona.

Menno moved into this area for the last years of his life. He was in Wismar until he had to flee following the debate with Micron in 1554. He then settled on an estate of Bartholomäus von Ahlefeldt located between Lübeck and Hamburg, where he built a printshop and was active in writing. Here he also died on January 31, 1561, and was buried in his own garden. The estate was laid waste during the Thirty Years' War, 1618-48, and the Mennonite congregation scattered. Today a monument to Menno Simons, the house where his printshop was located, and a huge linden tree called *Mennolinde,* mark the place.

### The Vistula Delta Settlements

Mennonites found refuge in another area along the coast of the Baltic Sea. Here again they were welcomed because of their farming and irrigation skill, but there was also more religious tolerance in the free city of Danzig, and on the large estates of the nobility. Many of these estates were in Poland and, for a time, it seemed that there might be as much religious freedom there as in Strassburg. Because of this, and because it was easy to follow the trade routes by water from Amsterdam to Danzig, many Mennonites and other Dutchmen came to the Vistula Delta in the 1530's and after.

A Mennonite congregation was soon established and grew rapidly. Close ties were maintained with the churches in the Netherlands, as the many old letters still kept in Amsterdam show. Menno Simons visited the congregation in 1549 to aid in the solving of a church problem, and Dirk Philips actually lived in Schottland, a suburb of Danzig, approximately from 1561 to shortly before his death in 1568. Church centers were established around the cities of Danzig and Elbing, and further east near Koenigsberg. Mennonites were usually not allowed to settle in the cities themselves, and were constantly subjected to oppressive measures by church leaders of the state church. Still, they remained a large and significant group until World War II, most of the Mennonites who went to Russia in the eighteenth and nineteenth centuries coming from these congregations.

### Divisions in the Brotherhood

Under the pressures of finding itself as a movement in the

midst of persecution, internal problems also arose to trouble the Dutch Mennonites. To some these problems simply proved that the early vision had been lost, to others they were an unfortunate but human and necessary part of growing up to Christian maturity as a brotherhood. We have already seen how extreme positions arose with David Joris' belief in prophecy and Adam Pastor's tendency to unitarianism and how these movements were rejected by the main body under Menno's leadership. But where do you stop, when you begin to separate from those with whom you disagree? Much of the history of the Mennonites in the Netherlands from 1555 to 1650 shows that there was no clear and simple answer about where to stop breaking fellowship.

In the disputes of this period some weaknesses became clear. The need to maintain purity in beliefs and practices, for example, is a demand which the church and the Christian ought to feel at all times, but how can this be prevented from becoming an unfair judgment of others who are also striving sincerely but find different answers? For some the church as an organization which demands complete agreement and purity overruled their love and concern for persons who needed fellowship and support. There were also personal rivalries, though not immediately recognized as such. Even great leaders such as Menno, Dirk Philips, and Leonard Bouwens were not free of this weakness which led to tension and an unforgiving spirit.

A significant source of their difficulties arose from their refugee life and persecutions. As people moved, they took with them the customs of their native land, customs which sometimes became a source of friction in new surroundings. Thus, for example, the Flemish from Belgium were rather quick-tempered and emotional in expression; they enjoyed fine clothing and good food. The northern Frisians, into whose territory they came, were reserved and did not easily show their feelings; they were not as open in their anger, but when aroused did not easily forget it. They were less concerned about how they dressed, but had fine household goods and linens. And these differences rubbed the wrong way despite the common Anabaptist faith which these people shared.

There were also differences in how the faith was to be lived. Some people wanted to try new ideas and practices; others wanted to hold to the tried and true ways of the past. Both groups undoubtedly loved the church, but these attitudes were sufficient cause for disagreements. It must be remembered that these people had, for the most

95

part, suffered persecution and believed strongly in their doctrines. Those who were willing to face death for their faith were also often ready to break fellowship with a brother if they thought him wrong; it was the heritage of an age in which religious convictions ran deep, and tolerance was not a virtue.

*The Waterlanders:* The Mennonites of the Netherlands and north Germany today are unions of groups which were divided earlier. Such a division came about in the sixteenth century between the Waterlanders, who received their name from the lakes and rivers region in which they lived north of Amsterdam, and the followers of Menno Simons. The Waterlanders opposed the strict use of the ban and of shunning or avoidance. Menno himself would probably have worked with them, had it not been for pressure from Dirk Philips, and especially from the missionary Leonard Bouwens. Because the church must be kept "without spot or wrinkle" as the bride of Christ, the husband of Swaen Rutgers was banned about 1556 for a reason which has long since been forgotten. But she continued to live with her husband in spite of Bouwens' demand that she shun him; for this disobedience she was herself placed under the ban. In protest the more moderate believers among the Waterlanders left the movement to form their own group, which Bouwens unfortunately immediately called "garbage wagon"; that is, they no longer demanded a pure church. The Waterlander group nevertheless continued to grow, apparently representing the sentiments of a large number of Mennonites. Being opposed to Menno in this, though he was much more moderate than Bouwens, they obviously did not wish to be called Mennonites and were simply known as Waterlanders. They were the first group to hold church conferences with some regularity and with broad representation, beginning in 1568. Under the leadership of men such as Hans de Ries they actively sought unity among the various groups of Mennonites. Their own preferred name *Doopsgezinde*, meaning baptism-minded, is the name used by all Dutch Mennonites today.

*The Frisian-Flemish division:* Scarcely five years after the death of Menno Simons, a major division was in the making among those who were united under his leadership during his lifetime. It was the most serious split among the Dutch Mennonites and took the longest to heal, though no major differences in belief were involved. Both parties later divided again but these had less meaning for the Mennonites as a whole. The story of this split is tangled and the interpretation of events is not always clear. It may be, however, that a look at this situation can be of help in seeing how people who were probably right in principle acted wrongly and how difficult reconciliation becomes when divisions are allowed to continue.

A large number of Flemish Mennonites had come to Friesland, as indicated earlier, and placed much stress on local congregations. In 1560 the church councils in four cities—Harlingen, Franeker, Dokkum, and Leeuwarden—made an agreement to work together but, for some reason, kept the agreement a secret. Of the nineteen articles agreed upon, three dealt with the use of ministers in all four congregations, the support of the poor, and a procedure for settling disputes which could not be resolved locally. The Flemish, who had not been included, now wanted their minister included in the team with the others, but his service was called into question by the others because of the secret agreement. This disclosure of the agreement made the Flemish feel that they had been discriminated against. When the congregations were called upon to vote on the Flemish minister, the voting was not properly held and further difficulties resulted.

In this situation Jan Willems and Lubbert Gerrits of Hoorn were prevailed upon to come to Friesland to mediate, both parties having agreed to accept whatever decision they might arrive at. After a careful study the issues seemed clear to the men, and they called a meeting of reconciliation on February 1, 1567, which was well attended, also by outside visitors. After a careful introduction the Frisians were asked to kneel and pray for forgiveness for their error. Then they arose and the Flemish were asked to do the same; when the Flemish wanted to arise from their knees, however, they were told that the Frisians would help them up since they, the Flemish, had the greater guilt. Anyone who knew Flemish tempers should have guessed the result; some assented, but the majority were deeply indignant, and the split was far worse than before.

As final hope Dirk Philips came from Danzig to help, together with two other leaders from that area but no peace could be achieved. The Frisian-Flemish division spread across northern Europe, drawing other issues into it until few knew just how it had all started. The disunity spread within each group as well as between them until there were "Old Flemish" and "Soft or Young Flemish," "Old Frisians" and "Young Frisians," and other smaller splits occurred again from these subdivisions. The tragic, and in a way almost comic, point was reached in Emden, where minister Jan van Ophoorn finally banned everyone in the congregation except himself and his wife!

When people take their convictions seriously and seek purity, they may be tempted to make high demands on others. They may fail to recognize to what degree they have personal weaknesses. Factors such as rivalries between older and younger generations, between leaders, and between groups who rally around some particular idea or practice become occasions for pride and bitterness. Many Mennonites were lost to the Calvinists in the sixteenth century because of the quarreling and splitting. It may be that Mennonites have not yet fully solved the problem of how to be earnestly seeking purity and hold strongly to deep convictions, without splitting over differences between equally sincere believers.

### Hans de Ries and Unity

The picture of the church is not all as dark as the history of these splits makes it appear to have been. Men of broader vision and greater spirit tried to rise above the disputes and restore unity. Lubbert Gerrits, who was unsuccessful in healing the Frisian-Flemish division, later made major efforts for unity, but only the story of Hans de Ries will be told in some detail here. He stands as a symbol of others who shared his spirit.

Hans de Ries was one of the refugees who came north from Belgium, having been born in Antwerp on December 13, 1553. He was a member of the Reformed Church, even being called to the ministry among them, but he objected to their use of arms which they even brought into church to guard against an unexpected attack. The Mennonites he knew were too divided and rigid for him to join, however, until he came north and met the Waterlanders. In 1575 or 1576 he was baptized by Simon Michels and joined that group. Though he returned to Belgium and was married there, persecution which included the burning of his close friend Hans Bret, caused him to flee again. He settled in Alkmaar but spent the years from 1578 to about 1600 in Emden and in traveling from that city. In a sermon shortly before his death in 1638, the octogenarian shared how the poor and suffering church of his youth had now become rich and socially acceptable but how much spiritual vigor had been lost in the process. It was out of this concern to remind children of the heritage of their martyr parents that he had already in 1615 published a history of martyrs which became the basis for the larger and more popular *Martyrs Mirror* by J. van Braght. He also produced a hymnal which went through six editions after the first printing in 1582.

In Alkmaar he helped draft the first-known Dutch Mennonite confession of faith and subsequently became instrumental in formulating additional confessional statements. Mennonites were opposed to confessions lest they replace the Bible as the only authority, but many confessions appeared in the Dutch Mennonite congregations during this period nevertheless. They were not intended to measure the orthodoxy of one another. Confessions explained Mennonite interpretations on points under dispute; groups used them to discuss differences and find unity; and congregations used them both for joining with other congregations in fellowship and as expressions of a common faith for admitting others into membership. The primary test, however, continued to be a life of discipleship rather than assent to a set of propositions.

In his unity efforts Hans de Ries stands out more for his kind spirit than for his achievements. Thus, for example, he succeeded in 1601 in uniting some groups into what they called the "Pacified [Reconciled] Brotherhood," but those who did not join formed the "Separated Brotherhood." From 1610 to 1615 he worked hard to make it possible for the Brownists to join the Waterlanders; they were a refugee group from England who had come to believe at many points like the Mennonites and asked for permission to join them, which they eventually did. De Ries carried on a large correspondence in the interest of the church and was frequently called upon to mediate in difficulties as in Haarlem in 1608, Workum in 1618, and Amsterdam in 1626.

Hans de Ries, however, was not the only man working to bring unity to the Mennonites. As early as 1574 Jan Willems of Hoorn was able to get an agreement on the use of the ban which, many hoped, would make unity possible. The agreement was signed in the province of Groningen at Humsterland and was called the Humster Peace, but the Flemish elders would not accept it and attempts to make peace at Emden and Hoorn in 1578 failed. In 1591 the Concept of Cologne did lead to agreement among the High German and Frisian congregations, the Waterlanders later also joining them. In 1632 a confession was drawn up at Dordrecht and further unified the groups. This Dordrecht Confession came to be widely accepted among conservative Mennonite groups, partly because of its emphasis also on discipline and foot washing, two articles which are not found in some of the other confessions. The Palatinate and Alsatian churches adopted this confession in 1660, from where it was brought to America.

Another step toward unity was taken in 1626, when four ministers of the Flemish branch in Amsterdam sent a letter to all churches in the Netherlands asking what the marks of a Christian church are, whether only the Flemish congregations had them, and whether peace was forbidden by the Scriptures. The answers were not too satisfactory; so on September 16, 1627, they drew up a letter to prepare for peace and sent it along with a confession of faith which they had written. The confession was called the Olive Branch, having been drafted as a sign of peace. Other steps were taken until on October 2-5, 1630, the Flemish and Frisian High German congregations joined them.

These various attempts at union did not bring all the Mennonites together. Two more centuries were to pass before that could happen, yet the forces were working for unity and overcoming the tendency to move apart. By mid-seventeenth century the Dutch Mennonites were entering more fully into the total life of the country and no longer spending most of their energy on internal disputes. They entered upon a Golden Age, if one measures it in terms of achievements in commerce and culture. Not all of this Golden Age brought gain to the church, however, as Hans de Ries had also said.

### The Golden Age

The last Dutch Mennonite martyr died in 1574. With the winning of Dutch independence from Roman Catholic Spain, Prince William of Orange established a policy of toleration which soon benefited the Mennonites. In the city of Middelburg the local authorities had closed all shops owned by the Mennonites and were attempting to force them into military service, but on January 26, 1577, Prince William wrote a letter ordering them to be left in peace so long as they remained quiet and useful citizens. The Union of Utrecht in 1579 provided that each person should be allowed to remain free in his religion.

These actions did not mean that all oppression had stopped, but the Mennonites were no longer forced to go to prison or to the stake for their faith. The Reformed ministers continued to harass them considerably, even rudely interrupting their worship services to ridicule them, but the government increasingly came to their defense. Full freedom of worship, however, did not exist for them until the nineteenth century.

Mennonites nevertheless soon made a place for themselves in the life of the nation. The overseas trade with Greenland and whale and herring fishing were almost completely in Mennonite hands. Most of them did not engage in trade with the United East Indian Company because ships had to be armed with cannons or travel under armed escort to guard against pirates and Mennonites had still retained their nonresistant heritage. They did, however, carry on the less profitable, but still valuable East Sea trade. They were also active in ship-building and in the lumber business. In Amsterdam and along the Zaan River they were leaders in the food industry, and in Drenthe they constituted the backbone of the textile industry.

For the most part, Mennonites were highly literate, partly from a desire to read the Bible and martyrologies, but also by way of overcoming their social disadvantage. In the seventeenth century a high percentage of the medical doctors in the Netherlands were Mennonite, this being one of the professions open to them. Since doctors were the best educated men in a congregation, they often served as pastors at the same time. As engineers the Mennonites made significant contributions to the draining of swamps. Many also engaged in agriculture and became recognized leaders in it.

In the fine arts Mennonites soon contributed a number of well-known names also. Carel van Mander was a poet and painter from the Old Flemish of Haarlem and lived from 1548 to 1606. Jan Luyken, who lived from 1649 to 1712, was also known for his work in both fields; the etchings for the second edition of the *Martyrs Mirror* were made by him. The man who ranks among the Dutch people as Shakespeare among the English was Joost van den Vondel, 1587-1679, whose parents fled from Antwerp because of their faith. He was a deacon among the Waterlanders, but left them to become a Roman Catholic about 1640. Other painters and etchers were Solomon van Ruysdael from 1602 to 1670, and Govert Flinck, at least in his youth, 1615-60. It is doubtful whether Rembrandt, 1606-66, was ever a member of a Mennonite congregation, but he had many close associations with them which no doubt affected the religious content of his paintings.

All this progress in material and cultural ways was not pure gain. A century or more after the Mennonites suffered deeply for their faith, they were tolerated and many were wealthy. Many no longer believed deeply in the things for which their fathers had died. Ease and luxury had done what persecution could not do. Galenus Abrahams, a leading minister in Amsterdam, proposed that the devil had found a clever way of dealing with the Mennonites; he stopped persecution and led them to become interested in the material things of the world. The words of Hans de Ries were clearly to the point when he said, "The goods are enriched but the soul is impoverished. Clothing has become precious but the internal decorations have perished. Love has cooled and diminished, and quarreling has increased."

In mid-seventeenth century the Dutch Mennonites had no serious threat to their life from without; leaders arose who tried to reverse the process of cooling off from within. They collected the stories of the martyrs, the writings of the heroes of faith, and wrote the history of their heritage in order to renew succeeding generations. They have left a rich treasure of works. All this, however, could not fully stem the tide of weariness from the quarrels within, and the persecution from without. The peak of membership and activity had passed, and the following century and a half were to witness a gradual, but continuing decline.

*Notes*
1. Pages 1008-24.
2. *Mennonite Encyclopedia*, II, p. 218.

## FOR FURTHER READING:

*The Mennonite Encyclopedia*, 4 vols.

*Mennonite Life* 3 (July, 1948), pp. 16-22.

A. L. E. Verheyden, *Anabaptism in Flanders, 1530-1650.* Scottdale: Herald Press, 1961.

T. J. van Braght, *Martyrs Mirror,* Scottdale: Mennonite Publishing House, 1951.

# Chapter 8

# A SUMMARY OF THE ANABAPTIST VISION

"ZWINGLI brought me into this thing," Conrad Grebel is supposed to have said about the beginnings of his reforming zeal, thereby acknowledging his dependence on the reformer. Each of the major branches of the sixteenth-century Reformation--Lutheran, Reformed, and Anglican--argued jealously the independence of their own origins as if the claim to have been directed by the Word of God would have been weakened by acknowledgment of dependence on one another. The Zurich Anabaptists were the only ones who made no bones about their indebtedness to others. Only when they became convinced that Zwingli was no longer willing to pay the price of obedience to his own best insights, did they let themselves be led into the creation of an independent movement. Therefore, as we try to identify and summarize those convictions which formed the center of what Harold S. Bender called "The Anabaptist Vision,"[1] we need to remember that it was not the intention of the Anabaptists to provide a full system of truth or an independent organization; they wanted only to correct the inadequaces of the other Reformation attempts which they saw around them.

## Scripture Alone

Every branch of Protestantism was committed to letting the Bible be the final rule for faith and practice. For the "official" Reformation, however, it was still the responsibility of political authorities to determine what was to be done about the truth found in the Bible. Thus Zwingli accepted a delay of eighteen months in the abolition of the mass because the government was not ready to move. This was the issue on the afternoon of October 27, 1523, as referred to in Chapter 2. *Zwingli:* "Milords [the city council ] will decide how to proceed henceforth with the mass." *Simon Stumpf:* "Master Ulrich, you have no authority to place the decision in the hands of Milords, for the decision is already made; the Spirit of God decides."

This exchange does not, as some scholars have thought, mark the clear and final break between Zwingli and his more radical disciples. It does, however, still symbolize the insistence of the Anabaptists that the authority of Scripture takes precedence even over the authority of government. This conviction, as we shall see later, has implications for the government itself--it will lead to the rejection of persecution, war, the oath, and the death penalty--but its first importance is for the church. The organization, the worship, and the doctrine of the church are not the prerogative of government. Although this position is widely accepted today, it was then held only by the Anabaptists.

## By the Power of the Spirit

If the Scriptures are to be the final guide for faith and practice, it is logical to ask how they are to be read since every preacher and every scholar has his own interpretation. The early answer of Luther and of Zwingli, an answer which they later abandoned but which the Anabaptists retained, was clear: in the gathered congregation. They believed that when Christians gather, the Word is preached, some listen, some prophesy, others weigh what is said (I Corinthians 14:29), and then the Holy Spirit, who is promised to those who gather in the name of Christ, will lead them to be of one mind. It was this conviction about the way in which the Holy Spirit leads in the congregation, which led the Anabaptists to reject any final authority of theologians or princes in the church. Nor was this simply a confidence in the democratic processes of majority rule; the Spirit would overrule human weakness and allow the will of God to become known in the situation in which they met.

This same vision of how the Spirit worked was also applied to problems and discussions in the larger brotherhood. We recall from Chapter 3 how such a unifying work of the Spirit was actually experienced at the Schleitheim conference in 1527, at Augsburg in the same year, and in the Strassburg conferences of the 1550's. The same method was used later in the reconciliation and unity meetings in the Dutch brotherhood. Whether the Dutch Mennonites were seeking agreement with the Reformed, or Pilgram Marpeck with the Moravians, the same method was used and the same goal sought after. Unity in the knowledge of the will of God was not to be reached by political or intellectual authorities, nor by religiously gifted leaders enforcing a correct creed, but by the working of the Holy Spirit among the brethren as they gathered to study the Scriptures.

### Following Christ in Life

Article six of the Schleitheim agreement states, "As Christ, our Head over us, is minded, so should we as members of His body be minded, that there may be no division in the body, by which it would be destroyed." Thus to follow Christ was not childish mimicry but necessary obedience in order that His body the church might be a unity in the world. It was the central argument of the Schleitheim agreement on the sword and the oath. This too had been learned from Zwingli who had said, "To be a Christian is not to talk about Christ, but to walk as He walked." [2] Better known is Hans Denk's motto, "No one may truly know Christ except he follows Him in life."

To see why "following Jesus" was a unique position we must be reminded of what the other churches were saying. The question of the sword is a good example. Whereas Jesus refused to bear the sword and so taught His disciples, Roman Catholics and Protestants alike were agreed that that was not a standard for the sixteenth century. Some appealed to the Old Testament warriors or to the example of honored Christian emperors like Theodosius or Justinian; some argued that reason or even natural behavior and instinct in a Christian society shows that someone must guarantee peace and order and have the physical power to enforce it. Some again felt that the existing social order was instituted by God and in such a way that if you were born a peasant God wanted you to remain a peasant, if you were born a prince God wanted you to be a good prince, and so on. The "vocation" or "station" in life has its own standards and, since it is established by God, must not be changed. Thus when the Anabaptists insisted on following strictly the words and example of Jesus, this was not easily understood nor accepted. Most could think of Jesus as a dying Saviour, or as a future judge, but not as someone to follow earnestly in life. Such an attempt seemed not only impossible to begin with since Christ was the Son of God but seemed also to lead back to the Roman Catholic system of saving works by which salvation could be earned.

The call to "follow Christ in life" may seem self-evident today, but for the Anabaptists of the sixteenth century it was a rare and daring claim, and a costly one, for the path of Christ led to the cross.

## Love

In the letter which Conrad Grebel and his friends wrote to Thomas Müntzer, referred to in Chapter 2, they said:

> The Gospel and its adherents are not to be protected by the sword, nor are they thus to protect themselves. . . . True Christian believers are sheep among wolves . . . they must reach the fatherland of eternal rest, not by killing their bodily, but by mortifying their spiritual enemies. Neither do they use worldly sword or war, since all killing has ceased with them.

To follow Jesus meant especially to bear the cross with Him, to love one's fellowmen absolutely, even at the cost of one's own life. This position has sometimes been called pacifism, but the term is inadequate because it places the focus on the political goals of peace rather than on the loving concern for persons and the refusal to harm them intentionally. Recently Mennonites in North America have spoken of nonresistance, a term which is also inadequate because it sounds passive and uninvolved instead of actively opposing evil. The traditional German Mennonite term *Wehrlosigkeit* (defenselessness) is a little better. The earliest Anabaptists seem to have had no term specifically for it; they spoke of surrenderedness (*Gelassenheit*), or of the cross, of "the faith and patience of the saints" (Revelation 13:10), or simply of discipleship. Today we might best speak of the Way of the Cross, of Agape (self-giving love), or of Suffering Servanthood. Jesus called it perfect (i.e., undiscriminating) love. Conscientious objection to military service and to war taxes, and the rejection of litigation (I Corinthians 6) have been its most obvious expressions in the past. A rejection of national, racial, and class selfishness and an active promotion of international and interracial reconciliation is the obvious modern extension of the disciple's love.

## Believers Only

Baptism was not the first difference to emerge between the Anabaptists and the reformer Zwingli, nor the logically most basic one, but it somehow became the most offensive issue. It was the first issue to call down governmental persecution and the one which was to give the young movement its name. In the above-mentioned letter which Grebel and his friends wrote to Müntzer, they said:

> We have learned that even an adult should not be baptized without Christ's rule of binding and loosing. Scripture tells us concerning baptism, that it signifies that through faith and the blood of Christ (as the one baptized changes his attitude and believes therein before and after the baptism) his sins are washed away; that it signifies that one is and should be dead to sin and should walk in newness of life and the Spirit.

The accent does not lie on the emotions involved in the conversion experience, nor on a discussion of what kinds of sentiments a child can or cannot have. The accent is positive; baptism has a clear, positive meaning. It points to forgiveness but also to a change of attitude, a determination to lead a new kind of life, and a commitment to the brotherhood (in "Christ's rule of binding and loosing"). That this commitment, which is required by the teaching and example of Jesus and the apostles, will not be made by infants need not be argued; it will not be made by all adults, either.

It follows that the church which is faithful cannot expect to be a large or powerful group. By no means could the true church be, like those churches supported by the state and practicing compulsory infant baptism, identical with the nation in membership. From this it follows further that the church must have its own distinct standards for organization, leadership, and membership; it must be *free* in two meanings of the term—membership must be voluntary, and its organization must be independent. This was precisely what all the reformers, like the Catholics, feared; they felt this would make the state pagan, and the church would be in danger of collapse if the alliance between the two were broken.

Thus the unique and fundamental meaning of believer's baptism is not just what it says about the individual believer—that his faith must be his own; it says something about the church—that membership is free and voluntary and that her only loyalty is to Christ.

### The Rule of Christ—Admonition

Article six of the Schleitheim agreement states that "In the law the sword is ordained over the wicked . . . and the secular governments are ordained to use the same . . . but in the perfection of Christ only the ban is used for the correction and exclusion of the one who has sinned." What the sword is to the compulsory community of the state, that the discipline of brotherly admonition is to the voluntary community of the church. The earliest Anabaptists referred to this practice of taking moral responsibility one for another as

"The Rule of Christ," referring to Jesus' words: [3]

If your brother sins, go to him alone . . .
If he listens to you, you have won your brother . . .
If he refuses to listen to you, take with you two or three . . .
If he refuses to listen to them, tell the congregation. . . .

The normal outcome of this approach to the brother is repentance and reconciliation; only in extreme cases will the ban (exclusion from the fellowship) result. The Anabaptists believed that this person-to-person and case-by-case means of restoration and education was the major tool for reformation of the church: "Discipline with the Word and establish a Christian church with the help of Christ and His rule, as we find it instituted in Matthew 18 and applied in the epistles." [4] We have seen that the reason for not baptizing infants was that they cannot voluntarily submit themselves to the "Rule of Christ." Since this practice of voluntary submission provides the *method* by which all other principles are applied, it is the key to the reformation of the church and its continuing faithfulness.

Membership is made meaningful to the individual by the fact that his brethren share with him in the responsibility for his discipleship. Only in this way does membership become important. For the state church reformers *church* meant that organization which, led by princes and scholars, provided for correct preaching. It needed no membership of its own since all men were its responsibility, whether they agreed or not. For the Anabaptists the church was a visible fellowship, separate from the state and other powers in society because its membership is voluntary and because the gathering of such a distinct, visible, caring, and sharing brotherhood is God's saving purpose in the world.

With the passing of time it was possible for this redemptive vision of the "Rule of Christ" to be lost. The ban could be applied woodenly, by a minister acting on his own without congregational approval, and on the basis of rules rather than in open reconciliation with the offender. The result would be an attitude of punishment rather than restoration. When this happened, particularly in the Netherlands as we have seen, both the meaning of discipline and the unity of the brotherhood were lost. It was on this point that the Swiss and German Anabaptists rejected the rigor of these Dutch practices in 1557.

*Never Alone*

From the very beginning the Anabaptists spoke of community of

108

goods as a necessary part of the Christian life. By this they did not mean, at first, a common treasury for the whole congregation and its needs; nor did they ever mean what some feared, a revolution to abolish private property as a pattern for a whole society. They were clear, however, that no Christian can call his property his own. He is responsible for his stewardship, not only in some vague way to God, but also concretely to his brethren and to anyone in need. Where there is need he will give without hope of return. Thus when the common treasury was established in 1528, under the pressure of banishment from Nikolsburg, as seen in Chapter 4, this was no radical innovation but only a further step in the direction already established. The reasoning behind this general Anabaptist teaching on property followed several lines. Love for the brethren demands a willingness to share with them (I John 3:17); the Lord's Supper itself expresses this sharing of worldly goods. Jesus' teaching on Mammon (Matthew 6) and on the conditions of discipleship (Mark 10:21-31) makes it clear that our property is a major focus of our self-centeredness, search for security, and idolatry. If Christ is truly our Lord, our hold on our possessions (or their hold on us) must be loosened. They also studied carefully the example of the early church as recorded in Acts 2:44 ff.; 4:34 ff. and, while not taking it as a legal command in every detail, came to see it as a powerful demonstration of the truth that economic sharing and vital apostolic obedience belong together.

## Only a Beginning

The vision of the Anabaptists has been sketched here only as it appeared in the very earliest period of the mid-1520's. It was not meant to be a complete charter for the founding of a denomination. On many points, such as the deity of Christ, the authority of the Scriptures, atonement by the death of Christ, and others, the Anabaptists agreed with other Protestants. They wished only to complete the process of reformation and purification which the others had begun and failed to finish. In the mid-1520's they still hoped to win others to this vision, and there was no desire to create a separate denomination. When the pressure of developments forced them unavoidably to the forming of a separate movement, other kinds of growth naturally followed. The scattering of the brethren, the small groups which were inevitable and necessary, the different geographic and hence cultural environments added new insights to the movement and broadened the vision, as we have seen in the preceding chapters.

Any listing of how the original vision was filled out and tested in concrete experience over all Europe would include the pre-Reformation mysticism of Hans Denk with his stress on the importance of the living Word. It would include the arguments on such issues as freedom of the will and original sin in which he, together with Balthasar Hubmaier, furthered theological understanding. Such a listing would include the missionary zeal of Hans Hut, together with his deepening of the meaning of suffering; it would include the concerns of Pilgram Marpeck, Menno Simons, and a host of others for the wholeness of the brotherhood and the fullness of its witness.

At other points the passing of time helped to clarify the boundaries of the Anabaptist movement, showing what belonged in and what did not. The stiffened practice of the ban in the Netherlands, as also the overrigorous legalism among some of the Swiss Brethren, muddied the waters for a time, but these were, nevertheless, signs of the love they had for the church. The peaceful and revolutionary Anabaptists were clearly and finally distinguished from one another with the collapse of Melchior Hoffman's separate movement and the tragedy of Münster, though their opponents seemed unable to distinguish between them. Similarly the claims of David Joris helped the main body to reject the temptations of "new revelation" in favor of careful Biblical interpretation, while the straying of Adam Pastor into Unitarianism warned of the dangers of rationalism. Pilgram Marpeck's successful identification of the issues separating Anabaptism from Spiritualism and the way in which he pointed up the consequences of the doctrine that the true church must remain invisible strengthened the Anabaptist sense of purpose and mission in the world.

At still other points local adaptations were made without really changing the essence of the movement. This may be said of Hoffman's view of the incarnation, of the institution of formal community of goods in Moravia, and later of the use of confessions among the congregations in the Netherlands in which beliefs held in common with other Protestants were included.

It is significant, however, that through all of this broadening and deepening, the essentials of the original vision were retained and clarified, standing the test of adaptation and of persecution without basically changing in nature. The central understanding of the church's way in the world, which was first hammered out in the mid-1520's, survived.

*Notes*

1. First printed in *Church History* (March, 1944), XIII, pp. 3-24. This very basic article has been reprinted numerous times and widely accepted as an accurate and authoritative statement. See, e.g., Guy F. Hershberger, *The Recovery of the Anabaptist Vision*. Scottdale: Herald Press, 1957, pp. 29-54. Also available as a separate pamphlet from Herald Press, Scottdale, Pa. 15683.
2. Ulrich Zwingli, *Works,* III, p. 407.
3. Matthew 18:15-18.
4. From Grebel's letter to Müntzer, September, 1524.

## FOR FURTHER READING:

*The Mennonite Encyclopedia,* 4 vols.

*Christian Living* (May, 1954), pp. 8-10; (August, 1954), pp. 10, 11; (June, 1955), pp. 24, 25.

*Mennonite Life* 5 (October, 1950), pp. 40-43; 9 (January, 1954), pp. 42-44; 10 (April, 1955), pp. 61-64; 15 (October, 1960), pp. 182-85.

J. C. Wenger, *Glimpses of Mennonite History and Doctrine.* Second revised edition. Scottdale: Mennonite Publishing House, 1947.

Franklin H. Littell, *The Anabaptist View of the Church.* Hartford: American Society of Church History, 1952. Reprinted as *The Origins of Sectarian Protestantism.* New York: The Macmillan Co.

# Chapter 9

# MENNONITES IN EUROPE
# 1648-1815

UNDER THE IMPACT of martyrdom, internal divisions, and accommodation to their environment the strength of original Anabaptism had gradually been lost in the four generations from 1525 to 1650. New movements were arising, however, and capturing elements of their spirit. The Baptists emerged with a concern for believer's baptism and congregationalism, the Quakers with a strong peace emphasis. Pietism came to stress the importance of an inner relationship to God. These movements were not without influence upon the Mennonites, but rationalism also came and had a particular effect upon the congregations in the Netherlands. The Swiss and South German Mennonites were best able to preserve their traditional way of life during this period and, to some extent, also the congregations in eastern Europe in Prussia.

## The South

*Switzerland:* Though Switzerland had been the cradle of Anabaptism, only the groups in the rural cantons of Zurich and Bern remained in 1648. This decline in membership was due, in part, to the strong emphasis upon military preparedness among the Swiss and the consequent pressure upon nonresistant Anabaptists. But the separateness of the congregations from the rest of the people and their culture also made them appear unpatriotic to the nationalistically minded Swiss population. The resulting pressure to conform led many to give up their faith and many others to preserve it through emigration. But emigration itself was very difficult, becoming possible only after 1642 through the intercession of the Dutch Mennonites with the Swiss authorities. Until 1661, most of these emigrants came to the Palatinate from Zurich.

As a result of these developments only the Bern Mennonites remained in Switzerland in late seventeenth century. Efforts to win them to the state church through persuasion and persecution continued. Innumerable mandates of suppression were issued against them in the seventeenth and eighteenth centuries. The persecutions of 1671, 1691, and 1711 were particularly tragic. A special commission was established to deal with them from 1699 to 1743. While the death penalty was no longer applied, other severe measures were taken against them. Many were sent to the sea as galley slaves. Many were imprisoned. They were frequently branded on the forehead to identify them as undesirables. No one was allowed to give them board or room. Those who reported them to the authorities received a reward. Mennonite children were considered illegitimate and had no rights before the law, not even the inheriting of their parents' property. They could not be buried in the community cemeteries. Thus it is clear that those who could, emigrated, especially since they were welcome in southern Germany and in Prussia because of their agricultural skill.

Most of the Swiss Mennonites were farmers, though there were some craftsmen, especially linen weavers, among them. Because of the persecution few were able to secure an education, in consequence of which very few writers arose among them. In matters of faith they simply adhered to the 1527 articles of Schleitheim, and in their worship the martyrologies of their fathers, to which they added from time to time, were important. The *Ausbund* was their hymnal. Eventually they also began to use a Reformed Church hymnal containing translations of the psalms, but they usually tore out the front page to eliminate the identity of the book. Use of the 1632 Dordrecht Confession may have begun as early as 1691. Later Pietism influenced the congregations in the direction of a simple, emotional, and inner piety, possibly through the reading of the devotional tract, *The Wandering Soul,* written by John Philip Schabalie in 1635 and printed later in the German language.

*Alsace:* In 1648 the Treaty of Westphalia gave Alsace to France, except Mulhausen which returned to the Swiss Confederacy. This political division also had its effect upon the Mennonite congregations, but they continued to meet as best they could. The record of a ministers' meeting held in 1660 shows the seriousness with which

113

they worked at matters of faith. Names represented at the meeting were Egley, Frick, Habich, Husser, Muller, Ringer, Schmidt, and others. The Dordrecht Confession, which the Flemish Mennonites had prepared in 1632, was adopted for use by the Alsatian congregations. We note further from the record of the meeting that a vigorous discussion was held on the nature of the church, including baptism, swearing of oaths, the ban and avoidance, foot washing, and the nature of Christ. Foot washing, which had been neglected, was reinstated as a Biblical ordinance. Questions about the nature of Christ were not fully resolved at this meeting. At issue, presumably, was the question about whether Christ had received His flesh from Mary or from heaven, a question which had been discussed vigorously among the Dutch Mennonite congregations during and following the ministry of Menno Simons.

Meanwhile Mennonite refugees continued to come into the region. Among them was Jacob Ammann (b. 1644), who soon became minister and elder of the congregation in Markirch. There he became troubled over the lack of church discipline in his and other Alsatian and Swiss congregations. Appealing to the Dordrecht Confession which the congregations had now adopted, he insisted that church discipline should include avoidance, i.e., that members have nothing whatever to do with a transgressor who had been excommunicated. In its strictest form this meant that even family members must avoid him, making him eat, sleep, and live completely alone. This was to force him to repentance. Ammann also insisted that all congregations should practice foot washing, that members wear simple clothing including beards for the men. Though he met with considerable opposition, particularly from elder Hans Reist in Switzerland, he traveled through the churches in Alsace and Switzerland to share his convictions, frequently banning those who disagreed with him. Numerous attempts were made at reconciliation, Gerhard Roosen even coming from Hamburg for that purpose, but without success. Gradually this division became sharper among the churches with most of the Alsatian congregations following Ammann, while most of the Swiss and South German congregations opposed his teaching. From this time (ca. 1700), his followers have generally been known as Amish Mennonites, or simply Amish.

Soon after this division the Amish faced the threat of withdrawal of the privilege of military exemption in Alsace, i.e., France. Though they appealed this decision, they were informed that they must leave the country. In preparation for this all families were registered by the authorities. Some did leave, but most of them managed to stay, though the instruction to leave was repeated in 1744, 1766, and 1780. It appears that their neighbors were jealous of their economic successes and reported them to the authorities but that the owners of the estates they were farming interceded for them because of their agricultural ability.

Two Amish conferences were held during this period, one in 1759 in Alsace and the other in 1779 in the Palatinate. A leading man among them during this period was Hans Nafziger, who was elected minister in 1731 and ordained as elder soon after. It is he who wrote the detailed statement of how an Amish congregation was to be organized and which has become the pattern for most of their congregations from that time to the present. The first Amish Mennonites probably came to Pennsylvania in 1720. Large migrations to America came later in the eighteenth and to mid-nineteenth century. Settlements were also established in Canada, as well as in Ohio and other midwestern states.

*The Palatinate:* The Palatinate of South Germany seemed to be a veritable crossroads for Mennonites in the seventeenth and eighteenth centuries. During this period one finds Swiss Mennonites, Hutterian Brethren from Moravia, Dutch Mennonites, and refugees from other areas all together in this region. The estate owners apparently even welcomed heretics such as the Mennonites were considered to be, if they could work to restore the land after the devastation of the Thirty Years' War. An edict of toleration was issued in their behalf in 1664 by elector Karl Ludwig of the Palatinate. This allowed them to worship in their homes but not to baptize and required the payment of an annual tax for the privilege of toleration. There is a story of how the elector was riding across his lands one day and came to a Mennonite farm. One of his aides whispered the rumor that the Mennonite was so wealthy because of his skill in making counterfeit money. When the elector confronted the Mennonite with this charge, the farmer simply showed him his blistered hands and said. "All the money I possess has come from this soil through the work of my hands under the blessing of God." According to the records there were twenty-seven congregations with a total of 618 families in this area by mid-eighteenth century. One of their number, David Moellinger (d. 1787), is known to this day as the "father of Palatine agriculture." The Mennonite name Detweiler likewise became synonymous with good farming at this time.

Here as in other congregations of southern Germany, Pietism

115

came to have particular influence among the Mennonites. Leaders in this movement were Peter Weber (d. 1781) and Adam Krehbiel (d. 1804). The leading Pietist John Henry Jung-Stilling was a personal friend of Moellinger. It was among these congregations also that the prayer book, *Ernsthafte Christenpflicht* ((serious attention to Christian duty), was published in 1739, followed by other prayer books later. Of great significance for their congregational life was the publishing of the *Martyrs Mirror* in 1780 through the efforts of Weber and Hans Nafziger.

## The North

*The Netherlands:* In the south the inner life of the Swiss congregations was less open to outside influences than that of their brethren who left to settle in Alsace and the Palatinate. In the north, however, it was the mother congregations in the Netherlands who were influenced, rather than the colonies in Prussia which had sprung from them. Here Galenus Abrahamsz de Haan (d. 1706) assumed leadership after the Thirty Years' War, being known as "the last prophet among the Anabaptists." He was a medical doctor ordained to the ministry in the Flemish congregation known as *The Lamb* in Amsterdam. Through him the Mennonites soon came into contact with the English Quakers. In an account of a visit with Galenus the Quaker patriarch George Fox reports that the former asked Fox to take his eyes off him, for they bothered him! Through Galenus the Dutch Mennonites also had contact with the Collegiants, an unorganized lay movement concerned with deepening of the spiritual life. It was his openness to the Socinian brethren from Poland, however, who were anti-Trinitarians, which brought him into difficulties, though he did not agree with them about the nature of Christ.

In time a serious division arose among the Mennonites in Amsterdam. Those worshiping at *The Lamb* church, and led by Galenus, stressed the importance of right Christian living, while those worshiping at *The Sun* church stressed the importance of right doctrine, calling for adherence to the old confessions and traditions of the past. Galenus finally wrote a clarifying statement in 1699, in which he listed the differences between Mennonite doctrine and Reformed or other groups as consisting of (a) the supremacy of the New Testament over the Old Testament; (b) believer's baptism; (c) non-swearing of oaths; (d) nonresistance. The conservatives soon replied with their own statements and a history, written by Herman Schijn (d. 1727), which erroneously linked Anabaptism to the twelfth-century Waldensians.

In addition to these somewhat polemical writings a host of devotional and worship literature appeared among the Dutch Mennonites at this time. These included the *Wandering Soul* and *Martyrs Mirror* already referred to, numerous hymnals, and a collection of writings from Menno Simons known as the *Little Menno*. These selections from Menno, which were chosen to stress the importance of conversion and discipleship, helped to shape the life and thought of European Mennonites for many years. A strong Pietist emphasis came to be felt in the Dutch congregations through *John Deknatel* (d. 1759), a minister at *The Lamb* church who had experienced conversion under the influence of the Moravian (Herrnhuter) Brethren.

The Dutch Mennonite congregations were also influenced by their economic experiences. Since they had earlier not been allowed to enter such professions as teaching, nor to hold any public offices, many had become traders, i.e., businessmen. By mid-seventeenth century many of them, having now long enjoyed toleration, became quite wealthy. This in turn led to social, cultural, and educational interests and influence. With many members becoming well-educated, the demand for trained ministers arose. For a time members who were medical doctors were ordained as those having received the most training, though it was not theological. By 1735, however, a seminary was founded in Amsterdam under the leadership of *The Lamb* congregation to provide leaders and to prevent the continuing loss of their young men who were seeking theological training in the Remonstrant Church seminaries. With this development the office of elder soon disappeared completely. Beautiful churches now arose, including the one built in Rotterdam in 1773, and with the new buildings came the desire for musical instruments. In 1765 the first organ was installed in Utrecht, to be followed by Haarlem in 1771, and eventually in most congregations. Audible prayer also gradually replaced the traditional silent prayers of the congregation.

Out of the stress upon discipleship among the Dutch Mennonites arose a strong concern for mutual aid. Not only did they seek to meet the needs of unfortunate members among themselves, but they also sent relief to the congregations in the Palatinate in 1696 as well as to Prussia and Poland in 1711 and 1713. The aid given to the Swiss has already been referred to. An administrative organization for relief abroad was established in 1725. A society was founded to aid the families of men lost at sea. Pieter Teyler van der Hulst, a Mennonite leader, established a foundation in Haarlem in 1778 to support museums and scientific research. This foundation is still active. There was genuine concern to use their wealth responsibly as Christian disciples. Through all these activities and resources Mennonite cultural, social, and even political influence in the Netherlands grew stronger than Mennonites have enjoyed anywhere else at any time.

In spite of all these developments a decline set in among the congregations. Church discipline became lax, as did the observance of traditional ordinances such as foot washing. Mennonite traders and shipowners began to arm themselves, putting cannons onto their ships, because of pirates. When the privilege of nonresistance was withdrawn by the state in 1799, very little objection was heard from the Mennonites. Membership declined sharply, forcing congregations to join together to maintain their programs. Some left for social or economic reasons, some because their heritage no longer meant much to them, some because the Reformed Church seemed to offer more spiritual stimulation. And so, while there had been some 160,000 Mennonites in the Netherlands in 1700, by 1808 there were only 26,953. One hundred congregations became extinct in those 108 years. A gradual recovery was to set in, however, leading to a baptized membership of 40,000 in 1964. The founding of an all-Mennonite conference known as the *Algemeene Doopsgezinde Societeit* (ADS) in 1811 became the first of many developments which helped to reverse the decline.

*The Lower Rhine:* The city of Krefeld was destined to become one of the key centers of Mennonite activity in the Lower Rhine region in the seventeenth century. Because it was under the sovereignty of the Dutch House of Orange many Dutchmen, including Mennonites, found their way to the city. Among these was Hermann op den Graeff, a competent Mennonite businessman, who came there either in 1607 or 1608. He not only founded his business but established a Mennonite congregation in the city, with close spiritual ties to the Flemish Mennonites. In 1632 he signed the Dordrecht Confession in behalf of the congregation. Numerous new members were added in 1654 and the following years of that decade when Mennonites were expelled from the neighboring duchies of Juelich and Berg. Since these refugees were more High German than Flemish, they gradually turned the life of the congregation in the direction of north German Mennonitism. An open and tolerant attitude to matters of faith became a distinguishing mark of the Krefeld congregation from this time on. In 1693 they were allowed to build a fine church on one of the main streets of the city.

A period of intense prosperity began for Krefeld and the Mennonites when the city came under Prussian control in 1702. Most of the Mennonites in this area were linen weavers, though some, like the von der Leyen family, specialized in silk. In 1731 this family founded the Frederick and Henry von der Leyen company which came to be known internationally for its silk products. For a time the company employed over 3,000 workers, almost half of the population of the city. Special privileges were granted to the Mennonite congregation by Frederick William I of Prussia because of the von der Leyens and in 1721 and 1738 he visited their plant. Later Frederick the Great likewise visited them in 1751 and 1763, presenting them an oil painting of himself. In due course the family was knighted because of their achievements and became a part of the German nobility.

Meanwhile the life of the congregation also changed, particularly through the influence of other religious movements. From 1670 to 1683 the English Quakers worked in that area, influencing some and actually causing some to leave the Mennonite Church. Eventually thirteen families followed the invitation of William Penn and settled in Pennsylvania in 1683 to become the first group of German settlers in America. From 1705 to 1725 some of the Mennonites came under the influence of the Dunkards, now known as the Church of the Brethren, who practiced immersion. The mysticism of the poet and hymn-writer Gerhard Tersteegen also influenced the congregation from 1735 to 1769. The Mennonite meetinghouse was one of the few places where he was allowed to preach. This mystic piety soon prepared the way for rationalism. Through the generosity of the von der Leyen family an organ was installed in the church in 1768, and from 1770 graduates of the Amsterdam Mennonite seminary were engaged as ministers. By late eighteenth century one Mennonite mansion after another was being built on Frederick Street, the most imposing one being the von der Leyen "castle" which today serves as the Krefeld city hall. To it Conrad von der Leyen would invite representatives of all confessions in the city for conversations in an effort to encourage tolerance and mutual understanding. A cluster of small congregations formed around Krefeld in the Duchy of Cleve, including one in Emmerich in 1676, Cleve itself in 1681, Rees in 1738, and others. Most of these groups received financial help and spiritual encouragement from the Amsterdam and Krefeld congregations.

South of Cologne, on the right bank of the Rhine, lay the Duchy of Wied. Following the destruction of the Thirty Years' War, Count Frederick (d. 1698) built a new capital on the Rhine in 1653, calling it Neuwied. To rehabilitate his lands he invited whoever would come to settle, including Mennonites, to whom he granted special privileges in 1680. His nephew, Count Alexander, who ruled from 1737 to 1793, caused the Mennonites to build a church near his castle in the same architectural style. Leader of this congregation during this period was Lorenz Friedenreich of Switzerland, a Pietist who maintained intimate contact with like-minded brethren in Holland and the Palatinate. One Peter Kinzing (d. 1816), a member of this congregation, became noted for his skill in watchmaking. The records also show that the German literary giant Goethe once visited the congregation and subsequently wrote about the "wonderful honesty and integrity" he had seen there in the faces of the Mennonites.

*East Friesland:* In mid-sixteenth century East Friesland became a haven for Mennonites who fled the Netherlands to escape the tyranny of the Spanish occupation. Consequently there were Mennonites in this area throughout the seventeenth century, and several congregations continue to this day. During the early days numerous families had located in the villages of the Krumhorn west of Emden, but by mid-eighteenth century only four city congregations remained in East Friesland, namely, Leer, Emden, Norden, and Neustadt-Goedens. Among these Emden was the center of most activity. Though several graduates of the Amsterdam seminary served these congregations, the members were careful to resist outside influences. Menno Simons' understanding of the incarnation was not forgotten. Church discipline was taken seriously. One elder, Jan van Ophoorn (d. late sixteenth century), was so rigorous in his exercise of discipline that he apparently banned all other Flemish and Frisian congregations as well as all members of his own Emden congregation, except his wife and himself. He died misunderstood and in poverty.

While the Mennonites were generally tolerated in this area, every change of government required a renegotiation of their privileges and the paying of additional compensatory taxes. Nevertheless, these families prospered. As in Krefeld, so here most of them were also weavers, though some became quite wealthy in the whaling industry. Here too the Mennonites began to build beautiful church buildings, installing organs, and calling trained seminary graduates to serve them. One of these men, Hinderk Waerma (d. 1741), representing the old Flemish tradition, prepared a Dutch-French confession of faith in 1757 for use by his congregation. The Emden church experienced a division 1692-1732 over the issue of silent or audible prayer during the worship services. While the traditional form had been silent prayer, the progressive Waterlander Mennonites had shifted to audible prayer early in the seventeenth century under the influence of elder Hans de Ries (d. 1638). This influence was now asserting itself in Emden, which was itself a Waterländer congregation.

In 1720 Joachim Christian Jahring (d. 1729), a Lutheran pastor in the area, described the Mennonites as follows:

As is generally known, their life and conduct is praised by many, and it is indeed true that they lead an honest and disciplined life. If differences occur with others over financial affairs, they seek private settlement rather than a decision of the courts. They are never heard to swear, nor do they have disputes and violence among themselves. They seek with all diligence to avoid immorality in every respect. So far as their economic life is concerned most of them are engaged in trade, which they carry on in as large a scale as opportunity provides. Because of this many are very wealthy, which is also enhanced by their frugal living. Some support themselves through farming, linen weaving, bakeries, etc.

*Hamburg and Schleswig-Holstein:* Anabaptists from the Netherlands and the Lower Rhine had been fleeing to Holstein as a sanctuary from the early days of the movement in the sixteenth century. In Fresenburg near Oldesloe, where Menno himself had spent his last days, a congregation flourished until 1656, in Luebeck until 1720. Particularly attractive were the lands under Danish sovereignty and congregations arose at Glueckstadt on the Elbe, at Friedrichstadt on the Eider River, and of course in Altona near Hamburg.

Though Mennonites had received an invitation with special privileges from Duke Frederick in 1623 and settled in the Friedrichstadt area, the high point of their congregational life was reached only in early eighteenth century. Already in 1698 the Frisian, Flemish, and High German groups had united as one congregation. By 1708 they had their own meetinghouse with a cemetery, the tombstones of which still testify to their faith and life of that time. They also established two homes for orphans, widows, and others without income. Here, as elsewhere, the records indicate that they acquired an excellent reputation through quiet living and intense devotion to agriculture and other peaceful vocations. For a time the same issues confronting the Amsterdam congregations were faced here, but their decisions eventually favored the more conservative position of *The Sun* congregation rather than that held by de Haan. In mid-seventeenth century a serious problem also arose when the magistrates refused to give legal sanction to marriages performed by Mennonite ministers, making their children legally illegitimate, but toleration was finally won.

Mennonites were entrusted with public offices in this area sooner than almost anywhere else in Europe. As early as 1607-8 Jan Coodt Classen near Eiderstedt achieved public recognition in municipal affairs. In 1680 a Mennonite became a member of the city council, followed by others including Nicholas der Ovens who became mayor of Friedrichstadt in 1711. At the same time, however, serious reverses were being felt within the congregation itself. Many young people had apparently been marrying members of the Lutheran state church who thereupon also became Mennonites. In 1751, however, a royal mandate decreed that all marriage partners had to become members of the state church if not already so. This led to a rapid decline of Mennonite membership. Thus, while Friedrichstadt counted 178 members in 1703, they counted only 30 members in 1803, one hundred years later.

A large congregation also arose in Altona. With its adjoining city of Hamburg, Altona enjoyed free city status, both cities governing their own affairs. As traders Mennonites soon found their way to Hamburg-Altona. A special edict favoring them was issued in Altona in 1601 and four years later in Hamburg, as a result of which many Mennonites came to settle there. Though these groups belonged to different traditions, i.e., Frisian, Flemish, and High German, they soon merged into one congregation which located in Altona, while many of the members lived in Hamburg. Coming from the Lower Rhine and the Netherlands, these immigrants naturally brought with them the textile industry as also an interest in shipping and commerce. Some were engaged in whaling expeditions to the coast of Greenland and apparently did very well financially. The profits of the Mennonite whaling crews were so substantial in 1675, in fact, that they enabled them to build and completely pay for a new church structure.

An insight may be gained into the life of the congregation through the experiences of two prominent families among them, the Roosen and van der Smissen families. The Roosens came to Altona in 1611 and for 300 years provided strong leadership in the congregation. Prominent among them was Gerhard Roosen (d. 1711), who firmly resisted the immersionist teachings of the Dunkers and the mystical piety of the Quakers around them. At the age of ninety he published a catechism for use in membership classes. This catechism went through many editions and was even translated into the English language. The tenor of this catechism, as of his other writings, was one of accommodation, however, it being Roosen's concern to make Mennonitism appear harmless and as nearly like other Protestant groups as possible. One might describe his catechism as Mennonitism in a minor key (Friedmann).

The van der Smissens came from a patrician family in Brussels and settled in Altona in 1632. Henry (d. 1737) brought fame to the family name through his involvements in the textile and bakery industries. He became so active in rebuilding the city following the Swedish-Danish War of 1712-13 that he was given the honorary title of cofounder of the city. The van der Smissens have been active in the Hamburg-Altona congregation since that time. The life of the congregation would, in fact, be almost unimaginable without the van der Smissen and Roosen families. In 1868 members of the General Conference Mennonite Church persuaded C. J. van der Smissen to come to America as director of the Wadsworth Institute (Ohio), the first Mennonite school for higher theological education in America.

*West Prussia:* In 1642 King Wladislaw IV of Poland issued an edict favoring Mennonite settlements in his lands. From the wording of this edict it becomes clear that they had won the respect of their government, and of their neighbors. This became true particularly through their work in draining the swamp lands bordering the Vistula and Nogat rivers, turning erstwhile useless lands into profitable pastures and wheat farms. The cost, however, was high and countless numbers died of swamp fever during the first generation, the estimate of deaths going as high as 80 percent of the settlers for a time. Toleration was the reward granted them for their labors.

This tolerant attitude can be seen, for example, from their experiences in the city of Elbing which belonged to the Hohenzollerns. As early as 1585 two Mennonites were given citizenship in the city, and five years later the congregation was allowed to build their own church. The city council in Danzig likewise was tolerantly disposed toward them but frequently forced to exert pressure upon them to retain favor with the guilds and others who were jealous of Mennonite prosperity. Because of these pressures Mennonites could not receive citizenship in the city of Danzig as late as 1800 and normally had to live on the outskirts of the city.

Persecution was particularly persistent in Danzig. During the Swedish-Polish War of 1655-60, and the Polish War of Succession, 1733-35, many of their houses were destroyed by the war and by those who resented them as a people. In 1660 they were charged by the city with having proselyted and baptized a Roman Catholic woman. Expulsion seemed imminent. The charge could not be proved, however, since the woman herself denied having been rebaptized at all. Similar problems arose again and again, usually initiated by those who were envious of their economic successes. Perhaps the Mennonites, on the other hand, failed to take time for their poorer, non-Mennonite neighbors and scorned them for their poverty. It was also unfortunate that anti-Trinitarianism was strong in that area and that Mennonites were sometimes confused with this movement. Repeated hearings were held to discover their theology, but no anti-Trinitarianism could be found in their doctrines and they stoutly denied it as well. For them Christ was indeed the incarnate Son of God who with the Father God and Holy Spirit constituted the eternal Trinity.

With the eighteenth century came greater tolerance. This immediately led to the building of churches in many places, though only simple sheds were permitted at first. Thus Thiensdorf built in 1728, Rosenort in 1754, and Fuerstenwerder, Heubuden, Ladekopp, and Tiegenhagen in 1768. In 1783 a second meetinghouse was built in the country, near Elbing. During this period also the congregations gradually shifted from the use of Dutch to German in their worship services. Of significance for the Mennonites was the transfer of sovereignty of this area from Poland to Prussia in 1772 and the subsequent edict of toleration issued by Frederick the Great in 1780. This and later edicts, nevertheless, did not long satisfy the Mennonite conscience, and by 1789 the great migration to Russia was under way.

*East Prussia:* In early eighteenth century the plague decimated the population of East Prussia. To revitalize his lands Frederick I invited any who would come, but especially also the Mennonites, to settle in that region. The first Mennonites arrived from Switzerland in 1711 but did not stay long. They were followed by others from West Prussia in 1713, who settled in the Memel region near Tilsit. By 1724, however, they were forced to leave again because they refused to become soldiers. This expulsion was revoked in 1740, and they returned to establish thriving agricultural communities in the Memel River valley. By 1765 there were 570 members in this region. Congregations had now been established in Königsberg, Brenkenhofswalde, Franztal, and other locations. It was here also that they came into close contact with the Moravian Brethren (Herrnhuter), from whom they learned the practice of child consecration but also acquired a new concern for missions and for the establishing of their own schools in order to preserve their heritage. Gerhard Wiebe (d. 1796) of West Prussia wrote a catechism which was used much in this area and which later found its way to America among the Amish congregations.

As we observe the Mennonites in Europe from 1648 to 1815 we note the following phenomena among them: (1) dispersion continues, but toleration is gradually achieved in most places; (2) general economic prosperity which makes them attractive to governments, but stirs envy in the hearts of their neighbors; (3) in the major cities some Mennonites achieve civic prominence and are honored as leading citizens; (4) there is a general numerical decline among them which, if it had continued, would have made them extinct in Europe today; (5) numerous outside influences help to shape their religious life in addition to their economic environment, notably Pietism, Quakerism, and rationalism; (6) prominent leaders arise from time to time who, through their writing and active participation in the life of the congregations, give new vision to their people; (7) some of these leaders, and some of the outside movements, brought divisions into the life of the congregations, but by 1815 the impact of tolerance and enlightenment was making it possible for most of the Mennonites to overcome their earlier schisms; (8) some of this new unity must also be attributed to the influence of Pietism among them, which had led to a recovery of Bible study, prayer, and a sense of mission among them.

FOR *FURTHER READING:*

*The Mennonite Encyclopedia,* 4 vols.

*Mennonite Life* 3 (April, 1948), pp. 10-17; 8 (January, 1953), pp. 24-30; 9 (October, 1954), pp. 156-61.

C. Henry Smith, *The Story of the Mennonites* (1950).

John Horsch, *Mennonites in Europe.* Scottdale: Mennonite Publishing House, 1942.

# Chapter 10

# THE MENNONITES
# IN RUSSIA

THE BEGINNING of Mennonite life in Russia in late eighteenth century is similar to the end of their organized life as a church nearly 200 years later in at least two ways: both periods were marked by poverty and suffering, and military action decisively helped to shape their destiny. In the beginning, poverty and suffering came as the natural accompaniments of pioneer life; in the end they came as the inevitable lot of refugees. In the beginning, the Russo-Turkish War (1781-92) pushed the Turks eastward and opened the vast regions of the Lower Volga and the Ukraine to the Mennonites; in the end World War I (1914-18), the Communist Revolution (1917-21), and World War II (1939-45) made the Mennonites victims instead of beneficiaries of the conflict.

In a way the experience of the Mennonites in Russia was similar to that of Job when he was stripped of his wealth, and said, "Naked I came from my mother's womb, and naked shall I return; the Lord gave, and the Lord has taken away; blessed be the name of the Lord." The Mennonites also believed that it was the Lord who gave, but they found it a little more difficult to recognize Him as the one who also took away.

The story of the Mennonite migration to Russia goes back to 1762-63 and the manifestos issued by Catherine II inviting Germans and other Europeans to settle and occupy the lands vacated by the Turks in southern Russia. Catherine II was the German wife of Peter III and succeeded him as ruler of Russia in 1762. Within ten years her invitation had resulted in the establishment of about

126

one hundred German colonies in southern Russia, but the Mennonites were not to come until the 1780's. Even then they were not motivated so much by the attractive settlement opportunity as by the pressure of events at home in Prussia. Growing military preparations in the face of a Europe made restless by the upheaval of the French Revolution made the nonresistant Mennonites apprehensive. Then, too, many were coming to be without land, and a Mennonite without a farm was like a rider without a horse. The problem arose from the fact that both military and church taxes were based on land ownership, and Mennonites would pay neither for support of the military nor for support of the state church. The more land they owned, the more difficult it became to finance military and church activities in Prussia, and they did already own approximately 300,000 acres. Consequently government controls prevented Mennonites from buying more land, but they had large families; what should young couples do for a living?

It is not surprising, therefore, that George Trappe, the special representative of Catherine II, found a very cordial reception among the Mennonites when he came to their Prussian communities in 1786. His reports of the settlement possibilities in the new Russian lands were enthusiastic, kindling a like response among those who heard him. At his urging some of the Mennonites appointed Jacob Hoeppner and Johann Bartsch to visit Russia and bring back a firsthand report. This they did, leaving on October 19, 1786, and returning just over a year later. They had many things to report—a visit with Catherine II herself, real travel difficulties, Hoeppner's broken leg—but most important of all, they reported very favorably about the lands they had visited and the agreement they had been able to make with governmental authorities in St. Petersburg.

The special charter of privileges granted to the Mennonites on March 3, 1788, and later reaffirmed by Tsar Paul I on September 8, 1800, did not vary significantly from the privileges granted to other immigrants. Russian colonial policy at that time aimed at a complete separation of all foreigners from the native population, as a result of which the colonies were quite independent in their affairs. This pattern appealed to the Mennonites, who cherished the right to control their own religious, educational, and civic affairs as they had been accustomed to doing it in Prussia. Among the privileges was the guarantee of complete religious freedom and exemption from military service for all time. There was also an interesting provision granting the Mennonites special permission to brew beer and vinegar and distill brandy, a trade for which they had already been famous in Danzig and Prussia in the sixteenth century. These special considerations were justified in the preamble to the charter as follows:

Conceding to the petition of the Mennonites settled in the New Russian territory, whose excellent industry and morality may, according to the testimony of the authorities, be held up as a model to the other foreigners settled there and thereby deserve special consideration; now therefore with this Imperial Charter we most graciously wish not only to confirm all their rights and privileges specified in the preliminary agreement concluded with them, but in order to stimulate their industry and concern in agriculture even more, to grant them also other advantages, as follows: (the listing followed). [1]

## The First Colony at Chortitza

Under these favorable conditions the first eight families, totaling fifty souls and including Hoeppner, left Danzig by wagon train on March 22, 1788. It took the group five weeks to reach Riga, less than 300 miles away, where they rested their horses for a month. The next 300 miles took six weeks, bringing them to Dubrovna on July 24, and since Russia was again at war with Turkey, they were forced to spend the winter there. More immigrants joined them in the months following, until there were 228 families in the Dubrovna camp.

For some reason there was not a single minister among all these people. Consequently four men were elected to read sermons they had brought with them, but this did not seem satisfactory to many. Soon there were also twelve couples wishing to get married. An offering was finally taken and sent back to Danzig with the request that it be used to send a minister to them. At the same time, however, the Danzig church had written that they should conduct their own elections for a minister. This was done and twelve names were submitted to Danzig, from which four were approved for ministry. One of them, Bernhard Penner, was later commissioned by letter to serve as elder.

Three weeks before Easter, 1789, the six most impatient families broke camp and set out for their final destination by sleigh and wagon. Travel was extremely slow, however, and eventually the rest of the group caught up with them, having grown larger meanwhile with other families coming direct from Danzig. Upon arrival at the land selected earlier by Bartsch and Hoeppner, they were advised to settle on the west side of the Dnieper River instead, the east side still being under military operations. A

Russian settlement director, who turned out to be greedy and inefficient, was appointed to help them. The new colony, which by now consisted of 400 families, finally located on the banks of the Chortitza River which was a tributary of the Dnieper River. Eventually the entire settlement came to be known as the Chortitza Colony, or also Old Colony since it was the first of the Mennonite colonies in the Ukraine.

Pioneering difficulties were so many in these early years that most of the immigrants became quite dissatisfied with their existence. Disease and death took a heavy toll. Rains made the mud huts even muddier. Horses were stolen or lost for lack of fences. Wood for construction was slow in arriving and of inferior quality. The promised government assistance of 500 rubles per family was delayed endlessly, much of it arriving eight years later. The people were very poor; even elder Bernhard Penner had to wear homemade sandals to church instead of shoes. Nevertheless, by the turn of the century the 400 families had become established in fifteen villages and were farming approximately 89,100 acres of land.

The problems of pioneer life were made more difficult by a lack of unity among the settlers. In time the frustrations of a large number focused on Jacob Hoeppner, who was accused of withholding funds from the others and of using the knowledge gained on his exploration trip for selfish ends. He was excommunicated from the church and denounced to the Russian authorities, who imprisoned him and made plans to send him into exile in Siberia. He was eventually released, however, and joined the church which had been established by the immigrants of Frisian extraction, though he himself was of Flemish origin. His land had been sold while he was in prison, and he lived the remaining years of his life in silence at Kronsweide. Some years after his death a beautiful monument was erected in his honor on the island of Chortitza in the Dnieper River.

Educational facilities and leadership were also totally inadequate in these early years. Primitive schools were established, but the children were frequently needed at home, and the teachers were appointed in a haphazard manner. The curriculum was limited and centered around the Bible and catechism. In most villages the same building was used for school and church meetings. These schools, as all affairs of the colony, were under the control of the Mennonites themselves, with little interference from the Russian authorities. To facilitate this control each village elected its mayor or *Schulze*, with an *Oberschulze* governing the entire colony. Through the

*Oberschulze* contact was also maintained with the Russian authorities in Odessa.

## The Molotschna Settlement

In spite of these hardships and problems more Prussian Mennonites became interested in establishing new homes in the Ukraine. Economic and religious restrictions were increasing in Prussia, and the reports from Chortitza were not sufficiently negative to discourage others from coming. Elder Cornelius Warkentin of Rosenort in Prussia had visited the Chortitza settlement in 1798, and had discovered the availability of a large tract of land 100 miles southeast of Chortitza on the Molochnaya River. With this news, others prepared to leave, and the first Molotschna group arrived in Chortitza in the fall of 1803. Their stay with these pioneers during the winter taught them many things which would make their own settlement less difficult. In the spring of 1804 they occupied their lands, soon to be joined by others, until 365 families had arrived from 1803 to 1806.

By now the Prussian authorities were becoming alarmed about the loss of some of their best citizens. The restrictions on land and taxes, which had been so troublesome to the Mennonites, were relaxed and a 10 percent tax was imposed on all immigrants leaving the country. These provisions, together with the Napoleonic War and Napoleon's march on Moscow in 1812, slowed down the movement but did not stop it altogether. By 1835 some 1,200 families had made their home in the Molotschna colony, settling in fifty-eight villages with an acreage of 324,000, thus constituting the largest settlement Mennonites were to establish in Russia. The villages of Halbstadt and Gnadenfeld served as administrative centers. Because this second movement included many teachers, ministers, and other aggressive community leaders, as well as being generally more prosperous than the 1788 movement, progress was rapid and the colony was soon thriving in every respect.

## Am Trakt, 1853, and Alexandertal, 1859

Two other colonies were established in Russia before the flow of immigrants from Prussia stopped, the Am Trakt colony in 1853, and the Alexandertal colony in 1859. The Am Trakt settlement was located near the Volga River in the province of Samara, receiving its name from the *Salztrakt,* a road which was used primarily to haul salt and which ran near the settlement. The first nine families arrived in 1853, followed by others until 197 families had located in ten villages by 1872. The original settlement privileges

130

were limited somewhat in that the immigrants had to make a deposit with the Russian embassy in Berlin against costs which the Russian government would have in their behalf. Exemption from military service was limited now to twenty years but available after that upon payment of a tax assessment.

Alexandertal, the last of the original Mennonite settlements to be established in Russia, was also located near the Volga River, not too far from the Trakt colony. It was named after Alexander II, who was ruling Russia at that time, and who showed considerable favor to the Mennonites. Settlement privileges were more limited, and the settlers had to buy their own land, but 106 families had come to the colony nevertheless by 1870. Marketing problems, and some internal tensions due to the religious fanaticism of Claasz Epp, limited progress in both colonies for a time, but strong leadership helped to place them on a permanent basis by the 1880's. Among the outstanding leaders of the Am Trakt settlement were Johannes D. Dyck (d. 1898) and Johann Bergmann, the former being decorated three times by the Russian government for pioneering achievements. He had spent over a decade in America before settling in the Volga region.

With these settlements the Mennonite immigration to Russia came to a close. By this time the threatened loss of exemption from military service was to lead 18,000 to America as will be seen in the following chapter. That some Mennonites were sufficiently attracted to come to Russia, while others were, at the same time, sufficiently threatened to leave, is an interesting commentary on Mennonite (and human) nature. In part it was a question of values. Sometimes spiritual values came first; sometimes material values seemed to dominate. Usually it was difficult to distinguish clearly between them. It is interesting to note that at this very time another large Mennonite group in Prussia possibly as many as 3,000, were considering settlement in Russia and were ready to forgo exemption from military service, provided they would be allowed special tax and settlement privileges.

In all four colonies the difficult pioneer years gradually gave way to years of remarkable prosperity. Whereas the settlers had originally occupied themselves primarily with small crafts and industries including silkworms, the development of Black Sea ports by Russia gave the Mennonites the possibility of grain production and export. The rich Ukrainian soil was ideally suited for the production of hard winter wheat, for which there was increasing demand all over

131

Europe. With economic prosperity also came greater attention to educational, religious, and cultural affairs. Stronger leaders with better training began to emerge, and the economy was better able to support the increasing cultural and socio-religious activities.

### Johann Cornies, 1789-1848

Among these emerging leaders none influenced the settlements more than Johann Cornies, who was appointed mediator between the Russian government and the Mennonites by the czar at the age of twenty-eight. In that capacity he became, in a sense, director of the growth and development of the Mennonite communities in their economic and educational activities, thereby also influencing their religious life.

Johann Cornies was born in Prussia in 1789 and accompanied his parents to the Molotschna settlement in 1804. After his preliminary grade school education he worked for a year as a laborer in a flour mill, then began marketing agricultural produce in nearby towns. Following his marriage in 1811, he settled on a farm in Ohrloff, a village of the Molotschna colony, but without intending to limit his activities to that location. Soon he was renting large tracts of government land for sheep and cattle grazing, including a 9,000-acre tract by 1830. Among his primary interests were the improvement of horses and livestock and the establishing of nurseries for trees and other horticulture. The government soon recognized his outstanding abilities and gave him almost unlimited authority to promote good agricultural practices among the Mennonites and beyond. In 1817 he was made permanent chairman of the Agricultural Association, which came to include all of the economic and cultural activities of the colonies.

Under the umbrella of this association Cornies founded a society for Christian education in 1818, an organization which was eventually to control all of the educational activities in the Mennonite colonies. Under its auspices the first secondary school was founded in Ohrloff in 1820. Through his efforts curriculum reform was undertaken, as was better teacher training, and the groundwork was laid for an excellent school system. Among his specific contributions was a major document on "General Rules Concerning Instruction and Treatment of School Children," containing much excellent counsel for teachers in relation to their school responsibilities.

With his knowledge, drive, and power of position Cornies influenced not only the Mennonites but also the Hutterites and various

Russian ethnic groups including the Doukhobors and Molokans. Special instruction in agriculture was given to Russian boys and girls in the Cornies home where they were temporarily employed, and Cornies did need many workers. At the time of his death in 1848, he was cultivating about 25,000 acres and keeping some 500 horses, 8,000 sheep, and 200 other head of cattle.

## Growth in Russia

The large number of children in most Mennonite families in Russia led to a very rapid increase in population and a consequent continuing need for more land since the vast majority gave little thought to any occupation other than farming. The original 10,000 settlers had grown to 34,500 by 1859 but had added very little land to the original acreage. There were, of course, men like Cornies who rented or purchased large estates wherever they could and farmed on a large scale. It is estimated that by 1900 there were as many as 384 such large estates, totaling approximately one million acres, but these estates were the exception. The government regulations stipulated that the original 176-acre plots of land for each family were not to be subdivided by the colonies.

The result of this policy was that many families were soon without land, and without land they became, in a sense, second-class citizens in the land-conscious Mennonite communities. These landless families were given a garden plot at the outskirts of the village and were, for that reason, known as *Anwohner* (marginal people). The landed farmers, on the other hand, were known as *Wirte* or landlords. While the former had no vote since the franchise was based on land ownership, they were obliged to pay taxes which were based on population. The situation became most acute in the Molotschna colony where there were 2,356 landless workers and 1,384 landed farmers in 1865.

The Molotschna landless appealed to St. Petersburg where they received a sympathetic hearing. With pressure from the government, the colony divided up the 64,500 acres of communal land which the landed farmers had been using thus far, into 88- and 40-acre tracts for the landless. But this was only a temporary solution. With a vision they had not shown before, the two oldest colonies initiated a vigorous program of fund-raising among their established families for the purchase of large tracts of land in other areas of Russia. Here they established the landless and young people in what came to be known as "Daughter Colonies." The new settlers were given ten years to pay for their lands, the proceeds being used for the purchase of more land. While the first daughter colony to be established was Bergthal in 1835, more than forty-five had been added a century later in the Ukraine, Crimea, Caucasus, south central Asia, and in Siberia. In Siberia Mennonites from all of the four old settlements founded the large Slavgorod-Barnaul colony in 1908, with fifty-nine villages on 135,000 acres of land.

## Religious Developments

The plight of the landless in mid-nineteenth century gave impetus to a growing restlessness within the church itself. In those years religious organization paralleled community organization; citizens of the community were almost certainly members of the church also. As the *Oberschulze* (mayor) was in charge of civil affairs, so his counterpart the elder was in charge of the church and, therefore, a powerful figure. The elder was assisted by ministers and deacons who together constituted the *Lehrdienst* (teachers) and who, as preservers of the tradition of the fathers, frequently became defenders of the *status quo*. In describing the difficult pioneer era, one writer has said:

Under these circumstances a slow stagnation crept into the intellectual and spiritual life of the group. When missionary David Schlatter visited the colonies in 1825, he reported that the church had lost its salt. But the spiritual life was to sink even lower during the next two decades. What impact could have come from the Russian culture was lost since the settlers did not know the Russian language. . . . By 1845 only one item had been printed by the Mennonites in Russia. . . . Continued intermarriage within the group led to a unique self and group consciousness. To be a Mennonite meant not primarily religious but ethnic relations. [2]

The dissatisfaction of many with this low spiritual state was increased by the failure of the church to champion the cause of the poor, who were all members of the one Mennonite church. The economic and educational progress made under Cornies' leadership clashed increasingly with the spiritual traditionalism of the church and finally stirred the people to action.

*Kleine Gemeinde:* As early as 1814 a break had occurred in unity of the Mennonites in Russia but had not prevented the later break in 1860. Klaas Reimer, a young minister who came to the Molotschna Colony in 1804 from Danzig, was appalled at the low spiritual life that developed among the immigrants, especially the lack of personal morality and ethical concern. He also opposed Mennonite contributions to the Russian government to win the war against Napoleon. He was particularly opposed to use of corporal punishment by the civic Mennonite leaders, believing that since all were church members, only excommunication should be used to discipline offenders. In reaching these conclusions he was guided by a serious study of the Scriptures and a diligent reading of the *Martyrs Mirror,* indicating his central concern to have been the restoration of authentic Biblical-Anabaptist Christianity. Finding little response in the church, he began meeting separately with like-minded members in 1812, and by 1814 they were organized as a separate group. The others mockingly called this minority group the *Kleine Gemeinde* (small church), a name which the group itself soon accepted fully as indeed indicating the true nature of the faithful church in a hostile world. (The group is today known as the Evangelical Mennonite Conference.) In 1869 a group broke with the *Kleine Gemeinde* over the mode of baptism and formed the Krimmer [Crimea] Mennonite Brethren.

*Mennonite Brethren Church:* Another division which grew out of this restlessness, and eventually affected all of the Mennonite communities, was the organizing of the Mennonite Brethren Church on January 6, 1860. In 1834 Wilhelm Lange, a Mennonite elder in Germany and former Lutheran, had led a group to the Molotschna settlement to found the village of Gnadenfeld (field of grace). Through contact with Moravian pietism in Germany, these settlers had brought with them a strong spiritual concern and religious fervor, and in turn provided contact with other evangelicals traveling through the area. Among these latter travelers was Eduard Wüst, a German pietist, who was soon conducting a series of meetings among the Mennonites. His messages stressed repentance and conversion and called for a life consistent with Christian faith. His meetings led to Bible study and prayer cells. When these Brethren, as they called themselves, despaired of working renewal among the Mennonites, they took the un-pietistic step of establishing their own organized brotherhood in 1860, with eighteen charter members. Their story will be told in detail in Chapter 15.

*Other signs of renewal:* The invigorating forces which gave birth to the Mennonite Brethren Church did not bypass the other Mennonites known simply as *Kirchliche,* i.e., Church Mennonites, or Mennonite Church. New spiritual concerns began to emerge among them also, undoubtedly stimulated by the challenge of the division. In 1883 all of these congregations united to form a conference in order to work together in the fields of education and charity. The conference took as its motto, "In essentials unity, in nonessentials liberty, in all things love." In addition to renewed attention to education, a concern also developed for missions and evangelism. Though the Mennonites were forbidden to proselyte among members of the Russian Orthodox Church, a significant outreach began among their neighbors, at times leading to imprisonment and even exile for the Mennonite missionaries. Although the Mennonites in Russia had been supporting the Amsterdam Mennonite Missionary Society since 1854, no missionary had been sent by them until 1871, when Heinrich Dirks went to Sumatra. His return ten years later, and appointment as elder among the home congregations, added considerably to their sense of mission. Dirks was followed by at least twenty-eight workers to Java and Sumatra, and one to Egypt. The much smaller Mennonite Brethren Church was also active in mission work during this time, having sent out twenty-two workers to India, and two to Africa by 1914.

This new vitality was sparked by the work of numerous men who felt deeply the inadequacies of their brotherhood but decided not to break with it. One of the foremost among these men was Bernhard Harder (d. 1884). Harder had also been inspired by the preaching of Eduard Wüst and became a powerful evangelist among the congregations without stressing separation as a mark of renewal. He was roundly criticized by many in the Mennonite Church for sounding too much like a Mennonite Brethren, and by the Mennonite Brethren for not joining them, but he coveted all the open doors he could find and had ready access to most Mennonite congregations of that time. Though he was a teacher by profession, he occasionally interrupted his teaching for longer periods to pursue evangelism, being supported during those times by a special group of friends. He has been called the greatest evangelist and pulpit man to arise among the Mennonites in Russia. In the course of his ministry he wrote many poems and hymns, of which over 1,000 have been published. [3] On September 27, 1884, he returned ill from a series of meetings in which he had preached four times daily and died of pneumonia five days later.

Two other developments in the life of the church at this time were the flight into the wilderness of a group under the visionary Claasz Epp, Jr., in 1880, and the establishing of the Evangelical Mennonite Church, generally known as the *Allianz Gemeinde,* in an attempt to overcome the separatist spirit in the settlement, in 1905. Epp was an able leader and farmer who became captivated with the books of Daniel and the Revelation. Under pressure of the events which caused many to leave for America, Epp was led to believe that deliverance from the great tribulation of the last times would come in the east, not in the west. Thus to go to America was to run away from the Lord. Consequently he led a small group deep into Asiatic Russia in search of the haven *(bergungsort)* which the Lord was to have prepared for His people, the Mennonites. Another group, which had joined them from the Molotschna Colony, settled in Aulie-Ata in Turkestan, while Epp pressed on to Ak-Mechet in the Khanate of Khiva. After untold hardship and suffering some eventually found their way to America anyway, but Epp died lonely and under excommunication in 1913, having climaxed his vision by proclaiming himself to be the Son of Christ and the fourth person of the Trinity.

## *Economic and Social Progress from 1850 to 1920*

The high point of community development among the Mennonites of Russia was reached during this period from mid-nineteenth century to the Bolshevik Revolution. As indicated above, the establishing of daughter colonies continued rapidly under the pressure of a high birth rate. The most comprehensive statistics of Mennonite life in Russia were taken for the decade of the 1920's and constitute an invaluable study of the socio-economic conditions at that time. From them it appears that there were 120,000 Mennonites in Russia after World War I, of which 75,000 lived in the Ukraine and 45,000 in Siberia and other parts of Russia.[4] This does not, of course, include the 18,000 who emigrated to America in the 1870's.

The agricultural development promoted by Johann Cornies made possible and necessary a limited industrial program also. Mennonites concentrated on the production of agricultural machinery primarily and the processing of their own agricultural products. Thus by early twentieth century they had seventy large steam-powered flour mills, factories whose combined output was, for example, 15,000 mowers and 10,000 plows annually, creameries, and other industrial projects. Six percent of industrial production in Russia was carried on by the Mennonites. But the vast majority of them were farmers. It has been estimated that the industrial wealth, which accounted for 50 to 75 percent of total Mennonite assets; was in the hands of 2.8 percent of the people. Some of them were very wealthy.

This flourishing economy made possible civic and educational programs unmatched anywhere in the Mennonite world at that time. Mutual aid, homes for the aged, orphanages, hospitals, includ-

137

ing a mental hospital, a school for deaf-mutes, a girls' school, and a school of business for young men were only a part of the vast provisions the communities made for their people. By 1914 they had 400 elementary and thirteen secondary or high schools, two teachers' colleges, four trade schools, one Bible school, and negotiations were soon to be carried on with the government for permission to establish a seminary. In addition there were approximately 250 Mennonite students attending higher Russian institutions and some fifty in seminaries and universities abroad. It is clear that all of these institutions could not have been supported adequately except by congregations who were experiencing a recovery of their spiritual life and were willing to sacrifice for these causes. This willingness was verified further by their support of some 12,000 Mennonite young men in the forestry and medical corps during World War I which, in 1917 alone, cost the congregations three million rubles.

### Developments to 1930

Meanwhile the Russian reform and nationalization program which had begun in 1866 was also affecting the Mennonites. The government-sponsored agricultural reforms led, for example, to a change in regional administrative boundaries as a result of which Mennonites began to find themselves a minority in a local Russian administrative unit. Where they were in the majority they were now forced to keep all records and official correspondence in the Russian language. They had also to contribute to the tax support of local political and welfare and educational institutions as well as supporting their own. The fact that many of the landless now received the franchise, moreover, threatened the traditional balance of power in the Mennonite communities.

The biggest threat to the Mennonite way of life, however, lay in the requirement that Russian be taught in all schools and that Russian teachers would be provided where Mennonite teachers were not qualified. Russian had been used in some Mennonite schools as early as the 1830's, and many more used it by the 1860's, but from 1881 the State Department of Instruction kept close watch over the Mennonite schools, and in the 1890's all instruction came to be in the Russian language, with the exception of Bible and German as a language. It is possible that this development conditioned the Mennonites to see the German language as an essential part of the Mennonite faith itself. Elder Leonhard Sudermann spoke for many in 1873 when he said, "those of our young people who enter Russian high schools are lost," but a Mennonite opponent of this view wrote in 1874:

It has been shown that the dear, honorable bishop was wrong. Our American brethren confess that it is much more difficult to keep their young people in the congregations than in Russia. . . . The number of those who have left the Mennonite faith while studying at Russian schools, or later . . . is very small. More have been lost from those who did not attend Russian schools . . . although these too have been few.[5]

Most of the Mennonites, nevertheless, had completely learned to identify themselves in terms of their totally self-sufficient and exclusive Mennonite communities. The changes which were coming among them, therefore, threatened to assimilate the Mennonites into the Russian population which seemed to many to forecast an end to their historic faith as a people.

The climax of this development was reached with the passage of the universal military service law of 1874. In anticipation of its passage the Mennonites sent five delegations to St. Petersburg from 1871 to 1873 to plead for the old privileges. We can appreciate the displeasure of the president of the Imperial Council when he discovered that two of the leading elders could not speak Russian to him though they had lived in Russia all their lives. Eventually the delegations were promised an acceptable form of alternative service instead of military training, but even this was more than some could tolerate. They asserted that they did recognize government as necessary, they did obey it whenever possible, and they did pray for it. They also cited the official recognition given to them following the Crimean War of 1854-56, when they had made major medical and food contributions and had cared for 5,000 wounded which were brought to their colonies from the nearby front. Section 157 of the law of 1874 did provide for alternative service by the Mennonites, but those who felt this to be a violation of conscience, or an indication of further threats to their faith, emigrated to the United States and Canada as will be seen in the following chapter. This group totaled 18,000. Among those who remained was a critic who charged that too many Mennonites identified their faith with the German language, whereas in Christ there should be neither Jew, nor Greek, nor Scythian, and then he added:

Thank God that they went. It was good for them, their children, and for America. They have calmed their conscience . . . and America has received many good farm families to Kansas, Nebraska, Dakota, Minnesota, etc., who will make these states rich. . . . It was also good for us and for Russia; their stubborn piety could no longer be met with the concessions they demanded, the like of which are almost impossible to grant in a modern European nation."

Meanwhile the involvement of the Mennonites with their Russian environment increased. The Mennonite hospitals served many non-Mennonites, business contacts with others increased, and friendships developed as the Russian language ceased to be a barrier: Thousands of Russians served the Mennonites as farm laborers and household help and, in many cases, became very fond of each other. Among Mennonite intellectuals were many who admired Russian literature and read deeply in Russian history to understand the soul of the nation. In the Russo-Japanese War of 1904-5, the families of Russian soldiers from Mennonite areas received very substantial monetary and food aid from the colonies. All of this involvement, however, was not sufficient to close the social, cultural, and economic gap that existed between the Mennonites and their neighbors. The peasants and many Russian officials were jealous of Mennonite achievements, piqued also no doubt by a certain Mennonite hauteur and condescension which implied their feeling of superiority.

These attitudes, together with Mennonite wealth, brought great difficulty to the colonies with the coming of the Bolshevik Revolution in 1917. As German-speaking people the Mennonites were suspect as enemies of the state in its war against Germany; as prosperous farmers and businessmen they were soon suspect as enemies of the revolution as well. For a time the struggle between the Red and White Russian armies centered in the Ukraine, the battle front having moved back and forth as many as twenty-three times in some Mennonite areas. With this devastation came pillaging by ruthless bands of robbers and opportunists, one of the most dangerous being Nestor Machno, a political prisoner whom the revolution had released from Siberian exile and who was out to take his revenge on society. Machno knew the Mennonites well, having worked for them as a young man; he even spoke the Low German language. In his opinion he had been underpaid by them and was now collecting his wages with the help of thousands of peasants. As a result of this reign of terror hundreds of Mennonites were killed (240 alone in Zagradovka in November, 1919) and countless villages completely destroyed.

During these dark hours most of the Mennonites, encouraged by their leaders, sought to remain true to the principle of nonresistance and of love for the enemy. For a minority of young men, however, this was too difficult to accept in the face of murder, rape, and wholesale plunder. With earlier advice and some equipment from the German forces they organized what was known as the *Selbstschutz* (self-defense), and gave armed resistance to Machno, particularly during the winter of 1918-19. Mennonite church conferences later condemned the *Selbstschutz* as both a tactical blunder and a violation of historic Biblical nonresistance.

A terrible famine swept over Russia from 1921 to 1923 in the aftermath of the revolution and thousands of people died. In desperation the Mennonites sent four brethren to North America to plead for help from the Mennonite churches. The Mennonite Central Committee, which was organized in 1920 in response to this request, sent immediate help and averted heavy casualties among the Mennonites in Russia as well as aiding non-Mennonites wherever possible. Clayton Kratz, one of the relief workers from Pennsylvania, disappeared mysteriously late in 1920 and was never heard from again. It is estimated that no less than 2,200 Mennonites perished in Russia during these years as a result of war, famine, and the typhus epidemic which scourged the land. The four men who had been sent for help had, in the meantime, explored settlement possibilities in Canada and by 1923 a steady flow of immigrants was on their way to join those who had settled there in the 1870's, as will be seen in the following chapter.

Those remaining in Russia began the difficult task of rebuilding their communities. An agricultural association was organized to co-ordinate their concerns and to speak unitedly in their behalf. It also became a channel for emigration which made it suspect in the eyes of the authorities. An office was established in Moscow to provide liaisonship with the new government. In 1925 this office began publishing *Der Praktische Landwirt* (The Practical Farmer) to encourage the Mennonites and keep in touch with them. Another publication, *Unser Blatt*, was begun the same year to speak to spiritual needs and issues. 1925 was also the year of the last large Mennonite church conference in Russia.

With the initiation of the first five-year plan on October 1, 1928, which included forced collectivization of their farms, new efforts were made by many to leave Russia. In a desperate attempt to escape some 13,000 Mennonites made their way to Moscow in the fall and winter of 1929, but only 5,677 managed to get to Germany, from where they were sent to Canada and South America. More might have been allowed to leave if Germany and Canada had been quicker to grant visas, but these nations were having unemployment

141

and other problems of their own as a result of the depression. A few were able to leave in 1930 before all emigration from Russia was stopped, bringing to 20,201 the number who had come to Canada from the time the movement began in 1923. Approximately 600 made their escape eastward across the Amur River into China.

The 8,000 Mennonites who had gone to Moscow but had been unable to leave returned to their homes, but many did not arrive there, being sent on to prison or exile and hard labor in the forests of the north. These were followed by countless others who were considered obstacles to the complete collectivization of Soviet agriculture. Many of the exiled never returned. Meanwhile the terrors of collectivization were followed by another famine in 1932-33, in which from five to eight million Russians died, including over 100,000 German-speaking people. The world Mennonite brotherhood was again able to send some help to the Mennonites in Russia.

## From 1930 to the Present

Spiritual poverty followed close on the heels of physical suffering. In the new society Christian concepts of right and wrong, property, marriage, education, responsibility, and freedom were changed. Revolutionary rights replaced human and civil rights. An unprecedented moral and spiritual decline set in among the Mennonites. Many mothers whose husbands had been deported had all they could do to provide daily bread for their children, while the children grew up without proper parental attention and without Christian training. By 1935 a majority of the churches were being used as clubhouses, stables, theaters, or granaries. Membership in these congregations had declined rapidly because of the antireligious propaganda and other threats to the faith. Many strong leaders had escaped to Canada, and those who remained were soon in exile. Non-Mennonites settling in Mennonite villages contributed further to the cultural disintegration of their communities. Some Mennonites also participated actively in the new social revolution. The purges of 1937-38, which victimized over seven million Soviet citizens, also hit the Mennonites. Many of the remaining leaders and ministers were sent into exile. While the exact number may never be known, we do know that in those two years the Chortitza settlement alone lost 800 men. The stories of many of these have been told in a new two-volume *Martyrs Mirror*.[7]

With the coming of World War II in 1939, the complete dissolution of the Mennonite communities was only a matter of time. Many were evacuated into Asiatic Russia in 1941, to escape the German front. For those remaining, the German occupation gave a brief period of relative freedom. While Russians suffered miserably at the hands of the Nazis, German-speaking peoples enjoyed numerous privileges; churches were reopened and religious instruction introduced into the schools. Soon, however, the rigors of war and occupation made the German rule almost equally oppressive. With the German retreat following the battle of Stalingrad in the winter of 1942-43, many ethnic Germans including some 35,000 Mennonites were evacuated westward by the retreating German armies. This retreat soon turned into a mass disorganized flight characterized by panic and terror. Hundreds of refugees died, while scores of families were separated. In the closing days of the war and its aftermath thousands were also forcefully repatriated into Russia and only 12,000 were later found in the western zones of Germany. Most of them subsequently migrated to South America and to Canada, as will be seen in Chapters 11, 14, and 19.

Little is known of the Mennonites in Russia immediately after World War II ended in 1945, except that there was continued suffering during the fourth five-year plan, 1946-50. Following the death of Joseph Stalin in 1953, there was an internal relaxation and amnesties were granted to the inmates of many of the labor camps in 1953, 1955, and 1957. Although they were not permitted to return to their former homeland in the Ukraine and the Volga region, they were at liberty to establish new homes. Many of them moved to the USSR of Kazakhstan in central Asiatic Russia, frequently worshiping with Baptist congregations. An additional concentration of Mennonite families seems to have occurred in southwest Siberia. A few were allowed to join their families in Canada, and six families were reunited when those living in Canada returned to Russia.

Contacts had meanwhile also grown between the Baptists in Russia and the Mennonites in North America; a Mennonite delegation visited Russia in 1956, in 1958, and again in 1966, while the Baptists visited Mennonites in the United States in 1964. The contacts confirmed that, while the Mennonites were losing their identity in many ways, there were religious services here and there in homes and in simple meetinghouses. The degree of religious freedom depended on the local authorities. Most of the active leaders were untrained, and some were women. The Russian language had almost completely replaced the German among them, and Mennonite young people were attending universities as well as entering the various professions. Economically there was improvement as conditions in

Russia improved generally after 1955.

In the 1960's some Mennonites were reported to be moving back to the Ukraine, but the past could not be recaptured. With the former settlements dissolved, the Mennonite ethnic culture thoroughly disrupted, and Mennonite religious life disintegrated, it appeared that their witness in Russia was drawing to a close after nearly 200 years. It was not known, however, how many faithful might still be witnessing to their faith, regardless of where they were, as they had opportunity.

*Notes*

1. Quoted in David G. Rempel, "The Mennonite Colonies in Russia: A Study of Their Settlement and Economic Development from 1789 to 1914." Unpublished PhD dissertation, 1933, Appendix II.
2. Gerhard Lohrenz in *A Legacy of Faith,* C. J. Dyck (ed.) (1962), p. 173.
3. Heinrich Franz, ed., *Geistliche Lieder und Gelegenheitsgedichte* (1888), and P. B. Harder, ed. *Kleines Liederbuch: Geistliche Gelegenheitslieder* (1902).
4. Adolf Ehrt, *Das Mennonitentum in Russland.* Langensalza: Julius Beltz, 1932, pp. 91-95.
5. P. M. Friesen, *Die Alt-Evangelische Mennonitische Bruderschaft in Russland (1789-1910).* Halbstadt: Raduga, 1911, pp. 500, 501.
6. *Ibid.,* p. 501.
7. A. A. Toews, *Mennonitische Martyrer,* I (1949), and II (1954).

*FOR FURTHER READING:*

*The Mennonite Encyclopedia,* 4 vols.

*Mennonite Life* 3 (July, 1948), pp. 30-47; 3 (October, 1948), pp. 5-10; 4 (January, 1949), pp. 22-27; 4 (October, 1949), pp. 28-33; 6 (July, 1951), pp. 28-37; 10 (January, 1955), pp. 14-30; 14 (July, 1959), pp. 138-40; 17 (July, 1962), pp. 126-33.

Frank H. Epp, *Mennonite Exodus.* Altona, Manitoba: D. W. Friesen & Sons, 1962.

C. Henry Smith, *The Story of the Mennonites* (1950).

———, *The Coming of the Russian Mennonites.* Berne, Indiana: Mennonite Book Concern, 1927.

# Chapter 11

# THE MENNONITES COME TO NORTH AMERICA

AFTER ALL the weary struggles of the Mennonites in Europe to achieve national homes where they might live in peace with their families, and after enduring the discomforts of petty persecution and the poverty which followed the endless wars of the European lands where Mennonites lived, the opening up of the New World of America sounded too good to be true! Mennonites crossed the Atlantic in a number of more or less well-defined waves. These Atlantic voyages were not to be taken lightly, for they were made in sailing ships which took two or three months for each trip. Dried food had to be eaten, the water supply was often inadequate, and disease frequently struck the travelers causing some to be buried at sea. But the poverty of the Mennonites in Europe in the 1700's, the desire to escape the militarism of Europe in the 1800's, and the communism of Russia in the 1900's were so strong that about 64,000 Mennonites gladly undertook to endure the rigors of ocean travel in order to come to the New World of freedom and unparalleled opportunity. Let us look more closely at the story of these movements by first listing the eight major "waves" of immigrants and then discussing them separately in greater detail.

## Immigration

*Wave 1.* From the area of the Lower Rhine, with such centers as Krefeld, about 100 Mennonites came to America in the period from 1683 to 1705. They settled in Germantown, a Quaker village north of Philadelphia (now within the city of Philadelphia), where the first permanent settlement of Mennonites in the New World was made. The first preacher in Germantown, William Rittenhouse, seems to have been chosen in 1690, but in the absence of a bishop no baptismal services were held until 1708, nor were any communion services observed until 1708. Upon written authorization from Mennonite leaders in Europe a later preacher, Jacob Gottschalk, finally did baptize applicants for membership and observed the Lord's Supper, 1708. In that year the first Germantown Mennonite meetinghouse was built of logs. This building was replaced by a lovely stone structure in 1770, which is still in use.

*Wave 2.* Immigration now got into second gear. The first wave involved only a hundred people. Now several thousands came, mostly from 1707 to 1756. They were all of Swiss origin and some of them came directly from their beloved Swiss mountains while others came from the Palatinate along the Rhine River. The Palatinate (*Pfalz* in German) was a land where a German dialect was spoken which the pioneers brought along to Pennsylvania. This dialect is properly known today as Pennsylvania German or Pennsylvania "Dutch" (*Deutsch* in German; it is not a form of Holland Dutch). It is estimated that from three to five thousand Mennonites came to Pennsylvania in this period--3,700 might be a good guess. Included in the group were about 300 Amish who came over from about 1720 and from about 1740 had several congregations in southeastern Pennsylvania.

*Wave 3.* After the time of Napoleon, from about 1815 to 1860, Amish Mennonites of Swiss background left Alsace, Bavaria, and Hesse, and settled in Ohio, Ontario, Indiana, and Illinois. They totaled about 3,000 persons. Later, around World War I, most of these Amish Mennonites united with the Mennonites of Waves 1 and 2, to make the present (Old) Mennonite Church.

*Wave 4.* About 500 Mennonites left Switzerland, largely between 1830 and 1860, and settled in Ohio and Indiana. Those who settled in Wayne County, Ohio, are largely (Old) Mennonites today, while those in Adams County, Indiana, are now affiliated with the General Conference Mennonite Church.

*Wave 5.* Possibly 300 Mennonite "stragglers" of Swiss extraction left the Palatinate in the general period, 1865-95, and settled in Ohio, Indiana, and Illinois.

*Wave 6.* Now the immigration shifted into high gear. In the early 1870's it began to appear that Russia might go back on its promise to grant the Mennonites permanent military exemption.

146

From 1873 to 1884 some 18,000 Mennonites, largely of Dutch (Holland) stock, left Russia and settled in the prairie states and provinces of North America: possibly 10,000 in Minnesota, South Dakota, Nebraska, and Kansas, and about 8,000 in Manitoba. Accompanying this vast group were about 400 Swiss Mennonites from Galicia and Volhynia in Poland; they settled in Kansas and South Dakota.

*Wave 7.* After World War I, from 1922 to 1930, another 25,000 Mennonites fled from Russia to escape from communism, and 21,000 of them settled in Canada, with the remainder going to Paraguay, Brazil, and Mexico.

*Wave 8.* During World War II, in 1941-43, an additional 35,000 got out of Russia with the help of the German army, but in a tragic manner almost two thirds of them were forcibly repatriated by the Russian army, while some 12,000 eventually made their escape to Canada (over 7,000) and to South America.

In summary about 8,000 Swiss Mennonites of Waves 2 to 5 came to North America, an additional 46,000 emigrated to North America from Russia in Waves 6 to 8 (of which 36,000 settled in Canada), while an additional 10,000 located in South America: making a grand total of 64,000 Mennonite immigrants to North and South America, 1683 to the present.

*Early Settlements in Pennsylvania*

As we saw earlier, the first permanent settlement of Mennonites in North America was made at Germantown, a village about seven miles north of the city of Philadelphia, in 1683. But the little group of Mennonites had only the reading of sermons by a lay brother, Dirk Keyser, and perhaps others, until 1690 when they chose William Rittenhouse as their first minister. As early as 1702, before the first meetinghouse was erected by the Germantown Mennonites, various families began to move to Skippack in what is now Mont- gomery County, some twenty miles farther north. The Skippack settle- ment prospered while the Germantown congregation remained rather small, perhaps never having had over 100 members. Around the middle of the nineteenth century the organized life of the congrega- tion faltered and died, but a few members lived on to affiliate with the revived congregation which eventually was set up. The Germantown congregation is now affiliated with the General Con- ference Mennonite Church.

The Skippack congregation did not long remain the only Mennonite church in southeastern Pennsylvania. Soon there were a number of congregations in what are now Montgomery, Bucks, Chester, Berks, Lehigh, and Northampton counties, many of them established in the first decade or two after 1720, especially those in Montgomery, Berks, and Bucks counties. Franconia Township (in what is now Montgomery County) was created in Philadelphia County in 1732. Franconia Township contains an ancient congregation of Mennonites called the Franconia Mennonite Church, and nearby is the village of Franconia as well. For almost two centuries the settlements which are here being described were often referred to as Skippack, but eventually the conference came to be known as the Franconia Conference because the semiannual ministers' meetings always were, and still are, held in the Franconia meetinghouse, near the village of Franconia, in Franconia Township.

Beginning in 1710, twenty years after the first American Mennonite preacher was chosen at Germantown, and eight years after the Skippack settlement was begun, a new Mennonite settlement was started about sixty miles west of Philadelphia in what was then Chester County, Pennsylvania, but is now Lancaster County. The very first settlement in the area was made near the present village of Strasburg, not far from what was originally called Hickory Town, now the city of Lancaster. The earliest Mennonite settlements in what is now the huge Lancaster Conference were made in the valley of the Pequea (pronounced PECK-way) Creek. Within two decades of 1710 a large and strong chain of Mennonite settlements had begun in various directions from Hickory Town. By mid-eighteenth century Mennonite settlements were spreading west of Lancaster County into the present counties of York, Adams, and Lebanon.

Franconia and Lancaster have different family names. Common names in Franconia are Alderfer, Allebach, Bergey, Cassel, Clemens, Clemmer, Derstine, Detweiler, Fretz, Funk, Gehman, Haldeman, Hunsicker, Moyer, Nyce, Oberholtzer, Rittenhouse, Swartley, Wismer, Yoder, and Ziegler. Common Lancaster names are Brackbill, Brubaker, Burkholder, Buckwalter, Charles (Karli at first), Eby, Erb, Eshelman, Garber, Graybill, Groff, Habecker, Herr, Hershey, Hess, Hoover, Hostetter, Kreider, Lehman, Lichty, Martin, Mellinger, Risser, Rutt, Sensenig, Shenk, Shirk, Snavely, Weaver, Wenger, and Zimmerman. Franconia and Lancaster also differed slightly in religious practices; foot washing was seldom observed among the former before 1900 but continuously among the latter. There were also slight differences in the German dialects spoken. In both conferences all services were conducted in German until the 1875-1925 period, when the older German-speaking ministers died and the younger men could no longer preach in German.

### The (Old) Mennonites and Amish Spread Out

As will be seen in the following chapter, these eastern settlements became the parents of a growing number of congregations in the central and eventually western states and in Ontario. Since colonial families were usually large, often with twelve or more children, daughter congregations were established wherever the young couples moved in search of more land.

*Virginia:* Within a generation after settling in Lancaster County, in the early 1700's, this search had led to settlements in Page County, Virginia, where thirty-nine families prospered until a terrible Indian raid occurred in 1758, followed by a second raid in 1764. In this second raid the Indians were led by a white man on a bloody rampage which was to cost many lives. Preacher John Rhodes was killed in the doorway of his home and his wife and son in their yard. A son who climbed a tree to see what was happening was shot in the tree and killed. Still another son was shot and killed as he tried to swim across a river. Later they killed two daughters and another son whom they had taken as captives. A fourth captive was later released by treaty. The most remarkable escape was made by a daughter Elizabeth, who seized her baby sister and ran into the barn, barricading it against a pursuing Indian. While he ran away, presumably to get fire to burn down the barn, Elizabeth escaped through a hemp field with her sister, and fled twelve miles to a married brother's home. Those were rugged days! Other settlements were made in Virginia, the most successful being those in Rockingham and Augusta counties about the time of the Revolutionary War.

*Southwestern Pennsylvania and Maryland:* In the 1760's and 1770's Mennonites and Amish began to settle in southwestern Pennsylvania and in Maryland to form what has been known since 1954 as the Allegheny Conference. As early as 1735, Lancaster Mennonite families began to locate in Franklin County, and by the time of the Revolutionary War they were also settling in adjoining Washington County, Maryland. Neither settlement became strong until the 1790's, the centers of the two groups being Chambersburg in Pennsylvania and Hagerstown in Maryland. In approximately 1810-1830 they formed the Washington-Franklin Conference.

*Ontario:* The Mennonites of the 1700's had a warm feeling for England because of the generous recognition of conscience on the part of the British authorities. Most of the Mennonites quickly transferred their loyalty to the new American government after the Revolutionary War, but there were some who decided to stay under the British flag. As early as 1786 a few families made the trek into the wilderness of Upper Canada, now Ontario. About sixty persons were at Vineland by 1800. Numerous other settlements were also established in Ontario, the largest of which was to be in Waterloo County, beginning in 1800. These early pioneers were cheated by a man who sold them land which was found to have a $20,000 mortgage on it. This was more than they could undertake to pay; so two men returned to Lancaster County and told their sad story to the church there. Members of the various congregations immediately formed a company to help their Ontario friends. The mortgage was paid off, and 60,000 acres of land purchased, helping the Ontario brethren to a good start. One of the outstanding leaders in Waterloo County was Bishop Benjamin Eby (d. 1853), of Ebytown, later Berlin and, since 1917, known as Kitchener. In the 1820's these groups were joined by Amish Mennonite immigrants from Europe, who remained separate for a century until 1922, when they formed the Ontario Amish Mennonite Conference. In 1959 they united with the (Old) Mennonite General Conference and in 1963 changed their name to Western Ontario Mennonite Conference. In the 1890's the Ontario Mennonites began moving westward also, settling in Alberta and Saskatchewan. The Alberta-Saskatchewan Conference was organized in 1907.

*Ohio:* While the Ontario movement was under way, others pressed west into Ohio. The first settlers from the Franconia and Lancaster conferences began to reach Fairfield and Perry counties in Ohio in 1799. Both Mennonites and Amish settled in Ohio. Among the latter were both the Old Order Amish and the less rigid Amish Mennonites. While the former were strict congregationalists with no district conferences and worshiping in homes, the Amish Mennonites adopted the English language, Sunday schools, and church buildings. In the years 1916-27 they were to merge with the (Old) Mennonites. Among the major Amish Mennonite congregations which emerged in the 1800's were Oak Grove in Wayne County, Apostolic Mennonite (now General Conference Mennonite) in Butler County, Beech in Stark County, Martin's Creek in Holmes County, and others. In contrast with the Mennonites, very few Amish Mennonite congregations became extinct.

*Illinois:* As in Ohio, both Mennonites and Amish Mennonites settled in Illinois, largely in the 1830's and 1840's. The Amish Mennonites arrived first, coming from Alsace-Lorraine, Hesse, the Palatinate, Bavaria, and Switzerland, with the greatest number from Alsace. The first congregation to emerge was Partridge, which is represented today in the large Metamora church. One of the strongest leaders in the history of the Illinois Amish Mennonites was Joseph Stuckey (d. 1902), often called "Father Stuckey." In the course of time he found himself somewhat out of step with the other leaders of the Midwest and ultimately withdrew from the Amish Mennonites to form the Central Conference Mennonite Church (name adopted in 1914). In 1946 this group affiliated with the General Conference Mennonite Church. A second leader among the Amish Mennonites was John Smith (d. 1906), whose son C. Henry Smith (d. 1948) has been called the "dean" of American Mennonite historians.

In the 1840's the Mennonites followed their Amish Mennonite brethren into Illinois. Perhaps the oldest Mennonite congregation was Union in Tazewell County, whose bishop Jost Bally (d. 1878) was an immigrant from Bavaria in 1847. The first meetinghouse was built in 1858. Other congregations which emerged were Freeport in Stephenson County, a congregation made famous by its able minister and bishop J. S. Shoemaker (d. 1936), as also the Science Ridge and Morrison congregations in Whiteside County. Small congregations arose near the town of Gardner in Grundy County, and Cullom in Livingston County.

*Indiana:* Mennonites and Amish also came to Indiana in the 1840's. A few feeble settlements had been established in 1838, when Swiss immigrants from the Jura in the canton of Bern began to settle in Wells and Adams counties. The Adams County Swiss Mennonites are now well known through the large Berne congregation with over 1,300 members. This congregation affiliated with the General Conference Mennonite Church in 1872, twelve years after the founding of the conference. A strong leader in the history of the Berne church was S. F. Sprunger (d. 1923). A few families from Lancaster County and the Shenandoah Valley began to settle near Arcadia, between Kokomo and Indianapolis, in 1838 but the congregation remained weak and died out by 1900.

The strongest settlement of (Old) Mennonites in Indiana was made west of Goshen in Elkhart County, beginning about 1840. The first preacher, an old bishop named Martin Hoover (d. 1850),

151

arrived with his married son in 1845. In 1848 two more preachers, Jacob Christophel and Jacob Wisler, came. Christophel was an 1818 immigrant from the Palatinate who had first lived in Pennsylvania; Wisler had been born in Bucks County, Pennsylvania, and ordained in Ohio. Wisler became the first active bishop of the (Old) Mennonites in Indiana, serving the church for two decades until his withdrawal in 1872 to found the Old Order Mennonites who were determined not to adopt the Sunday school. The real successor to Wisler was the able John F. Funk (d. 1930), preacher and publisher from Chicago, who came to Elkhart in 1867, and like Wisler a native of Bucks County, Pennsylvania. Among the Mennonite churches which emerged west of Goshen were Yellow Creek, Holdeman, Olive, Christophel, Blosser, Elkhart, and Nappanee. An interesting immigration from the Netherlands took place in 1853 and 1854 when a number of conservative Frisian Mennonite families came to Elkhart County. In 1889 the Christophel and Blosser (Old) Mennonite congregations merged to form the Salem church, and the Frisian congregation was absorbed into the Salem (Old) Mennonite congregation. In addition to Bishop John F. Funk, special mention must be made of the first outstanding evangelist of the (Old) Mennonites, John S. Coffman (d. 1899).

Amish families began moving into Indiana in 1841. The story of how this migration came about is interesting. It begins with the crowded situation of the Amish farmers in Somerset County, Pennsylvania. In 1840 a group of four Amish men left Somerset County on an inspection trip to find new lands on which to settle. They went to Pittsburgh and by boat down the Ohio River to the Mississippi, and from there to Iowa. From Iowa they journeyed to Indiana. When they came to Elkhart County, they decided they had found the "Promised Land." Full of joy they returned to Somerset County and prepared to move to Indiana the next year. The 1841 caravan from Somerset County to Elkhart County consisted of eight adults and sixteen children, the four family heads being Preacher Joseph Miller, Deacon Joseph Borntreger, Daniel S. Miller, and Christian Borntreger. When they reached Holmes County, they spent a week visiting the Amish there, doing their washing, and baking fresh bread. Then they set off again with their teams, spending their last night on the state line south of White Pigeon. On June 29, 1841, they drove into Goshen. They lived in huts three miles south of Goshen for a few months but that fall moved to the farms they bought east of Goshen. The two ordained men settled in Clinton Township, Elkhart County, while the two other families went ten miles to the northeast and located in Newbury Township, Lagrange County. They held their first Amish Service that fall in the home of Daniel S. Miller in Lagrange County. Other Amish settlers soon arrived, and the church grew rapidly.

*Iowa:* By 1839 the wave of Mennonite westward migration had reached Iowa with the arrival of John C. Krehbiel from the Palatinate in Germany. Settling at West Point in Lee County, he drew others after him until they were ready to organize a church in 1845, a step which was postponed until 1849, however, because of the murder of their minister. Amish settlers first came around 1840, also locating in· Lee County. The strongest Mennonite settlements emerged in Johnson and Washington counties with vigorous congregations also in Henry and Iowa counties. Several settlements proved not to be permanent with the continuing westward migration to Missouri and Kansas.

*Missouri:* About the time of the Civil War Amish Mennonites and Mennonites also began to make small settlements in Missouri. An Amish Mennonite settlement was begun in Hickory County in western Missouri in 1856 or earlier. The Cass County settlement, begun in 1860, was greatly strengthened by the arrival of Bishop J. C. Kenagy of Ohio in 1868. A few years later Mennonites from Adams County, Indiana, Polk County, Iowa, and Rockingham County, Virginia, began to move into Morgan and Moniteau counties, Missouri, and out of this mixture came an (Old) Mennonite church, Mount Zion, and a General Conference Mennonite church, Bethel. The man who did much to build up the church in Shelby and Marion counties was Benjamin Hershey (d. 1888). Lancaster County, Pennsylvania, Mennonites established the Palmyra congregation in Marion County in the 1880's.

*Kansas:* Mennonites began to move to Kansas in the early 1870's. M. W. Keim and his friends from Johnstown, Pennsylvania, bought 5,000 acres in Marion County during the winter of 1869-70, but their little colony did not prove permanent. In 1873 Bishop Daniel Brundage (d. 1895), the father of the (Old) Mennonites in Kansas, arrived in McPherson County. Brundage came from near Toronto, served as a preacher at Markham, Ontario, and then in Elkhart County, Indiana, from 1858 to 1869. After four years in Missouri he gave seventeen years of most effective leadership to the Kansas settlement, returning to Elkhart County in his old age in 1890. About the time of his return to Indiana a substantial

Amish migration from Ohio, Illinois, and Iowa began to Harper County in Kansas, some also settling near Milford in Nebraska.

*Other areas:* While the (Old) Mennonite and Amish settlements have never been numerous west of the Mississippi River, they have nevertheless located in many states in addition to those already mentioned. In 1956 there were approximately 11,400 baptized (Old) Mennonites west of the Mississippi and over 5,000 west of Ontario in Canada. The largest of these, as of the Amish settlements, were in Kansas. But the westward movement continued, and by 1900 congregations had been established in the Dakotas, Montana, Colorado, Washington, and Oregon. By that time both (Old) Mennonites and Amish had also settled in Oklahoma, to be followed later by congregations being established in Arkansas, Texas, Florida, and California. By the mid-1960's few states remained where descendants of the early immigrants from Switzerland and Germany had not established thriving communities and active congregations, and Quebec had been added to the four provinces on the (Old) Mennonite map of Canada.

## The Coming of the Mennonites from Russia

We have seen in Chapter 10 how and why the Mennonites went to Russia from Prussia beginning in 1789 and continuing to mid-nineteenth century. By the time the last immigrants had arrived in Alexandertal in 1870, the first contingents were ready to move on to America. One of the major events in North American Mennonite history in the years from 1873 to 1950 was the coming of no less than 46,000 Mennonites from Russia to the central provinces and states in what was described above as Waves 6, 7, and 8. While their coming added significantly to Mennonite life in the United States, the locating of 36,000 of them in central Canada actually began an entirely new chapter in their own religious life as well as in the life of their new homeland. Most of these immigrants eventually affiliated either with the General Conference Mennonite Church or the Mennonite Brethren Church, though some remained independent or belonged to the *Kleine Gemeinde*--now the Evangelical Mennonite Conference.

*From 1873 to 1884:* During this period approximately 18,000 Mennonites came to the central states and provinces from Russia, of whom 8,000 settled in Manitoba, 5,000 in Kansas, 1,800 each in Minnesota and the Dakota territory, and the rest in Nebraska with a few in Iowa. They came because a new military law which became effective in 1874 seemed to threaten their exemption from military service. Section 157 of that law actually provided for alternative service in forestry or medical work, but they were not accustomed to alternative service and were afraid this was simply the beginning of an end to their coveted religious freedom. Other motives were also involved in their leaving: the increasing pressure upon minority groups to assimilate with the Russian population, land hunger resulting from the high Mennonite birth rate, and an unwillingness or inability to deal creatively with the problems of a changing society.

The way to America had been prepared by twelve deputies who had been sent to spy out the land. These men were very much encouraged by the brotherly attitudes of the American Mennonites and by favorable settlement opportunities. Their return in September, 1873, marked the beginning of the emigration. While Canada had gone further in guaranteeing religious freedom than the United States because each state had to pass its own legislation, more settled south of the 49th parallel to escape the isolation and harsh winters they anticipated in Manitoba. At least one of the deputies would be extremely surprised if he saw Manitoba today, for he wrote very negatively about his impressions. Winnipeg, he said, "is only a small town," and as he traveled across the lands reserved for them, his diary reports:

> The people are lazy farmers of mixed Indian blood. . . . The land does not seem bad. . . . The wheat stand was small but looked fresh and healthy. One could also see considerable unthreshed wheat left from the previous year. . . . We continued our journey through many muddy and marshy places. . . . The roads were very bad. . . . We came to a house where only the wife was at home. . . . They had been living in Canada for two years. . . . She praised the country, very likely because she wanted neighbors. . . . This region seemed more subject to drouth. . . . The mosquitoes were so bad that one could hardly defend himself. [1]

His inspection report concluded with the remark, "To most of us Manitoba country was not to our liking, but seven of the brethren liked it." Since there were only twelve deputies, the majority actually preferred Manitoba. On his return trip through the Dakotas the deputy wrote that they saw some grasshoppers, "but not as many as in Manitoba." In strong contrast to this pessimism is the report of the Governor General Lord Dufferin after a visit to the Mennonite settlements in Manitoba in 1877, only a few years after their arrival:

155

Although I have witnessed many sights to cause me pleasure during my various progresses through the Dominion, seldom have I beheld any spectacle more pregnant with prophecy, more fraught with promise of a successful future than the Mennonite settlement. When I visited these interesting people they had been only two years in the province, and yet in a long ride I took across many miles of prairie, which but yesterday was absolutely bare, desolate, untenanted, the home of the wolf, the badger, and the eagle, I passed village after village, homestead after homestead, furnished with all the conveniences and incidents of European comfort, and of a scientific agriculture; while on either side of the road, cornfields ripe for harvest, and pastures populous with herds of cattle stretched away to the horizon. Even on this continent—the peculiar theater of rapid change and progress—there has nowhere, I imagine, taken place so marvelous a transformation. [2]

Reports from the other settlements in the United States were equally glowing. In 1883 one Kansas writer said that "the sight of their [Mennonite ] fields and orchards, their trim buildings hedged in with mulberry, is like a glimpse of some fair new land of promise." A few years later *The Daily Record* of Lawrence, Kansas, reported:

After sixteen years those Mennonites are with us still. They abided and toiled in Marion, McPherson, and Harvey counties . . . went on tilling their 100,000 acres of land : . . and every fall, no matter what the season, wheat has been brought to the Newton market in untold quantities from that settlement. . . . The Mennonite says nothing, but goes on marketing his fat cattle, his corn and wheat. . . . [3]

The wheat was the new, hard winter wheat which they had brought with them from Russia, and for which they were to become modestly famous.

The Mennonites of Ontario and in the United States had given real encouragement to the immigrants, having raised over $100,000 for their transportation and settlement costs. In 1873 they had set up a Board of Guardians to administer this aid in the United States and a similar committee in Ontario. John F. Funk, the publisher-editor in Elkhart, Indiana, who had been a most vigorous and able champion of the immigration, began a new paper called *Die Mennonitische Rundschau* in 1880 for the Mennonites from Russia. It was hoped that this paper would help to overcome the geographical separation of the immigrants from each other and from the American Mennonite communities. The new settlements continued to prosper and congregations arose quickly. In 1882 they founded a school for higher education, which was to become Bethel College of Newton, Kansas. Several years later a deaconess hospital was established in the same city. Another school, which was to become the Mennonite

Collegiate Institute, was founded in Gretna, Manitoba, in 1889. Soon the new immigrants seemed to be not only fully at home in the North American environment, but also surpassing the economic, social, and spiritual levels of their former home.

*From 1922 to 1930:* Meanwhile events in Russia were leading to the second major Mennonite exodus, bringing an additional 21,000 persons to Canada and some 4,000 to South America. It must be remembered that 70 percent of them had not emigrated in the first movement. Some had stayed because they were too comfortable to leave, some because they did not sense a threat to their freedom in the way those who left did, and some stayed because they felt that to be the will of God. Among these last were those who believed that God had called the Mennonites to Russia for a purpose and that leaving would be running away from God. One elder wrote, "Some consider it a matter of conscience to go; I consider it a matter of conscience to stay. . . . We are to be the salt of the earth, and salt is needed here as much as anywhere else." He added that the Mennonite witness had opened the door to religious freedom in Russia, and who could tell what God would yet do in that land because of this.

Even the most sturdy became concerned, however, with the bitter civil war and the establishing of a communist government in Russia after World War I. They sensed immediately that more would be at stake than the loss of exemption from military service, an exemption which was, in fact, maintained until the late 1920's by the new government; at stake would soon be the right to an undisturbed church life, the right to have their own church institutions to care for the sick, handicapped, and aged, the right to nurture their children in the Christian faith, and other rights which they considered essential to their identity and survival as a Mennonite people. Consequently a commission of four men was sent to North America by the Mennonite congregations, as we have seen in Chapter 10, and made arrangements for their coming to Canada. Others, however, still hoped to stay and carried on difficult negotiations with the young government. A petition in 1925, for example, pleaded, "Give us our children, give us freedom to train and educate them in accord with the commands of our conscience," but their hopes were not to be fulfilled in the new emerging social order. Thus they began to leave the land they had grown to love, at first reluctantly and in small groups, selling their lands to other Mennonites eager to extend their holdings; but soon reluctance turned to haste, and haste

157

to panic until all emigration was stopped in 1930.

The life of those settling in South America will be told in Chapter 19. Those coming to North America all settled in Canada except perhaps 100 who were allowed to enter the United States for special reasons. The Canadian Board of Colonization, which had been organized under the chairmanship of David Toews to raise the necessary funds for travel, made valiant efforts in settling the newcomers on prairie farms. With the depression and drought years of the early 1930's, however, many relocated in Ontario and British Columbia. In keeping with their life in Russia, they again established schools, homes for the aged, and hospitals together with their constantly increasing congregations from the Pacific Ocean to the Great Lakes. An increasing number of their children acquired advanced training as teachers, doctors, social workers, and in other professions, but they remained essentially a rural people until World War II. With few exceptions, they were only moderately successful financially during the first two decades, but a strong spiritual life was apparent in many of their congregations. During this period most of their worship services were conducted in the German language, with lay ministers carrying primary responsibility.

*From 1946 to 1954:* As indicated in Chapter 10, approximately 35,000 Mennonites in Russia were evacuated to Poland and western Europe by the retreating German army following the Battle of Stalingrad in 1943. Of these, some 23,000 were later returned to Russia by the Russian and Allied troops, but approximately 12,000 remained in the west. Most of these wished to join their relatives in Canada, but health and other reasons prevented many from going. Rather than stay in Europe, they chose to settle in South America and nearly 5,000 located in Paraguay, Uruguay, and Argentina. Over 7,000, however, did come to Canada and were soon scattered across the land with friends and relatives, most of them preferring to live in cities where work could be found. With hard work and high postwar wages most of them were soon financially independent. Since few of them had settled in closed communities, they did not build their own churches but joined the Mennonite churches around them. Because of their urban living, acculturation was extremely rapid among them as they settled down to become Canadians in the full sense of the word.

*For Conscience Sake*

All of these migrations, both to North America and within

158

its boundaries, show the Mennonites to have been a people on the move. A study of their history reflects an endless pilgrimage from one corner of the earth to the other. We have seen, for example, how the first immigrants were ready to leave Russia for America by the time the last had come to Russia from Prussia. Similarly, the immigrants to Canada in the 1920's and again in the 1940's came just in time to buy up the farms of those Mennonites leaving for Paraguay and Mexico. From their sixteenth-century European origins the Anabaptist-Mennonites have spread to Asia, North America, South America, and even Australia. Africa was seriously considered at one time. Until recently the Mennonite self-image which has emerged because of these migrations has been that of pilgrims and strangers in a hostile world, the church in the wilderness seeking to remain pure for the coming of the Bridegroom, Christ. Harold S. Bender once wrote:

It is not that Mennonites do not love the soil or have no sense of home and homeland. Nor is it that they have not loved the men and women of the lands in which they have lived, or that they were unwilling to stay and carry on even after difficult circumstances. It was the hostile world around them which would not tolerate them, which forced them to go, which was unwilling to let them stay and maintain a faith and a spirit which was a challenge to its own system. [4]

It is clear that freedom of conscience was central to these migrations, particularly if conscience is defined to include the economic, social, and other conditioning factors which shaped their life together as much as pure religious convictions. And conscience worked differently with different people, as we have seen, urging some to leave for the sake of their faith and some to stay for the same reason. How can it be shown that those who left a country first were more faithful to their God than those who stayed the longest and often perished for their faith? The faith and beauty but also the agony and pathos of those who were forced to make a decision one way or another are reflected in the words of a young colonist in Mexico:

Great-grandfather migrated with his family from Prussia to South Russia via the wheelbarrow route. He lies buried there. Grandfather with married sons and daughters came to Canada in 1873. He sleeps beneath the soil in Manitoba. Now father, an old man, has brought his family to Mexico where he is starting all over again. [5]

Notes
1. Quoted in C. J. Dyck, "For Conscience Sake?" an unpublished paper (1965), from J. M. Hofer (ed), "The Diary of Paul Tschetter, 1873" (July, 1931), V, p. 204.
2. Quoted in Dyck, Ibid., p. 24, from E. K. Francis, In Search of Utopia. Glencoe, Illinois: Free Press, 1955, p. 79.
3. Quoted in Dyck, Ibid., p. 25, from Helen B. Shipley, "The Migration of the Mennonites from Russia, 1873-1883, and Their Settlement in Kansas," MA thesis (1954), p. 184.

4. In Sanford Calvin Yoder, *For Conscience Sake.* Goshen, Indiana: Mennonite Historical Society, 1945, p. viii.

5. *Ibid.,* p. 234.

## FOR FURTHER READING:

*The Mennonite Encyclopedia,* 4 vols.

*Christian Living* (June, 1956), pp. 14-16; (July, 1961), pp. 14-17.

*Mennonite Life* 2 (October, 1947), pp. 41-43; 5 (July, 1950), pp. 6-11; 7 (October, 1952), pp. 170-75.

J. C. Wenger, *The Mennonite Church in America.* Scottdale: Herald Press, 1966.

Frank H. Epp, *Mennonite Exodus* (1962).

C. Henry Smith, *The Coming of the Russian Mennonites* (1927).

—————————, *The Story of the Mennonites* (1950).

*Mennonite Life* 1 (January, 1946), maps and charts.

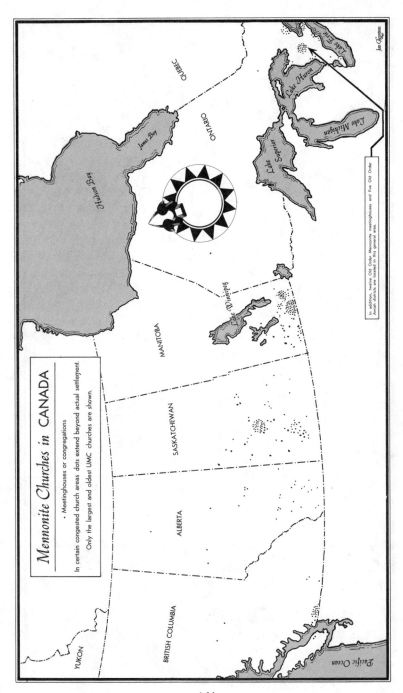

Mennonite Churches in CANADA

· Meetinghouses or congregations

In certain congested church areas dots extend beyond actual settlement. Only the largest and oldest UMC churches are shown.

In addition, twelve Old Order Mennonite meetinghouses and five Old Order Amish districts are located in this general area.

Jan Gleysteen

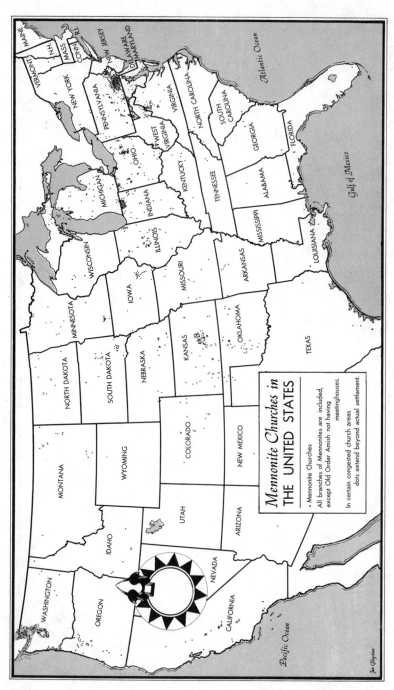

Mennonite Churches in
THE UNITED STATES

• Mennonite Churches:
  All branches of Mennonites are included,
  except Old Order Amish not having
  meetinghouses.

In certain congested church areas
  dots extend beyond actual settlement.

# Chapter 12

# THE (OLD) MENNONITE CHURCH

EXCEPT for a few Dutch and North German (Lower Rhine) families who settled at Germantown and from there spread out into the Franconia Conference to the north of Philadelphia, the members of the (Old) Mennonite Church are almost pure Swiss in origin. We have seen earlier that the first members in Switzerland were called *Täufer* (Baptizers) or Anabaptists but that they preferred to be known simply as Swiss Brethren. In Germany and the Netherlands the Anabaptists were also known as *Wiedertäufer* (re-baptizers), or *Taufgesinnten, Doopsgezinden* (baptism-minded). After 1545 the Dutch Anabaptists, and eventually the Germans, came to be called *Mennists* or *Mennonists* after Menno Simons. Since Menno Simons had nothing to do with the Swiss Brethren, however, how would they be known after they came to America? The question was complicated, in a way, by the fact that the very first Anabaptist descendants to settle in America were from the Dutch wing at Krefeld, hence Mennonites.

One of the earliest Mennonite documents in America is the 1724 deed for the land on which the first Germantown meetinghouse had been built in 1708. In it the land is described as belonging to the "Meeting of the people called Mennonist (alias Menisten)"--which means that the congregation was known as Mennonists or as Mennists. The word "Mennisten" was pronounced, Men-NISHT-eh, in German, causing some people to think that the name of the church was Men-NEESHT! In the English edition of the Dutch Mennonite Confession of Faith, adopted at Dordrecht in 1632, and printed in English in

163

Amsterdam in 1712 for distribution among their English neighbors by the Germantown Mennonites, the church members are described as "harmless" (that is, nonresistant) Christians, "Known by the name of Mennonists." (The Pennsylvania Mennonites had this same booklet reprinted in Philadelphia in 1727.) The 1738 Alms Book of the Skippack congregation refers to the members of the church as *Taufsgesinden,* which is a variant spelling for *Tauffsgesinnten* (1748 *Martyrs Mirror* title page, which adds, "Or Nonresistant Christians"). When the children of Bishop Henry Funck published his book on how Christ fulfilled the Old Testament, 1763, they described their late father as a "Minister [*Lehrer*] of the New and Old Testaments of the Church of the Believers on Jesus Christ which are nicknamed *Wiedertäuffer* or Mennonists." A common name for the church in Pennsylvania deeds of the 1700's was Mennonist Society. Mennonites did not like the German word *Kirche* for their brotherhood; so in English they used the Quaker term *Society* rather than the English word *Church* which for the Mennonites meant state church.

Finally, perhaps before 1800, the Mennonites of Pennsylvania began to call themselves Old Mennonites (*Alt-Mennoniten* in German). The later schismatic groups, such as the Herrites in Lancaster County, or the larger Oberholtzer body in Franconia, were then dubbed the New Mennonites. The main body actually became fond of the name, Old Mennonites. They used it on cornerstones of meetinghouses, on tombstones of ministers, and in common speech. The word was acceptable until various bodies of Mennonites who withdrew from the Old Mennonites from 1872 to 1901, because they rejected the Sunday school and other changes which came with the "Great Awakening," came to be called Old Order Mennonites. Then some Old Mennonite leaders became sensitive about the word "Old," fearing, no doubt, that it would confuse the larger mother body with the Old Order children who opposed the Sunday school. Men like Bishop Daniel Kauffman, editor of the church paper, often wrote the name Old in parentheses, thus: (Old) Mennonite Church. Harold S. Bender, a more recent leader in the group, did not want the word Old in any shape or form; so he insisted that the *Mennonite Encyclopedia* refer to the group as the Mennonite Church (MC). In various parts of the church, particularly in the large Lancaster and Franconia conferences, people (both members and nonmembers) commonly call the church members "Old Mennonites" to this day, however.

164

## Composition

The Mennonites of the Lancaster Conference, some fifty miles west of Philadelphia, and reaching on west, consist almost wholly of Swiss families, as their family names indicate. In the Franconia Conference there are a few Dutch and Lower Rhine family names. Looking at the entire membership of the (Old) Mennonites, apart from the missions of the last seventy years, the church is almost pure Swiss by ethnic origin and was German in culture from 1683 until almost 1900. The language spoken at home was the dialect of German spoken in the Palatinate, and to this Palatine German many English words were added in the course of the centuries. A Mennonite speaking this so-called Pennsylvania German would indicate that he must now *die Car griege so dass ich die Train nemme' kann* (get the automobile to take the train). All church services were conducted in Palatine German--often modified more or less by the German of the Bible.

## Original Settlements

The oldest conference of the Old Mennonites, Franconia, began in 1683 and became the Germantown congregation north of Philadelphia, and from there a daughter congregation, Skippack, was started in 1702. In the next few decades the other old congregations of the Franconia Conference were established: for the most part in what are now Montgomery and Bucks counties in Montgomery (then Philadelphia) County: Worcester, Plains, Salford, Towamencin, and Franconia; and in Bucks County: Rockhill, Line Lexington, Blooming Glen, Doylestown, Deep Run, and West Swamp. Small Mennonite settlements were also made in neighboring counties, such as Chester (Coventry and Vincent), Berks (Hereford), Lehigh (Upper Milford and Saucon), and Northampton (Settlement and Siegfried). But the bulk of the Mennonites of the Franconia Conference live within a fifteen-mile radius of the town of Souderton, which is in Montgomery County but near the Bucks County line.

In 1710, just eight years after the Germantown Mennonites started the Skippack settlement, Swiss and Palatine families (all of Swiss ethnic origin) started a new settlement near the present town of Strasburg in what is now Lancaster County (then Chester). Here the Willow Street or "Brick" congregation developed. Other congregations soon emerged, such as New Danville, Byerland, Abbeyville, Mellinger, Millersville, Habecker, Masonville, Landisville, East Petersburg, Chestnut Hill, Landis Valley, Hess, Hammer Creek, Weaverland,

Groffdale, Metzler, and Bowmansville: all in present-day Lancaster County. New settlements were also soon made in York and Adams counties (Bair's Codorus, Stony Brook, and Bair's Hanover), as well as in Lebanon County (Shirksville and Dohner).

## Colonization

Within two decades after settling in Lancaster County, Pennsylvania, some enterprising Mennonites had found their way to Page County, Virginia. Here the early settlements in Page, Shenandoah, and Frederick counties died out, while the congregations in Rockingham (Trissels, Pike, and Weavers) and Augusta (Springdale and Hildebrand) flourished. The scattered congregations of the Allegheny Conference, largely in southwestern Pennsylvania, were founded for the most part around the time of the Revolutionary War (1775-83) and the following years. The Mennonite churches of the Washington County, Maryland, and Franklin County, Pennsylvania, Conference were established for the most part a little before 1800. Although scattered Mennonite families were in Franklin County by 1735, the main migration to the area did not take place until the 1790's. The Ohio congregations of Mennonites began to spring up in the early years of the 1800's, and the Amish followed their Mennonite brothers into Ohio as early as 1808. The Amish settled in Illinois in the 1830's and the Mennonites in the 1840's. Mennonites began to locate in Indiana in 1838, and the Amish followed in 1841. Mennonites reached Missouri in the 1850's, Kansas in the 1870's, and Oregon in the 1890's as discussed in Chapter 11.

The distribution of the (Old) Mennonites in North America is as follows, all statistical data being taken from the 1964 *Mennonite Yearbook:*

| Conference | Organized Congregations | Dependent/ Unorganized Congregations | Baptized Members |
|---|---|---|---|
| 1. Franconia | 33 | 17 | 5,470 |
| 2. Lancaster | 130 | 70 | 15,864 |
| 3. Washington-Franklin | 15 | 8 | 1,739 |
| 4. Allegheny | 34 | 12 | 3,412 |
| 5. Ohio & Eastern | 75 | 41 | 12,655 |
| 6. Ontario | 31 | 12 | 4,152 |
| 7. Western Ontario | 13 | 1 | 2,549 |
| 8. Virginia | 56 | 30 | 4,887 |
| 9. Indiana-Michigan | 55 | 46 | 9,949 |

| | | | |
|---|---|---|---|
| 10. Illinois | 33 | 5 | 3,572 |
| 11. North Central | 13 | 4 | 664 |
| 12. South Central | 40 | 2 | 3,077 |
| 13. Iowa-Nebraska | 30 | 2 | 4,146 |
| 14. Alberta-Saskatchewan | 11 | 10 | 918 |
| 15. Rocky Mountain | 15 | 1 | 1,073 |
| 16. Pacific Coast | 24 | 4 | 2,306 |
| 17. South Pacific | 8 | 2 | 545 |
| 18. Conservative | 52 | 33 | 6,074 |
| 19. Churches Abroad | | | 8,943 |

*Summary:* Total baptized members in the USA, 75,433; in Canada, 7,619; in the younger churches abroad, 8,943: total, 91,995.

## Church Government

When the Mennonites began to come to America a little before 1700 and in the following years until the middle 1700's, there were no district conferences in Europe. The first American Mennonites were congregationalists in church government. Occasional ministers' meetings had been held in Europe to discuss various issues, however, and the same was soon true in Pennsylvania. In the year 1725, for example, sixteen ministers from five congregations or settlements in southeastern Pennsylvania held a ministers' meeting and adopted the Dutch Mennonite Dordrecht Confession of Faith (1632) as their doctrinal standard. They wrote a quaint endorsement of this Confession of Faith: "We the hereunder written Servants [that is, Ministers ] of the Word of God, and Elders in the Congregation of the People, called MENNONISTS, in the Province of Pennsilvania [sic!], do acknowledge, and herewith make known, that we do own the afore-going CONFESSION, APPENDIX, AND MENNO'S Excusation, to be according to our Opinion; and also, have took the same to be wholly ours. In Testimony whereof, and that we believe the same to be good, we have here unto Subscribed our Names." Then follow the names of five Lancaster ("Conestoga") bishops, two Franconia bishops, and nine Franconia preachers.

Other ministers' meetings were held, both in the Franconia and Lancaster settlements. In the course of time these meetings were held regularly, each spring and fall, both in Franconia and Lancaster. Sooner or later, perhaps from the very beginning, the oldest bishop in terms of service presided. The first man to sign the above-mentioned confession in 1725, was the first man to serve as an American Mennonite bishop, Jacob Gottshalk (d. 1763), who began

167

to baptize and administer the Lord's Supper in 1708 at Germantown. There was no prepared program of addresses at these ministers' meetings, no written agenda, no constitution, no secretary, and no minutes, indeed, no officers of any sort. In a general way the bishops served as leaders, with the senior bishop presiding. What are now spoken of as the semiannual meetings of conference were therefore at first unofficial and informal ministers' meetings to discuss the life and welfare of the congregations of the area. In the course of the decades, however, these ministers' meetings grew in prestige and influence and eventually became church synods or district conferences which increasingly set the disciplinary standards for the congregations of *the regions involved. For a century and a half, or longer, no disciplinary standards were printed and adopted. Lancaster adopted its first *Rules and Discipline* in 1881 and Franconia followed a few decades later.

The (Old) Mennonites therefore have a form of church government which is difficult to name. It is neither purely episcopal, synodal, nor congregational, but a combination of all three. The district conferences now set the basic disciplinary standards for the congregations. The bishops, assisted by the deacons, attempt to carry out these standards in the congregations of their charge. Major matters of policy are, however, subject to congregational discussion and decision. This type of church discipline involves an intricate system of checks and balances, with some variations in different parts of the church. Some conferences put more weight on the authority of the bishops and on the decisions of the conference; others are more inclined to stress congregational government.

*Organization*

The (Old) Mennonites have a total of over 1,200 congregations, largely in the United States, but including some in Canada and others in the mission fields such as India, Argentina, and Tanzania. Two thirds of these congregations are fully organized, while some four hundred are emerging, being not fully organized, or still dependent on a mother congregation or a mission board. These congregations had a combined membership of about 92,000 in 1964. In the year 1720 there were no Mennonite organizations in North America other than the several dozen congregations. By 1820 the older district conferences, such as Franconia, Lancaster, Washington-Franklin, and possibly Ontario, had emerged, and Virginia and Ohio soon followed.

Between 1875 and 1895 the three historic boards of the (Old)

Mennonites were organized in their earliest forms: Publication, 1875, Mennonite Publishing Company; Missions, 1882, Evangelizing Committee; and Education, 1895, Elkhart Institute Association. These three boards took their present form as follows: Mennonite Publication Board, 1908; Mennonite Board of Missions and Charities, 1906; and Mennonite Board of Education, 1906. In their earliest forms the three boards, therefore, antedated the Mennonite General Conference which had its preliminary meeting in 1897 and was formally organized in 1898. The three older conferences, Franconia, Lancaster, and Washington-Franklin, did not formally and fully unite with the General Conference. The three boards listed above have never voted to come under the jurisdiction of the Mennonite General Conference, this being an example of the system of checks and balances in the (Old) Mennonite Church.

The basic work of the Mennonite Church is, of course, done in the local congregations. The district conferences fulfill a unifying and directive role in the life of the local congregations. The boards serve the district conferences and congregations by performing tasks which it would be impractical for a single congregation to perform and which are best performed by representatives of the entire church. Although the General Conference does excellent work through its committees, commission, and board, it is advisory in character in relation to the congregations and district conferences of the denomination. The major committees and organizations of the General Conference are: (1) Peace and Social Concerns, (2) Worship, (3) Historical and Research, (4) Ministerial, (5) Church Welfare, and (6) Commission for Christian Education; also (7) a board, parallel to the other three boards, but in this case under the General Conference: Mennonite Mutual Aid and its subsidiary corporations.

In 1949 Mennonite General Conference also created a General Council, composed of several dozen church leaders including the executive committee of the General Conference, one representative of each organization (committee, commission, board) under the General Conference, one from each of the three historic boards of the church, and one representative from each district conference of the denomination—whether or not each district conference is officially affiliated with the General Conference! The Women's Missionary and Service Auxiliary (WMSA) is attached to the General Mission Board, and the Mennonite Youth Fellowship (MYF) is attached to the Mennonite Commission for Christian Education.

## Statistical Data

The giving of the (Old) Mennonites is now about five million dollars a year, which is almost five million more than a century ago, but this is still far short of a tenth of the earned income of the group. About 100,000 pupils are enrolled each year in the summer Bible schools conducted by (Old) Mennonites, while Sunday-school enrollment is about 128,000. About 2,500 converts are baptized every year, and fifty ministers are ordained, of which 10 to 15 are seminary trained.

## Four Major Leaders

*John Fretz Funk, 1835-1930:* The most important figure in the life of the (Old) Mennonites in the nineteenth century was John F. Funk. Born in Bucks County, Pennsylvania, he took summer courses at Freeland Seminary (now Ursinus College), and taught school three years. In 1857 he moved to Chicago and entered the lumber business, working first with his brother-in-law, Jacob Beidler, and soon going into business for himself but with a partner. Converted in 1858 under Presbyterian influence, he returned to his home church, Line Lexington in Bucks County, and was baptized a year later. In 1864 he started the first successful church periodical of the (Old) Mennonites, the English *Herald of Truth,* and its German twin, the *Herold der Wahrheit.* That same year, 1864, he also married his second cousin, Salome Kratz (d. 1917), one of his former pupils. They had six children, four of whom died in childhood. In 1865 Funk was attending the services of a small Mennonite congregation in a schoolhouse near Gardner in Grundy County, Illinois. There John M. Brenneman ordained him to the ministry. Two years later Funk, then thirty-two, sold out his lumber business in Chicago and established his home and a printing business in Elkhart, Indiana. Here he lived the remaining sixty-two years of his life, dying in his ninety-fifth year.

Funk started the publication work of his denomination, first as an individual, then in partnership with his brother Abraham, and finally as the Mennonite Publishing Company in 1875. In 1908 he sold his periodicals to the young Mennonite Publication Board which had its publishing house at Scottdale, Pennsylvania.

Funk also had a vision for building up the spiritual life of his denomination through Sunday schools. He had been an ardent Sunday-school worker for D. L. Moody in Chicago and knew the value of the Sunday school. Indeed, he had regularly attended three Sunday schools in Chicago: as a pupil in one, as a teacher in a second, and as the superintendent of a third! By personal urging and by public appeals through his *Herald of Truth,* Funk was a leading figure in helping the (Old) Mennonites to establish Sunday schools throughout his church from east to west, largely in the period 1865-95.

As early as 1882 Funk led the Indiana Conference to set up an Evangelizing Fund to send preachers to neglected communities and members. This fund was administered by an Evangelizing Committee which ultimately developed into the general mission board of the (Old) Mennonites, the Mennonite Board of Missions and Charities.

Funk also felt that it would be a help to the unity of the (Old) Mennonite Church to create a General Conference. Consequently he mailed from his Publishing Company office a letter to the ministers of the church asking for their reaction to the plan of setting up a General Conference. The response was favorable, a number of district conferences appointed representatives to do the initial planning, a number of committee meetings were held, a preliminary meeting was held at the Pike meetinghouse, Elida, Ohio, in 1897, and at the first regular session of the Mennonite General Conference in 1898, Funk preached the conference sermon.

No one can estimate the influence of John Fretz Funk on the (Old) Mennonite Church. He was more than any one man the founder of the publication and mission work of the (Old) Mennonites and the strongest promoter of the Sunday school. He and Daniel Brenneman also held the first series of evangelistic meetings (then called Protracted Meetings) in the (Old) Mennonite Church: Masontown, Fayette County, Pennsylvania, 1872. He also served a vigorous ten-year period as a bishop in the Indiana Conference, 1892-1902. In Chapter 11 we saw his work with the immigrants from Russia, and his founding of a paper in their behalf. His biography was published in 1964 and was entitled, *Bless the Lord, O My Soul.*

*John S. Coffman, 1848-1899:* One of Funk's most effective colleagues was John S. Coffman of the Shenandoah Valley, Virginia. Born in Rockingham County, Coffman early became a successful schoolteacher and an effective preacher. Funk urged him to locate in Elkhart and help in his publication work. Coffman made the move in 1879 and for twenty years he was an influential teammate of Funk, promoting all good causes in the church, serving as assistant editor of the *Herald of Truth,* and writing Sunday-school lesson helps.

But Coffman's greatest contributions came in still other lines of

Christian service. Daniel Brenneman had promoted an emotional type of piety and evangelism through which he eventually lost the confidence of many of his fellow ministers and was expelled in 1874 for his unwillingness to accept direction from them. Coffman knew this history very well, yet he became convinced that the church had to engage in evangelistic work or perish. He therefore fasted and prayed for the Lord to open the door for the desired "Protracted Meetings." And open it did! In 1881, just two years after he came to Elkhart, the small Bowne congregation in Michigan invited him to hold a series of meetings. This he did, and with good success. Other churches heard of this pioneer evangelist, and they too called for Coffman to come and hold meetings. A handsome, well-built man with an open countenance, clear gray eyes, and a pleasant personality, Coffman was also a man of much prayer. Sometimes he prayed all through the night instead of sleeping. And yet he was also a man with a keen sense of humor with which he held and delighted his audiences. The result of all this was that he was a man of unusual effectiveness in the pulpit—undoubtedly the most effective preacher in the (Old) Mennonite Church in the last quarter of the nineteenth century. He gathered hundreds of fine young people, many already married, into the church. And just as significant, he helped to create a new image of a Mennonite. For he was friendly, progressive, intelligent, well-dressed, and favorable to higher education.

It was in the field of education that Coffman made his final contribution. A Mennonite osteopathic physician, Dr. Henry A. Mumaw (d. 1908), had founded a small school in 1894, with the rather pompous title, Elkhart Institute of Art, Science, and Industry in Elkhart, Indiana. A year later he turned it over to a self-perpetuating board of trustees known as the Elkhart Institute Association. In 1896 Coffman became the president of this board and guided the school with a firm and able hand until his death three years later. This service on the part of Coffman cost him much, for some of his former friends and supporters turned away from him when he became the open champion of higher education in the church. Coffman's address on the occasion of the dedication of the Elkhart Institute building in 1896 was entitled, "The Spirit of Progress," and it testifies effectively to the power and strength of the vision which possessed him.

In many ways Coffman served as a balance wheel to his employer and fellow minister, John F. Funk. Funk's junior by thirteen years, Coffman possessed in a remarkable degree a number of the gentler virtues which Funk may have lacked. Perhaps the word which would best characterize Coffman was "gracious" or "winsome," while Funk gave the impression of an iron will, although accompanied by a large heart, to be sure.

*Daniel Kauffman, 1865-1944:* The third major figure in the molding of the (Old) Mennonite Church was one of the many converts won by John S. Coffman, Daniel Kauffman, a native of Juniata County, Pennsylvania, and the son of David D. Kauffman and his wife, Elizabeth Winey Kauffman. In 1866 David Kauffman and family moved to Elkhart County, Indiana, and three years later to Morgan County, Missouri. There David served as a preacher and bishop. Son Daniel attended the Missouri State University and earned the degree Principal of Pedagogics. From the ages of eighteen to thirty-two Daniel Kauffman was a schoolteacher in Missouri, serving part of this time as county superintendent of schools. For a time he conducted a private business college at Garden City, Missouri, In 1887 Kauffman married Ota J. Bowlin who bore him two children, a son and a daughter. She passed away in 1890. That same year he was converted, standing to accept Christ with his sleeping son James in his arms. In 1892 he was ordained to the ministry, having given up his planned political career soon after his conversion. He also remarried in 1892, this time to Mary C. Shank who bore him six children. In 1896 he was ordained a bishop in the church and served in that capacity for forty-eight years. He served as editor, first of the *Gospel Witness,* which was published at Scottdale from 1905 to 1908, and then of the merged *Gospel Herald,* after the purchase of Funk's *Herald of Truth.* In the long span, 1905-43, more than any other man, "D. K.," as his friends knew him, served as the chief leader and the major voice of the (Old) Mennonite Church. A man of great poise and dignity, a quiet man by nature, he was nevertheless, a most effective team worker. At one point he is said to have been a member of twenty-two committees and boards. He was four times moderator of Mennonite General Conference, including the first official sessions in 1898, and three times he was called upon to preach the conference sermon. He was also the author of twenty-two books and pamphlets. More than any man had ever been, he was the spokesman of his denomination. Among his books may be mentioned, *Manual of Bible Doctrine,* 1898; *A Talk with Church Members,* 1900; coauthor, *Mennonite Church History,* 1905; *Bible Doctrines Briefly Stated,* 1908; editor, *Bible Doctrine,* 1914; *The Conservative Viewpoint,* 1918; *The Mennonite Church and Current Issues,* 1923; *Doctrines of the Bible,*

1928; *My Vision of the Future* (a booklet setting forth his non-millennial position), 1938; *Fifty Years in the Mennonite Church,* 1941; and *The Devotional Side of Life,* 1942.

Daniel Kauffman was a true church statesman. He saw more clearly than most people the basic spiritual issues which the church was facing, and he quietly took a courageous stand for what he believed was right. He loved people, and was a good arbiter in cases of tension and misunderstanding, a true peacemaker. He was basically conservative, yet he would gladly make concessions in religious practice in order to maintain the unity of the church. His delivery in speaking before an audience was unhurried, thoughtful, and forceful. Like all human beings, he could make mistakes--and one of his "slips of the lip" was made at his home congregation at Scottdale: "We must," he urged his audience, "press on with fresh veal and zigor!"

John F. Funk was the great organizer of the church, founding its publication work, and its mission outreach, as well as the Sunday-school movement of the (Old) Mennonites. John S. Coffman was the pioneer evangelist and man of prayer, and the chief promoter of the Elkhart Institute, which in 1903 was moved to Goshen, Indiana, and renamed as Goshen College. Daniel Kauffman was the statesman of the church who labored to consolidate the gains of the "Great Awakening" which came to the church in the latter decades of the nineteenth century, to clarify the doctrinal position of the brotherhood, and to maintain its unity. Who would be the fourth spiritual giant to lead and bless the group?

*Harold S. Bender, 1897-1962:* The fourth leader was to be Harold S. Bender. Born in Elkhart, Indiana, when Funk was sixty-two, when Coffman was forty-eight, and when Kauffman was thirty-two, Harold was a brilliant and gifted boy. At the early age of twelve he accepted Christ as his personal Saviour and was received by baptism into the membership of the Prairie Street Mennonite Church, the congregation in Elkhart which had been founded by John F. Funk about twenty-six years before Harold's birth. Harold was an able student, graduating from Elkhart High School in 1914, and from Goshen College in 1918, in spite of taking out a year to teach in the Thorntown (Indiana) high school, 1916-17. In August, 1922, he received the Bachelor of Divinity degree from Garrett Biblical Institute; in May, 1923, the Master of Theology degree from Princeton Theological Seminary; in June, 1923, the Master of Arts degree from Princeton University; and the Doctor of Theology degree from Heidelberg University, Germany, in 1935. In 1923 he married Elizabeth Horsch,

174

daughter of the Mennonite historian, John Horsch of Scottdale, Pennsylvania. They became the parents of two daughters.

Harold Bender was first of all an outstanding teacher at Hesston from 1918 to 1920 and at Goshen from 1924 to his death. He had the art of mastering his field of study so thoroughly that he was not bound to the textbook or to the outline of anyone; he came to class with a clear grasp of what he wished to share with his students, and he was able to do so effectively. As a teacher he was a competent lecturer, rather than a teacher who "discussed" the field with his students. Yet he stimulated interest and learning. He taught in many fields but excelled in Bible and church history.

Second, Harold Bender was also an able college administrator. When Dean Noah Oyer died in 1931, Harold Bender was placed in his chair, in which position he came to be known far and wide as Dean Bender. During his years in office the college received accreditment from the North Central Association.

Third, Dean Bender inaugurated at Goshen College in 1933, a theological course four years in length and leading to the Th.B. degree. Gradually this course was strengthened until a college degree was required for admission, the B.D. degree was offered, and the name of the Bible School was changed to the Biblical Seminary. The Seminary also achieved accreditment from the American Association of Theological Schools.

Fourth, Dean Bender put his hand to the writer's and editor's pens. His most outstanding book was his definitive biography of the chief founder of Swiss Anabaptism, Conrad Grebel, written in German in 1935, and published in English in 1950. But we must go back to 1924 for the founding of the Mennonite Historical Society at Goshen College, and to 1927 for the establishment of the leading journal in its field, *The Mennonite Quarterly Review*. Dean Bender served until his death as president of the society and editor of the *Review*. He was also the longtime chairman of the Historical and Research Committee of Mennonite General Conference. But his really huge contribution was as primary editor of the four-volume *Mennonite Encyclopedia*, published 1955-59.

Fifth, Dean Bender was an ecumenical Mennonite leader. He was assistant secretary and executive committee member of the Mennonite Central Committee (MCC) from 1931 until his death in 1962. In 1939 he became secretary of the Mennonite Central Peace Committee; and in 1942 chairman of the MCC Peace Section, and he retained that position until his death. In 1944 he was ordained to the ministry in

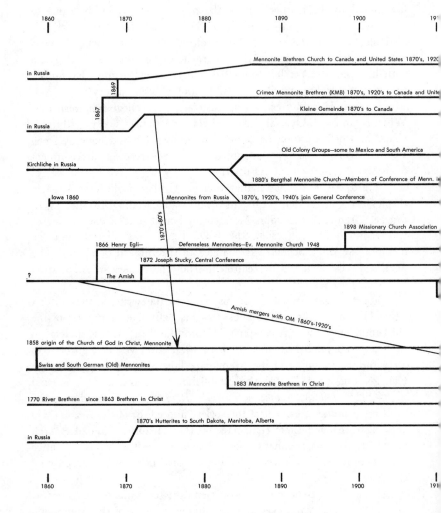

1860    1870    1880    1890    1900    19

Mennonite Brethren Church to Canada and United States 1870's, 192C

in Russia

1869

1867

Crimea Mennonite Brethren (KMB) 1870's, 1920's to Canada and Unite

Kleine Gemeinde 1870's to Canada

in Russia

Old Colony Groups—some to Mexico and South America

Kirchliche in Russia

1880's Bergthal Mennonite Church—Members of Conference of Menn. i

Iowa 1860    Mennonites from Russia    1870's, 1920's, 1940's join General Conference

1870's-80's

1898 Missionary Church Association

1866 Henry Egli—    Defenseless Mennonites—Ev. Mennonite Church 1948

1872 Joseph Stucky, Central Conference

?    The Amish

Amish mergers with OM 1860's-1920's

1858 origin of the Church of God in Christ, Mennonite

Swiss and South German (Old) Mennonites

1883 Mennonite Brethren in Christ

1770 River Brethren    since 1863 Brethren in Christ

1870's Hutterites to South Dakota, Manitoba, Alberta

in Russia

1860    1870    1880    1890    1900    191

176

1960

Since 1959 Evangelical Mennonite Conference

1936-37 Ev. Menn. Mission Conference

joins GC 1946

sh

ve Amish Mennonite Conference

# :NNONITE FAMILY TREE IN NORTH AMERICA

since 1947 United Missionary Church

1920       1930       1940       1950       1960       1970

his "Mennonite Church (MC)," as he preferred to call it, and at about that point he entered the most strongly ecumenical phase of his ministry. Beginning in 1945 he made annual trips to Europe for shorter or longer visits, largely devoted to MCC and Mennonite World Conference concerns. Indeed he was president of the 1952, 1957, and 1962 sessions of the World Conference. In 1948 he helped launch the German Mennonite periodical, *Der Mennonit* (The Mennonite). In 1949 he became chairman of the International Mennonite Peace Committee. His 1943 presidential address at the American Society of Church History was entitled, "The Anabaptist Vision," which soon became internationally known as a magnificent statement of what Anabaptism really was. Perhaps the cause dearest to his heart was the Biblical Seminary at Goshen College, and when its deanship was separated from the office of the college dean in 1946, he elected to go with the seminary, rather than to stay with the college. He was also delighted with the leading of the Lord when the Goshen College Biblical Seminary and the Mennonite Biblical Seminary of the General Conference Mennonite Church became the Associated Mennonite Biblical Seminaries in 1958.

Sixth, Dean Bender was a man of action. In addition to all his other projects--Peace Committee of Mennonite General Conference, Relief and Service Committee, Mennonite Central Committee, Mennonite Board of Education, General Council of Mennonite General Conference, Mennonite World Conference, and many other similar activities--he still found time to be the major figure in the establishment of Bethany Christian High School, by the High School Board of the Indiana-Michigan Conference, serving also on its board of control, from its beginning until his death.

He had his critics, of course, for how could a man be as active as he was without arousing criticism? Students were sometimes annoyed that he seemed so certain of what courses they ought to take, or what positions they should accept, and someone half-humorously one day dubbed him with the label, "The pope," which title was well known on the campus, beloved as he was at the same time.

And so Harold S. Bender was the outstanding scholar-leader of the (Old) Mennonites, the one who really led the intellectuals of the church to drink at the refreshing fountain of Anabaptism; he was the ecumenical Mennonite, who was personally a staunch (Old) Mennonite, and who was able at the same time to put a warm arm of love around all the Mennonites of all lands on the earth. He told the huge throng at the Seventh Mennonite World Conference at Kitchener a few weeks before his death that he was sometimes accused of being a "Mennonite Ecumaniac," and if loving all the brethren made him that, he added, then he would plead guilty!

Who is or will be the successor of Dean Bender? It is unlikely that there will be any one person as outstanding in the life of the brotherhood as were the four leaders just described. The leadership of the church is becoming much more diffused, which is really a wholesome development. The church is growing larger, there are more able leaders, and as the institutions of the church grow, fewer and fewer men will have the time, energy, or inclination to immerse themselves in so broad a spectrum of activities as did Funk, Coffman, Kauffman, and Bender.

*Group Characteristics*

In a general way, (Old) Mennonites have a strong historical consciousness. They are keenly aware that their spiritual forefathers suffered and died for the faith and fled from one land to another in search of religious liberty. Many public prayers make fervent mention of and give thanks for the fact that we in this land may worship God according to the dictates of our conscience and with no fear of being harmed or molested.

(Old) Mennonites also have a strong sense of mission. They believe in the doctrines of the Scripture as understood historically, and they want to bring people of all lands and cultures to this same nonresistant Christian faith. Prior to 1940 three foreign missions were established, one before 1900, and one each in the next two twenty-year spans. Since 1940, however, about thirty countries have been entered with the Gospel. No cause appeals to Mennonite giving as much as missions. Because of this a high premium is also put on higher education. The average couple will borrow money, even mortgage their house or farm, in order to assist their children to get university degrees. Large numbers of young people are entering such service professions as the ministry, medicine, social work, and teaching. With other Mennonites the (Old) Mennonites emphasize the simplicity of the Gospel, · reading the Bible in faith and obedience. Like the Church of the Brethren, they have a simple hermeneutic, that is, taking the Bible at face value. And so if it commands foot washing or anointing with oil, they practice these rites as a church.

(Old) Mennonites have developed deep social concern. They are distressed that anyone should be made to suffer for creed or color. They are eager to see all citizens everywhere enjoying the full benefits of citizenship. Likewise they desire to alleviate the distress of poverty, of warfare, and of natural disasters. They strongly support with personnel and funds such relief agencies as the MCC and Mennonite Disaster Organization. Young men accept the alternative to military service provided in the United States by federal law and a good portion serve their two years without pay in service projects at home and abroad. Many enter Pax service, which is Christian social and relief service abroad. Many young women are also serving in Voluntary Service.

(Old) Mennonites find deep satisfaction in their simple worship service. The entire congregation joins in the singing of four-part music, usually sung a cappella. The pulpit is placed in the center of the platform symbolizing the centrality of God's Word as it is read and expounded. Historically everyone knelt for prayer, but in the latter half of the twentieth century reverence for God is generally expressed by standing during prayer. Traditionally the worship service was held every two weeks, but in the last generation all churches have been meeting for worship every Sunday morning, as well as for Gospel services of testimony and praise, sometimes with an evangelistic sermon, every Sunday night. The midweek meeting is commonly devoted to Bible or mission study and to prayer.

The (Old) Mennonites have a strong publishing program supported by a loyal reading constituency among its members as well as by others. A quick review of the books and pamphlets issuing from Herald Press at Scottdale, Pennsylvania, will indicate the importance they attach to the teaching and witness value of good literature.

*FOR FURTHER READING:*

*The Mennonite Encyclopedia,* 4 vols.

*Christian Living* (January, 1954), pp. 22-25; (August, 1954), pp. 18-21; (September, 1954), pp. 24, 25; (August, 1955), pp. 6-9; (October, 1959), pp. 28, 29, 34, 39.

*Mennonite Life* 2 (January, 1947), pp. 24-27; 18 (January, 1963), pp. 18-42.

*Mennonite Yearbook,* edited by E. D. Zook. Scottdale: Herald Press, annual.

J. C. Wenger, *The Mennonite Church in America* (1966).

_____, *Glimpses of Mennonite History and Doctrine* (1959).

# Chapter 13

# THE AMISH

THE NAME AMISH is a nickname for the followers of Jacob Ammann, a Swiss Brethren (Mennonite) elder or bishop. Born at Erlenbach in the canton of Bern, he was an able man with a strong sense of right and wrong. Somehow he always took the stricter side where there were differences of opinion over doctrine. He was much in favor of nonconformity to social customs, stressing the importance of an untrimmed beard and plainest clothing and headgear.

With the early Anabaptists Ammann taught that discipline was the spiritual weapon given to the church to overcome evil among its members. He believed, however, that excommunicated members ought to be shunned also, that is, the church members should avoid eating with them, doing business with them, and should break off all social fellowship. Up to this point the Swiss Brethren had simply barred an expelled member from the Lord's Supper but had continued to love him and work with him. It is possible that Ammann got some of his ideas from the Dordrecht Confession (1632), and from Menno Simons' *Foundation Book* published in German in 1575.

In any case, Ammann made a tour of the Swiss Brethren congregations in 1693, to win the preachers and elders to his views on shunning. Worse than that, he began to excommunicate all those who refused to agree with him. The leader who withstood him finally was Hans Reist, a mild-mannered man by nature, but unwilling to allow Ammann to impose his radicalism on the congregations. To Reist the older and traditional disciplinary views were truly Biblical and had to be preserved. The result was a division in the Swiss brotherhood, which also spread to the congregations in Alsace and the Palatinate. The Reist followers were later nicknamed *Knöpfler* (those having buttons on their coats), while the followers of Ammann were called Amish, and later also *Häftler* (those using hooks and eyes instead of buttons). The Reist-Ammann controversy has long been forgotten in Europe, but over 20,000 baptized Amish members with another 10-15,000 unbaptized children live in America.

## Emigration to America

Amish settlers began to locate in Berks County, Pennsylvania, as early as 1720, but no congregation was organized until 1749, when Jacob Hertzler (d. 1786) came to America from Switzerland via the Palatinate. He may have been ordained in Europe. In any case, he immediately took charge of the little Northkill Amish group near his farm "Contentment," two miles west of Hamburg. In 1766 Richard and Thomas Penn donated twenty acres of land near the Hertzler farm for church purposes, and the Amish immediately built a log schoolhouse.

In 1750 Jacob Mast (d. 1808) came to Berks County at the age of twelve, and together with his parents, a brother and four sisters, joined the Amish group at Hamburg. But trouble soon arose when the Indians returned to claim their ancestral lands. Consequently the Masts moved on to near Morgantown, where Jacob eventually became the second Amish bishop in America, with oversight of the Northkill, Maiden Creek, Tulpehocken, and Conestoga groups in Berks County, Goshen in Chester County, Compasville and White Horse in Lancaster County. In Berks County only the Conestoga congregation thrived, the others dying out when the Amish moved elsewhere.

Among the family names represented in these early groups were: Beiler, Burke, Detweiler, Hertzler, Kauffman, Kurtz, Lapp, Mast, Stoltzfus, Stutzman, Yoder, and Zook. Christian (Christel) Stoltzfus (d. 1832), who came to Philadelphia with his father Nicholas in 1766, became a bishop later, as did also Johannes Blanck (John Plank).

## Migration in America

The Amish settlement in southeastern Pennsylvania flourished. Today some 4,000 are located in the area, mostly in Lancaster and Chester counties. Beginning in the 1760's Amish settled in Somerset County, many coming directly from Hesse in Germany in the period 1830-60. By the 1790's they were settling in the "Big" (Kishacoquillas) Valley in Mifflin County and by 1810 had reached Union County, as well as Fairfield County in Ohio.

The large Lancaster County Amish settlement was destined to be surpassed eventually by the settlement in Holmes County, Ohio. The movement to Holmes County began from Somerset County a little before 1810, but grew rapidly after the War of 1812. The new Ohio community eventually spread into Tuscarawas and Wayne counties and today has a total baptized population of 5,000.

Early in the 1840's other Amish families from Somerset County, and some from Holmes County in Ohio, began to locate east of Goshen in Elkhart and Lagrange counties, Indiana, with the latter settlement growing to 3,000 baptized members by 1964. Another strong settlement was made in Marshall County near Nappanee, Indiana, in the late 1840's, a settlement numbering 750 baptized members in 1964. Other settlements were established in Allen, Adams, Howard-Miami, and Daviess counties in Indiana. Amish settlements were also made in Michigan, New York, Illinois, Iowa, Kansas, Nebraska, and South Dakota, as well as in the province of Ontario. The three strongest settlements, however, were those in Lancaster, Holmes, and Lagrange counties.

The Amish were not spared division among their ranks. In Indiana it became evident that those who came from Pennsylvania had slightly different attitudes and customs than those who came from Ohio, and the central issue was soon the extent to which time-honored traditions needed to be kept as part of the true faith. In 1845 a division occurred between the more progressive and more conservative members, but the schism was happily ended two years later through the mediation of three Amish leaders from Ohio. A second and more serious division occurred in 1854 and has not yet been healed. The progressives gradually dropped the strict and all-embracing Amish discipline on clothes and other aspects of life, took a favorable attitude toward the adoption of English in worship, and eventually began to build meetinghouses. These people came to be known as the Amish Mennonites and merged with the Mennonites of Indiana in 1916, as we have seen in Chapter 12. Other schisms occurred among the Amish of Ohio and Pennsylvania between 1850 and 1875, and similar mergers occurred also. The Western District Amish Mennonites, embracing scattered congregations from Illinois to Oregon, merged with the Mennonites of their respective areas in 1920-21, while the eastern Amish Mennonites of Ohio and Pennsylvania merged with the Ohio Mennonites in 1927. Meanwhile the Old Order Amish pursued their quiet and unchanging pattern of life, happy in the knowledge that the Lord was pleased by their 'utter nonconformity to the fashionable and wicked society.

## The Faith of the Amish

*Convinced Christians:* It is sometimes almost forgotten that the Amish are Christians. Sociologists become fascinated with various customs and attitudes of the Amish and sometimes think of them only as a continuation of European rural and peasant folkways. But the Amish accept the fundamental doctrines of New Testament Christianity. Their doctrinal position, in contrast with their religious practice in the area of dress, modes of transportation, and the like, is quite similar to the doctrinal position of the Mennonites. As we saw in earlier chapters the Mennonites and the Amish had a common history in Switzerland from 1525 until the tragic division of 1693.

Amish, therefore, accept the basic doctrines of Christianity: the existence of a personal God who created the universe, who sustains it, and who is sovereign in human history; the creation of man in the image of God; the fall into sin involving all posterity in sin and depravity; God's redemptive purpose for mankind, shown in His several covenants with Abraham and his family (Israel), and culminating in the new covenant made by Jesus Christ in His death; salvation through repentance from sin, and faith in Christ as Lord and Saviour; the Christian life as one of holiness and love; the reality and objective significance of prayer; the acceptance of the church as the body of Christian believers, obligated to follow Christ and ready to bear the cross of suffering—which is potentially the lot of His disciples; the awareness that the struggle of the church with sin and unbelief is but temporary, and that Christ will return in glory to raise the dead, judge the world, and usher in His eternal kingdom. Other doctrines could, of course, be added but this is enough to show that the Amish are strictly Christian in their basic doctrinal position.

*Nonconformity:* Among the concerns which the Amish have for the life of robust Christians is nonconformity to the world. They point to Romans 12:2, which in their German Bibles means something like "do not fashion yourselves in accordance with the world." That is, dare to be different. The Amish leader is not impressed if someone points out that they are simply wearing the clothing of the rural areas of the Palatinate and Switzerland in previous centuries. That may well be true, he will reply, but in those days many people conformed to the will of God in their plain and simple dress. Since that day society has gone wild in fashions, luxury, and wealth, and people generally have become worldly in their dress. This indicates clearly that their hearts are cold spiritually and conformed to this sinful world. "We Amish," he may add, "are minded to maintain our simple, modest, and plain dress until the end of time. We cannot do less, according to the light we have, and be pleasing to our kind heavenly Father. Why should we follow after the fashions of the world? They are not based on Christian principles and, as one of our most helpful books, the *Martyrs Mirror,* says, are as changeable as the moon. Furthermore, we prefer hooks-and-eyes on our coats and vests, for buttons originally had a military flavor, and we can see no good reason for using them now."

*Wholesome living:* Another point on which the Amish feel strongly is the necessity of maintaining rural life. They reason like this: God's open country is a great place to live; here we are less in danger of being corrupted by the worldly and sinful ways of the cities; here we live close to the soil, watching the weather changes of our God, observing the continuous growth of our crops and our livestock, and of our precious sons and daughters; here we always have plenty of hard work for our children, and that is a good thing to keep them out of mischief and delinquency. The country is a wonderful place for growing sons and daughters. In addition to wholesome work, they have opportunity for hunting, fishing, rearing a calf, local ball games, parties of Amish young people, and the like. There is no place as desirable as the farm. It is all right to enter such trades as carpentry, if one can do so while maintaining a rural base. Anything which does not call for higher education is legitimate: a small business like harness-making, or being a blacksmith or welder, or painting buildings; but any profession which would call for higher education is suspect. The wisdom of this world has a corrupting influence on the soul of man; it tends to make him proud, dissatisfied with the Amish way of plainness and simplicity.

*Congregationalism:* Simplicity applies not only to the Amishman's clothing and mode of life, however, but equally to the way the church is set up and operated. The typical Amish congregation has from fifty to ninety members, served by self-supported ordained men. Under normal circumstances the average congregation has a chief shepherd, the Full Minister *(Voller Diener* in German; bishop, for lack of a better term, in English), two Ministers of the Word, and a Minister to the Poor (deacon). Upon the Full Minister, who is voted for as a nominee, selected from the nominees by lot, and ordained for life to this heavy responsibility, rests final responsibility for the spiritual care of his flock. It is he who is responsible to see to it that everything is done which is humanly possible to keep all members on the strait and narrow way which leads to life eternal in the glory world. This is no trivial undertaking, and he is keenly aware of the 'deceptiveness of the world, the flesh, and the devil. He determines with much prayer to do his best as a spiritual watchman over his people. And the people want him to be just such a watchman. They feel for him when the lot falls on him, and they seek to uphold him by their moral support and by prayer. He is the chief disciplinarian, although the Minister to the Poor, who is charged to see to it that the widows, orphans, and needy are always adequately cared for, also serves as his right-hand assistant in the area of discipline. The Ministers of the Word are the teachers and interpreters of the Word of God. This teaching is no private enterprise, for it is his solemn responsibility to teach correctly and safely within the doctrinal and ethical understandings of the brotherhood. When a sermon is finished he wants to be able to hear the warm endorsement of his fellow ministers that the message was sound, that it was the Word of God which will stand for time and eternity.

The Amish read nothing in the New Testament about synods, district conferences, or, much less, of a General Conference of the church of Christ. And since this also happens to have been the polity of the Mennonites for the first two centuries, it seems entirely proper to the Amish to continue in the good arrangement which they have always held. Final authority rests with the bishop and his local congregation. They decide everything which needs to be acted on. There is no need of any person, committee, or conference to tell the local assembly of believers what their decision ought to be. Each congregation (and bishop) is keenly aware that it is being observed by neighboring congregations of Amish believers, and each group is sincerely concerned to be faithful to the Lord of the church and to His holy Word. This leads to a remarkable uniformity, reinforced, as Amish church life always is, by a strong church tradition. Furthermore, without in any sense denying the validity of congregational church government, Amish ministers in a given region hold occasional ministers' meetings to discuss the issues of the day and to counsel with one another. But there the meetings stop. They are not bodies with binding ecclesiastical power.

*Enjoying life:* It should not be thought that all of Amish life is deadly serious. Amish children run and play and laugh and have fun just as other children do. Amish young people have their parties and folk games which they enjoy every bit as much as anyone else. Amish adults will half-jokingly refer to slightly differing customs in other parts of their church, such as commenting with a smile on the faster mode of singing in Iowa than in some other areas, perhaps calling the fast singers, *"Die stoltze Iowäers"*--those proud people of Iowa! And when a group of Amish come together to rebuild a barn which burned down--it would seem like a major sin against a brother not to rebuild his barn *gratis*--the men, although working hard, will also have time for a little good-natured teasing, and perhaps a few harmless pranks. On such occasions the women will do their share by providing such a hearty meal that a city dude could not enjoy all of it. The capacity of these sturdy sons of the soil is quite adequate for any challenge their good wives can prepare.

*Alles Deitsch:* The Amish feel that it would be tragedy to give up the German language. It would have a disruptive influence on their church life; they are comfortably familiar with their beloved German *Bivel* (Bible), and they would not wish to hear God's Word in any other language, least of all in the language of the worldly English around them! Furthermore, all the good devotional and doctrinal and catechetical books and booklets of the Amish are in German. And so it is natural, wise, and prudent to do as the fathers did, hold on to the German. In Adams County, Indiana, the Amish are descended of Swiss immigrants, hence employ Swiss German in their services, but elsewhere the Amish speak Palatine German, commonly nicknamed Pennsylvania "Dutch." Ralph Charles Wood has made the *Gospel of Matthew* available in Pennsylvania Dutch, and this is a good exhibit of the dialect at its best. There are many English words in it, but the good Amish minister will tend to improve the dialect by introducing German words from the Bible, rather than to preach in the "pure" dialect. Most of the listeners consequently think he is preaching in High German rather than Pennsylvania Dutch, but many Amish would have real difficulty understanding modern High German. Singing in their worship services is slow, almost melancholy, and usually from the *Ausbund* of 1564, one of the oldest Protestant hymnals in the world.

Amish worship services are usually held every other Sunday morning, taking three or more hours. Where houses are too small they are held in barns or sheds, church buildings being considered evidence of straying from the Most High, who does not dwell in temples made by men's hands, as the Word of God states.

*Total simplicity:* If an Amishman were told that technology had now made manual labor unnecessary, he would be sad. Did not God command man to till the earth in the sweat of his face? Work is good and wholesome; more than earning a living, toil itself is good for people. Without manual labor man's wicked flesh would assert itself even more diabolically than at present. For the Amish work is not an unfortunate calamity, but a blessing of God. There have been cases of Amish people selling their land when oil was discovered under it; they did not wish to receive unearned money, and perhaps lose their soul through the spiritual corruption which wealth would certainly bring. So the peaceful Amish farmer plows with horses, harrows with horses, plants his grain with horse-drawn planters, harvests his grain with horse-drawn binders, and does a maximum of hand labor, made possible largely by the many children most Amish families have. As the Amish farmer grows older, he often sits in his rocking chair, reading his Bible, or glancing over the nearest thing to an Amish newspaper, the Sugarcreek (Ohio) *Budget,* turning the pages with his huge gnarled hands. But his children are well and strong; the livestock and crops on his farm are thriving under the care of the next generation. His heart is at peace. The drone of an airplane high in the sky seems far away, and it actually is for him. Soon he and Mamma will move into the *"Gross-Dawdy-house,"* just as his parents did thirty years before, and one of his strapping big boys will marry and take over the management of the farm. He will continue to help feed the stock, assist with the milking and other chores as long as he is able. And Grandma will knit mittens and sweaters for her many grandchildren. Their steps are slow, but they have lived a good life, God has been good to them, and they trust that all will be well when they step into the other world at the death of the body.

*What about miting?* We have seen earlier in this chapter how important church discipline and shunning were to Jacob Ammann and his followers. The German word for shunning is *Meidung* (pronounced MY-doong), but in Pennsylvania Dutch it is pronounced MITE-ing. This is one of the few Amish practices which seem harsh and unloving to the wider society, but the Amish would reply that they have no choice in the matter. They do not shun excommunicated members because they are holding a grudge against them, or because they wish to be harsh with the sinning brother who has become the slave of drink, or some other sin. They practice miting out of simple obedience to what they understand the New Testament to

188

teach. And they would be quick to point out that the intention is not to ruin the former member but to bring him to see the gravity of his sin and lead him to repentance. Amish leaders can point to numerous cases in which miting did seem to bring such apostate members to genuine repentance and change of life. The total number of persons excommunicated by the Amish is actually small.

## An Amish Library

What books do the Amish read? Though they are not highly educated people, they do see the importance of being well-informed Christians and good farmers, which requires some reading. Most of their books are German, of course, beginning with the Bible. Like the early Mennonites, they prefer the old Swiss German Bible of Froschauer (1529, New Testament 1524) of which many reprints were made, but Luther Bibles are much easier to obtain in America and, therefore, common among them. Ranking next to the Bible in terms of its influence upon them throughout history is the *Martyrs Mirror*, first published in Dutch in 1660, but in many German editions since then.

Beyond these two standard volumes many Amish homes possess several or all of the following books as well: the prayer books *Christenpflicht* (Christian Duty), and *Geistliches Lustgärtlein* (Garden of Spiritual Desire), which are also used in worship; the *Liedersammlung* as second hymnal in addition to the *Ausbund;* the *Foundation Book* of Menno Simons, or even his complete works; the *Enchiridion* or Handbook of Christian Doctrine of Menno's colleague Dirk Philips; the catechism of Gerrit Roosen, the Bible history *Wandelnde Seele,* and the devotional book *Güldene Äpfel in Silberne Schalen.* Also present would be *Raber's Calendar,* an almanac and Amish congregational directory.

For the sake of the farm many Amish homes also possess Baer's annual *Agricultural Almanac,* and practically every Amish home subscribes to the *Budget,* a newspaper catering to the Amish, and printed in Sugarcreek, Ohio. In this periodical are found a constant stream of letters which tie the scattered communities together, as well as news of church services, reports on crops and the weather, trips, and accidents. The *Budget* even contains Amish poetry, a sort of peasant ballad describing in a rather emotional and colorful manner the illness, accident, or death of some Amish person, and frequently capped with an earnest spiritual admonition.

It must be emphasized, however, that reading is a sort of luxury with the Amish, a form of spare-time recreation. The concept of being a well-read person would look suspiciously like an effort to get out of work to an average Amishman. Reading is something to do during a winter storm, or on a Sunday afternoon, or on a quiet evening. The Christian life is to them not a matter of much book learning, but rather of simple obedience to God's will. And the biweekly sermons serve adequately to keep them aware of what obedience to this divine will involves.

### The Amish Personality

Anyone with the tact to really become acquainted with the Amish, especially if he can speak the dialect, will discover in the typical Amishman a man of sincere faith, with a devout heart, and an honest soul. He may also strike the average American as quiet and timid, and this not without cause. It may be that the long years of suffering and persecution in Europe, especially in Switzerland, have left their mark on the Amish personality and, some think, upon Mennonites also. And so the quiet Amishman behind his large beard does indeed size up his visitor carefully, being on the alert against smooth sales talk, and fully assuming that when the visitor is through with his pleasantries he will try to sell him something. The freedoms of democratic America have not yet served to bring the Amish out of their shell, and the abuses of persecution long ago as well as the ridicule and misunderstanding they themselves experience in our culture have not helped to relieve them of the tendency to distrust strangers.

While Amish children grow up in the carefully protected environment of their semi-closed communities, a little imagination will show how difficult it must be to keep them happy in the Amish faith in the midst of the surrounding social and cultural influences. The pressure to conformity is strong, and sometimes leads to a reaction among them, taking the form of minor vandalism or the use of strong drink by minors. Obviously, what might appear to be normal deviancy in other communities is seen as darker and more sinful than it really is when it happens among the Amish. Often the older members are not inclined to worry too much about such youthful exploits, for they know that the young man will soon find an Amish mate, after which he will "settle down" both socially and spiritually. On the other hand, if an Amish youth begins to do serious Bible study, his folks may become afraid that he is considering uniting with the Mennonites. Most of the Amish children actually unite

190

with the church of their fathers, turn to the Lord in repentance and faith, and live a sober Christian life of separation from the world with its temptations. John A. Hostetler, the foremost American authority on the Amish, attended an Amish baptismal service in Indiana, and published an account of his experience, now reprinted in J. C. Wenger, *The Mennonites in Indiana and Michigan,* pages 387-91.

*FOR FURTHER READING:*
The Mennonite Encyclopedia, 4 vols.
*Christian Living* (March, 1954), pp. 6, 7, 40; (July, 1955), pp. 4-7; (September, 1956), pp. 4-6; (January, 1962), pp. 28, 29, 39.
John A. Hostetler, *Amish Life.* Scottdale: Herald Press, 1965 (17th printing), a brief popular treatment.
───────────, *Amish Society.* Baltimore: Johns Hopkins Press, 1963.
An interesting and informative novel entitled *Rosanna of the Amish,* Scottdale, Herald Press, 1961, has been written by J. W. Yoder, son of an Amish preacher.

# Chapter 14

# THE GENERAL CONFERENCE MENNONITE CHURCH

THE MENNONITES living near the Mississippi River in Illinois and Iowa were lonely. Most of them had come from the South German province of Bavaria, Palatine, and Hesse between 1830 and 1850, to find freedom and prosperity on the American frontier. Family names among them were Wittmer, Eyman, Weber, Galle, Ruth, Hege, Schmidt, and above all Krehbiel, a name going back to the Crayenbühl family which fled from Switzerland to the Palatinate in the seventeenth century. The Mennonites who had come to Pennsylvania a century earlier carried the same names, and many of them came from the same South German provinces, but they were different because of their experiences. While those who came in the eighteenth century lived in closed, self-sufficient Mennonite settlements, those who came after 1830 had experienced the spiritual and intellectual freedom which had arisen in Europe after the French Revolution of 1789. They were beginning to be citizens of this world while still being pilgrims on their way to the world beyond.

True to their Mennonite tradition, the immigrants began to organize churches as soon as they arrived in the Middle West. One congregation was organized at West Point, Iowa, in 1849, with two men chosen as ministers. A small log cabin church seating thirty people was built four miles from town. Because it was located on the edge of a wooded area the congregation was often referred to as the *Busch Gemeinde,* i.e., bush church. Another congregation, called Zion, was organized nine miles from the first, in Franklin Town-

192

ship, in 1852. They were allowed to use a German Lutheran church building on alternate Sundays until their own building was completed in 1855. A third congregation was organized at Summerfield, Illinois, across the river from St. Louis, in 1858. Krehbiels were among the leading men in all three congregations. There were other Mennonites and Amish in these communities also, families who had moved west from Pennsylvania and Ohio, but because of their different background and experiences these German immigrants did not seem to have much contact with them.

Because fellowship was necessary for Christian growth the three congregations at West Point and Summerfield tried hard to overcome their geographical and spiritual isolation. In 1853 the West Point and Franklin Township congregations united to form the *German Evangelical Mennonite congregation* with a total of 181 members. Since the two churches were nine miles apart, they continued to meet separately but had annual conferences together. By 1859 they felt a strong urge to do something concrete in home and foreign missions. They became convinced that they needed to be united in order to undertake such work. Three resolutions were adopted at the conference that year: first, to take an offering for missions on the first Sunday of every month; second to take offerings for the support of a minister who could be asked to visit the scattered Mennonites in the Middle West; and third, to appoint a business committee to take care of these affairs and to "correspond with other Mennonite churches and invite them to join this union." When minister Jacob Krehbiel I sent these resolutions to be published in the Mennonite paper, *Das Christliche Volksblatt*, he added a letter saying:

May the Lord lend His blessing to this small beginning, that eventually a common bond of brotherhood bind all our Mennonite communities to work unitedly that the brethren living in isolation may receive the pure Gospel, and thereby the scattered sheep be held for our church. [1]

Almost unknown to these congregations was the fact that four years earlier, in 1855, a similar unity had been achieved by the congregation in Wadsworth, Ohio, with several Mennonite congregations in Ontario. The minister of the Wadsworth congregation was Ephraim Hunsberger, a real frontier preacher who felt Mennonites were too slow in spreading the Gospel. The leader of the participating Ontario congregations was Daniel Hoch, a zealous evangelist who disturbed many Mennonites with his emphasis upon prayer meetings, freedom of expression in church meetings, and holiness. Here too missions and unity received primary attention. Hoch himself was commissioned as itinerant evangelist and union negotiations were begun with the East Pennsylvania Conference. At the third meeting of this group, which was known as the Canada-Ohio Conference, approval was given to a proposal which had appeared earlier in *Das Christliche Volksblatt*. The proposal began with the words, "Let all ministers of the various branches of the denomination cultivate a fraternal confidence toward each other and abandon all prejudice." It further urged the preparation of a confession of faith and added that "all those who will accept this confession and unite upon it shall be considered the real Mennonite denomination."

### John H. Oberholtzer, 1809-95

There was another group involved in unity negotiations, a group which was to have a major part in bringing about the forming of the General Conference. This group was under the leadership of John H. Oberholtzer, minister of the Swamp Mennonite Church near Quakertown, Pennsylvania. It is interesting to note that while this group was deeply interested in *union* with other Mennonites, their own little East Pennsylvania Conference had originated in 1847 after a *break* with the older and larger Franconia Conference.

Oberholtzer was born on January 10, 1809, in Berks County, Pennsylvania. His great-grandfather Jacob Oberholtzer had come to Philadelphia from Switzerland in 1732. Young John received the best education a farm boy could acquire during the winter months in the German church school. By the time he was sixteen years of age he was himself employed as a teacher every winter until he was ordained as a minister in 1842. But this teaching had its own problems. For a time his classroom was the second floor of a hog barn on the farm of John Ritter. It seems that the older boys enjoyed asking for permission to leave the room and then used the occasion to stir the swill barrel downstairs until the hungry pigs were in a real uproar waiting to be fed. Classes naturally had to be dismissed for the remainder of the period because of the noise and dust. This practice became such a nuisance that the school had to be discontinued at that location. Since the school year was short and the salary small, young John also learned the locksmithing trade, later establishing his own shop near Milford Square. This skill became his main financial support for thirty years.

His call to the ministry came through the lot. Since the minister of the Swamp church was over eighty years old, the congregation nominated fifteen members of the church as possible ministers, John among them. Though he had real misgivings about calling ministers by the lot, there was really nothing he could do about it since that was the way tradition demanded. When the fifteen candidates were together, each was given a Bible, but only one had the lot in it. This was a slip of paper on which the words of Proverbs 16:33 were usually written: "The lot is cast into the lap, but the decision is wholly from the Lord." John drew the lot. One Sunday morning about six weeks later John was told, upon arriving at the church, that he was to preach his first sermon that morning. Silently he called upon God for help and chose as his text Ephesians 2:8, "For by grace you have been saved, through faith." After the service he overheard the remark, "That was a scholarly sermon," and since scholarship was seen as a sign of pride the remark obviously meant that it had been a bad sermon. Yet he himself had experienced real divine help in this hour, having claimed the promises of Joshua 1:5 and Hebrews 13:5.

Nevertheless, he continued in his ministry but felt increasing opposition to his thinking. He was an able preacher and administrator, with many new ideas which he believed to be Biblical. He was young and possibly somewhat impatient with the old forms of worship and community life. More and more he found himself distinguishing between practices which were followed from force of habit only, without clear Biblical precedent, and those which he found in the life of the early church according to Acts and the epistles. Why, he asked, should ministers wear different coats than laymen, why should no minutes be kept of church meetings, why is a church constitution sin, and why could Mennonite ministers not have Christian fellowship with other ministers except Quakers? There were other lesser things which troubled him, and personality clashes must have been inevitable. He could not get used to the authority of the bishops, believing rather that the entire congregation should decide all major issues in the church. And slowly the fellowship was broken, though several attempts were made at reconciliation. Like Oberholtzer, Christians have often believed so strongly that they have been more willing to break fellowship with each other than to give up what they considered to be Biblical and right. God does expect His children to be faithful, but He never expects them to stop loving each other.

This had indeed been a difficult time for the Mennonites in

Pennsylvania. Being both hard-working and frugal they had become quite wealthy. Religious freedom meant for them the freedom *not* to change their old customs. In describing this time one writer says, "From 1683 to the ordination of John H. Oberholtzer, almost 160 years later, no significant changes were made, and no one intended to make any. The Bible had not changed; why should anyone introduce any innovations?" [2] The War of Independence had cut them off from stimulating contacts with their European brethren, and the democratic American environment seemed foreign to them. Missions were not undertaken; education was suspect; prayer meetings were frowned upon. Members were forbidden many things that seemed harmless, such as picnics or celebrations, farm exhibitions and poultry shows. But all this must not be taken as a lack of spiritual interest. There was, on the contrary, very strong Christian conviction, but they lacked the ability to distinguish meaningfully between the good and the bad which the new situation brought to them. The unfamiliar constituted a threat to the faith because they were so conscious of a heritage to preserve. And so the faith was seen as a timeless deposit to be guarded zealously from the world, rather than as a living power meant precisely for the world in its lostness. The consequent stress upon external forms and customs left too little freedom for the renewing work of the Holy Spirit.

A particular problem among the two groups was the constitution Oberholtzer had written for adoption by the conference. Known as the *Ordnung,* it not only gave full authority to the entire congregation instead of to the bishop but also proposed the keeping of minutes, regular elections, and a modification of the use of the lot in choosing ministers. It urged a greater openness to other Christians, also suggesting that Mennonites might marry outside of their church so long as it was "in the Lord." It was clear that the *Ordnung* would lead to less separation from the world and greater adaptation to their American environment. With this, it seemed, would come a loss of the heritage of faith through outside influence. By 1847 the rupture was complete and the representatives of fourteen congregations met to form a new organization which they called the East Pennsylvania Conference of the Mennonite Church. Soon this group became known as the *New* Mennonites to distinguish them from the *Old* Mennonites, though neither group really considered the other to be true disciples of Menno any longer.

In addition to leading the affairs of the new conference and ministering to his own congregation, Oberholtzer now worked tirelessly for spiritual renewal. He was to establish one of the first American Mennonite Sunday schools, he ordered Mennonite literature and catechism materials from Europe to teach young people the meaning of their faith, and he carried on a vigorous correspondence with Mennonites scattered throughout the Middle West. Particularly important was his founding of a newspaper, *Der Religiöser Botschafter*, in 1852 by which it became possible to reach the most scattered believers with greetings and spiritual help. Four years later the name was changed to *Das Christliche Volksblatt* and continued successfully under the editorship of Oberholtzer.

## A General Conference Is Born

The initiative toward union came from the two congregations at West Point, Iowa, with the editorial support of Oberholtzer. Having themselves united in 1853, they published the minutes of their 1859 conference which invited others to join them and announced the next meeting for "the second day of Pentecost in 1860 at West Point." Neither the Canada-Ohio Conference nor the East Pennsylvania Conference took much notice of this invitation. Shortly before it was to meet, however, the latter group adopted a motion stating that "Since the Iowa conference has come to notice, it is agreed that ministers who wish may attend voluntarily." At the last minute friends raised enough money for Oberholtzer to go the conference.

When the conference convened, only the two sponsoring churches and four visitors, including Oberholtzer, were present. Five sermons were preached before they turned to the agenda of four points. These were the organization of a missionary society, the establishing of a training school for Christian workers, the formation of a historical society, and the publication of tracts. During the conference a committee of five was appointed to draw up a plan of union by the following morning. This they did and the resulting plan, with six points, was adopted without much change. Its provisions were to make it possible to work together on all important matters without violating the congregational freedom of the churches. Uniformity in all things was not considered necessary for cooperation. It was agreed to work earnestly in home and foreign missions and to establish a school for the training of Christian workers just as soon as possible. It was also agreed to meet again the following year at Wadsworth, Ohio. John H. Oberholtzer was elected chairman of the new conference.

A significant decision of the 1861 conference was the appointing of Daniel Hege as *Reiseprediger*, i.e., a traveling minister for the conference. It was to be his duty to travel through the Mennonite communities to promote unity, evangelism, and the need for a stronger educational program. In speaking of this need before the conference he said:

> If we Mennonites are not to increase our guilt by longer neglecting the duty of missions as commanded by our Lord . . . we must, not singly, but as a denomination, make missions the work of the Lord by our people. If we would undertake our mission duty, we first need Christian educational institutions. But to found and carry on institutions . . . demands not only active interest, but also much money, and for that, church-wide participation and unremitting sacrifice is required as well as unity. [3]

Because of the Civil War Hege was unable to begin his journey immediately, but in May, 1862, he set out to visit the churches in the Middle West, the East, and in Ontario. He normally conducted at least four preaching services each week and as many as fifty and sixty house calls. In every home he challenged them to give to missions and education, sharing with them his vision of a united Mennonite Church forgetting its differences in the work of the kingdom. He was very well received in most places after he had presented his case, though questions and criticism were often leveled at him before they discovered his fine Christian spirit. In November he returned home to Summerfield, planning to finish the work in Iowa by the end of the year, but he took seriously ill and died of typhoid fever on November 30. His itinerant ministry had made a deep impression upon the churches, however, so forceful that Oberholtzer wrote, "If the aims of the general conference of Iowa and Ohio are ever accomplished, then Brother Hege stands forever as one of the first men who helped break through the opposition." In a way Hege represented in himself the vision of the young, emerging conference at that time with his interest in missions, education, and unity.

We have seen earlier that the initial membership in the conference consisted of two kinds of groups: American Mennonites who had become dissatisfied with the traditional patterns of their Swiss and South German immigrant fathers, and groups coming from the same South German area one hundred years later, in mid-nineteenth century. Ten years after its founding the General Conference thus consisted of some twenty congregations with approximately 1,500 members. To these were later added as a third group the congregations in Ohio, Indiana, and Missouri which had come directly from Switzerland between 1817 and 1854. It was from the Swiss congregation at Berne, Indiana, that S. F. Sprunger (d. 1923) was to come. Known as Samy to most people, he had a great influence upon the conference through his deep spiritual concern and evangelical power. The fourth and by far the largest group to join the conference were the Mennonites from Russia. The history of their experiences has been told in Chapters 10 and 11. Leaving Russia to escape the military draft and the threat of gradual assimilation into their surrounding culture, the first groups arrived in the United States and Canada in 1873. During the ten following years a total of 18,000 were to come, 10,000 settling on the frontier lands west of the Mississippi in Dakota, Nebraska, and Kansas, and 8,000 locating in Manitoba. A large number of these soon joined the General Conference. An additional 20,000 immigrants came to Canada from Russia in the 1920 decade and 7,000 in the 1940 decade, many of these likewise affiliating with the conference. By 1964 two thirds of the membership in the General Conference was of Russian Mennonite background.

The coming of these immigrants has been described in detail by C. Henry Smith in *The Coming of the Russian Mennonites* (1927) and Frank H. Epp in *Mennonite Exodus* (1962), the former dealing with the first movement and the latter with the movements of the 1920's and 1940's. Each of these movements called forth men of vision who were willing and able to direct them and who frequently risked a great deal to bring them to pass. Prominent in the movement of the 1870's was Cornelius Janzen (d. 1894), a man of courage and ability who was exiled from Russia for encouraging the Mennonites to leave and who himself settled in Beatrice, Nebraska. Central to the movement of the 1920's was the life and work of David Toews (d. 1947) who came to Kansas from Russia via Asia at the age of fourteen, moved to Canada as a young man to teach school, and came to be known as the Moses of the Mennonites before he died. Traveling far and wide from his modest home in Rosthern, Saskatchewan, in the interests of the emigration he soon had many friends and helpers, even in Ottawa. When he borrowed nearly $400,000 in the name of the Mennonites to make the coming of these emigrants possible, he also had numerous enemies among his own people. Total borrowings and interest were to grow to 1.9 million dollars before all was repaid in 1946, one year before his death. Central to the emigration of the 1940's were B. B. Janz (d. 1964) and C. F. Klassen (d. 1954), both members of the Mennonite Brethren Church, but especially the work of the Canadian

199

Board of Colonization which had been established by David Toews. The human drama of these migrations was real and gripping, much stronger than fiction.

Other smaller groups also joined the General Conference in addition to those already mentioned. There were immigrants from Prussia to both Canada and the United States in small numbers from the 1870's to the 1940's. In 1946 the Central Conference with 3,211 members primarily of Amish background joined. Later some 3,000 Prussian and Russian Mennonites, who had settled in Uruguay and Paraguay after World War II, were received into the conference. Together with the increase through nurture and evangelism, all of these groups totaled approximately 56,000 members in 370 congregations in 1964. This did not include 23,000 members added through overseas missionary activities, nor approximately 5,000 members of the Bergthal and other churches who were a part of the Canadian conference but not the General Conference. In North America the heaviest concentration was in the Middle West, stretching from the Prairie Provinces in Canada through the Dakotas and Nebraska to Kansas and Oklahoma.

## United to Serve

"From the very beginning of the General Conference," wrote J. W. Kliewer, chairman of the Mission Board for twenty-five years, "missionary interest has been the cement that has held this structure together." As has been seen, missions and education were indeed the primary motives leading to union. The wide variety of ethnic and cultural backgrounds of the groups joining the conference indicated that something stronger than family relationships was drawing them together. Nor were they uniting simply for the sake of unity, as their minimal organizational machinery verifies; they did not adopt a formal constitution for thirty-six years. They united in order to do together that which none of them could do alone. A constant theme of their early correspondence and conferences was that they needed each other to carry on the work of the Lord.

American Christians were long familiar with the idea of missions, but the Mennonites were too isolated by their own cultural patterns to be inspired by them and the mission zeal of the sixteenth-century Anabaptists had long been lost. The Dutch Mennonites, however, being more open to the influence of others, had organized a missionary society in 1847, and sent their first missionary Pieter Jansz

200

(d. 1904) to Java in 1851. The Mennonites in Germany and Russia soon supported this work. It is likely, therefore, that the immigrants coming from South Germany to West Point and Summerfield in mid-century had brought an interest in missions with them. In 1853 Oberholtzer published an article about Methodist mission work, the first of many on this subject. At the 1858 meeting of the East Pennsylvania Conference he was asked to write to the European Mennonites for information about their missionary activities. Their response was an invitation to join in the work with the Dutch, German, Austrian, and Russian Mennonites who were already supporting it. The following year the Ontario Mennonites organized the "Home and Foreign Mission Society of the Mennonites," and in 1866 the Pennsylvania Mennonite Mission Society with seventy-two charter members was organized in Oberholtzer's church. Nevertheless, it was to take until 1872 before the first missionary candidate was available.

The founding of an educational institution was seen as part of their interest in, and preparation for, missions. For a time this absorbed all the energies of the new conference. Mennonites had generally been opposed to higher education. They believed that much learning made people proud and prevented them from seeing simple spiritual truths. The persecutors of the sixteenth-century Anabaptists had, for the most part, been learned men. Faith, the Mennonites had come to believe, was not so much independent study and intellectual understanding, but a matter of the heart and of obedience to the requirements of the church. The new conference, however, saw education as inseparable from missions; those chosen for this work should be well prepared. The institution they wanted to establish was to be a missionary training school, missions meaning not only bringing the Gospel to distant lands, but working with the unevangelized at home, and even gathering indifferent and scattered Mennonites.

At the conference sessions of 1863 a report was received from the committee which had been appointed to study the school question. This report called for the school to be built at Wadsworth, Ohio, as soon as possible and to be named the "Christian Educational Institution of the Mennonite Denomination." Funds were immediately solicited and the building was finished in time to be dedicated at the next conference session in 1866. Classes began in 1868 with twenty-four students and six teachers. That same year Carl J. van der Smissen was called from a pastorate in northern Germany to be principal. The curriculum was divided into three departments—theology, German, and English. Under the latter department were included most of the subjects normally taught in academies and colleges at that time. That the field of education was indeed new to Mennonites became clear when the school had to be closed in 1878, after eleven years of operation, because of financial and internal problems. But this first attempt was not without results. A total of 209 students had come under its influence, including the first missionaries to be sent out and many others who were to assume leadership in the conference. The school taught the people to give of their money and to think in terms of missions. Consequently the same session which closed the school in 1878, authorized the Mission Board to establish another school at a more favorable location but no immediate steps were taken.

With the coming of the Mennonites from Russia in 1874-83, many new congregations were added to the conference together with fresh enthusiasm for missions and education. Because they had conducted their own schools in Russia for over one hundred years, they were familiar with school problems and procedures. By 1877 a committee had been appointed to study the possibility of founding a school for higher education in Kansas. That school opened its doors in 1882, and eventually became known as Bethel College. They also brought a limited mission interest with them, stimulated in Russia by German pietism and by the work of the Dutch Mennonites. In 1868 Henry Dirks, the first Mennonite missionary from Russia, had gone to the Java field. The financial help which they received from their American brethren upon arrival in the Middle West accustomed the latter further to sacrificial giving, which directly benefited the mission cause a few years later. All of these factors caused the Pennsylvania minister N. B. Grubb to write that "It was not until the Russian brethren had come to America and united with the General Conference that the cause of missions took definite action and the spirit of missions became fact." [4]

Judged by modern standards the beginning was slow and painful. The mission societies of 1859 and 1866 had confined their activities primarily to fund raising and the publishing of articles about missions. Now, in 1872, S. S. Haury, a former student of the Wadsworth school, declared his intention to become a missionary and to prepare for this by further studies in Barmen, Germany. The conference thereupon promptly established a Mission Board of five members to work with him, also agreeing to support him financially during his studies. Following his return in 1875, he was ordained and commissioned to find a suitable field. Since the Mission Board preferred to begin their own work rather than lend him to the Dutch for work in Java, he spent five difficult years in this search. When the door seemed to close for work among the American Indians, he made a 9,000-mile trip to Alaska, but since the Presbyterians were already locating there he returned to explore the Indian territory further. Finally, in 1880, the way opened for him to locate at Darlington, Oklahoma, to work among the Arapahoes. There were many hardships. A fire claimed four lives, including his own child, and destroyed the new mission building. But the work prospered and by Christmas, 1882, fourteen workers were on the field.

Overseas work began in 1899 when famine relief was sent to India, followed by mission workers in 1901; in 1911 the Central Conference, later to merge with the General Conference, began work in the African Congo; in 1914 the work begun earlier in China by private persons was taken over; soon after World War II work was begun in Colombia, South America, Japan, and Taiwan. In 1964 the Mission Board had a budget of $979,322, this being 65 percent of the total budget for the conference, plus nearly $100,000 raised by a very active Women's Missionary Association for this cause. There were 209 workers on the field in that year.

With the increase in conference activities came the need for a clear understanding of responsibilities such as a constitution helps to provide. The first formal constitution was consequently written and accepted in 1896, providing for the boards of Home Missions, Foreign Missions, Publication, and a Business Committee. In order to preserve the congregational autonomy so dear to General Conference people the constitution provided that the conference could *advise* but not *legislate,* the final authority still remaining in the hands of the congregations. After continuing revision to meet new situations the constitution established four boards to carry the work: Missions, Christian Service, Education and Publication, and Business Administration. A fifth board was set up to carry responsibility for Mennonite Biblical Seminary.

The program planning and administration of the General Conference boards was carried on by an executive secretary for each board, together with his staff at Central Offices in Newton, Kansas. These plans, including the budget, were studied and approved at an annual Council of Boards meeting. In 1964 the conference budget was approximately one and one-half million dollars of which 65 percent went for missions, as indicated, 17 percent for the work of the Board of Christian Service, 11 percent for the Seminary, and 7 percent for the Board of Education and Publication. Total contributions of conference members for all causes in 1964, including local congregational causes, amounted to slightly more than six million dollars. The two conference papers were *The Mennonite* and *Der Bote*.

## Faith and Life

At a centennial study conference in 1960 the following statement of goals was adopted as expressing the hopes and vision of the people of the General Conference:

As we of the General Conference stand at the threshold of our second century, we look back to the work of those who walked before us, faithful in the cause of Christ and His church. We also look up in gratitude to our heavenly Father for His merciful guidance in the century now closing; and we look forward humbly to the century ahead, aware of the far-reaching warfare we may be called upon to wage against unprecedented demonic power.

So we stand at the threshold, seeking inspiration from the past and praying for God's strengthening in the present and the future as we surrender ourselves in deeper discipleship to Him who is our Saviour and Lord, dedicating ourselves to

WITNESS

to the saving power of Jesus Christ our Lord
to the unity of all believers in Christ
to the Gospel of peace and reconciliation through Jesus Christ
to the priesthood of all believers

to the growing multitudes in our cities
to all who have not heard the Gospel
to each succeeding generation

against the spirit of materialism of this age
against the spirit of exclusivism in our fellowship
against the spirit of division in the Christian Church
against the rising tide of moral laxity

through personal evangelism
through the witness of the printed page
through our institutions of higher learning and all conference institutions
through the efforts of the conference in the area of Christian service

by reaffirming our faith in the inspiration and authority of the Scriptures
by dedicating ourselves anew as disciples of Christ
by living a life of dedicated stewardship
by keeping open our hearts to the regenerative and sanctifying work of the
Holy Spirit
by strengthening the Christian family
by manifesting concern over social evils of our culture
by a prophetic witness to state and society.

These goals represented dedication to greater faithfulness. A spirit of repentance and hope was evident at the study conference which adopted them. This was not unusual since self-criticism had been common in the General Conference from the beginning. At its best this critical self-awareness had represented an openness to the leading of the Holy Spirit and the kind of looseness to tradition which made change possible with a minimum of threat. There had also been real freedom of discussion and expression. At times, however, this self-critical tendency became a sign of insecurity and lack of conviction about reasons for the continuing existence of the conference. Because of the variety of ethnic backgrounds of the congregations, self-criticism also reflected a certain lack of unity within the conference itself, fostered in no small measure by outside influences to which General Conference people have been particularly open because of their polity, doctrine, and their desire to be relevant to the needs of the world in which they lived. Nevertheless, guilt and repentance were signs of spiritual health. Repentance has been the first requirement for renewal of the church in every age.

As indicated earlier, the General Conference was from the beginning committed to the necessity of education for the continuing personal and congregational growth in faith and discipleship. In spite of this conviction there were many failures to counter positively, through a dynamic program of Christian nurture, the pressure of the secular and the religious environment upon young and old alike. There occurred what might be called a dilution of the historic and Biblical faith, with a consequent shift in values and loyalties. The coming of World War II (1939-45), for example, showed how the teaching of Biblical nonresistance had been neglected by the churches, in that one half of the young men of draft age rejected that position. The congregations which were less conformed to their socio-religious environment, however, and lived primarily in rural areas with large Mennonite centers, had a better record, particularly in Canada and the American Middle West.

A remarkable strengthening of the educational program occurred in the twenty years following that period. In cooperation with other Mennonite groups attractive and well-written study materials were prepared for all ages of primary Sunday schools. A Mennonite Boys' League for ages nine to eleven and twelve to fourteen was organized and quickly adopted by many congregations. Each of the districts of the conference established one or more retreat camps with an active summer and, in a few cases, all-year-round program, the effects of which were soon felt in a new depth of faith and commitments of many of the attendants. A conference-wide Young People's Union (YPU) gave program and project inspiration to the local YPU groups; a Student Services program aimed at establishing contact with all General Conference college and graduate students, of which there were approximately 1,000 in conference schools in 1964 and nearly twice that number in non-conference institutions, many of them in graduate schools.

This recovery of interest and vision naturally led to increased financial and student support for the conference-related Bible schools, high schools, and colleges. There were four Bible schools: Bethel in British Columbia, Menno in Alberta, Swift Current in Saskatchewan, and Elim in Manitoba. The three high schools were also in Canada: Rosthern Junior College in Saskatchewan, Mennonite Collegiate Institute in Manitoba, and the United Mennonite Educational Institute in Ontario. The Canadian Mennonite Bible College opened its doors with a four-year program in Winnipeg in 1947. Two four-year colleges, Bethel at North Newton, Kansas, and Bluffton in Bluffton, Ohio, became increasingly significant in the educational task of the conference, as did the Junior College and Academy at Freeman, South Dakota. In 1945 the conference opened the doors of Mennonite Biblical Seminary in Chicago, relocating in 1958 to Elkhart, Indiana, in order to work together with the (Old) Mennonites and others in the training of Christian workers.

There were other signs of new life and vigor in the conference. As the hundreds of men who had been forced to think about their faith in the Civilian Public Service (CPS) camps of World War II returned home, they brought new conviction and zeal to the work of the church. Soon these were joined by a constant stream of young men and women who had spent two or more years abroad in service under the Mennonite Central Committee (MCC), either as relief or voluntary service (VS) workers, or under Pax or Teachers Abroad Program (TAP). In their work they had rubbed shoulders with other

Mennonite and non-Mennonite Christians, they had seen the depth of human misery everywhere, and they had seen the power of faith. There was hardly a congregation in the conference which did not have one or more young persons serving abroad or in VS at home in any given year. This confrontation with the physical and spiritual needs of humanity invariably changed these persons, and when they returned they helped to inspire those who had stayed at home. Never had a ˙church given more opportunities for witness and service to its members than the Mennonite Church after World War II. It was clear these persons could not have worked abroad except for the sacrificial giving of the congregations and frequently also parents and families who undertook real hardship to let their young people go.

In all of these activities the local worshiping congregation continued to be the heart of the conference life, providing an increasing number of workers and growing financial support. There still seemed to be a shortage of both, however. While these congregations continued to cherish their autonomy and occasionally reversed tendencies to centralization, there was increasing cooperation among them, and a growing reliance upon District and General Conference administrators for program and other help. Worship patterns continued largely as in the past, usually under the leadership of trained and salaried ministers, except in Canada where the lay ministry was being retained in many congregations. Preaching seemed to be Biblically based, though more topical and inspirational than exegetical and didactic. The role of lay people in the church was being stressed vigorously. Baptisms were usually performed at Pentecost, though some were establishing a year-round membership class with baptism whenever a believer was ready for it. The age of baptism also seemed to be rising slightly after having sunk to fourteen and even thirteen years, except in Canada where it continued to remain sixteen or over in most congregations. Midweek Bible study and prayer meetings continued, but attendance was generally weak. The Sunday morning church school, on the other hand, continued strong on all levels. A slow but continuing increase in membership was being experienced. By 1960 some 11.5 percent of the members in the five United States district conferences had been born to non-Mennonite parents.

There were continuing problems, of course. The growth in membership was still slow and some members were constantly being lost to other churches or to secularism. Urbanization was proceeding so rapidly that only 30 percent of General Conference people in the United States were farming in 1960, and this occupational mobility brought many changes to the churches and the demands upon them. The materialism of the American-Canadian environment was constantly tempting the faithful to conform to its selfish standards. With the increased understanding among Mennonites came the question of the nature of the unity that should be sought. Voices were even being heard that the conference had fulfilled its calling and should now be dissolved to merge with other Mennonite groups. In a way, however, the recognition of these problems, and the openness with which they were being faced, were an encouraging sign of the continuing power of the Holy Spirit at work among the churches.

*Notes*
1. S. F. Pannabecker, *The Development of the General Conference of the Mennonite Church of North America in the American Environment.* Unpublished PhD dissertation, Yale University, 1944, p. 204.
2. J. C. Wenger, quoted in "General Conference Mennonite Church." *The Mennonite Encyclopedia,* II, p. 465.
3. Pannabecker, p. 219.
4. E. G. Kaufman, *The Development of the Missionary and Philanthropic Interest Among the Mennonites of North America.* Berne, Indiana: Mennonite Book Concern, 1931, p. 103.

*FOR FURTHER READING:*

*The Mennonite Encyclopedia,* 4 vols.

*Mennonite Life* 2 (April, 1947), pp. 29-34, 37-43; 6 (April, 1951), pp. 16-19; 15 (April, 1960); 18 (April, 1963).

The papers of the Study Conferences held since 1953, and available from the conference offices at 722 Main Street, Newton, Kansas.

H. P. Krehbiel, *The History of the General Conference of the Mennonites of North America,* 2 vols. Newton: Mennonite Publication Office, 1898 and 1938.

# Chapter 15

## THE MENNONITE BRETHREN CHURCH

ALTHOUGH spiritual life was at a low ebb in the Mennonite colonies of South Russia, there were strong influences for renewal also, as we have seen in Chapter 10. The sermons of Ludwig Hofacker were read by many ministers in private as well as in public meetings. These sermons were not spectacular in style but stressed the need for repentance and forgiveness. Tobias Voth, the first teacher of the Ohrloff high school, manifested strong pietistic leanings also and organized evening services, mission fellowships, and youth meetings.

The village of Gnadenfeld, which had been influenced by Moravian pietism in Germany, began observing harvest-thanksgiving Sundays annually at which particular emphasis was given to the subject of missions. Preachers from surrounding non-Mennonite churches were sometimes invited to speak at these occasions, among them Eduard Wüst, a Lutheran pietist serving a nearby separatist Lutheran church. Wüst was a dynamic speaker, with strong convictions, stressing free grace and holy living. His style and message presented a sharp contrast to the more unassuming, conventional preaching of the Mennonite ministry and led many Mennonites to a conversion experience, following which they witnessed to their faith in a free and open manner.

Under the influence of these pietistic brethren, lay evangelism was introduced into the villages from Gnadenfeld. House visitations were made and meetings held in homes to which unbelievers could be invited. Larger prayer and Bible study meetings were initiated on

Saturday afternoons in order not to conflict with the regular Sunday worship services. Pastor Wüst was present at many of these meetings, usually assuming responsibility for preaching and teaching if he could come.

Many of the elders in the church appreciated Wüst's message. Even August Lenzmann, an influential elder at Gnadenfeld, expressed his willingness to cooperate with Wüst. When criticism was expressed over the extreme emotionalism in the group meetings, Lenzmann defended Wüst by attributing the deviations to a misunderstanding of the nature of free grace. This criticism was, however, confirmed by P. M. Friesen when he wrote that "Sanctification, to which he [Wüst ] referred and which he earnestly practiced, was not preached in a systematic way nor was it in proper relationship to his joyful and evangelical sermons of grace."

Wüst died in 1859, but his conventicle groups continued to meet. Since they addressed each other as Brother, they came to be known as the Brethren. Increasingly they became discouraged with the opposition of many of the leaders in the church and charged them with unspirituality. This, in turn, led to estrangement and separation, which prevented the new spirit from working its way into the church as a whole. With the growing separation, the new group felt drawn more closely to each other and this encouraged them to observe the Lord's Supper together late in 1859 under the leadership of Abraham Cornelsen, a schoolteacher. Since none of the church elders had been present, this procedure was considered highly irregular and calls for discipline were heard. Elder Lenzmann consequently invited the offenders to a hearing, at which six of the brethren promised to refrain from further irregularities, pledging obedience to all things not contrary to their conscience and the Word of God.

Elder Lenzmann and other ministers in Gnadenfeld were, however, deeply concerned for reconciliation and worked to this end. Their efforts were thwarted by the demands of the church majority that private communion services must be discontinued, while the Brethren insisted they could no longer have fellowship with the entire membership of the large church. On January 6, 1860, the Brethren met in a private home to discuss the possibility of organizing a separate fellowship of believers. A document, addressed to the elders of the church, had been drawn up by Abraham Cornelsen and was considered carefully. Attention was called to the persecution which might follow formal separation. A prayer session followed. Finally, toward evening, the document was laid on the table and signed by eighteen of those present, several of those present refraining, however. Of these, nine added their signatures two days later.

The document accused the church of being in a state of growing corruption and its leaders of tolerating this condition of spiritual decay. There seemed to be little quarrel over doctrine, the primary concern centering around moral and ethical laxity among church members. The statement consciously stood for historic Anabaptism-Mennonitism in its discussion of baptism, communion, foot washing, election of ministers, church discipline, and other issues. In addition to the signatures, the document named a committee of three who had been appointed as spokesmen for the new group.

The signers of the document could hardly have anticipated the results which would follow immediately. Since the elders either refused to admit the moral and spiritual decay charged to the church, or were defensive about it, the document was considered a serious attack against them and the establishment. Consequently, at a meeting of elders on January 18, a statement was drafted which placed the entire matter into the hands of the civil authority in the colony, the *Gebietsamt,* i.e., the state. This statement was signed by five elders, several others saying they needed "more light on the matter." It was clear that the five wanted the new group to be disciplined by force in order, as the statement said, "to bring them back from the error of their ways."

In thus turning a religious issue into a state, *viz.*, colony matter, the elders did what the Anabaptists had experienced so harshly at the hands of the establishment in the sixteenth century, they identified the cause of the church with that of the state. But this violated a very basic conviction of the Anabaptists, who rejected the jurisdiction of the state in matters of faith. Not all of the elders were in agreement with the action of the five. Even before the January 18 meeting, the Ohrloff-Halbstadt church council had pleaded for tolerance and urged that efforts should not be directed against the new group but against the evils they were criticizing. Many were troubled by the issue but seemed unable to do anything about it; little was known about the entire problem in the two colonies on the Volga River.

Meanwhile the colony administration accepted the responsibility given to it by the elders and asked the Brethren for an explanation. In their response of January 23, they declared that they would gladly have remained in the church, but since the ministers were not obedient to the Word of God, they felt compelled to leave. They also declared

211

their intention to remain Mennonites. The colony administration, however, invoked Article 362 of the Penal Code of 1857, which dealt with secret societies, against the Brethren. Religious meetings not sponsored by the established church were forbidden. But physical suffering followed. P. M. Friesen speaks of "continuous examinations, threats, imprisonments, sentences to hard labor, and starvation." Abraham Cornelsen, the father of a large family, was banished from the colony and spent a long time among one of the surrounding nomadic tribes. Others were ruined economically. Since legal travel documents were denied them, the Brethren were unable to leave the colony, yet staying became unbearable.

The revival which began in the Molotschna Colony had its counterpart in the Chortitza Colony, though the two movements were not related at first. Church conditions were no better in the one colony than in the other, and provided ample room for criticism. Unfortunately the Chortitza movement, centering in the village of Kronsweide, embodied emotional excesses which led to a false freedom and to immorality which, of course, brought further disrepute upon the movement. In the village of Einlage, however, sanity prevailed and the renewal group there disassociated itself from the others. It appears that the Einlage group was influenced by the German Baptists through periodicals which they had been receiving from them. In spite of these distinctions, the Brethren in Chortiza had as hard a time of it as those in the other colony. Wilhelm Janzen was given ten lashes and jailed in an unheated room, while his overcoat was taken from him.

### Early Organization and Recognition

One of the first problems which faced the Brethren was a lack of strong leadership. On May 30, 1860, an election of ministers was held by the Molotschna group. Three of them immediately disqualified themselves for office, though they had seemed likely candidates, because they had earlier given a promise to the Inspector of Colonies not to organize a church without official permission. Consequently Heinrich Huebert and Jacob Becker were elected and ordained three days later. While there are no official records of the ordination itself, unofficial reports indicate that the oldest member of the group, Franz Klassen, upon the request of the others, laid his hands on the two candidates and, with earnest prayer, dedicated them to the ministry of the church. Though the elders had been invited to the ordination service, none were present. The historian P. M. Friesen considered this election and ordination to constitute the official organization of the Mennonite Brethren Church.

Now began a long struggle for official government recognition of the new group, which would force the Mennonites to also recognize them. Failing this, they stood in danger of losing all of their special privileges as Mennonites. Repeated trips to St. Petersburg showed the government to be both friendly and helpful, and contact was also made with the Baptists. The colonies, on the other hand, tried to prevent the government from granting the desired recognition and identified them as no longer being Mennonites but "a new sect." At home the Molotschna colony administrator asked the elders to choose between two options for the new group: expulsion from the colony or recognition, apparently hoping thereby to prepare the way for the first option to be implemented. Meanwhile the Brethren had also presented a petition to the Czar in the spring of 1862.

A break came in the tense situation through the leadership of the well-known teacher and minister Johann Harder (Chapter 10). In a letter of November 12, 1862, to the colony administration he wrote:

Following the general conference held on the 11th of October, 1862, in the colony administration building, in which the administrator proposed that the Mennonites which had left the corrupt churches be either banished from the colony or recognized as a congregation with equal rights; our congregation, having had the matter presented to them, declared that since the former is not scriptural, it is willing to accept the latter on the condition that their confession of faith, should they be asked for the same, be in accordance, essentially, with ours.

As a result of our request the seceders have declared in writing that the *Confession of Faith of the So-Called United Flemish, Frisian, and High German Anabaptist Mennonite Church*, published by the congregation of Rudnerweide, South Russia, was their own. Consequently, nothing hinders the Ohrloff-Halbstadt congregation from recognizing the Mennonites in question as an independent congregation of which I now, according to our verbal agreement, wish to inform the colony administration.

This recognition was a direct challenge to the five elders who had signed the objection, and they drafted a lengthy reply. In it they accused the Brethren of acting without the sanction of ordained leadership, particularly in observing communion. The reply further referred to improper conduct in the meetings of the Brethren and to the practice of rebaptizing persons who had already been baptized in the Mennonite Church. A last attempt to suppress the movement was made by the administration of the colony late in

213

1863, by ordering village officials not to recognize marriages performed by the Brethren, and to record the children of such marriages under the mother's name as in the case of illegitimate births. This instruction roused the Brethren to send a petition to the government, which was answered on March 5, 1864, with the coveted official government recognition that they were still considered Mennonites in the full sense of the word.

The period of litigation had come to an end, but the division remained. Bitterness and strife continued for a time, but gradually church leaders of both groups again began working together in matters of common interest to them all.

### Doctrine and Church Government

*Baptism:* The question of the mode of baptism was not an issue for the first group of Brethren; the original document had simply stressed the importance of believer's baptism. Jacob Reimer, one of the signers, had, however, come to question sprinkling or pouring as a Biblical mode already in 1837. As an eighteen-year-old, before his baptism, he had read the biography of Anna Judson and had expressed the desire to be baptized by immersion. When he asked whether there were still people who baptized by immersion, his father answered that he had known such people in Prussia.

The first baptism by immersion occurred in the Molotschna Colony in September, 1860. The memoirs of Jacob Becker, one of two baptized at that time, throws some light onto the developments which led to the introduction of the practice of immersion in the Mennonite Brethren Church. He writes:

We knew nothing of immersion until the first Sunday in September, 1860, when two sisters who had not been baptized in the Mennonite Church applied for baptism. After the church had examined them, I received the charge to baptize them. Then brother Johann Claassen came to me and asked me: "According to which form do you intend to baptize?" He went on to say: "The way the church baptizes is not scriptural." These were strange words to me.

Claassen then gave Becker a pamphlet on baptism which he studied carefully and gave to his neighbor, Heinrich Bartel. From it both received the conviction that they themselves would need to be baptized before they could baptize others. Fearful lest the elders would interpret this as proof that they were indeed introducing a new religious fellowship, they read the works of Menno Simons to see whether he confessed baptism in water. Becker found a reference

214

in which Menno stated that although the mode of baptism had changed several times since the apostolic age, it had originally been in running water. From this the Brethren concluded that they were in agreement with Menno and that they now had good historical backing for immersion, while still remaining Mennonites.

When Becker brought his convictions to the attention of the Brethren, many agreed with him, and it was decided that he should baptize the women by immersion. He himself, however, felt that he would first need to be immersed, before he could so baptize others. Consequently he writes:

On a day of the second week of September, a wagon load of Brethren drove to the water. First, we knelt by the water in prayer. Then we stepped into the water. Jacob Becker baptized brother Bartel, and then Bartel baptized Becker. The latter then baptized three sisters by immersing them backwards three times.

The early Brethren did not make immersion obligatory for those who had already been baptized by sprinkling or pouring in the Mennonite Church. Heinrich Huebert, one of the eighteen and later the first minister and elder of the church, was rebaptized in May, 1861, the year following his election as a minister. Johann Claassen, who was always highly recognized among the Brethren, was not baptized until June 30, 1862.

Early Mennonite Brethren historians note the fact that the conviction to baptize by immersion came to them independent of direct Baptist influence from the outside. However, since Johann Claassen had been in fellowship with the Baptists in St. Petersburg, it is quite possible that they influenced him in his understanding of the Scriptures at this point. In the Chortitza Colony the question of baptism emerged later, after Abraham Unger, a leader among the Brethren, had corresponded with a German Baptist minister in Hamburg. Eventually the insistence upon immersion as a prerequisite for membership also came from Chortitza, where the Einlage group made immersion a requirement for participation in communion. The churches in the Molotschna Colony were more tolerant on this issue, and until 1863, it was still possible for non-immersed persons to fellowship with the church. However, the advocates of immersion as a prerequisite for membership and the proponents of close communion were finally successful in establishing these practices in the church.

*Extremism is overcome:* Meanwhile the emotional excesses referred to earlier were leading to a crisis in the young movement. Members involved in this overenthusiasm, which came to be known as the

215

*fröhliche Richtung* (joyous movement), called themselves the "happy" ones, and "strong" ones. Several of the leading men were drawn into this circle, though Elder Heinrich Huebert was a staunch opponent and declared it unbiblical. The moderates, however, were unable to stem the tide of emotionalism and soon leadership fell to the radicals both in Chortitza and Molotschna. Those who did not participate in the movement were excommunicated. All social contacts were forbidden to the elect, and even the greeting of a relative on the street was considered to be fellowship with the world.

Johann Claassen, who was in St. Petersburg at this time, wrote strong and pleading letters to these new leaders, but without effect. By spring, 1862, their excesses reached tragic proportions. The doctrine of "liberty in Christ" was interpreted to mean that all usual proprieties between men and women could now be disregarded. The saved, after all, were free from the flesh. This attitude led one of the radicals to engage in sexual immorality. He was excommunicated by his own group, and the case served as a deterrent to the entire radical movement among the Brethren.

In June, 1865, five brotherhood meetings were held and a sixth one on August 4. One meeting, begun on Saturday afternoon, lasted throughout the night. The following day, Sunday, was observed as a day of repentance and prayer. Letters of repentance were written to church and government leaders. And so ended a most unfortunate and shameful chapter in the early development of the Mennonite Brethren Church.

*Baptist influence:* During these early years the inexperienced Brethren often turned to their Baptist contacts for help and counsel, those in the Chortitza Colony being particularly open to them. It was natural, therefore, that Abraham Unger should write to Hamburg for counsel in connection with the extremist problem, from where the Baptist August Liebig arrived to help them in the spring of 1866. Finding the Chortitza Brethren somewhat bewildered and disorganized, he began to preach and to organize brotherhood meetings to bring order into the movement.

Many of the Brethren were opposed to formal organization of any kind, lest it hinder the free work of the Holy Spirit, but Liebig served as chairman of the meetings and took the opportunity to show them parliamentary procedure. Minutes were also kept at his request. After two weeks' stay, however, the authorities arrested him and deported him back to Germany, but even in that brief time he had given invaluable aid and counsel to the Brethren.

Unger stayed in touch with him by letter, and in 1869 the Baptists sent J. G. Oncken to South Russia to organize the scattered Baptist groups. A special meeting was called for October 18, 1869, at which meeting Oncken ordained Unger as elder, Aron Lepp as minister, and two men as deacons. The Molotschna Brethren also desired Oncken's services, but the aging minister was anxious to return to Germany before winter set in.

Oncken's visit proved to be a mixed blessing. He stimulated the Brethren spiritually, and helped to organize them further. But he smoked, and his influence inspired several of the Brethren to follow his example. Also, since he was a Baptist, many considered those who had been ordained by him to be Baptists as well. Furthermore, he seems to have had a negative influence upon the traditionally Mennonite belief in Biblical nonresistance. The anti-Oncken group finally won, and the ordained men were considered still to be Mennonites. The brethren who smoked were excommunicated. The Brethren continued to cherish fellowship with the Baptists but favored organizational separation from them. They had chosen to remain Mennonites and were not to be deterred from this decision.

*Allianz Gemeinde:* Very little genuine fellowship existed between the Mennonite Brethren and other Mennonites. With the growing convictions about immersion and close communion an increasing rigidity led to exclusivism and consequently isolation. After the crisis of emotionalism had passed, Johann Claassen and Jacob Reimer ceased to be very influential, and a new set of leaders emerged. Many of them were limited in their theological understanding and carried the pure church concept to such extremities that fellowship with other Christians was impossible. A reaction came to this in the *Allianz* or alliance movement.

There were other Brethren in addition to Claassen and Reimer who favored wider contacts than the new leadership wanted. One of them was Christian Schmidt, an evangelist sometimes called "the Wüst of the Mennonite Brethren." Schmidt worked toward fellowship with all true believers, irrespective of their church affiliation. At one of the annual conferences of the Brethren several of these ecumenically-minded persons announced their intention to practice open communion, and the service was held in 1899. The repercussions were almost immediate, and the congregation of which the evangelist Jacob W. Reimer was a member was asked to discipline him by the others. But the congregation loved Reimer and refused to do this.

As this spirit of tolerance spread, a group of the Brethren met on May 16, 1905, to organize the "Molotschna Evangelical Mennonite Brethren Church," a fellowship dedicated to serve all Mennonite believers, regardless of the mode of baptism practiced by them. The group soon came to be known as the *Allianz Gemeinde*, i.e., alliance or unifying church. Its single requirement for membership was the new birth, and this also meant open communion. Immersion was practiced, but members who had been baptized by another mode were not required to submit to immersion. The office of elder was abolished. In one way this group represented another division, but in another it served as a wholesome corrective to Mennonite Brethren exclusiveness, constituting a bridge between the Mennonite Brethren and the other Mennonite churches. After the migration to America in the 1920's most of the members of this group joined Mennonite Brethren congregations. Those who migrated to Brazil joined the congregations of the General Conference Mennonite Church, while those in Paraguay have remained independent.

*Krimmer [Crimea] Mennonite Brethren:* Another group born in the midst of revival and closely related to the Mennonite Brethren Church in thought and practice was the Krimmer [Crimea] Mennonite Brethren Church (KMB). The village of Annafeld in the Crimea experienced a revival, and Jacob A. Wiebe was converted. A potential leader, Wiebe became a dominant figure in the new movement. He had had previous contacts with the *Kleine Gemeinde* (see Chapter 10), and had been impressed by their piety, and so invited Elder Johann Friesen to visit Annafeld and to organize the new group into a *Kleine Gemeinde* congregation. This was done in 1867, with Wiebe as its first minister.

Since many of the members had been baptized before experiencing a conversion, the question of rebaptism was raised. Elder Friesen would not condone a second baptism; so the group commissioned one of its own brethren to baptize Wiebe, who in turn baptized eighteen others, on September 21, 1869. The group chose the name *Brudergemeinde* (Brethren Church) and, to distinguish it from the other Mennonite Brethren, added the geographical designation *Krimmer,* i.e., from the Crimea. The contacts with those other Mennonite Brethren, however, were few, though they agreed doctrinally except on immersion, which the new group practiced kneeling and immersing forwards. Rigorous austerity in dress and life, coupled with strict church discipline, marked the KMB's even more than the Mennonite Brethren.

With the immigrants of the 1870's, which have been described earlier, were also numerous Mennonite Brethren and KMB families. One of the first of these was Peter Eckert, a Mennonite Brethren elder who arrived in Kansas in 1875, bringing a number of families with him. The group was of Lutheran background and had become Mennonite through the early revivals and evangelistic efforts which followed 1860. Eckert was a tolerant and open-minded Christian and, therefore, made an attempt to form one group with the KMB families who had located nearby in the village of Gnadenau, fourteen miles northwest of Peabody, in Marion County, but they preferred to remain separate.

In 1876 some seventy-five additional families arrived from Russia. Although the majority were from the Volga area, a number had also come from the Kuban and Chortitza colonies. Those from the Volga and the Kuban settlements immediately joined Eckert's group, but the Chortitza families remained separate. The reason for this seems to have been the close feelings not shared by the others. From 1874 to 1880 a total of approximately 200 Mennonite Brethren families came to the Middle West, including Elder Abraham Schellenberg of the Molotschna, who exerted a very stabilizing influence in the new settlements.

After these congregations had become established, a general desire was expressed for the organization of a conference of local churches. The first meeting for this purpose was called by Peter Regier and eleven delegates representing the churches in Kansas and Nebraska. Because of inadequate representation and decisions made which later conferences could not approve, this meeting has not been accepted as an official conference. The first official conference was held in Henderson, Nebraska, in 1879. From that time on they were held annually until 1909, and triennially thereafter.

There were also Mennonite Brethren families among the 8,000 immigrants who settled in Manitoba in the 1870's migration, as well as *Kleine Gemeinde* and KMB's. Four years after the first Mennonite Brethren conference in 1879, Heinrich Voth of Minnesota was sent to Manitoba to evangelize among these Mennonites, with the help of David Dyck, one of the immigrants. The first converts coming from this work were baptized at Burwalde, near Winkler in Manitoba, in 1886. Later, Gerhard Wiebe, an immigrant of 1888, was supported by the conference in an evangelistic ministry. The first congregation was organized at Burwalde, with smaller congregations organized at Plum Coulee in 1897 and Kronsgart in 1898. From these centers workers were sent to Saskatchewan, where congregations were established in Rosthern and Herbert.

By 1900 membership in the Mennonite Brethren churches in North America was a little over 2,000. Annual conferences made it possible for them to carry on projects in missions, evangelism, and literature. In 1903, the conference delegates were asked to consider the possibility of dividing the total constituency into district conferences which could convene annually, and to have the entire conference meet every three years. No agreement was reached, however, and the question was tabled. Meanwhile a constitution was written, and accepted in 1908. The following year the projected division was carried out with the establishing of the Southern, Central, and Northern District conferences. At the 1911 conference in Rosedale, California, the Pacific District was added as a fourth conference.

The migration of the 1920's brought many additional Mennonite Brethren families to Canada and, from 1930 on, also to Paraguay and Brazil in South America. Those settling in Canada soon established strong congregations in the Prairie Provinces and, after the depression forced many to move to British Columbia and Ontario, also in those provinces. On the prairies, Winnipeg emerged as the largest urban concentration of Mennonites, including the Mennonite Brethren, where many became leaders in business and a wide variety of the professions.

On June 9, 1930, a group of fifty-five brethren met in the village of Gnadenheim, Fernheim Colony, Paraguay, to organize the Mennonite Brethren Church in that land. Leaders in this movement were Heinrich Pauls and Gerhard Giesbrecht. The newly organized group adopted the constitution they had brought along from Russia. With the founding of Friesland Colony in Paraguay in 1937, active Mennonite Brethren congregations were established in that area also, under the leadership of Kornelius Voth. When more settlers arrived after World War II, the Volendam Mennonite Brethren Church was organized in 1947 and the one at Neuland Colony in 1948.

The first Mennonites to settle in Brazil arrived in January, 1930. An intimate relationship was maintained among the Mennonite Brethren, Evangelical Mennonite Brethren, and Mennonite churches. However, efforts to organize a united Mennonite Church failed and the Mennonite Brethren Church was officially organized in the Krauel Valley under the leadership of Elder Jakob Huebert. Several Mennonite Brethren churches were then organized in other districts. The district around Curitiba had attracted many Mennonite settlers from the Krauel and the Bougueirao Mennonite Brethren Church was organized, with Peter Hamm as its leader. Later, the churches at Guarituba and Neu-Witmarsum were established; also, the churches of Villa Guarira and Xaxim. One of the larger Mennonite Brethren churches in Brazil is the Bagé church, founded in 1949 in the province of Rio Grande do Sul. Smaller congregations now exist at Blumenau, Saltobach, and Sao Paulo.

Several Mennonite Brethren churches have been established in Uruguay as well. The first church was organized in 1950, among the immigrants coming there directly from the Danzig and Prussian settlements which had been abandoned. Congregations were later also established at Gartental and Montevideo.

According to the official statistics for 1963, the total number of members in North and South America was 29,914. An even larger membership had grown up through missionary activity, until the Younger Churches added 32,199 to the American figures for a world total membership of 62,113. Included in this total were the KMB's, who had merged with the Mennonite Brethren Conference in 1960.

*Distinctive Characteristics*

While Mennonite Brethren stand fully in the Anabaptist tradition together with the other Mennonite groups, the following characteristics may be pointed up as distinctive in emphasis and spirit, not as differences in basic doctrine. [1]

*Bible-centeredness:* Frequent Bible study sessions with discussion of Biblical passages have given directives to Mennonite Brethren for faith and life. They have often resulted in mutually binding covenants and have thus given direction to daily living and corrective discipline. These Bible studies, rather than preaching services, have frequently led visiting inquirers to receive Christ.

*Personal conversion:* Definite decision with reference to receiving God's redeeming grace is the prerequisite to Mennonite Brethren church membership. This represents a different course than entry into the church through mastery of a catechism. The converted can usually state time, place, and specific insight into God's Word in reference to the turning point. This is followed by a public confession of this experience and baptism by immersion.

221

*Discipleship and church membership:* Practical holiness was no new teaching for the nineteenth-century Mennonites of Russia. But there was laxity in emphasizing actual, loving, corrective discipline of the spiritually sick. The Mennonite Brethren insisted then and now that "new life" within the "re-born" is shown by a new sense of direction through the dictates of the Holy Spirit. Discipleship implies that the brethren place themselves in a corrective discipline toward each other within the church—a willingness to receive and to give exhortation. This entire spiritual transformation means a refusal to be molded by world goals and ambitions. Christ-directed goals and ambitions hold supremacy.

*Missions:* From the beginning, Mennonite Brethren have held the missionary mandate to be obligatory for all Christians. Disciples are called to use whatever gifts they have to bring people into living fellowship with Christ and the church. A result of this orientation is the fact that more than one half of the conference membership is outside North America today. At present, more than 200 Mennonite Brethren are evangelizing in countries other than their own. In addition, more than 700 are giving their full time to missionary and related causes as they build and establish churches in their own country. Each of the approximately 600 churches in the world increasingly considers itself a mission post for contacting the unreached. Members are encouraged to regard themselves as Christ's ambassadors in areas where they live and work in their daily routine.

*Freedom of spiritual expression:* An open sharing in the warmth of brotherly fellowship is encouraged by Mennonite Brethren in expressions of testimony, prayer, aspirations, calls for intercession, and new insights from God's Word. There is a closeness of clergy and laity. Lay ministers have often been elected from the body of the congregation. Qualifications have included not only knowledge of the Scriptures and leadership ability, but also—primarily—spiritual qualities evident in their daily lives, in their dealings with people and situations.

*Cooperation in Christian concerns:* In the first decades, the Mennonite Brethren of Russia participated with Baptists in a missionary program in India. Similar cooperation has continued through the years. Today, in Japan, India, the Congo, Paraguay, Brazil, Peru, Colombia, and Israel, Mennonite Brethren cooperate in one or more areas of missionary endeavor with various evangelical agencies. Some conference-supported missionaries serve under interchurch administration.

222

The North American Mennonite Brethren are associated with the Evangelical Foreign Missions Association and with the National Association of Evangelicals. A part of their ministry of compassion to the world's needy is channeled, along with that of other Mennonite groups, through the Mennonite Central Committee. In local areas, churches associate themselves with evangelicals in social concerns, service, outreach, and witness.

It is true that these high goals and vision have often not been reached. The vision, however, is still there. It is there to give renewed perspective to the mission that Mennonite Brethren feel God has given them to accomplish. While the particular emphases outlined are not peculiar to this group, the combination of these emphases in one body is unique and represents the thrust that continues as the prayerful aspiration of the Mennonite Brethren.

## The Present Witness

The present *Constitution* of the conference divides it into three area conferences: Canada, United States, and South America. The European area conference has been organized but does not yet function as a part of the total conference. Other area conferences are expected to join as soon as they feel ready to do so.

The first missionary to be sent out by the congregations in North America was N. N. Hiebert, who went to India in 1899. Today the work of missions includes Brazil, Colombia, Paraguay, and Peru in South America; Mexico, and work among the Latin people of Texas, in North America; sixty-two church centers are active in the Republic of Congo in Africa; ninety church centers in India, and nine in Japan. Five churches in Germany and Austria comprise the European outreach. The total missionary force in 1963 numbered 242, with an annual budget of over three-quarter million dollars.

The Mennonite Brethren began publication activities in 1884, when the conference elected a committee of three to arrange for the editing and printing of a church paper, the *Zionsbote*. This paper was published in German until January 1, 1965, when it was discontinued. *The Christian Leader* was first published in English as a monthly periodical (1936-48) and since 1948 twice a month. In Canada the German family paper, *Die Mennonitische Rundschau,* originally founded by John F. Funk, as we saw in Chapter 10, is published by the Christian Press of Winnipeg, a publication house owned by the Canadian area conference. *The Mennonite*

*Brethren Herald* is the English language Canadian periodical. Two publishing houses serve the Mennonite Brethren: the Mennonite Brethren Publishing House in Hillsboro, Kansas, and the Christian Press in Winnipeg, Manitoba. The Mennonite Brethren of South America cooperate in the publishing of the *Menno-Blatt*.

The United States area conference presently supports Tabor College in Hillsboro, Kansas, a four-year liberal arts institution founded in 1908. Pacific College in Fresno, California, an outgrowth of the Pacific Bible Institute, is also a four-year liberal arts school. Both institutions have been accredited by their respective regional accreditation associations. The Mennonite Brethren Biblical Seminary was established in Fresno, California, in 1955 and presently serves the United States area conference as a training school for ministers and missionaries. The Mennonite Brethren Bible College of Winnipeg, Manitoba, was founded in 1944 as a Canadian area school. In 1961, the arts division of the Bible College was affiliated with Waterloo Lutheran University, a chartered degree-granting university in Waterloo, Ontario.

Relief and welfare activities are carried out through the General Conference Board of General Welfare and Public Relations. In its foreign relief effort the conference is affiliated with the Mennonite Central Committee.

*Notes*
1. Adapted from "The Story of the Mennonite Brethren Church" pamphlet. Used by permission.

*FOR FURTHER READING:*

*The Mennonite Encyclopedia*, 4 vols.

*Mennonite Life* 14 (October, 1959), pp. 176-78.

John H. Lohrenz, *The Mennonite Brethren Church*. Hillsboro, Kansas: The Mennonite Brethren Publishing House, 1950.

Delbert Wiens, *New Wineskins for Old Wine*. Hillsboro: Mennonite Brethren Publishing House, 1965.

*Chapter 16*


## THE SMALLER MENNONITE
## AND RELATED GROUPS
## IN NORTH AMERICA


IN ADDITION to the three larger Mennonite groups and the Amish, which have been discussed in the preceding four chapters, there are other branches of the Anabaptist-Mennonite family tree which need to be known for a proper understanding of the legacy of sixteenth-century Anabaptism in our day. Attention has already been given to the origins of the Hutterites in Chapter 4 and to the *Kleine Gemeinde* in Chapter 10. The latter changed their name to Evangelical Mennonite Church in 1952, and in 1959 to Evangelical Mennonite Conference. The total baptized membership of these smaller Mennonite groups in North America is approximately 41,000 including those in Mexico and British Honduras but not the Bergthal Church, which is part of the Conference of Mennonites in Canada. This is roughly one fifth of the total baptized membership of the Mennonite churches in North America. The four Mennonite-related groups to be discussed in this chapter totaled approximately 36,400 members in 1964.

The uniqueness of these smaller groups will be seen in the following brief discussion of their historical development and present emphasis. Often the specific emphasis of a group arose in response to the particular cultural and geographical environment in which it found itself, rather than in a negative response to what other Mennonites were saying. Other differences emerged from the variety of ways in which congregations in the same environment responded to the same challenge because they were independent and free to act as they thought best. Different leaders also had different visions for the church, and obedience meant different things to them depending on their background, character, and use of the Scriptures. To some obedience meant the establishing of communities which were isolated from the world either by geographical location or by language and other cultural barriers. In time this isolation obviously had its effect on their life and thought. To other groups obedience meant going into the world with the good news, and the ensuing influence of their environment often changed them radically, some even leaving the Mennonites in their desire to be faithful to the heavenly vision.

We cannot conclude from these reasons for the differences among them, however, that the Mennonites were not interested in unity, but that they gave a higher priority to obedience as they saw it. It may be that the heritage of suffering and persecution influenced them more than they suspected, or that their stress upon the importance of love as a doctrine made it easier to forget it in practice as they labored to establish the disciplined and faithful church. If spiritual unity is considered a primary goal of the church, most of the Mennonites were far more united than might appear from an organizational chart; it was, in fact, their very oneness which accented the image of their diversity.

### Groups of Swiss Ethnic Origin

*Reformed Mennonite Church:* John Herr of Lancaster County, Pennsylvania, founded the Reformed Mennonite Church in 1812. His father Francis had been excommunicated from the Mennonite Church earlier for reasons which are not entirely clear but seem to have centered around his conviction that the Mennonites had forsaken the faith of Menno Simons, especially in their lax discipline of erring members. Francis had subsequently met in homes with his followers until his death in 1810, after which his son John continued as leader. In 1812 the group elected him minister and bishop, though he was unbaptized. One of the members subsequently baptized him even as the Swiss Brethren had done in 1525. The group was variously spoken of locally as "New" Mennonites, or *Herrites,* but eventually came to be known as the Reformed Mennonites.

In doctrine the Reformed Mennonites seek to return to what they believe was taught by Menno Simons, whom they regard very highly. Their basic position is spelled out in the *Restitution,* a book which indicates clearly where they believe the church needs restoring. It seems to them that the rest of the Mennonites have left the true faith because most of them vote, some take part in local political issues, all have fun and tell stories, and some neglect the Biblical requirements of foot washing, the kiss of peace, and strict discipline including shunning. The church has no Sunday-school work, no youth work or mission activities, concentrating its efforts primarily in the Sunday morning worship service. Young people are active participants in the normal life of their community until they join the church, at which time a radical transformation in attitudes, dress, and social relations is expected, which may be one reason why many find it difficult to join the church of their fathers. As a result, there has been a steady decline in membership in the twentieth century, until only 800 remain. Of these, about 200 are located in Ontario, and most of the rest in Pennsylvania, with a few scattered families in Ohio, Indiana, Illinois, Michigan, and New York. A church paper, *Good Tidings,* was published from 1922 to 1932.

*Stauffer Mennonite Church:* An even smaller group than the preceding, totaling only 300 members who are continually plagued by disunity among themselves, the Stauffer Mennonites originated in a break from the Lancaster Mennonite Conference in 1845. The original schism arose from a dispute over an orphan child, and the continuing disunity has caused them to be named variously after their leaders, either as Rissler Mennonites, or Weaver Mennonites, or Stauffer Mennonites. The largest group is also known as Pike Mennonites after their meetinghouse located in Lancaster County, Pennsylvania. In dress and living customs they somewhat resemble the Old Order Amish, as also in their patterns of worship.

*Church of God in Christ, Mennonite:* Originating in Wayne County, Ohio, in 1859, this group is also known as the *Holdeman Mennonites* after the founder John Holdeman (d. 1900), Like the preceding two groups it protested against the seemingly low level of spiritual life in the church, but unlike the former, its central thrust arose from a deep religious experience rather than from misunderstanding among the leaders. John Holdeman had a deep religious experience at the age of twelve. At twenty-one he was baptized and reconsecrated himself to the work God would have for him. He felt a strong calling to preach; but the church had not, and might never call him to the ministry. At the same time, he was appalled at the traditionalism he found as he entered into the life of the congregation as a new member. His concerns were not shared by the leaders, however, and he soon faced the necessity of either giving up his vision of what the New Testament church should be like or breaking the fellowship.

After much prayer and inner struggle he chose the latter course, calling separate meetings in homes for those of like concern. Because he wanted to see his church directly in line with the New Testament church, he called it the Church of God in Christ. To avoid being confused with other churches of God, and to show that they cherished the Anabaptist heritage, the name "Mennonite" was added later. The Dordrecht Confession of 1632 was adopted as spiritual guide, to which was added a particular emphasis on nonconformity to the world in dress and all of life, one of the more obvious marks being the wearing of beards by all male church members. Strong stress was placed on the actual study of Menno, to the point where some even shared his understanding of the incarnation. The strong Anabaptist emphasis on discipleship has led to a warm fellowship among the Church of God in Christ, Mennonite congregations and a gentleness in human relations which makes visitors feel unusually welcome among them.

The spiritual concern of John Holdeman led to missionary activities from the beginning. After a slow beginning in 1859, the church won numerous members from other Mennonite churches, especially the *Kleine Gemeinde* in Manitoba and Kansas soon after their arrival from Russia in the 1870's. An energetic mission program, including a hospital and several schools, is carried on in Mexico since 1927. More recently work was begun in Haiti, and since 1963, an active program of cultural and spiritual help is being carried on in Nigeria. In 1965-66 they sent a delegation around the world to pursue contacts arising from radio and Bible lessons and explored the possibility of new mission programs in Egypt, India, and other countries en route. The church also participates fully in the work of the Mennonite Central Committee in relief and peace programs around the world. In 1964 there were 498 members in Mexico, 1,778 in Canada, and 5,370 in the United States, for a total of 7,646 in all.

*Evangelical Mennonite Church:* The impetus leading to the founding of this group in 1864 was again a personal experience of deep spiritual significance, this time on the part of Henry Egly, an Amishman near Berne, Indiana. Because of his leadership they were frequently known as the "Egly Amish" but called themselves the Defenseless Mennonite Church of North America until 1948 when they adopted the present name. This use of the name Defenseless was probably the most accurate translation of the

German *wehrlos,* which is today translated as nonresistant. As in the case of John Holdeman, so Egly charged the church with indifference in things spiritual, especially in forsaking the genuine inheritance of the Mennonite fathers. Among these important essentials was the new birth. Soon those who felt as he did, and who had experienced conversion themselves, joined him in separate meetings which led to their formal organization as a group.

A strong conservatism prevailed in dress and doctrine during the early years, but gradually the distinctive external marks of faith were discarded, including bonnets and beards. The practice of the holy kiss was largely abandoned, musical instruments were introduced into the worship services, and English replaced the German language. The early zeal, however, continued. Several preaching services were held every Sunday, Sunday schools were organized in the 1870's, and regular evangelistic meetings were held once or twice annually. Missionary work was begun in what is now the Republic of Congo, Africa, in 1896. Out of this program the Congo Inland Mission was organized in 1912, in cooperation with the Central Conference of Mennonites, now part of the General Conference. This work grew to where there were over one hundred missionaries in the Congo in 1964, despite the difficulties which followed in the wake of Congolese independence in 1960. Since 1949 mission activities have also been carried on in the Dominican Republic.

The first annual conference of the Defenseless Mennonites was held in 1883, but formal organization was not completed until 1908. Publication of the first conference paper began with the *Heils-Bote* in 1897, but the name was later changed to *Zion's Tidings* and is now called *The Evangelical Mennonite.* In 1964 the total membership was 2,475, located primarily near Berne, Indiana, Archbold, Ohio, and Gridley, Illinois.

*Old Order Mennonites:* A series of divisions resulted from the decision of a few leaders to oppose the introduction of the Sunday school and other progressive arrangements into the (Old) Mennonite Church in the period from 1872 to 1900. These years, which Harold S. Bender sometimes called the Great Awakening in his church, brought severe stress to many by threatening the long unchanged traditions to which they had become accustomed. Four protest groups eventually emerged as separate churches and are together often called the Old Order Mennonites, because of their desire to preserve the old order of life and faith. They have no formal conference organization which unites them, however.

The first group arose from divisions in Indiana and Ohio in 1872 under the leadership of Jacob Wisler; the second in Ontario under Abraham Martin in 1889; the third in Lancaster County, Pennsylvania, under Jonas H. Martin in 1893; and the fourth in Virginia under Gabriel D. Heatwole in 1900. In some places members of these groups are called Wisler Mennonites, in others Martinites, and in Ontario Woolwichers, after Woolwich Township in Waterloo County. While some use only horse and buggy for transportation, others use automobiles but paint the bumpers black. This has earned them another name among the people—the Black Bumper Mennonites. The strong conservatism in external things and the inability to adjust to the changing times have led to further painful divisions among these groups. In 1964 the total membership of the original four groups and their subdivisions was estimated to be approximately 7,100.

### Groups of Dutch Ethnic Origin

*Old Colony Mennonites:* Many of the immigrants coming to Manitoba in the migration of the 1870's were from the Chortitza settlement which was also known as the Old Colony, since it was the oldest Mennonite settlement in Russia. They were joined by immigrants from the two daughter colonies of Chortitza, Bergthal and Fürstenland. The Bergthal group settled on the East Reserve some thirty-five miles south of Winnipeg and came to be known as the Bergthal Mennonite Church; the Chortitza and Fürstenland groups settled on the West Reserve, west of the Red River, and came to be known as the Reinland Mennonite Church after the municipality of Reinland, in which many of them lived.

A decade later, in the 1880's, about one half of the Bergthal settlers moved into the West Reserve areas occupied by their brethren from the other two groups. Problems soon developed because of the progressive spirit of many of the Bergthal members who were willing to abandon the old pattern of settling in villages in favor of the individual farm pattern prevalent in Manitoba. Many of the Chortitza and Fürstenland leaders saw a real danger to the faith in the scattered farm life. As early as 1880 the Reinland Mennonite Church had made willingness to live in closed villages a test of membership, causing many to join the Bergthal Church. Some of the progressive Bergthal members constituted an additional threat in their attitudes to education. Instead of being content with the simple seven-month school led by untrained teachers under the supervision of the elder, they desired teachers who could pass government inspection and were not opposed to receiving tax support.

By 1890 a major regrouping of loyalties occurred among all of them, including the Bergthal Church. Bergthal members living in the West Reserve and opposed to the new progressive movement came to be known as the *Sommerfeld Church,* after their elder who lived in the village of Sommerfeld. Bergthal members living in the East Reserve and sharing the same fear of progress came to be known as the *Chortitza Mennonite Church,* after their elder who lived in the village of Chortitza. The progressives in both Reserves retained the name of *Bergthal Mennonite Church,* while the largest and most conservative group of all came increasingly to be referred to as the *Old Colony Mennonites.*

Following this regrouping the Bergthal Mennonite Church moved forward rapidly. Local schools were improved and a high school, later to be known as the Mennonite Collegiate Institute, was established in Gretna in 1891 with H. H. Ewert (d. 1934), a Kansas Mennonite educator, as principal. Ewert was also appointed government inspector of all Mennonite schools in Manitoba. In 1903 he became one of the founders of the Canadian Conference of Mennonites, now affiliated with the General Conference Mennonite Church, together with Peter Regier of the Rosenort church in Saskatchewan and David Toews, the "father" of the Mennonites in Canada. In 1929 a Bible school was begun in Gretna and relocated to Altona in 1940, where it is known as the Elim Bible School. By 1964 the membership of the Bergthal Church had grown to about 3,000.

In the meantime many Old Colony families had moved to Saskatchewan, settling in the Rosthern and Swift Current areas. The coming of world War I in 1914, however, revived their concern over education. Schools failing to meet government standards were to be subjected to official control, and English was to be the language of instruction in all subjects except religion. It was clear that most of their schools would not meet minimal government standards. When numerous petitions to the provincial authorities in Manitoba failed to bring any promise of relief in this threatened area of the faith, a delegation left for South America on July 15, 1919, to explore the possibility of settlement in those lands. Neither Brazil, Uruguay, nor Argentina seemed willing to grant the desired privileges, however, and the search continued. By 1921 it was clear that Mexico was to be the new haven of refuge to which these people could escape and by 1926 approximately 4,500 moved to that land, as will be seen further in Chapter 19, the first trainload having left Canada on March 1, 1922. Nevertheless, the continuing pressures in Canada led to further search, and in 1926 the first contingent left for Paraguay, where good settlement possibilities seemed to exist. This movement will also be discussed in Chapter 19.

In 1964 the total baptized membership of these groups in North America, which includes Mexico, was approximately as follows: Old Colony Mennonites: 3,000 in Canada and 9,000 in Mexico; Sommerfeld Church: 2,500 in Canada and 350 in Mexico; Chortitza Mennonite Church: 1,600 in Canada; and the Reinland Mennonite Church with 800 members in Canada. The Bergthal Church had, as indicated, moved rapidly into the twentieth century, providing many leaders in education, as well as in church and community affairs, and working vigorously through the Canadian Conference it had helped to found earlier.

*Evangelical Mennonite Mission Conference:* In the preceding paragraphs we have seen the Old Colony Mennonites as the most conservative and the Bergthal Church as the most progressive of the immigrants of the 1870's, with the Sommerfeld and Chortitza groups somewhere between these two on questions of change. In 1936-37 a split occurred in the Sommerfeld Church as a result of the evangelistic work of I. P. Friesen of Rosthern, Saskatchewan. Under the impact of his three-year ministry people were changed and became willing to break with the traditionalism of the past. Their church, however, remained intransigent until the new believers eventually formed a separate group called *Rudnerweide Mennonite Church,* after the village of Rudnerweide in Manitoba, Russia, and Prussia. In 1961 the name was changed to the Evangelical Mennonite Mission Conference (EMMC).

In contrast to the mother church, the new group immediately carried a strong missionary concern, as also interest in education and discipleship. It appeared to be a genuine recovery of the vision of the sixteenth-century Anabaptists at many points. The EMMC became particularly active in working with the brethren they had left in the old church and eventually also established churches among them in Saskatchewan. In 1964 the EMMC included approximately 2,000 members in twenty-four congregations and twenty missionaries abroad.

*Evangelical Mennonite Brethren:* Another of the groups arising to work for renewal among the immigrants of the 1870's, the Evangelical Mennonite Brethren founded their own church at Mountain

232

Lake, Minnesota, in 1889 under a slightly different name, changed it later, and in 1937 adopted their present name. For a time they were also known as the Brudertaler Church. Reasons given for the initial break were insufficient emphasis upon the new birth in their old church, too much conformity to the world, and the lack of Scriptural church discipline. The form of baptism has remained optional, either by immersion or by pouring.

With the break came a strong emphasis on education and missions, though most of their missionaries served under other boards. The A. F. Wienses were among the first Mennonites to work in urban areas when they located in Chicago in 1906. Though the conference numbered only some 3,300 members in 1964, it sent out and supported over sixty missionaries. In addition it cooperated in the support of numerous Bible schools, including those at Dalmeny, Saskatchewan, Steinbach, Manitoba, Meade, Kansas, and Omaha, Nebraska. Its congregations were scattered through the entire Middle West, from Manitoba to Kansas, with some also in the Pacific northwest. In 1953 a loose federation was entered into with the Evangelical Mennonite Church, which was rescinded a few years later, primarily because of the distances separating the congregations of the two groups. The conference paper is the *Gospel Tidings*.

### Groups Related to the Mennonites

*United Missionary Church:* Until the present name was adopted in 1947, this church was known as the Mennonite Brethren in Christ Church, which in turn had originated in 1883 through the merger of the Evangelical United Mennonites with a Brethren in Christ group in Ohio known as the Swankites. The Evangelical United Mennonites had, in turn, originated from earlier divisions and mergers. One historian has aptly characterized this process of division and union among these groups as follows:

In the case of each division the cause was somewhat the same—a large body desiring to cling to the established methods, with a smaller body wishing to adopt a more aggressive, evangelistic type of work. This in each case eventually led to an estrangement resulting in division. It should not be thought that insignificant trifles produced these ruptures. There was generally a pronounced difference of spirit that only showed itself in little things that then became the occasion of difficulty. [1]

Much of the impetus for the new spiritual vigor of the Mennonite Brethren in Christ Church came from contacts with Wesleyan piety and church organization, together with an emphasis upon holiness

233

prevalent among some Methodist churches. Under this influence the Anabaptist ingredient of the faith grew less with the passing of time, and few contacts were sought with the Mennonites. The change of name was adopted in 1947. The Pennsylvania Conference withdrew from the United Missionary Church in 1952, only to adopt the name Bible Fellowship Church in 1959.

In addition to the usually accepted evangelical doctrines, a strong emphasis is placed upon sanctification as a second work of grace following regeneration. Baptism is by immersion. Annual camp meetings have become standard procedure for church renewal and membership recruitment. These camp meetings, together with other forms of evangelism, have led to a vigorous growth of the church until it numbered 12,000 in 1964. This missionary activity is a primary concern of all members, with over one hundred workers on foreign fields and a strong church extension program at home. Two periodicals, the *Gospel Banner* and *The Missionary Banner,* serve the churches. Several schools are maintained, including Bethel College, a four-year college in Mishawaka, Indiana.

*Missionary Church Association:* The MCA originated in Berne, Indiana, in 1898, when several members of the group now known as the Evangelical Mennonite Church were excommunicated. The reason for this discipline was their belief in the necessity of baptism with the Holy Spirit after regeneration as a separate work of grace. They had also stressed the importance of divine healing, immersion as the only valid form of baptism, and had developed some new insights into the Second Coming of Christ. Several ministers of the General Conference Mennonite Church were also influenced by these questions and joined the movement in its early years.

Like most of the other schismatic groups, the MCA soon manifested a vigorous interest in mission work and by 1964 was supporting over one hundred missionaries abroad. Many of these had been trained in its own school, the Fort Wayne Bible College of Fort Wayne, Indiana. Members of the MCA numbered approximately 8,000 in 1964, scattered over many of the states but not in Canada. The official church paper has been *The Missionary Worker* since 1904.

*Brethren in Christ:* A revival movement went through the Lutheran, Baptist, and Mennonite communities in Lancaster County, Pennsylvania, in 1770, promoted by Philip Otterbein and the Mennonite Martin Boehm. Boehm was excommunicated by the church in 1777 for his part in this work and later founded the Evangelical

234

United Brethren (EUB) Church together with Otterbein. As a result of the work of these men and others, "Brethren" gathered together in an informal manner and to worship at different points in Lancaster County. One of these groups met in western Lancaster County near the Susquehanna River and was thus referred to as the River Brethren. Eventually these Brethren broke their relationship with Boehm, at which time Jacob Engle, who was probably a Mennonite, assumed leadership of the group. They continued to be known as River Brethren until 1863, when the present name was officially adopted.

The original River Brethren combined an eighteenth-century pietistic emphasis on the crisis conversion experience with the Mennonite-German Baptist understanding of the church and the relationship of the church to the world, thus being indebted both to the Anabaptists and to the Pietists. This emphasis continued throughout most of the nineteenth century, with the central concern being the actualizing of the true church or the visible people of God. In the latter portion of the nineteenth century, however, conservative, revivalistic, and individualistic Protestantism began to have a telling impact on them, as also upon the Mennonites. From about 1870 to 1910 many changes were introduced into the Brethren in Christ Church, Sunday schools were begun, as were home and foreign missions, protracted meetings, a church school, and a church paper.

Of these changes, the one that made for denominational uniqueness was that of Wesleyan holiness. It encountered great resistance but finally won the day. In the process the emphasis was moderated. The basic impact of Wesleyan holiness, when compared with the Mennonite point of view, was that it gave to the Brethren in Christ orientation a greater emphasis on emotion and feeling. By way of example Mennonite sermons were almost always more rational and placed greater emphasis on discipleship and on the "ought." Wesleyan holiness also made the Brethren in Christ appear more individualistic than the Mennonites, among whom the concept of the church was stronger.

The period from 1910 to 1940 in Brethren in Christ history was a time of consolidation and expansion. Very few new programs were begun, but the ones accepted between 1870 and 1910 were digested and worked into the fabric of the church. Since 1940 a greater degree of interest in outside affairs and movements became apparent. In 1942 the Brethren in Christ joined the Mennonite Central Committee, and the National Association of Evangelicals and

National Holiness Association about 1948. They have worked closely with Mennonites in the fields of peace education and the Mennonite World Conference.

Brethren in Christ congregations are scattered over thirteen states and two provinces in Canada, totaling 9,378 members in 1964. Two high schools and Messiah College at Grantham, Pennsylvania, are maintained. Missionary work has been concentrated primarily in India and Rhodesia, with a strong emphasis on education. An official conference paper, *The Evangelical Visitor,* has been in circulation since 1887.

*The Hutterites*: The origin of the Hutterian Brethren, and the history of their development to the time of their ultimate suppression in Europe, has been discussed in Chapter 4. This included the fact that by 1590 they had established some eighty Bruderhofs (colonies), totaling about 15,000 persons, in southern Moravia and Slovakia. After more than one hundred years of persecution, however, they had been all but wiped out. It is believed that there were only nineteen Hutterites left in 1756, but in that year they were joined by fifty-six Lutherans who gave new life to the movement. In 1770 all of them settled in the Ukraine under the generous provisions of Catherine II, as we saw in Chapter 10. Here they abandoned the practice of communal living for a period of forty years, simply living in villages as the Mennonite and other settlers did.

In the 1870's the entire group, which by that time numbered approximately 800 persons, joined the Mennonite emigration to North America. Since their representatives on the Russian Mennonite delegation sent to investigate settlement possibilities in 1873 had not been impressed with Manitoba, they located primarily in the Dakota territory. Here half of them settled on private farms and became known as Hutterite Mennonites and Krimmer (Crimea) Mennonites. The others, however, returned to the colony pattern of settlement. John A. Hostetler, one of the foremost authorities on the Hutterites today, has written as follows concerning their experiences in America:

Since their initial settlement in South Dakota, the brethren have located in various parts of the Northwest. During World War I they were harassed by pressure groups who resented them because they were prosperous, they were German-speaking, and they were pacifists. Two young men died as a result of abuses in army camps. Most of the seventeen colonies moved to Canada from 1918 to 1923 but many later returned to the Western states. The Hutterites have generally prospered in North America. There were 170 colonies in 1965, of which 120 were in Canada. Alberta had 63, Manitoba 42, and Saskatchewan 15. In the United States they were distributed as follows: South Dakota 26, Montana 21, and one each in Minnesota, North Dakota, and Washington. The total population in 1965 was about 15,300. [2]

In faith and life the Hutterites continue the pattern of their sixteenth-century Anabaptist fathers, seeking to restore the true New Testament church. They cooperate with the public schools in a normal manner but do not permit pupils to leave the colony for high-school education. Some of the colonies offer a year or two of this higher training on their own. Hutterites also pay taxes, but as a group or colony rather than as individuals. Their land purchases have led to considerable misunderstanding among their neighbors, as a result of which the Alberta legislature has passed restrictive legislation, but other provinces and states seek to control their expansion through negotiation. The ideal colony is made up of from 90 to 130 persons. Families are very large, and with agriculture as the primary group vocation, it is clear that land is a basic need for their survival as a people. Of the 15,300 persons, approximately 7,000 were baptized members of the church.

A modern attempt to recapture the Hutterite ideal of communal living based on New Testament patterns was made by Eberhard Arnold with his founding of the Society of Brothers in Germany in 1922. Arnold, a leader in the Student Christian Movement of Germany, arrived at his vision independently but soon discovered Hutterian history and by 1928 had established contact with the Hutterites in America. In 1930 he was ordained in one of the Bruderhofs in Alberta, and commissioned to return to his work in Germany. Arnold died in 1935, and the Bruderhof was expelled from Germany under Hitler in 1937. The new Hutterites took refuge in England, establishing the Cotswold and Oaksey Bruderhofs, later also Wheathill and Bulstrode. When the pressures of World War II forced them to move again, they settled some eighty miles northeast of Asunción in Paraguay, near the Mennonite colony of Friesland. Here they founded the *Primavera* (meaning Spring) colony with three Bruderhofs, but economic and other pressures led to the disintegration of the settlement early in the 1960's. Some of the members migrated to America to join the existing Hutterite Bruderhofs, while others founded new ones of their own in the United States. Among these the Bruderhofs at Rifton, New York, Oak Lake near Uniontown, Pennsylvania, and in Connecticut continued to function actively. An attempt to reestablish a community near the original site in

237

Germany had to be abandoned about 1961-62.

*Notes*
1. J. A. Huffman, *History of the Mennonite Brethren in Christ Church,* 1920, p. 34.
2. John A. Hostetler, *Hutterite Life,* 1965, p. 12.


*FOR FURTHER READING:*
*The Mennonite Encyclopedia,* 4 vols.
*Christian Living* (January, 1962), pp. 14-17, 34.
*Mennonite Life* 3 (April, 1948), pp. 5-9; 16 (July, 1959), pp. 122-24.
John Penner, *A Concise History of the Church of God.* Hillsboro, Kansas: Mennonite Brethren Publishing House, 1951.
E. R. Storms, *History of the United Missionary Church.* Elkhart: 1958.
Walter H. Lugibihl and Jared F. Gerig, *The Missionary Church Association.* Berne, Indiana: Mennonite Book Concern, 1950.
A. W. Climenhaga, *History of the Brethren in Christ Church.* Nappanee, Indiana: Evangel Press, 1942.
Paul S. Gross, *The Hutterite Way.* Saskatoon: Freeman Publishing Company, 1965.

*Chapter 17*

# THE MENNONITE CHURCH IN LATIN AMERICA

NORTH AMERICANS have generally been so busy with themselves that they have tended to forget the vast lands south of the Rio Grande, yet in this region live over 200,000,000 people who are also Americans. In this area, which we know as Latin America, are twenty independent nations and Puerto Rico, which is a United States possession. These twenty republics are Mexico, Central America (Guatemala, Honduras, El Salvador, Nicaragua, Costa Rica, and Panama); the West Indies (Cuba, Haiti, Jamaica, and the Dominican Republic), and South America (Colombia, Venezuela, Brazil, Uruguay, Argentina, Chile, Paraguay, Bolivia, Peru, and Ecuador). Geographically this area also includes British, Dutch, and French Guiana, but the name *Latin America* is a cultural term derived from the fact that the three languages used here, namely, Spanish, Portuguese, and French, are *Latin* in origin. All together these republics make up a land area almost as large as Europe and the United States combined.

In this vast region climate and topography have played a decisive role. Latin America is 25 percent mountainous, almost 25 percent swampy, and about 10 percent desert land. The gigantic Andean mountain range on the west coast, the steaming jungles of Brazil, and the four great rivers--Amazon, Magdalena, Orinoco, and La Plata--have determined the flow of population, economic development, and political boundaries. Agriculture is still the dominant activity of the majority of the people, together with mining and the exploiting of raw materials for shipment abroad. In recent years great emphasis has been placed on industrialization as a means to economic prosperity, but extreme poverty is found everywhere except in certain sections of the cities. Ninety percent of the land is owned by ten percent of the people, leaving the majority of the people in a peasant status. [1]

The economic problems of Latin America are accentuated by a 2.9 percent annual population increase, which adds over five million persons every year. This rate of increase is higher than in any other major area of the world. One result of this high birth rate is that some 50.3 percent of the 200 million population are under twenty years of age.* The problems of sheer survival are enormous. A 1961 study reported that "at least 130 millions of Latin Americans suffer the pernicious consequences of malnutrition, that is, insufficient, incomplete, and unbalanced nutrition." [2] Educational facilities are completely inadequate even for elementary education, though the universities of Peru, Mexico, and the Dominican Republic are the oldest in the western hemisphere. Politics become volatile when people are hungry, unemployed, and only partially literate. While most of the younger generation are done with military dictatorships and suspicious of Marxism, they are not convinced that a simple transplanting of North American democracy will give them long-range solutions. A social revolution of major proportions is under way everywhere in Latin America.

Most Latin Americans consider themselves to be Roman Catholics, but for the majority this means very little. A Roman Catholic publication in 1955 gave the number of active participants in the life of the church as ranging from 15 to 30 percent of the people, dropping as low as 10 percent in some countries, including communicant children. [3] There is only one priest for every 5,000 members, and many of these priests have been brought from Europe since the Roman Church in Latin America is unable to supply enough workers from its own ranks. As a result of this shortage of workers secularism is the dominant orientation of the majority, though the cultural aspects of Roman Catholicism—laws, social institutions, language—permeate the life and thought of the people. One third of the Roman Catholics of the world live in Latin America. While Roman Catholics themselves referred to the church situation in Latin America as tragic not many years ago, there are signs that renewal has come to many aspects of its life and work in recent years. There is truth in the statement of a Catholic writer that "the renaissance of the Catholic Church in Latin America is well under way." [4] This renewal has come about in part through the successes of Protestantism, and in part through the new life given to the Roman Church by Pope John XXIII and the Second Vatican Council. An unprecedented use of lay people in the work of the church has taken place, making possible new approaches to education, social and economic problems, and other issues faced by the members.

Protestantism is strong and growing rapidly in Latin America. Estimates range from six million to over ten million members, constituting roughly five percent of the population.[5] The number of Protestants in Brazil, for example, grew from 175,451 in 1,618 congregations in 1937 to 1,763,142 members in 11,328 congregations in 1961.[6] Ninety percent of Protestant growth has come since 1916. There had been Protestants in Latin America throughout the entire colonial period, but active mission work began early in the nineteenth century through the efforts of the British and American Bible societies. By mid-nineteenth century the major Protestant denominations were establishing work in scattered areas, including primary and secondary schools, but interest in Latin America was small. This changed with the International Mission Conference in Madras, India, in 1938. By this time Protestant missionaries saw the possible loss of their fields in Asia because of Japanese military exploits and a new concern arose for other fields. Latin America was proposed and enthusiastically adopted. Tremendous activities followed, particularly after World War II. Two unique aspects of this work have been the close cooperation of the major Protestant denominations and the phenomenal growth of the Pentecostal groups. Roughly one third of the Protestants in Latin America today are Pentecostals.[7]

### Mennonites Move to Latin America

Mennonite settlers first came to Latin America after World War I. They were the Old Colony and Sommerfelder groups from Manitoba and Saskatchewan. The former had received their name in Russia by virtue of being the first group to settle there in 1789, the "Old" colony; the latter represented the conservative wing of a split which had occurred near Sommerfeld in the West Reserve of Manitoba in 1890. Both groups felt threatened by the new education law passed by the Manitoba legislature in 1915 providing for provincial control of education and the use of the English language in all schools. They considered this law to be a violation of the promises given to their fathers when they first came from Russia in 1874. The loss of German meant to them the gradual loss of their Mennonite faith and culture through assimilation into the Canadian environment. The Manitoba government had no desire to undermine the faith of any of her settlers, but there was a strong desire to create greater national unity through standardization of education and less emphasis upon the ethnic uniqueness of minority groups.

*Mexico:* With this apparent threat before them, the Mennonites sent out commissioners to find a new land of greater freedom. Numerous locations were considered, including North Africa and Australia. A team of six men explored settlement possibilities in several of the South American countries, including Paraguay, but finally returned with the recommendation to settle in Mexico. (See Chapter 16.) Mexico could be reached with little difficulty from Canada. Even more important was the fact that its president Alvaro Obregon had personally guaranteed to them all the rights and privileges they requested, including freedom of religion and full control of their own school program.

From 1922 to 1926 several thousand Old Colony and Sommerfelder Mennonites left Canada for Mexico, most of them settling in the state of Chihuahua. Others followed in a continuing stream, some settling south of the earlier colonies in the state of Durango. In 1948 a major movement, including 100 families of the *Kleine Gemeinde* who were troubled by the progressive thinking of some of their leaders, likewise left for Mexico. All of these migrations to Mexico, together with the high birth rate since the settlements began, brought the total number of Mennonites in that country to approximately 16,000 by 1950.

Most of these settlers were and remain farmers. Members who leave the colonies for the cities are not in good standing with the church. The village pattern of settlement which had prevailed in Russia and Canada was also followed in Mexico. Each village consists of from ten to thirty farms of approximately 160 acres and sufficient grazing lands for the village cattle. Corn, beans, and a variety of other crops are grown, but the climate is not suited to wheat production. Some modern machinery is used. The buildings are usually of adobe brick with a tin roof. Particular attention is given to the raising of cattle and horses. Cheese factories are scattered throughout the colonies.

All colony life is under the control of the church. Because of the geographical and cultural isolation, the ban is a much feared form of discipline since the delinquent has nowhere to go when he is excommunicated except into the strange and unknown outside world. Each village has its own school, but the teacher is selected at random and has no special training. A simple reader, the Bible, catechism, and hymnary are the basic study materials. Emphasis is placed upom memorization rather than upon independent thought. Very little reading is done by anyone in the colonies except for the *Steinbach Post,* which brings welcome news from Canada. Sunday morning worship services are usually two or more hours long with silent prayer, the reading of an ancient sermon, and exhortation to obedience by the ministers and elder.

A General Conference Mennonite church was organized in the city of Cuauhtémoc by Mennonites from Russia who were unable to go to Canada and came to Mexico in 1929-30. Some of the men who felt uncomfortable in the colonies have moved to the city and joined this fellowship. Five families of the Church of God in Christ, Mennonite (Holdeman) moved to Mexico from Oklahoma in 1927 to witness to the Mennonite settlers but soon shifted their attention to work with the native Mexican population. Extensive medical, educational, and agricultural assistance programs have been carried on by the Mennonite Central Committee for many years. In 1957 this work was transferred to the General Conference Mennonite Church.

Many of the settlers do not believe Mexico to be their permanent home and confidently wait for God to lead them on. During a prolonged drought in 1954 several hundred returned to Canada. Others began to settle in British Honduras in 1958 until over 3,000 persons had moved there from Mexico by 1964, establishing settlements to the north and to the west of Belize. In 1963 the Mennonite Central Committee transferred responsibility for aiding these settlements in British Honduras to the Eastern Mennonite Board of Missions and Charities of Salunga, Pennsylvania.

*Paraguay:* In contrast to the negative report which a delegation had brought back from Paraguay in 1920, six delegates who left Manitoba on February 11, 1921, brought back a very favorable description of Paraguay and many became eager to leave. Through the help of a New York banker, Samuel McRoberts, the Paraguayan government was asked to provide guarantees of full religious and educational freedom to the Mennonites if they should settle in Paraguay. This request was generously met by the Paraguayan Congress in its passing of Law No. 514 on July 26, 1921, the provisions of which are commonly referred to as the *Privilegium* by the Mennonites of Paraguay. With the passing of this legislation came a most cordial invitation to the Mennonites to make Paraguay

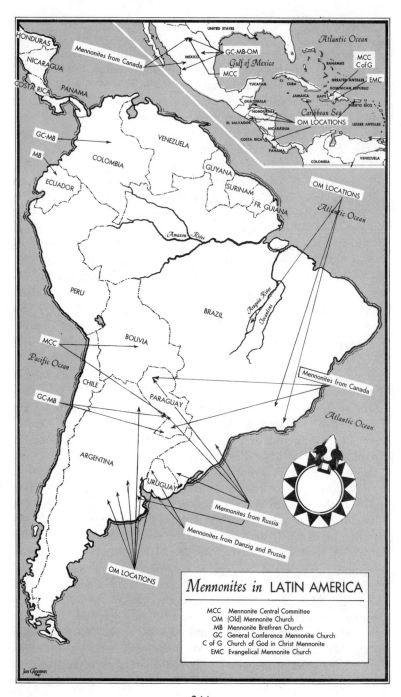

Mennonites in LATIN AMERICA

| | |
|---|---|
| MCC | Mennonite Central Committee |
| OM | (Old) Mennonite Church |
| MB | Mennonite Brethren Church |
| GC | General Conference Mennonite Church |
| C of G | Church of God in Christ Mennonite |
| EMC | Evangelical Mennonite Church |

their home. Economic conditions in Canada, however, delayed emigration until 1926, though large numbers did go to Mexico.

In the meantime banker McRoberts formed two land holding companies, the Inter-Continental Company in Winnipeg to buy the land of the emigrants in Canada, and the *Corporación Paraguaya* in Paraguay to sell them lands there in return. The first land purchased by the Mennonites consisted of 137,920 acres in the Chaco, approximately 155 miles west of the river landing at Puerto Casado, which in turn lay some two days and two nights by boat up the Paraguay River from Asunción, the capital city. The first group of fifty-one families (309 persons) left Altona, Manitoba, on November 23, 1926, followed by other groups totaling 279 families or 1,767 persons by 1930. Though they received a cordial presidential welcome in Asunción, the immigrants were soon to experience great suffering. Upon arrival at Puerto Casado they discovered that few preparations had been made for their coming. Worst of all, their land had not been surveyed by the *Corporación Paraguaya*. Sixteen weary months were to elapse before they could move to their farm locations in April, 1928. During this difficult period many became discouraged and returned to Canada, while 147 died of a typhoid epidemic. The majority remained, however, to establish Menno Colony with thirteen villages and learned to wrest a simple living from the region which had been known as the "Green Hell" prior to their coming. By 1964 the colony had grown to *ca.* 5,000 inhabitants owning nearly a million acres of land, of which some 20,000 were under cultivation. Schools, churches, and other social organizations had become well established, bringing to mind the words of Isaiah 35:1, 2: ". . . the desert shall rejoice and blossom; like the crocus it shall blossom abundantly."

A second colony known as *Fernheim* was established in the Chaco in 1930 by Mennonites from Russia. They had fled to Germany from their lands in 1929 in the hope of finding a new home in North America, but neither Canada nor the United States was willing to receive them at that time and they could not remain in Germany. (See Chapter 10.) Through the Mennonite Central Committee arrangements were finally made to have them settle in the Paraguayan Chaco. The government was willing to include this group also under the privileges of Law No. 514, and *Corporación Paraguaya* had sufficient land available. Consequently a total of 1,853 persons in 374 families made their new home in the Chaco in 1930. Though they were aided by the Menno Colony brethren,

245

pioneering hardships again took their toll, including sixty-five persons who died of another typhoid epidemic. Drinking water was so scarce from their only good well during the early months that a boy was at times stationed at the bottom of the well to dip the trickling water with a cup and gradually fill the bucket. Many of the immigrants were extremely frustrated with their location and economic potential, but few had sufficient resources to leave. In 1937 a group of 140 families relocated in East Paraguay in the hope of achieving greater economic success, founding what became known as colony *Friesland*. Through great sacrifice and unrelenting toil both colonies gradually became moderately well established. In 1964 Fernheim counted *ca.* 3,000 persons with some 8,000 acres under cultivation, while Friesland had just over 1,000 inhabitants and some 2,000 acres under cultivation.

A third wave of immigrants came to Paraguay from Russia after World War II, establishing colony *Neuland* in the Chaco and colony *Volendam* near Friesland in East Paraguay. Having fled westward before the advancing Russian armies, thousands of Mennonites from Russia had been crowded into Berlin and West German refugee camps awaiting resettlement. When emigration to North America seemed impossible, large numbers of them decided to go to Latin America. Consequently 2,314 persons in 641 family units, of which 253 were without father or husband, came to establish *Neuland* Colony between 1947 and 1950. During the same period 1,810 persons in 441 families founded the *Volendam* Colony, so named after the Dutch ship which brought them to the New World. Though the help of the previous immigrants made life much more bearable for the later groups than they themselves had experienced, many of the *Neuland* and *Volendam* settlers left at the first opportunity, some going on to Canada and others returning to Germany. Consequently the number of persons in *Neuland* was about the same in 1964 as when they first arrived in 1947-48, while *Volendam* counted approximately 750 in 1964.

There was a fourth wave of Mennonite immigrants to Paraguay. Like the first settlers, these came from Manitoba and Saskatchewan for the same reason as in 1926, *viz.,* to preserve their spiritual heritage through isolation from the corrosive influence of modern society and its effects upon their children. Nearly 1,700 persons left the prairie provinces in 1948 to settle on 27,500 acres of primitive forest land in eastern Paraguay some sixty-five miles east of Villarica. They came with substantial financial resources which made possible the purchase of modern farming equipment, but the agricultural patterns as well as the climate were so different from what they had been accustomed to that approximately one third of the immigrants returned to Canada. The remainder were able to establish themselves in two colonies, *Bergthal* and *Sommerfeld*, fifteen miles from each other.

All of these colonies—*Menno, Fernheim, Friesland, Neuland, Volendam, Bergthal,* and *Sommerfeld*—are predominantly agricultural communities with only sufficient industrial equipment to meet their own agricultural needs. With hard work and frugal living most of the colonists can claim to have their own daily bread and modest comforts. In an attempt to help meet their economic needs North American Mennonite businessmen formed a Mennonite Economic Development Association (MEDA) and are achieving significant results in partnership with the settlers. In the Chaco the primary cash crops are cotton, peanuts (oil), and kafir corn. In East Paraguay the acreage is much smaller but peanuts, sugarcane, and other crops provide some cash income, as does the sale of timber. In recent years the experimental farm in the Chaco has successfully developed a strain of wheat suited to that climate to the great joy of the people who had not forgotten the white loaves of bread they took for granted on the steppes of Russia. Manioc has replaced the potatoes of Europe and Canada. Fresh vegetables are strictly seasonal in the Chaco, but citrus fruits are available in abundance. Meat is the staple food of most major meals.

The educational program of all classes is completely under the control of the colonies themselves and is conducted primarily in the German language by their own teachers. As with the Mennonites in Mexico, only a few years of schooling are offered in the *Bergthal* and *Sommerfeld* colonies. A more adequate basic education is being achieved in the *Menno* Colony, though trained teachers are limited. In the other colonies the European system of six years' elementary and four years' secondary training is followed, with a two-year teacher-training course available to those who desire it. A cooperative Bible school is conducted in Filadelfia, the center of Chaco activities, during part of the year. Together with Mennonites in other lands in Latin America, a Bible Institute is operated in Brazil and a seminary in Uruguay, as will be discussed later. For advanced studies students travel to Europe or North America, though one Mennonite medical doctor has received his degree from the University of Paraguay.

247

Church activities are at the heart of social and community life in the colonies, with regular worship services held in many places. With the exception of *Bergthal* and *Sommerfeld,* an active Sunday school, prayer meeting, and midweek Bible studies program is carried on. The churches are organized into three major bodies and one smaller group. The conservative Old Colony and Sommerfeld churches have not formed an official conference but work together among themselves and maintain close relationships with their brethren in Canada. The Mennonite Brethren churches transferred as a body from Russia. The "Church Mennonites" (*Kirchliche*) of Russia remained independent in Paraguay until the 1950's when they joined the General Conference Mennonite Church of North America. The Alliance Church arose in Russia in 1905 in an attempt to bridge the gap between the Mennonite Brethren and the "Church" Mennonites, as was shown in Chapter 15, and continues as a small, independent group in Paraguay. A strong spirit of brotherhood among the churches has strengthened all of them in their ministry amidst most difficult hardships. Coordinating committees serve to unite church and mission activities of the several groups into a total ministry. An independently published biweekly, the *Menno Blatt,* keeps the scattered settlers in touch with each other and with the "outside" world. It has been a consistent promoter of unity, courage, and optimism.

Many of the Mennonites in Paraguay have become keenly aware of their missionary responsibility and numerous programs have been undertaken. A radio ministry and a bookstore are being supported in Asunción, as are several evangelism outposts. Other mission stations have been established in Itacurabí, Villa Hayes, and Cambyreta. The churches of the Chaco, with financial help from North America, have worked intensively over many years to evangelize the native Indian tribes. Difficulties with this Indian work have been prolonged and many. In 1958 Cornelius Isaak was speared to death by the Moro Indians. A breakthrough did come, however, even with the Moro tribe. By 1964 over 1,000 Indians from the Lengua and Chulupi tribes had been baptized and most of them resettled in villages. A medical and Gospel ministry is also being carried on among Paraguayans suffering from Hansen's disease (leprosy). This work was undertaken together with the Mennonite Central Committee in gratitude to Paraguay for admitting the Mennonites when no other nation seemed to want them.

*Brazil:* Among the Mennonites who left Russia for Germany in 1929 were about 280 families totaling 1,300 persons who chose to settle in Brazil instead of *Fernheim* in the Chaco of Paraguay. This became possible for them through the efforts of the German government and substantial help from the Dutch Mennonites. Land was secured for them in Santa Catarina, a state with a large German population in southern Brazil, and the first Mennonites arrived there on February 10, 1930. Two settlements were laid out, *Witmarsum* in the Krauel River valley and *Auhagen* on Stoltz Plateau, but neither seemed to prosper economically, though the forests, hills, and valleys constituted very beautiful scenery. The *Auhagen* settlers soon moved to the outskirts of Curitiba city and took up dairying on such a large scale that they eventually supplied over half of the milk required by the one-quarter million inhabitants of that city. The Witmarsum Colony also relocated, some establishing themselves sixty miles northwest of Curitiba in *New Witmarsum* and some near the Uruguayan border in *Colonia Nova* at Bagé. Some also found employment in the cities, particularly in Sao Paulo. Through these relocation efforts most of the immigrants were soon able to achieve economic independence. In 1964 the Mennonite community totaled some 3,500 persons but was scattered over much of south and central Brazil with primary concentrations at Curitiba, Bagé, and New Witmarsum. A biweekly paper *Bibel und Pflug* kept them in touch with each other and served to strengthen their spiritual life.

As in Paraguay, church and school activities are patterned after the traditional forms developed in the Mennonite settlements in Russia. Since all education is state controlled, however, the Mennonites have sought to preserve their values by having their teachers receive state training and certification and by bringing their own schools to meet certification requirements. In this way several excellent schools have been developed, including the elementary and high school *Erasto Gaertner* in Curitiba, and many non-Mennonites are being taught together with their own students. A Bible Institute has been established in Curitiba by the Mennonite Brethren churches of South America and in 1963 had fourteen students enrolled. An orphanage in the same city, likewise sponsored by the Mennonite Brethren churches, cares for approximately seventy children between the ages of four and seventeen.

Church activities are carried on in both the German and Portuguese languages. The pressures to acculturation are much greater than in Paraguay and young Mennonites consider themselves more Brazilian than German. Fortunately there is a growing cooperation with the larger evangelical Protestant community in Brazil, which helps to make their faith indigenous rather than extraneous to their culture. Difficulties have been encountered in securing conscientious objector classification for Mennonite men of draft age, due in part perhaps to the lack of conviction of some of the men themselves on this issue. For a time internal tensions among the churches prevented serious devotion to their teaching and witnessing ministries, but these problems have been overcome and a strong evangelical concern is evident among the congregations.

*Uruguay:* The settlement of Mennonites in Uruguay began in 1948 with the coming of 750 immigrants from Danzig and Poland. Together with all of their coreligionists they had been forced to leave these homelands in the closing days of World War II in 1945. Upon arriving in Uruguay they immediately found employment and by 1950 were able to purchase *El Ombu*, a 2,900-acre ranch northwest of Montevideo, with the help of the Mennonite Central Committee. In October, 1951, a second group of 431 came to join them, locating on an even larger ranch near Tres Bocas, and which they named *Gartental*. A third colony was established in 1955 on 3,600 acres some sixty miles northwest of Montevideo and named *Delta* after their Vistula Delta homeland in Prussia. All three of the colonies are primarily agricultural, growing wheat, peanuts, corn, potatoes, and other crops, as well as raising cattle and giving great effort to the establishing of a dairy industry. Except for help in purchasing land, most of the settlers were self-supporting from the beginning due to their energetic spirit and the rich economy of the country. Though some returned to Germany, the Mennonite census had grown to approximately 1,500 by 1964, of which total nearly 1,000 were church members. Most of these had affiliated with the General Conference Mennonite Church, a small group belonging to the Mennonite Brethren Church.

As in Brazil the schools are subject to state supervision and must meet national certification requirements. In 1956 Montevideo was chosen as the location for a seminary sponsored by the (Old) Mennonite and General Conference Mennonite churches of South America. It is known as the *Seminario Evangélico Menonita de Teología* and offers a three-year course of instruction to some thirty-five to forty students annually. Graduates of the seminary are in great demand throughout the colonies and on the vast mission frontier of South America. The Uruguay Mennonite churches give all possible support to this international school among them, finding their own life and concerns strengthened by its presence.

This, then, is the picture of the ethnic Mennonite groups in Latin America in 1964. To it should be added 800 persons living in Argentina, primarily in Buenos Aires, where an inter-Mennonite congregation has been established. With some 20,000 persons in Mexico and British Honduras, *ca.* 13,000 in Paraguay, 3,500 in Brazil, and 1,500 in Uruguay the total might be set at 38,800. To this might be added another 1,200, however, to include those in Bolivia and other scattered areas for an approximate total of 40,000 for all of Latin America. Church membership appears to be somewhat less than one half of this total.

### Non-Ethnic Mennonites in Latin America

With a task force of this size it might be assumed that a great evangelical witness is being given by these heirs of sixteenth-century Anabaptism. This is indeed true in some areas and becoming more so increasingly as North American Mennonite mission boards work with their brethren in Latin America in a united outreach. It must be remembered, however, that most of these communities came to these new lands as refugees and were for a time completely submerged in their struggle for existence and relative economic security. The rise of a Bible institute and seminary is a sign that they are girding for their calling to testify to their faith in a very secular and shallowly religious environment. Some forms of witness, nevertheless, like the work with the Indians of the Paraguayan Chaco, were begun almost the day of their arrival as immigrants. In the eyes of most Latin Americans, however, the Mennonites have until recently been seen primarily as good farmers and hardy pioneers, rather than as Protestant evangelicals with a faith to proclaim. They have appeared to be content to remain "the quiet of the land."

Long before the first immigrants came to Paraguay North American Mennonites were interested in Latin America as a mission field. One of the first missionaries described this interest as follows:

During the 13 years, 1904 to 1917, the movement developed that gave birth to the Argentine Mennonite Mission. Mennonite youth in Goshen College studied about the neglected South American continent. Churches and wide-awake individuals contributed to a fund for South American missions. The Mennonite Board of Missions and Charities in 1911 sent J. W. Shank as its representative on a six months' tour of investigation in Peru, Bolivia, Chile, Argentina, and Uruguay. Then followed a general solicitation campaign that brought over $20,000 for the new mission. By the late summer of 1917 the four missionaries under appointment, the T. K. Hersheys and J. W. Shanks, sailed to Buenos Aires, arriving on September 11.[8]

After language study and careful survey of possible locations the first work was begun in a semi-rural town called Pehuajó, some 200 miles west of Buenos Aires, in 1919. After ten years seven growing young churches, with outstations and Sunday schools, were in existence. In 1942 work was begun among the Toba Indians of the Argentine Chaco, and a little later, in Buenos Aires itself. By 1961 these efforts had multiplied the congregations to twenty-five with nearly 900 members and thirty Toba Indian congregations with over 1,000 members. A printing press and an orphanage had become part of the program as had a Bible school at Bragado, where workers were trained for the churches and the mission. From a small beginning the work has grown to where the churches have organized their own Argentine Mennonite Conference which carries on its own program in close cooperation with the (Old) Mennonite churches of North America.

An equally dynamic program was launched in Colombia by the General Conference Mennonites in 1943 and the Mennonite Brethren Church in 1946. Both groups established schools and orphanages, the General Conference Mennonites giving particular attention to the care of children of parents suffering from Hansen's disease (leprosy) near Cachipay. A second and third school were added later as were medical clinics. A Bible school is operated by the Mennonite Brethren Church. Almost from the beginning both missionary groups experienced strong opposition from authorities, at times even persecution. A 1959 report of the Evangelical Confederation of Colombia lists 115 Protestant Christians martyred, sixty-six churches destroyed, as well as robbery and vandalism almost without government intervention during the decade of severest persecution following 1945. During this period the government closed over two hundred Protestant schools, though 43 percent of the population was illiterate. Yet during this same period more believers were added to the Protestant churches than during the preceding ninety years. With increased toleration, following in the wake of Vatican Council II (1962-65), the work has grown further in scope. By 1964 there were four churches and six meeting places with 281 members in the area of General Conference activity, six churches and four meeting places with 300 members in the areas of Mennonite Brethren responsibility. Indigenous conferences had been organized by both missions, and Colombian Christians were themselves reaching out to their neighbors with the good news in partnership with the workers from North America.

252

Different circumstances led to the beginning of Mennonite work in Puerto Rico in 1943. Mennonite conscientious objectors, who were not permitted to serve abroad in relief ministries, were invited to do so in Puerto Rico. Initially their program included medical, recreational, educational, and agricultural services at La Plata and surrounding regions. Two years later the Mennonite Board of Missions and Charities began work on the island, establishing a church at La Plata in 1947. In 1958 both the service and evangelism programs were united under this board, including the administration of a 32-bed hospital in Aibonito. By 1964 fifteen congregations with a membership of 622 had been organized. Of particular significance was the work of the Ulrich Foundation, a Mennonite nonprofit corporation established by interested businessmen in Illinois to promote charitable, educational, and medical work among those in need. This included the operation of a dental clinic. An aggressive agricultural and scientific research program was carried on by the Foundation in its efforts to promote the economic and social welfare of the people.

A radio program *Luz y Verdad* (Light and Truth) is prepared in Puerto Rico by Mennonite Broadcasts, Inc., the radio division of the Mennonite Board of Missions and Charities. It was begun in 1950 and by 1964 was broadcasting a thirty-minute program over seventeen Spanish-speaking stations and a fifteen-minute program over twenty-nine stations. A woman's program *Corazón a Corazón* (Heart to Heart) was added to sixteen stations in late 1964. Numerous other Mennonite radio programs are being broadcast over local stations. Since 1953 the Mennonite Brethren Church has helped to support with funds and personnel the German broadcasts transmitted over the powerful, nondenominational Christian radio station HCJB at Quito, Ecuador.

In addition to these programs and the witness carried on by the Mennonite settlers referred to earlier, numerous new mission efforts were initiated by the Mennonites from North America after 1950. In *Brazil* the Mennonite Board of Missions and Charities began work in 1954 at Campinas, Sao Paulo, and other places. Eventually a ministry to plantation workers developed, as did four bookstores including one in the new capital city Brasilia. An additional mission outreach was also established at Araguacema on the Araguaia River, south of the Amazon. In 1954 the same board also began work in *Uruguay* with the native people in Montevideo and surrounding towns. By 1964 four congregations with fifty-two members had arisen. The work seemed difficult because of the apparent indifference of the people to the Gospel. A continuing witness was nevertheless given, strengthened by the presence of the seminary community. Two city missionaries and a Bible school program for native children became the center of an active witness program carried on in Asunción, the capital of *Paraguay,* by the Mennonites of the city. There was also a mission to Russian immigrants.

To the north the General Conference and Mennonite Brethren mission boards both began mission work in *Mexico* in 1950. While the former concentrated their efforts on the Mennonite settlements, the Mennonite Brethren established four areas of evangelistic outreach, combining education, medical, and Gospel ministries. Considerable attention is being given to the preparation and distribution of literature. The Franconia Conference began mission work in Mexico City in 1958, and by 1964 had fourteen workers in the area. The Pacific Coast Mission Board of the (Old) Mennonite Church began work in Mexico in 1959, and by 1964 had founded three congregations, two Sunday schools, and a summer Bible school program in three locations.

In 1950 the Eastern Mennonite Board of Missions and Charities began work in *Honduras,* branching out from their center at Trujillo where a Bible Institute has been established. By 1964 numerous outposts had been occupied and some 125 persons baptized. A similar work was begun in *British Honduras* by the same board in 1960 and a church established in 1964. Much care is given to ways in which the conservative Mennonite settlers near Belize may be helped spiritually. In addition to these programs a small work was begun by the Krimmer Mennonite Brethren in *Peru* in 1946 both to the Choco Indians and the Spanish-speaking natives. The Conservative Mennonites (see Chapter 12) began work in *Costa Rica* in 1960.

Similar programs have been initiated in the Caribbean area. Both the (Old) Mennonite Church and the Brethren in Christ began work in *Cuba* in 1954, but Americans were forced to leave after the revolution. The former group also began work in *Jamaica* in 1955. The Church of God in Christ, Mennonite has begun work in *Haiti,* while the Evangelical Mennonite Church has been active in the Dominican Republic since 1945, having established thirteen congregations with 355 members by 1964.

All of these programs have had a significant impact upon their environment, though the number of members added to the church is not large, possibly between 4,000 and 5,000 in total. The significance lies in the fact that traditional Mennonitism has been able to

254

transcend its ethnicism in its efforts to be faithful to the great commission, and in so doing has started a chain reaction in many areas
of Latin America where new believers now take. a leading part in
the witness ministries of the church. This phenomenon is only a
part of the tremendous and growing strength of Protestantism in
Latin America in the twentieth century. A well-known Latin-American
churchman has written about this as follows:

The Protestant Reformation of the sixteenth century did not fail in
Spain; it was retarded, only to emerge triumphant years later in
Spanish America. Never before, throughout the four hundred fifty years
of its presence in history, has Protestantism reached such heights of
apostolic passion and ecumenical vitality as of today in Hispanic America. . . .

. . . The old doctrine of the universal priesthood of believers has become
flesh among the Latins, who have as a slogan "Every believer a preacher."
. . . Here we have the core of the fact: every Protestant down South
is a proselytist. . . . [9]

This optimistic assertion does not fully describe the Mennonite
Protestants, as the preceding pages have indicated, but it does
illustrate the courage and determination of several millions of
Christians in Latin America to communicate the good news of
Jesus Christ to their neighbors. Among these millions countless
Mennonites are giving inspiring and dedicated leadership, not only
by preaching to the people but also by living among them as
Latins themselves.

*Notes*
1. W. Stanley Rycroft and Myrtle M. Clemmer, *A Factual Study of Latin America.*
   New York: Commission on Ecumenical Mission and Relations, 1963, p. 2 ff., 83.
2. *Ibid.,* p. 89 ff.
3. *Ibid.,* p. 207.
4. Robert Wood, *Missionary Crisis and Challenge in Latin America.* St. Louis:
   Herder, 1964, p. 85.
5. *Ibid.,* 54.
6. Clyde W. Taylor and Wade T. Coggins, *Protestant Missions in Latin America.*
   Washington: Evangelical Foreign Missions Association, 1961, p. vi.
7. Rycroft and Clemmer, p. 219.
8. J. W. Shank, "Argentine Mennonite Mission," *Mennonite Encyclopedia,* I (1955),
   pp. 154-56.
9. Alberto Rembao, "The Reformation Comes to Hispanic America," *Religion in
   Life,* XXVII (Winter, 1957-58), pp. 45, 49.

## FOR FURTHER READING:

*Mennonite Encyclopedia,* 4 vols.

*Christian Living* (November, 1955), pp. 4-7, 40, 41; (December,
1955), pp. 6-9, 39-41; (January, 1956), pp. 14-17, 42-45; (February,
1956), pp. 14-17, 34, 35, 42-44; (March, 1956), pp. 16-19, 41-43;

(April, 1956), pp. 27-29, 45-47; (August, 1959), pp. 12-14; (January, 1960), pp. 14-17, 32; (February, 1960), pp. 4-7, 24-27; (March, 1960), pp. 12-15; (August, 1965), pp. 20-22.

*Mennonite Life* 2 (January, 1947), pp. 37-43; 2 (April, 1947), pp. 29-45; 2 (October, 1947), pp. 28-32; 3 (January, 1948), pp. 8-11; 5 (January, 1950); 7 (October, 1952), pp. 152-56; 10 (April, 1955), pp. 53-59; 13 (October, 1958), pp. 160-66; 16 (January, 1961), pp. 10-14; 16 (October, 1961), pp. 147-75; 21 (January, 1966).

A. Grace Wenger, *God Builds the Church in Latin America.* Scottdale: Herald Press, 1961.

J. Winfield Fretz, *Pilgrims in Paraguay.* Scottdale: Herald Press, 1953.

Henrique Ens and G. E. Reimer, *Jahrbuch der Mennoniten in Suedamerika, 1961.* Curitiba: Tipografia Santa Cruz Ltda., 1961.

Hyla S. Converse, *Raise a Signal.* New York: Friendship Press, 1961.

Dana Gardner Munro, *The Latin American Republics. A History.* New York: Appleton-Century-Crofts, Inc., 1950.

Paul Erb, *Our Neighbors South and North.* Scottdale: Herald Press, 1965.

# Chapter 18

# THE MENNONITE CHURCHES IN ASIA AND AFRICA

THE PEOPLE of Asia are justifiably proud of their ancient cultural heritage. Thousands of years before the American continents were known, great civilizations flourished in India, China, and the large peninsula between them. Any good museum with an Oriental section will quickly convince one of this. India's literary tradition goes back at least 500 years before the Old Testament and the Homeric epics. The Chinese were using movable type in printing books about 700 years before printing was invented in Europe and have a national literature equal to anything in the western world. The architectural wonders of Burma, Thailand, and Indonesia are accessible to us all through art books and encyclopedia.

Moreover the peoples of Asia have been as zealously religious as men elsewhere in the world. Hinduism and Buddhism, the main religions, are both much older than Christianity and have much in them that is both worthy and admirable. With the emergence of national independence for most of the Asian countries, these ancient religions are experiencing a revival, so that today Buddhists in Asia are sending missionaries to the United States of America! Islam, the youngest of the great world religions, is also again allying itself with nationalism and experiencing resurgence and growth.

The story of Africa is not quite like that of Asia, for here, with the one exception of Egypt, there existed no great civilizations in the past. Most of Africa lay in the Stone Age when Christian missionaries arrived. But Africa has another claim to fame--the earliest human fossils and evidences of human habitation. It was here, evidently, that man first learned to make tools and use them, and it was from here that he spread over the face of the earth. African religion was mostly of the animist variety, that is, belief that all natural phenomena are inhabited by spirits which need to be kept friendly by a variety of rituals and magic. But in Africa there is also Islam which was responsible for the destruction of the church in North Africa in the seventh century, and which in Africa today claims to be an African religion. It has gathered much strength in the last decade, especially across the northern two thirds of the continent, and has fed on that nationalism which regards Christianity as a tool of western imperalism.

The change of the Asian and African nations from colonialism to political independence hastened the process of change from mission to church in the whole of the Christian missionary enterprise. While there was some sentiment for the withdrawal of western missionaries from Africa and Asia, the wiser course has been recognized to be a partnership relationship, missionaries and native leaders working together as equals. Furthermore, the organizational structure of the newer churches in Asia and Africa has become western oriented, making it irresponsible for the western church to expect the younger churches to carry alone an institutional structure too big for their meager resources. Throughout Asia and Africa, therefore, we have today self-governing Mennonite churches, themselves assuming responsibility for mission work in their own countries, and gradually developing structures suited to their needs and tasks.

## Asia

*Indonesia:* For over a century there have been Mennonites in the world who were not white, German-speaking descendants of European ancestors. On March 16, 1854, Pieter Jansz, a Dutch Mennonite missionary, baptized five persons near Japara on the Indonesian island of Java. It was the beginning of the first "younger" Mennonite church. Soon there were to be others in India, Africa, South America, and elsewhere.

In July, 1851, Pieter Jansz and his young wife sailed quietly from Holland without a farewell. Although they knew they were going to Java, they had no idea where they would settle down. After traveling about the island, Jansz decided on the Muria Mountain area in the north central part as a suitable place for his work. Progress was difficult and very slow. Gradually Jansz developed a novel strategy which was put into practice about

1890 by his son. The Javanese who became Christians were settled in a colony because, argued missionary Jansz, it was very difficult for new Christians to live in a hostile Moslem environment and they could better grow as Christians if they lived and worked together. Actually anyone was free to join but all had to adhere to the Christian rules of the colony. The church developed slowly with help from Mennonites in Holland, Germany, Switzerland, and Russia both in missionaries and in money. By 1940, nearly a century after the beginning of the church, there were twelve congregations and about 1,200 members.

In addition to the Javanese Mennonite Church, a church developed among the Chinese in the neighborhood as well, primarily through the vision of a layman, Tee Siem Tat, who was a printer by profession. He began his work in 1918 and in 1927 a separate Chinese conference was organized. Except that Tee and others were baptized by a white missionary, this Chinese Mennonite Church was begun and is being continued without any missionary help.

The Javanese Mennonite Church became completely independent from the European church in 1940, although developments toward independence began in 1928. Almost immediately the new church faced severe tests. The Japanese invaded Java in 1942 and in the attending unrest Christians were cruelly persecuted by Moslems and much church property was destroyed. Japanese, Moslems, and Dutch all suspected the Christians of collaborating with the enemy. But the time of testing strengthened the church, and after peace finally came to Indonesia in 1949 a period of growth and expansion set in. Schools and churches were built, and medical service was again established with the help of the Mennonite Central Committee. Membership in the Javanese and Chinese conferences in 1952 was 3,500. In 1962 it was 8,400. Since 1949 American and European Mennonites have assisted the Indonesian church primarily in sending needed doctors, nurses, and teachers.

Two experiences have forced the Indonesian Mennonites to clarify for themselves their identity and their mission. First, the difficulties of independence as a church and the strain of the war years raised seriously the question about the justification for continued existence as a Mennonite Church. The Reformed Church in Java urged the Mennonites to join them, but at a conference in 1942 they overwhelmingly decided to remain Mennonites. A statement of faith drawn up at that time said: "We believe that God has helped us during all these difficulties, and that our church will now be used

259

by God to do the part of the task He has given to the church in Indonesia."[1]

The second experience was that of living and working as the church of Jesus Christ in the new Republic of Indonesia. One of the principles of Indonesia's "guided democracy" is belief in one great God. All religious groups including the Christian Church are called upon to participate actively in the construction of Indonesia, especially in the intellectual and religious area. The churches, including the Mennonite Church, are given certain privileges by the government in return, as it were, for their contribution to the life of Indonesia. The Mennonites share in the excitement of playing a meaningful part in the building of a new nation. This represents both an unparalleled opportunity and a subtle danger. It can mean the increased possibility of rendering the educational and humanitarian services so much needed today; it can also mean an identification with Indonesian nationalism which will prevent them from being truly the church which knows no national boundaries.

*Japan:* The growth of the Christian Church in Japan has always been slow. The Roman Catholic Jesuit mission of the sixteenth century won many converts, but it was soon destroyed by persecution. When Protestant mission work began in Japan in the 1860's, becoming a Christian was a crime punishable by death. This law seems not to have been enforced, however, and was soon removed. Progress, nevertheless, was slow, but after one hundred years of work, there were approximately 750,000 Christians in Japan in 1963--and 4,000 foreign workers.

The Mennonite Church in Japan is only fourteen years old, for it was in 1951 that the first converts were baptized. The Mennonite Brethren, General Conference, and (Old) Mennonites all felt compelled to send workers to a land which, immediately after the war, was open to the Gospel. Each group located on one of the main islands--the Mennonite Brethren on Honshu, the General Conference on Kyushu, and the (Old) Mennonites on Hokkaido. The Mennonite Brethren began work in the large urban area in and around Osaka, while the other two groups were strongly concerned to work in the rural areas.

This development reflects the general pattern of Christian work in Japan. In spite of strenuous efforts, no significant impact has thus far been made on the rural areas. Even though Stephen Neill, in his book *A History of Christian Missions* refers to the "rugged individualism" of the Japanese, it appears that the strong social

260

ties of the rural *buraku* (a group of households or families) make individual decision very difficult if not impossible. The *buraku* is a voluntary association for dealing with common concerns like funerals, festivals, the building and repairing of roads and bridges, home-building, seeding and harvesting. The religious is part of community life and therefore is also the concern of the *buraku*. Membership is voluntary, but once a family belongs to a *buraku* the individual is practically compelled to conform because of pressure from the other members. Open disagreement with a decision within the group is extremely bad taste and if persisted in leads to ostracism. In the rural areas, therefore, the main obstacle to the Gospel is not "rugged individualism" but the individual's submersion in the group which makes the individual decision called for by the Gospel most difficult. In the cities the *buraku* does not exist and individuals are freer from social restraint. No wonder then that the church is composed of the people who are socially uprooted in the cities. [2] This also means that church congregations tend to remain small because, as in any industrial society, people move around a great deal. Many of these are lost to the church eventually when they move to areas where there is no Christian congregation.

Although the Mennonite Church in Japan is only fourteen years old, these congregations established by the (Old) Mennonite and General Conference workers are completely independent administratively. The missionaries of these two conferences work as partners of the Japanese leaders, and are actual members of local Japanese congregations. The reason for this unusually rapid move toward independent status is that Japan is a highly literate country. Virtually everyone can read and write; many have high-school and university education. This means that the Japanese Christians can take charge of their own church life as easily as Christians in Europe or North America.

The high literacy and advanced technology of Japan also help to determine the manner of church growth. Missionaries do not normally engage in medical and education work as in Africa and other parts of Asia, these services being adequately provided for by the government. Consequently there is a strong emphasis on radio evange-lism and literature distribution--on a personal basis, through the mails, and by operating bookstores. Effective work is done through kindergartens operated by missionaries, frequently leading to the forming of Sunday schools and contacts with the whole family. Work among high-school and university students, often through the medium of English instruction offered by the missionaries, has shown itself to

261

be both rewarding and challenging.

The Mennonite Church in Japan will continue to be a cooperative work, with Japanese and North American Christians working side by side for some time to come. Even though it is an independent church, it continues to receive support from the churches in Canada and the United States. If, however, it should become necessary for the missionaries to leave, the work of the Mennonite churches would go on, for they are fortunate to have the leadership of trained and dedicated young men and women.

Although the three missionary groups included in this brief review work independently and pursue their goals in their own way, the General Conference and (Old) Mennonite groups work together in many ways. They have joined hands in the production and distribution of Christian literature and have sponsored a joint program of Christian witness in Tokyo. Special efforts have been made in recent years to teach the New Testament and Anabaptist doctrine of peace. This has produced a considerable interest in Japan, the only nation which directly experienced atomic destruction. But this is only the beginning. Perhaps, in the years to come, some of the younger Mennonite churches will teach the older ones how to come together in the spirit of Christ.

*China:* Although it is almost completely cut off from its sister churches elsewhere in the world, a Mennonite fellowship continues to exist in The People's Republic of China. That fellowship began in 1905 when H. C. Bartel, a member of the Krimmer Mennonite Brethren Church, began independent work in Ts'aohuen, Shantung province, in the hope of attracting Mennonite support. This work was adopted and supported by the China Mennonite Mission Society, an organization in which several Mennonite bodies participated. In 1909 and 1912 the General Conference and Mennonite Brethren began work with J. J. Brown and F. J. Wiens in Hopei and Fukien provinces respectively.

In all areas of Mennonite work, expansion was rapid during the first few decades, with considerable numbers of converts being baptized. The main methods of church extension were evangelism, medical work, distribution of literature, and education work at the primary and secondary levels. Immediate assumption of missionary responsibility by the Chinese themselves characterized the Chinese Mennonite Church, and the move to independence began early.

All of this subsequently proved to be of great importance since China has had a troubled history in this century. Serious political unrest nurtured by antiforeign feeling disturbed China in 1926 and 1927. In the early 1930's civil war, involving the developing communist power, ravaged a number of provinces. Added to this was the undeclared war between China and Japan which began in 1931, and which became a war of Japanese conquest in 1937. This unrest brought the work of the Mennonite Brethren to an almost complete stop. Then came World War II. In 1940 a number of missionaries were evacuated only to be interned by the Japanese. Others remained and moved into western China where Chiang Kai-shek ruled over what was called Free China. During all this time the Chinese Mennonite churches continued their work of preaching and living the Gospel under very difficult conditions. When the war ended in 1945, many of the missionaries returned to their old places of work. But the trouble was not yet over, for throughout the years of unrest since the early 1930's the communists had been establishing control over larger and larger areas of China. This provoked the civil war lasting from 1946 to 1950. Thus prompted, the Mennonite missionaries moved westward again to establish new work in Kansu and Czechwan provinces.

In 1948, just when the tide of the civil war turned to favor the communists, the (Old) Mennonite Church entered China with a mission at Hochwan in Czechwan province. But the days of the missionaries in China were numbered. Conditions became more and more difficult and missionaries began to go home or to other fields, leaving the Chinese Mennonite churches to carry on the "ministry of reconciliation" in a war-weary and exhausted land. The last Mennonite missionary to leave was H. C. Bartel, the founder of Mennonite work in China. That was in 1952. There were at that time over 5,000 Mennonite Christians in China. Occasional reports received since then testify to the continuance of the church, especially in the cities. It is to be hoped that the Mennonite Church also is alive and that someday soon we shall know more about its struggles and victories.

*Taiwan:* In December of 1949, Chiang Kai-shek and his army fled to Taiwan and China became a divided country. But the nationalist regime established on Taiwan provided Mennonites with one last opportunity to continue building the church of Christ in China. The Mennonite Central Committee established medical work on Taiwan in 1950, at the invitation of the Canadian Presbyterian Mission, and in turn invited the General Conference to undertake evangelistic work. This invitation was accepted and work began in 1954. The conditions seemed to call for personal evangelism, medical work, and literature distribution as the main methods of operation. A hospital, with a nursing program, and a bookstore have consequently been established as part of the total program of witness and service. In 1964, there were just over 300 baptized members united in the Fellowship of Mennonite Churches in Taiwan. The congregations carry on a full range of church activities under the guidance of many responsible Taiwanese leaders, and the church is already largely indigenous.

*Vietnam:* The Mennonite Church in Vietnam began with the entry of the Mennonite Central Committee in 1954. Three years later the (Old) Mennonite Church initiated work in Saigon. By 1964, a small fellowship composed mostly of young people had been gathered. Because of the war and political instability, however, progress was slow. Since most of the Vietnamese men were away fighting, few able leaders remained at home. As in Taiwan, so here English classes were proving popular, and over 200 students were enrolled. Considerable interest was also being shown in the reading room and lending library which had been established.

*India:* The largest Mennonite Church in Asia is in India. This is not strange, since India is the only land where war and suppressive measures did not interrupt the work. The first Mennonites came to India from America in response to the needs of thousands of victims of the famine in 1898-1900. Missionaries from the Mennonite Brethren, (Old) Mennonite, and General Conference Mennonite churches spent the first years in physically and spiritually exhausting work of feeding the hungry. They were faced with the complete care of many children orphaned by the famine. A number of these eventually became strong leaders in the churches.

The Mennonite Brethren churches are located in Andhra Pradesh, and have been unusually effective in winning others to Christ. The (Old) Mennonite work centered in Madhya Pradesh, and later a second field was opened in Bihar, while the General Conference missionaries also worked in Madhya Pradesh. In each case work began at one initial station and then branched out in all directions to the numerous villages of India. By 1964, the total number of members in all the Mennonite churches was 30,000, of which 23,000 belonged to Mennonite Brethren churches. In that year they also united to form a service agency known as the Mennonite Christian Service Fellowship of India (MCSFI), with headquarters in Calcutta. Through this agency they were able to speak unitedly to issues of common concern at home and abroad, and pool their resources when necessary in particular situations.

The primary methods of church extension in India have been personal and preaching evangelism, medical work, and education. Medical work soon occupied a central place, with hospitals and clinics being built, and mobile clinics put into operation. Nursing schools were begun to provide the necessary help for these institutions, and to bring health care into the villages. Special efforts were made early to help those suffering from Hansen's disease (leprosy). At first it was simply a matter of providing food and shelter, but treatment programs soon followed. With the advance of modern medicine, many could experience the arresting of their disease and return to meaningful living. Several missionaries received the Kaisar-i-Hind medal from the Viceroy of India for distinguished service to patients.

It is no accident that literacy is high among Indian Christians since the church in India has always considered education to be one of its first responsibilities. Primary and secondary schools came into existence in large numbers on the mission stations, as well as in the villages. Industrial schools were also begun to teach agriculture to the boys, and homemaking to the girls. In recent years Mennonites have jointly supported Union Biblical Seminary at Yeotmal by contributing funds, students, and faculty. The production of literature for use in school and church programs has also been carried on jointly by the various Mennonite groups.

Because of the devoted work of missionaries and national leaders and because of the strong educational program, responsibility for the Gospel ministry has been assumed fully by the Mennonite churches of India. More and more trained and capable leaders have emerged, so that one can truly speak of the Mennonite Church in India. In 1951 the (Old) Mennonite mission activities became the Mennonite Church of India. So did the missions of the other groups. Mennonite missions in India continue, but now as the joint work of foreign and national missionaries.

The last few years have brought about great changes in the areas of the Mennonite churches of Madhya Pradesh. Dhamtari, the first station of (Old) Mennonite activity, is suddenly near a center of steel production because of the presence of iron ore. Korba, one of the first General Conference stations, has become an electric power center because of large deposits of high quality coal in the area. It has attracted a large fertilizer plant and a technical institute. Suddenly a quiet rural area has become an industrial center.

This creates new opportunities as well as new problems for the church. A large number of technicians and workers from all over India came to Korba. They spoke different languages. Among them were Christians from various denominations. The language used in the Mennonite Church is Hindi which many of the newcomers did not know. How was the church to minister to these people? These new situations demanded the development of new methods. In 1958 a "church-in-the-house" was begun partly to deal with the language barrier, partly to overcome transportation difficulties. By early 1965, four such house churches employing different languages were meeting regularly for worship and study. Each one had a leader but members participated freely. They have also had joint meetings and have begun to collect money for a joint chapel. Because of the high literacy rate of the newcomers the Dhamtari and Korba churches have established reading rooms and bookstores to provide Christian literature. Graduates of Yeotmal Seminary are in charge of this work, seeking to meet the educated on their own level.

## Africa

From Asia we move across the Indian Ocean to the continent of Africa. Christianity is old in Africa, having existed there in some form ever since apostolic times. However, it was limited to the area bordering the Mediterranean and Red seas and did not penetrate into the interior of the continent until David Livingstone took it there between 1850 and 1870. Since then it has been as busy a place for Christian missions as any in the world.

*The Republic of Congo:* The Mennonite Church began in Africa in the Congo in the year 1912, but Mennonite missionaries had been there since 1890. In the year 1912, the Congo Inland Mission (CIM) was organized as the joint enterprise of the Defenseless Mennonite Conference (now the Evangelical Mennonite Church) and the Central Illinois Mennonite Conference (now part of the General Conference). The field is located west of the Kasai River, a large tributary of the Congo, and about 250 miles southeast of Kinshasa. By 1916 there were twelve converts. Progress was slow, for three years later membership stood at only sixty. With an increasing number of missionaries and developing Congolese leadership, it was possible to extend the field. A surge of new workers began early in the 1940's, and by 1964 over one hundred missionaries were working in the CIM field.

In the course of the years the Evangelical Mennonite Brethren,

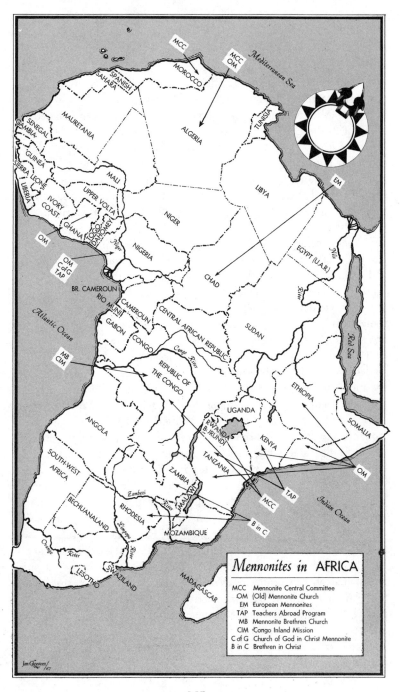

### Mennonites in AFRICA

MCC    Mennonite Central Committee
OM    (Old) Mennonite Church
EM    European Mennonites
TAP    Teachers Abroad Program
MB    Mennonite Brethren Church
CIM    Congo Inland Mission
C of G    Church of God in Christ Mennonite
B in C    Brethren in Christ

the General Conference Mennonite Church, the Evangelical Mennonite Conference, the Mennonite Brethren Church, the (Old) Mennonite Church, the Mennonite Brethren in Christ, and the United Missionary Society have participated in the work of the CIM either by membership or through individual workers. This has been one of the best examples of Mennonite cooperation. Since 1943 independent work by the Mennonite Brethren Church has been carried on adjacent to the CIM field on the west. Mennonite church membership in the Congo now stands at about 28,000. The work of church extension is carried on by means of evangelistic, educational, medical, agricultural, and literature work. A printing press at Charlesville supplies the literature. CIM is also cosponsor of the largest printing press in Africa, at Kinshasa, for the distribution of Christian and other wholesome literature.

Every country in Asia and Africa in which the Mennonite Church has been planted has had its own peculiar social, religious, and political crises. In the Congo it has been the continuing crisis brought about by independence in July, 1960. The problems and anxieties created by independence for the church were many. For some years prior to July, 1960, there had been progress toward an independent, self-supporting, self-governing church. In February of 1960 a meeting took place in Charlesville at which the national leaders were invited by the mission to assume full leadership with the missionaries remaining as counselors. The invitation was accepted with the knowledge of its importance and awareness of the weight of responsibility involved, and the Evangelical Mennonite Church of Congo came into existence. Although there was a definite connection between this move and the forthcoming political independence, no one could have guessed in February how important this action would turn out to be in July and August of that year. When the Belgians left, law and order crumbled rapidly, and missionaries were forced to leave. The responsibility for the church in Congo had been accepted by the Africans in February. In July it was forced on them in extremely dangerous and uncertain circumstances. But the responsibility was shouldered; the work of the church continued, and when the missionaries returned later in the year they found the church of Christ a living, active reality. This was followed by a very determined attempt at communist take-over; missionaries left and returned a second time. But the Mennonite Church in the Congo, strengthened and purged in the fires of civil war and national chaos, is an abiding reality.

*Eastern Africa:* Three Mennonite churches have emerged in eastern Africa since 1934—Tanzania, 1943, Ethiopia, 1948, and Somalia, 1953. Events have moved fast, for in only thirty years the church in *Tanzania* is a free, self-governing sister church of other Mennonite churches throughout the world. Perhaps this particular Mennonite church stands out as one that has grown rapidly through the impetus of a revival which began in those regions in 1942 and which had a profound influence upon the church. Through confession of sin and the resulting establishment of mutual trust, confidence, and love, the maturity and strength of the church was greatly increased. Its trans-national and trans-cultural concern could put to shame many churches of the traditionally Christian West. The rapid growth of this church has brought with it the problem of keeping up a high standard of Christian instruction for all the inquirers and the need for a sufficient number of qualified teachers. A fellowship of 4,000 members is gradually shouldering the responsibility for Christian witness in the new nations with Nairobi becoming the center of many significant new forms of witness.

The Mennonite Church in *Ethiopia* faces a different situation altogether. Ethiopia has a national Christian church which has existed there in unbroken succession since the fourth century. This gives it, at least partially, a Christian background which no other African country can claim. It also means that the government is very reluctant to allow missions from other churches to locate there. The Mennonite Church was granted recognition because the Mennonite Central Committee had begun a medical work which so impressed the emperor that he gave his personal attention to the Mennonite application for mission status. A small church of 250 members is now in existence, and the work of evangelism, healing, and education is being carried on in five locations.

*Somalia* is distinguished from the rest because it is a predominantly Moslem country, and because it is one of the poorest, driest countries in the world. Missions to Moslems have traditionally met with very small success, primarily because of the nature of Islam and because of its traditional hostility toward Christianity.

In 1950 two (Old) Mennonite missionaries from Tanganyika entered Somalia, then an Italian-UN trusteeship, to investigate the possibility of establishing a Christian witness. In spite of official warnings of the danger involved, and the difficulty of working in a Moslem area, they recommended to the Mennonite Board of Missions and Charities that mission work be started in Somalia. The

269

recommendation was accepted and the Mennonite Church became the first Protestant body to establish Christian work in that land. Two groups had begun work earlier but withdrawn. Work began in 1953 and slowly expanded into six stations. The work has been primarily educational and medical.

The warnings of the dangers involved in working among Moslems became tragically clear when in 1962 a fanatical Moslem attacked missionaries Mr. and Mrs. Merlin Grove, killing Mr. Grove and seriously injuring his wife. Despite this setback and a government curb on evangelism, the work in Somalia goes on. There were, in fact, signs that a breakthrough had been achieved and that the church was emerging strongly in spite of persecution and suffering.

*Ghana and Nigeria:* Among the youngest Mennonite churches are those in Ghana and Nigeria. The Mennonite Church in Ghana was in existence before American missionaries came there. It began through the work of a Mennonite layman, T. George Thompson, whose home was in Ghana, and who gathered a Christian fellowship in his home. In 1956 these believers were received into the Mennonite Church. Opportunities for mission work were plentiful, and within three years forty-five missionaries were working in the Accra area on seven stations. A strong emphasis was being placed on medical and educational work, but since the government was taking over these areas the emphasis of the work was changing in the direction of thorough training of local leadership. There are fifteen Mennonite churches in Ghana with 227 members.

In 1958 a call for help came to the Mennonite Church in Ghana from Nigeria. A considerable number of Christian congregations in Calibar Province asked for leadership and for medical and educational help. Missionaries from Ghana responded to the call, investigated, and proposed that help be sent. The story of this help is eloquently told by Irene and Ed Weaver in *The Uyo Story.* As they neared Uyo, which was to be the center of their work, they saw a roadside sign which read *Mennonite Church, Nigeria, Inc.* What a story! Some forty to fifty congregations of Christians already awaiting the first missionary! What a change from the early days of missionary work in Nigeria! But if there was a church already there, the first missionaries wondered if it was a burden or a blessing. For these were congregations that had broken away from the older Presbyterian and Methodist churches for various reasons. They were in charge of leaders who were poorly trained; their religion was a mixture of Christian faith and animism. And yet they wanted to be Christians;

they wanted Bible schools so that they could know more about what it means to be a Christian. On the other hand, the older missions did not welcome the Mennonite intention of starting work there. It would merely increase the confusion of Christian fragmentation further, they said. Other denominations had come and gone; these churches had been known by various names. Now they would be called Mennonite for a while and a few years later something else. What these churches needed to do was to repent and return to the established churches. A lot of heart-searching, conversation with older missionaries, praying, and agonizing took place. The people clearly needed help, but there was the bitterness of long division between Christians. What added to the disquiet and uncertainty was that the Nigerians seemed to be interested more in the social and religious respectability of association with an established church denomination than in the Gospel. They were more anxious about the benefits of western civilization than about being disciples of Christ. And yet there was that longing for schools so that they might know.

It was finally decided to stay and begin work in this complicated and difficult situation. A real ministry of reconciliation began to unfold between these leaderless, paganized Christians and the older missions. Medical work was begun in cooperation with the Presbyterians and leadership training began immediately. The Nigerian Mennonite Church now consists of twenty-five congregations with over 700 members and many more congregations waiting to join. Of the twenty-five to thirty missionaries on the field, only two families work directly in the church. The rest are working in supportive roles as teachers, doctors, and agriculturists in government and mission-sponsored institutions.

The Church of God in Christ, Mennonite also began mission work in Nigeria in 1963. A small church of thirty members has been gathered and efforts are directed at teaching and training these Christians so that they, in their turn, can become missionaries. This work is situated in the western and midwestern region of Nigeria. Literature distribution has been a strong emphasis in the program. Among the Mennonite-related groups working in Africa, the Brethren in Christ became particularly effective in Rhodesia, where they began work in 1897. In addition to other methods of evangelism, special attention was given to education. By 1964 over 20,000 pupils were enrolled in day school classes; church membership stood at 5,060, with an additional 4,030 in classes preparing them for membership. In 1964 also, the Mennonite Central Committee was deeply involved in agricultural, medical, and educational programs in Algeria and was supplying dozens of teachers, through its Teachers Abroad Program (TAP), to many of the new nations eager for their help. Relief help was also being given Morocco, Angola, Burundi, Republic of Congo, and other areas.

All of these developments were climaxed, in a sense, at Limuru, Kenya, in 1962 when representatives from 'all Mennonite groups in Africa met together for the first time. While the conference had been convened primarily to discuss the peace testimony Mennonites could give in volatile Africa, it soon became apparent that the representatives had many other problems they wished to share with each other. A second conference was therefore convened at Bulawayo, Rhodesia, in 1965, under African leadership, to provide opportunity of discussion on some of the critical issues facing the church in Africa. The following five problems emerged as common to all nations and groups present at the conference:

1. There is a growing awareness of the fact that Christianity must speak to all of life and must be relevant to everyday needs and problems.

2. The church is stretched far beyond its means and so has great difficulty expanding. It takes the full tithe of many, many members to support one highly trained pastor. Yet there is a reluctance to ask Western churches for large subsidies, and Western churches are honestly asking whether this is the way.

3. There is growing unrest on the part of the masses because, even after independence, they see their condition as wretched as compared to industrialized nations, and things are not improving. They wonder why. Can the rich Christian brother turn his back on the poor one, even though separated by an ocean?

4. Since independence the new nations find themselves in the East-West struggle. This arises out of their need for foreign capital. Also some non-African nations are still in Africa, speaking from a lofty position of power, and showing that power when necessary.

5. The problem of race relations is far from settled in Africa, and the rest of the world, for that matter. Africa is disturbed by what she sees in the world. How long are her children destined to be second-class citizens, at home and abroad?[3]

The conference decided also to continue its meetings in the future and organized the African Mennonite Fellowship (AMF) to aid in coordinating interchurch activities and to serve the churches when unified action is required. From this and the preceding chapter it becomes clear that the fellowship of the Mennonite Church circles the globe. Its members belong to many nations and races. Some 78,000 members of this fellowship are nonwhite, and nearly all are citizens of nations which have achieved political independence since 1945. This has had its effect on the church. Today it is no longer a matter of home churches—European and North American—and foreign missions. The fact is that Mennonite congregations throughout the world are working at witnessing to the reconciling love of God as partners, as fellow workers, sharing their resources, and bringing to the one task the special gifts given to each by Christ, the Head of the church. Workers will continue to go to Asia and Africa, to Europe and America, all working, not one for the other, but one with another in the service of Christ.

*Notes*

1. C. J. Dyck (ed.), *The Lordship of Christ.* Scottdale: Mennonite Publishing House, 1962, p. 273.
2. Paul W. Boschman, "Church Growth in Miyazaki." Unpublished paper, 1964, pp. 7-17.
3. *Messages and Reports, Africa Mennonite Fellowship,* Bulawayo, Rhodesia, March 3-10, 1965, p. i, ii.
4. The help of the (Old) Mennonite, General Conference, Mennonite Brethren, and Church of God in Christ, Mennonite mission board offices is hereby gratefully acknowledged as is the information received from the following individuals: John E. Beachy, India; Verney Unruh, Japan; Donald R. Jacobs, Tanzania; Chester L. Wenger, Ethiopia; Everett G: Metzler, Vietnam; Roland Wiens, Japan; Marian Hostetler, Algeria; Daniel I. Koehn and Edwin I. Weaver, Nigeria; Irvin L. Friesen, Congo.

## FOR FURTHER READING:

*The Mennonite Encyclopedia,* 4 vols.

*Christian Living* (August, 1954), pp. 30, 31; October, 1954), pp. 11-13, 27; (December, 1954), pp. 14, 15; (January, 1955), pp. 8, 9; (June, 1955), pp. 34, 35; (May, 1956), pp. 4-6; (June, 1956), pp. 6-9; (July, 1956), pp. 14-16, 32; (August, 1956), pp. 16, 17; (February, 1958), pp. 3-8; (April, 1960), pp. 6-9; (October, 1960), pp. 4-7; (November, 1960), pp. 8-10; (March, 1961), pp. 12-14; (April, 1961), pp. 14-17, 26; (May, 1961), pp. 24-27; (May, 1963), pp. 3-5; (March, 1964), pp. 3-6.

*Mennonite Life* 5 (July, 1950), pp. 10-32; 12 (October, 1957), pp. 147-92; 15 (October, 1960), pp. 154-63; 16 (April, 1961, pp. 51-96; 18 (October, 1963), pp. 153-56.

Stephen Neill, *A History of Christian Missions,* Pelican Book A628.

*Indonesia:*

Henry P. Van Dusen, "Indonesia Today," *Christian Century,* LXXXII (May 5, 1965), pp. 584-88.

_____, "The Outlook for Indonesia's Churches,"
*Ibid.* (May 12, 1965), pp. 616, 617.

*Taiwan:*

"The Mennonite Church in Taiwan," Board of Missions of the General Conference Mennonite Church, Newton, Kansas, 1964.

*India:*

Mary M. Good, ed., *The Mennonite Church in India.* Mennonite Board of Missions and Charities, Elkhart, Indiana, 1955.

S. F. Pannabecker, ed., *The Christian Mission.* Faith and Life Press, Newton, Kansas, 1961.

*Africa:*

Merle W. Eshleman, *Africa Answers.* Mennonite Publishing House, Scottdale, Pennsylvania, 1951.

James E. Bertsche, *The Profile of a Communist Offensive.* Congo Inland Mission, Elkhart, Indiana, 1964.

Edwin and Irene Weaver, *The Uyo Story.* Mimeographed account of beginnings in Nigeria. Available from the Mennonite Board of Missions and Charities, Elkhart, Indiana.

W. B. Weaver, *Thirty-Five Years in the Congo.* Congo Inland Mission, 1945.

*Messages and Reports, Africa Mennonite Fellowship,* 1965. Mimeographed. Available from the Mennonite Central Committee, Akron, Pennsylvania.

# Chapter 19

# MENNONITES IN EUROPE SINCE 1815

WHEN the Thirty Years' War ended with the Treaty of Westphalia in 1648, the age of nationalism in politics and denominationalism in religion had arrived in Europe. The meaning of these new forces for the states and churches became clearer by the nineteenth century, particularly also through the French Revolution, which was both a sign and a product of the new age.

The French Revolution (1789-99) was initially a struggle between the French people on the one hand and the king with his nobles on the other. The ideals of the Revolution had strong appeal to the masses and were embodied in the slogan *Liberty, Equality, Fraternity.* They seemed to agree with Christian teaching, but in the French context came more from social and political reformers who based their theory on natural law; since all men are born equal, no one has the right to make them unequal or enslave them.

When these ideals were combined with Napoleon's military and political plans, they brought both hope and new problems for the Mennonites. Persecution by death or imprisonment had ended, but the Mennonites were still second-class citizens whose privileges were restricted beyond those of others in most of Europe. Because of this they had withdrawn to isolated rural areas, where they remained unmolested as long as they remained "the quiet in the land." There were exceptions, of course, as we saw in Chapter 9.

The ideal of equality brought full citizenship to most people, but the granting of equal rights also meant accepting equal responsibilities, and among the latter military service was a primary duty.

Mennonites had always faced this requirement in some form, and had tried to meet it—sometimes by working out special exemptions, sometimes by cash payments, sometimes by hiring substitutes, sometimes by emigration, sometimes by dying for their faith. By the time Napoleon introduced universal military service, however, the first three options were becoming almost impossible to obtain. Some forms of alternative service were available in several countries, but they were related to the military and therefore usually unacceptable to the Mennonites. As defined in the nineteenth century, equality did not include freedom of conscience when it conflicted with the demands of the majority, and liberty was more national than personal.

In 1803, and again in 1805, the South German Mennonites decided, after much prayer and fasting, to ask Napoleon for some acceptable form of alternative service. Pastor Möllinger of the Ruchheim congregation was sent to begin negotiations with him to that end but was unable to even get to see him. Early in the nineteenth century the French Mennonites made five appeals to secure acceptable alternatives, in 1809, 1811, 1812, 1814, and 1829, but without any success. A regulation made in 1793 would actually have given them relief, but it was not observed by the authorities. Some Mennonites were still able to hire substitutes, but conscription left few available men at large, and the cost of paying a substitute soon became a heavy burden also. Some Mennonites doubted the virtue of the practice as well.

A course still open to many was the fourth option listed above—emigration, but many had come to love their environment and found it difficult to leave. We have seen from Chapters 10 and 11, however, that large numbers chose the fourth option. Only one group left from the Netherlands; in 1854, most of the members of the Balk, Friesland, congregation, consisting of fifty-two persons, settled near New Paris, Indiana, not far from Goshen. The large Amish migration described as "Wave 3" and the Swiss migration described as "Wave 4" in Chapter 11 were motivated primarily by these military pressures. The migration of large numbers of Mennonites from Prussia after 1789, and from Russia after 1870, was also caused in large measure by this problem, though other social and economic factors were also involved.

There were other Mennonite beliefs, in addition to nonresistance, which came to be seen differently by others because of the ideals of the French Revolution. Equality tended to mean uniformity; why should Mennonites be different from others and refuse to swear an

276

oath, or believe in the lay ministry? On the other hand, however, the lay ministry appealed to those who had imbibed something of the Revolution's anticlericalism, and to many equality also meant trusting each other—so why swear an oath at all? Most countries were still willing to make exceptions to the swearing of the oath, Switzerland by substituting a handclasp for it, France by requiring only the simple statement that one would tell the truth.

Migration siphoned off those who held most strictly to traditional Mennonite beliefs. The constant demands for conscription and for conformity in other ways nibbled away at the consciences of many until few Mennonites living in western Europe in late nineteenth century were willing to make an issue of military service any longer. In Switzerland noncombatant service became the rule for Mennonites, which had been provided in the constitution of 1848, and which Mennonites felt to be a recognition of their principles. The fact that Switzerland did not take part in either World War I or II has helped to support the idea that service in the Swiss military does not involve them in any real conflict.

In Germany and the Netherlands, where Mennonites were more fully accepted in industry, politics, and culture, more young men have willingly accepted military service as a duty. In 1848, a Mennonite deputy from Krefeld opposed in Parliament a request for special exemption from military service for the Mennonites, when it was introduced by a non-Mennonite from Danzig. The congregation at Emden had among its members Isaac Brons as president of the East Friesland Navy League in 1861, a major general in the army, and an admiral in the navy during World War I. By World War I, nonresistance was largely a historical memory for the Mennonite churches in Western Europe. It was no longer a living conviction. Most other distinctive Mennonite teachings and practices were in danger of suffering the same fate, or had already been lost.

### The Netherlands

The Dutch Mennonites had suffered a steady drop in membership during the eighteenth century. From an approximate high of 160,000 members in 1700, they dropped to less than 27,000 by 1808, or about one sixth of what they had been a century earlier. The Haarlem congregation, for example, had about 3,000 members in 1708, but only 488 in 1834. Even in rural Friesland membership dropped from 20,000 in 1666 to 13,000 in 1796. It was not until after 1830 that the decline was stopped. Later in the nineteenth century, beginning in 1855, but especially after 1880, the direction changed to where they again increased to 39,000 for the entire Dutch Mennonite brotherhood by 1964.

Much of this loss must be attributed to the impact of the Enlightenment on all of Europe, and including the Mennonites. The Enlightenment was an eighteenth-century movement characterized by love for the scientific method and a consequent questioning of anything which seemed irrational, including the authority of the Bible, the church, and tradition. The movement was strongest among the educated classes, and this included the Mennonite seminary in Amsterdam which had been established in 1735. Soon a reaction against traditional Anabaptist-Mennonite ideas and practices as old-fashioned set in among the congregations. Particularly noticeable among the Mennonites was also the individualism which the Enlightenment brought; everyone was free to do his own believing, to write his own confession of faith, and to interpret the Bible for himself by himself.

There were, nevertheless, those among the Mennonites who were not swept away by the flood of Enlightenment thought, though they could not stop its eroding effects on the brotherhood. A leader among these was Samuel Muller (d. 1875), a professor at the Mennonite Seminary and an able preacher. D. S. Gorter, another minister, wrote in 1856: "I do not want to be either liberal or orthodox . . . but only Biblical." A revivalistic movement called the *Reveil* found support in some sections of the brotherhood. Unfortunately the so-called orthodox were at odds among themselves over the kind of orthodoxy they felt ought to prevail. Some of these later organized an "Association for the Maintenance of God's Word in the Mennonite Congregations." Seeing this confusion, the enlightened rationalist was confirmed in the wisdom he believed he had shown in rejecting the church. A prophet arose in Jan de Liefde (d. 1869), but his voice went unheard--perhaps because it was too true. He charged that the Mennonites tolerated every heresy except infant baptism. In graphic language he wrote of a fishing boat driven before a storm and in danger of sinking, while some on board saw no danger, and the others could not agree on how to save themselves. He entitled the 110-page pamphlet, *Danger, Danger, and No Peace,* with the subtitle "A Word to Those Sleeping and Lulled to Sleep," but it went almost unnoticed. In desperation de Liefde left the Mennonites, and nobody responded to that protest either, but recent scholarship has finally recognized what it was that de

Liefde tried to do. [1] There were others like Taco Kuiper of Amsterdam, and Jan Hartog of Utrecht, who tried to maintain a more traditionally Mennonite position.

Interestingly enough, it was the Enlightenment spirit itself which helped to bring unity and recovery to the Mennonites in due time. Some of the increase in membership came from the Reformed Church, whose members were restive under an increasing stress upon confessions as tests of orthodoxy; but it was the tolerance of liberalism which finally brought the Dutch Mennonites together for the first time, ending divisions which had begun in the time of Menno Simons. This new unity marked a turning point in their life as a brotherhood, seen in the organization of the ADS *(Algemeene Doopsgezinde Societeit)*, a general conference of all congregations, in 1811. The growing unity and the financial needs of the Seminary and small congregations were the reasons for its founding. The ADS immediately set about strengthening the training of ministers, giving financial support to small congregations, and in other ways working for the health of the brotherhood.

Although many of the Dutch Mennonites had no interest in missions because of their liberalism, a small group was interested enough to organize the Mennonite Missionary Association in 1847. Many of these had already been instrumental in founding the Dutch section of the British Baptist Missionary Society in 1821 and now decided to transfer the assets to the Mennonites and to change the name, since they were almost the only supporters. They soon gained support from other European Mennonites, especially those in Germany and Russia. In 1851 P. Jansz was sent to Java to open the first field. The mission soon encountered difficulty because converts found it too difficult to live as Christians in a society run by Muslims. The mission continued, but new methods of approach were used after 1879, especially the establishing of an agricultural colony for the converts.

The Dutch opened a second field in Sumatra in 1871. It had only moderate success, and when financial difficulties came after World War I, it was turned over to a German mission society in 1928. The General Conference in America contacted the Dutch Mennonite Missionary Association when it first became interested in foreign missions. Some contributions were sent to that work by the General Conference and for a time the first American Mennonite missionary, S. S. Haury, considered going to Java under the Dutch Association.

279

The Mennonites in Holland have a long history of charity and service. During the nineteenth century they were in the forefront of a number of welfare activities. An Association for the General Welfare *(Maatschappij tot Nut van't Algemeen)* worked for improvement of the school system, as well as for a system of savings banks. Special efforts were being made to care for the old, the sick, and others in need, with some congregations adding social workers to their staff as these became available.

The Dutch story takes a new turn with the coming of World War I, though not directly related to it. During the war three young Mennonite ministers went to a Quaker center in England. The Quakers had experienced a spiritual decline in the nineteenth century and had established the center as a source of renewal among them. Though at least one of the Dutch ministers did not really expect much to happen, they all came back fired with a new idea for awakening the Mennonite brotherhood. Their work led to the *Gemeentedag beweging,* a Church Day Movement. On August 2, 1917, a conference in Utrecht launched the effort, with far-reaching results. A series of brotherhood houses have been built. Conferences, meetings, and vacations together have afforded new fellowship and the opportunity to work in bringing new life to the churches. An active program for youth grew out of a youth day held in 1922, leading also to renewed interest in the peace witness, in missions, in student work, and in other avenues of service and witness.

During the years between World War I (1914-18) and World War II (1939-45), a new direction was given to European theology as the weaknesses of nineteenth-century theology were discovered. Older beliefs were reexamined and put in terms understandable to the contemporary man. The Dutch Mennonites have had leaders who shared in these efforts and agree with much of them. They have helped to check the movement that led many out of the church.

The Dutch Mennonite Church is today the largest organized body of Mennonites outside of North America. One conference body includes all the Mennonites, which number approximately 39,000. Mission work has become a part of the work of the entire brotherhood. A relief organization for "special needs" collects money and goods and supports a variety of projects. A Fellowship for Mennonite Brotherhood Work acts as a clearinghouse for much lay activity sparked by the Church Day Movement. A weekly paper, the *Algemeen Doopsgezind Weekblad,* serves a variety of needs, carrying special inserts from the different groups such as missions, as well as church news and announcements.

In 1922 the Dutch Mennonites organized a Work Group of Mennonites Against Military Service and reorganized its work after 1945. By 1964 the group had a membership of about 700, but with a much larger support among the churches. They hold regular conferences, orientation meetings for prospective conscientious objectors, camps for young people, and service projects. In 1963-64 they built their own camp on the island of Texel.

The youth work has grown until they had about 2,100 members in three groups in 1963, these groups being the Elfregi Federation—the scout group, the Mennonite Builders Federation for club work with ages 12-18, and the Mennonite Youth Union for ages 18-35. In 1952 all of this work was brought under a central program called the Mennonite Youth Agency. In addition they have 8,000 children in Sunday school and 5,000 taking catechism out of a total of approximately 15,000 young people.

A Federation of Mennonite Sisters Circles was organized in 1952. Many of the circles are much older, but they now share ideas and have a mass meeting nationally every five years. As many as 2,400 women from all over the Netherlands gather for these national Sister Circles days. In 1963 over 4,300 women were enrolled as members of 200 circles.

## Germany

The Mennonite churches in northern Germany had much in common with the Dutch and differed very little from them in their activities and spiritual direction. They maintained close contact with the Dutch congregations and reflected the same influences which had shaped their coreligionists in the Netherlands. In southern Germany, on the other hand, Mennonites continued to be a rural people with quite different attitudes and values. The nineteenth century brought more toleration for them, but migrations continued because of military conscription and because of economic needs. In addition to the steady flow to North America, some moved to the east along the Danube, settling as far away as Galicia in Poland.

In addition to the long-standing influence of pietism among the southern congregations, the Baptists also began to influence the Mennonites. They appealed to the Mennonites because of their warm personal religious life and their stress upon the Scriptures. Adult baptism, and the belief that the church is composed only of believers, also agreed with Mennonite views. On the other hand, the Baptists did not stress discipleship in the way Mennonites had been taught, nor did they believe in nonresistance. By mid-nineteenth ) century congregations in the Palatinate were employing salaried ministers, but in other parts of south Germany many congregations continued to use the lay ministry pattern to the present time. A few of these ministers had received their training at the Mennonite Seminary in Amsterdam, but more were trained in Baptist and related pietistic schools in south Germany and Switzerland.

During this entire period the *Weierhof* came to be a most significant center of south German Mennonite life. Michael Löwenberg (d. 1874) was minister and teacher on this estate, also establishing a training course for ministers. He had a vision for the founding of a secondary school and seminary and became a pioneer in Mennonite education in south Germany. After 1884, Ernst and Gustav Göbel carried on the work, developing it to where the *Weierhof* became the largest private school in the Palatinate. It was a boarding school, and also accepted non-Mennonite students. From it came a host of church leaders, and the school itself provided a center for renewal activities among the congregations.

One of the outstanding leaders who worked from this center was Christian Neff (d. 1946). Neff was ordained at the *Weierhof* in 1887 and soon became known for the depth of his spiritual concern and his vision for the Mennonites of Germany. In addition to his pastoral and conference duties, he was an earnest and able scholar. It was he who first envisioned the compilation of an encyclopedia about the Mennonites, beginning the *Mennonitisches Lexicon* in 1913. It was Neff also who first envisioned a conference of Mennonites around the world and called the first meeting of the Mennonite World Conference in 1925, in Switzerland. He was constantly active in historical writing and research, in editing journals, hymnbooks, and other literature for the needs of his people, while at the same time teaching in the *Weierhof* school and serving as pastor of the *Weierhof* congregation for nearly fifty-five years.

Under his influence, and together with others of like mind, the German Mennonites also showed signs of renewal, even as the Dutch. In 1924 a relief agency called *Christenpflicht* (Christian Duty) was organized by them to help the Mennonites in Russia. A Mennonite historical society was founded, which began publishing a periodical in 1936. A retreat and Bible study center called the *Thomashof* was founded near Karlsruhe in 1920. The *Gemeindeblatt der Mennoniten,* a church paper founded in 1870, continued to serve the congregations, and a youth paper called *Junge Gemeinde* was founded in 1948. Support was given regularly to the German missions committee, and through it to the international Mennonite missions committee (EMEK). Mennonite students from Germany regularly found their way to the Bienenberg Bible school in Switzerland, an international school which the German Mennonites helped to support.

World War II took a heavy toll of the German Mennonites. All of those living east of the Oder-Neisse rivers were driven west and now live in West Germany. Their coming added to the congregations already established but also brought new problems to them. Help was given in material aid, in the building of houses and old people's homes, and in resettlement abroad. The uprooting and moving of these people is a mosaic of a thousand tragedies. In the worst days some committed suicide, but others endured and triumphed over despair. Their courage has strengthened the church and inspired many. Together with the aid the established Mennonite congregations were challenged to give, these experiences have brought new vigor to the German Mennonite congregations. Not least among the influences to renewal was the work of the American Mennonites in Germany in a variety of forms. In 1963 the German Mennonites established their own material aid center, had their own voluntary service program, and had in many ways grown to be partners with their brethren in North America in ministering to a world in need. Their total membership in 1964 was approximately 12,000.

## France

The French Mennonites had a troubled history in the nineteenth century. Most of them had come from the Berne district of Switzerland, settling in the more isolated areas of the Vosges Mountains in the province of Alsace, although some moved on northwest to Lorraine, and some later moved to the interior of France. Montbéliard became an early refuge. Since 1912 it has been the largest and most compact Mennonite settlement in France.

Being few in number, and scattered over these regions, the French Mennonites were hard put to retain their faith. They were often surrounded by French Catholics who envied their prosperity and took numerous occasions to molest them. They also suffered because of the wars which swept over their area. While they were not heavily affected by the Napoleonic wars except through the conflict over military service, the wars of 1870, 1914, and 1939 all ravaged their lands. Most difficult of all was the changing political status of Alsace and Lorraine, whereby its ownership was thrown back and forth between France and Germany, accompanied by all the hatred engendered by the wars. By the end of the nineteenth century French Mennonitism was at a low ebb. Available statistics place the number of French Mennonites at 4,450 in 1810. An official government source listed them as numbering 5,044 in 1850, undoubtedly including children. A German source gives their number as 3,143 in 1892. Intermarriage with non-Mennonites, French nationalism, and continuing migrations added to the problems already mentioned. The Mennonites in German-speaking France have tried to retain the German language. Those among them who felt more French than German, as well as their non-Mennonite neighbors, resented the German invasions of 1870, 1914, and 1940. This expedited the transition from German to French. In French-speaking areas, during the language transition between 1870 and 1914, baptismal candidates had to learn the Dordrecht Confession in German and respond to baptismal questions in German, even though the young people no longer really spoke or understood the German language.

By the turn of the century several factors and the work of two men began to lead to a strengthening of spiritual life among the French Mennonites. There was, first of all, the influence of other groups such as the Salvation Army and the Baptists, to which the Mennonites had always been open. The immigration of a number of Swiss Mennonite families into Alsace also brought fresh life among them. It ended those distinctions in dress which had still prevailed, and with it the external evidences of the Amish background of the group. To these influences must be added the work of Valentin Pelsy (d. 1925) and Pierre Sommer (d. 1952). Sommer had been deeply influenced by Christian Neff at the *Weierhof*. In an effort to unite the scattered groups these two men initiated the organization of the French Mennonite conference in 1901. In the same year Sommer founded *Christ Seul* (Christ Alone), a paper promoting Christian living and meaningful congregational activity. Though its publication was interrupted several times, it became a major organ of renewal, with Sommer editing it until 1941.

Other activities followed the work of these two men. First one and then a second minister was employed to visit the scattered families and congregations, a mission committee was formed, a youth committee and a relief organization were set up. Two orphanages were operated together with the Mennonite Central Committee at first, and since 1959, independently of outside help. The two conferences in France, one French-speaking, the other German-speaking, cooperated in most of these projects. Financial and student support was also given to the European Bible school in Switzerland after its establishment in 1951. In 1964, the total French Mennonite membership was approximately 2,700.

## Switzerland

The story of the Swiss Mennonites from the time of Napoleon to the present is quickly told; the effects of toleration on the practice of nonresistance have already been told, and much of the rest of the story is included in the chapters telling of their emigration to France and America. Those who did not emigrate had withdrawn to remote mountain regions, where they developed thriving farming communities. Except for nonresistance, they were able to preserve much of the heritage of their Anabaptist fathers, which continued to make them suspect in the eyes of their neighbors. At times their relative prosperity also caused them to be envied and discriminated against even in the 1960's. By mid-twentieth century urbanization had led to the establishing of numerous congregations in cities also. Officially they are not known as Mennonites, but as *Die Altevangelische taufgesinnte Gemeinden der Schweiz* (the old evangelical, baptism-minded congregations of Switzerland). All of the congregations are united in a conference organized in 1780, which had a total membership of approximately 2,000 in 1964.

From 1946 to 1952 the Swiss Mennonites had much contact with the North American Mennonites through the Mennonite Central Committee which had located its European headquarters in Basel. In 1951 Basel became the location of a European Mennonite Bible school, which relocated to the *Bienenberg,* a huge building at Liestal, near Basel, in 1957. The fifth meeting of the Mennonite World Conference was held at St. Chrischona, near Basel, in 1952. The conference also held a memorial service for Felix Manz, usually considered to have been the first Anabaptist martyr when he was drowned in Zurich in 1527.

Between 1832 and 1835 Samuel Fröhlich (d. 1857), a Reformed minister, organized a new group called the *Neu-Täufer* (New Baptists) or *Fröhlichianer.* About half of his initial membership came from Mennonites in the Emmental region who were dissatisfied with the low spiritual life in their congregations. Emigration soon scattered the new group, however, many moving to Hungary and Yugoslavia, while others moved to Ohio, New York, and Illinois, from where they scattered to other states and Canada. The groups in Hungary and Yugoslavia have grown to several thousands in number and manage to retain many of the early Anabaptist emphases in a remarkable way. They are the only Slavic people knowing Anabaptist doctrine and seeking to follow it.

The groups which came to America in 1846 and later have been known as "New Amish" or Apostolic Christians. Two or three families also came from the German-speaking area of Lorraine and settled in Canada. They have no direct connection with the Amish but in their attempt to reform the church on the apostolic pattern have many practices which Jacob Amman and his followers brought from the same area of Switzerland.

### Luxembourg

There were fewer than one hundred baptized members of the Mennonite Church in Luxembourg in 1964, and most of these were descendants of three families which had come there in the nineteenth century. Several meeting places had been established, including a small stone chapel built on a farm with the help of a voluntary service camp in 1953-54. In 1946 these groups started an annual Bible conference, which helped to keep the faith alive among them and served as outreach center to others.

### Other Developments

*Mennonite World Conference:* Nationalism, especially in the nineteenth century, divided Europe, and with it the Mennonites, but a new beginning became possible after World War I. Contacts increased, and under the inspiration of the historical studies of Christian Neff at the *Weierhof,* a conference of all Mennonites of Europe was called in Switzerland in 1925 to commemorate the four hundredth anniversary of the origin of Anabaptism in Zurich. Attendance was small, with only one representative from America. The second session was held in Danzig in 1930 to consider how world Mennonitism might help the Mennonites in Russia and those who had just left it. The third was held in Amsterdam and Elspeet in 1936, to commemorate the four hundreth anniversary of Menno Simons' break with the papacy. World War II interrupted the series, but the fourth session was held at Goshen, Indiana, and Newton, Kansas, in 1948. At this conference Harold S. Bender emerged as the spiritual father of the conference, succeeding Christian Neff who had carried primary responsibility for the first three sessions. In 1952 and 1957 the sites for the sessions returned to Europe, with the first at Basel, and the second at Karlsruhe, Germany. The seventh was held in Kitchener, Ontario, in 1962, and the eighth was scheduled to meet in Amsterdam in 1967.

From a small beginning, oriented primarily to the pursuit of historical interest, the conference had grown to become a worldwide fellowship with representatives from South America, Asia, and Africa on its General Council together with Europeans and North Americans. Significant issues of the faith were being discussed at its sessions, and members from around the world shared their problems and joys with each other privately, in small groups, and on the conference floor. Without in any way binding the member churches to itself organizationally, the conference was proving to be a helpful channel furthering inter-Mennonite understanding and spiritual growth.

*European Mennonite Evangelism Committee:* Known from its German title as EMEK, this committee was set up in 1952 to coordinate the mission work of the churches in the Netherlands, Germany, France, and Switzerland. It continued the mission cooperation begun among the Mennonites in the nineteenth century, as noted earlier. Particular support has been given to the Dutch work in Indonesia and New Guinea. The French have shown particular interest in the Chad in Africa. A Dutch family was also sent to Ghana to work in the Islam project, a joint undertaking of many mission groups. EMEK also served increasingly as liaison office with its counterpart COMBS in North America, providing considerable coordination of effort on the part of Mennonites in their worldwide witness.

*International Mennonite Peace Committee:* The IMPC was organized in 1936 in the Netherlands, immediately following the third Mennonite World Conference. In 1949 representatives of most of the European and American Mennonite groups met in the Netherlands to reorganize this committee, in order that the cause of peace might be promoted more effectively. Annual meetings were projected and have been held since 1961, an information bulletin was begun, and aid was given to conscientious objectors having difficulty with their respective governments.

Relatively few Mennonites in Europe had chosen nonresistance in the twentieth century. In World War I Pierre Kennel, a French Mennonite, refused the call to army service and was dismissed from his teaching position at the University of Geneva as a result. His own congregation did not support him in his stand. There were a handful of conscientious objectors in World War II, but these were led to their conviction individually, rather than because it was a Mennonite tradition. Active peace groups have now grown up in both Germany and the Netherlands to promote nonresistance and to aid young men in questions relating to military service. By 1964, legal provision had been made for conscientious objectors in the Netherlands, France, and Germany.

*Relief and service:* The European Mennonite relief commission was begun in 1954, as a result of interest aroused at the Mennonite World Conference in St. Chrischona in 1952. Mennonite Voluntary Service was organized in Europe in the same year, although cooperative work had begun earlier with the North American programs. In 1961 a Trainee Exchange program developed. It had begun in 1950, with European and other Mennonites coming to the United States and later also to Canada, but since 1961, North American trainees also go to Europe for a year, working on farms or in industry, or other jobs in which a real exchange of ideas and understanding is facilitated.

*Publication:* In 1948 the Mennonite Central Committee began a paper to serve the refugees from Russia and elsewhere during their stay in the refugee camps and in the early years of pioneering in South America. By 1957, an inter-Mennonite publishing committee was formed to sponsor it. Similarly, the Mennonite Central Committee started a Christian education materials program in 1950, which developed into the Agape Verlag, a publishing company with an advisory council from Swiss, German, French, and American Mennonites. Some financial support continued to be provided by the Mennonite Publishing House at Scottdale, Pennsylvania.

*North American mission work in Europe:* Work in Sicily was begun by the (Old) Mennonites in 1949, Belgium in 1950, Luxembourg in 1951, England in 1952, and France in 1953. Activities were also carried on by them in Germany. Most of the work in these countries was an outgrowth of relief ministries in these countries. The work in Luxembourg and France was carried on in cooperation with and at the request of the Mennonites in those countries. The Conservative Amish Mennonite Conference cooperated with the (Old) Mennonites in Luxembourg but carried on an independent program at Espelkamp and Berlin in Germany. The Mennonite Brethren organized a conference of churches which had arisen from mission work in Germany and Austria after World War II.

288

In review it may be said that persecution had driven most of the Mennonites in western Europe to the farms and mountains. Except for the Mennonites in the Netherlands and northern Germany, they had been isolated from the main stream of history. Persecution and isolation led them to a formalism which centered primarily in the attempt to preserve the faith among themselves. The greater freedom of the nineteenth century exposed them to other influences around them. In the south and east, pietistic influences were strong, while the theological liberalism of the Enlightenment made its inroads in the north and west. Nationalism and cultural influences also had a bearing on their development.

Despite these weaknesses, the Mennonites in the isolated byways of Europe did preserve a memory that might otherwise have been lost. When they were either isolated, or too much a part of a nation, they tended to decline in numbers and lost their vitality. Meetings with other Mennonites and a study of the past stimulated new life among them all. The disappearance of divisions was sometimes simply the result of a lack of conviction, and such unity did not greatly help the church, but when differences were overcome to achieve a larger goal, the unity became fruitful. Similarly contact with other Christian groups stimulated the Mennonites, but sometimes it led to divisions, sometimes to the loss of their heritage. It seems that those groups were most in danger of outside influence which had become formal and rigid in their own internal life.

In 1964, the total number of baptized Mennonites in western Europe, not including Russia, was approximately 60,000. There were many signs of recovery and renewal, as we have seen. Causes for the emerging of new life in the church were difficult to define precisely, but several of these have been indicated. The European Mennonites show that though they seemed at times to be asleep the Spirit of God could bring new life to them in a new age through the influence of other Mennonites and non-Mennonites, through the forces of their environment, through suffering, through dedicated leaders, and through a remembering of their past. The full flowering of this new vigor would become clearer in the second half of the twentieth century.

Notes

1. Frits Kuiper, "The Discordant Voice of Jan de Liefde," in *A Legacy of Faith*, C. J. Dyck (ed.), pp. 159-68.

*FOR FURTHER READING:*

*The Mennonite Encyclopedia,* 4 vols.

*Christian Living* (September, 1954), pp. 20, 21; (November, 1964), pp. 28, 29.

*Mennonite Life* 2 (January, 1947), pp. 8-14; 3 (January, 1948), pp. 12-22; 7 (April, 1952), pp. 56-62, 7 (July, 1952), pp. 103-6; 14 (January, 1959), pp. 19-28; 18 (October, 1963).

C. Henry Smith, *The Story of the Mennonites* (4th ed.), 1957, pp. 218 ff., 237-345, and 464-526.

John Horsch, *Mennonites in Europe* (1942).

# Chapter 20

# MENNONITES IN THE
# NORTH AMERICAN ENVIRONMENT

SINCE MENNONITES came to North America from many different regions of Europe and over a period of more than two hundred and fifty years, from 1683 to 1950, as we have seen in earlier chapters, they naturally brought with them a variety of cultural forms and religious concerns. Their subsequent choice of location in the vast lands of the United States and Canada further determined their development and added to the variety among them. Yet in spite of these historical and geographical differences Mennonites have much in common because of their faith and because they have been a cohesive and homogeneous ethnic group throughout much of their history. The following description of their life in the North American environment, therefore, deals briefly with some of their common experiences and concerns in an attempt to see them in their present context from the perspective of their Anabaptist heritage.

## *The American Way of Life*

Most of the Mennonites came to the United States and Canada to escape European intolerance and persecution. It was difficult for them to leave their homes in Germany, Switzerland, France, Prussia, and Russia but force of circumstances *pushed* them into the New World to preserve their faith. Yet there were also *pulling* forces which attracted them—economic opportunity, relatives, and most of all the prospect of establishing the ideal Mennonite community on the frontiers of civilization. They yearned for freedom without having the vision of a democratic society, desiring only to be left alone to worship God according to their conscience and their tradition. For most of them being a Mennonite was something they inherited, rather than being a deliberate choice made by each individual between several religious options. All members of the relatively closed Mennonite community were considered either actual or potential members of the church also. For many of them non-Mennonites were a threat to the faith, necessitating withdrawal from the "world" with its temptations and sin. Marriage with non-Mennonites, for example, was strongly opposed and sometimes led to excommunication because the new partner was considered to be worldly and an outsider, usually designated by the terms *Weltmensch* and *Engländer* respectively.

*Economics:* From this perspective the agricultural economy was long considered ideal by the Mennonites. For over three hundred years farming was considered to be *the* Mennonite way of life and the rural community the indispensable form of organizing their common life. Initially, to be sure, Anabaptism had been an urban movement carried by men who were fully at home in the world of men and ideas, but under the pressure of persecution it quickly became rural, surviving best in small, isolated ethnic communities. The Dutch Mennonites constitute a partial exception, but they too had a heavy concentration in rural areas. Throughout most of the seventeenth, eighteenth, and nineteenth centuries to be a Mennonite almost invariably meant to grow up in an agricultural community. So strong was this heritage that many believed Mennonites could not survive in the cities; they would either be lost to the church, or compromise the essentials of Mennonite doctrine to the point of irrelevance.

All this began to change in the twentieth century. Following World War II, urbanization took place on an unprecedented scale in North America. As farms became more difficult to acquire and to operate profitably, Mennonites too found their way to the cities, serving in the professions, in business, or attending schools of higher learning. While the degree of urbanization varied from group to group, the phenomenon itself was common to all but the most conservative groups and the Amish. By 1959, for example, the General Conference Mennonites had more members in city churches than in either country or town churches.[1] According to the 1963 family census in the (Old) Mennonite Church only 38.9 percent of 4,139 employed heads of homes were farmers. Another illustration of this movement was the city of Winnipeg, which by 1964 had no less than twenty-two churches representing all of the Mennonite groups in the area. By this time, too, most of the churches being received into membership of the various Mennonite conferences in North America were urban churches.

This movement to the cities and consequent shift in the vocations of many Mennonites tested their faith and moral values in a new way. As tensions increased between inherited values and the common social values of their environment, some gave up any pretensions of having a unique faith and left the Mennonite Church. Others became what might be called *marginal* Mennonites, retaining a certain nostalgic love for the tradition which nurtured them but discarding most of its claims upon them as outmoded and narrow limitations upon their freedom. Many, however, took up the challenge of relating their heritage in a meaningful way to their environment and to the world in the second half of the twentieth century. Some of the most penetrating critics of Mennonitism were among this last group, appealing to the Biblical and early sixteenty-century Anabaptist models in their call for renewal. The recovery of interest in what the Biblical and Anabaptist fathers had really been saying, a recovery in which the work of Harold S. Bender and others played a significant role, became a major source of renewal together with a new interest in Biblical studies.

It may, therefore, be said that the history of North American Mennonitism in the twentieth century was in part a history of their accommodation to the American environment. Sometimes this accommodation was only an adding or recognizing of the values of others around them, sometimes it led to actual assimilation of these values with their own, and sometimes it led to full secularization with a rejection of the heritage of faith. But in part this history was also one of spiritual renewal which made the Mennonites conscious of the unlimited opportunities for witness and service in the cities. In this renewal the threat of urbanization was turned into an asset as they drew upon their Biblical and historical roots for help and guidance.

*Language:* Many of the Mennonite immigrants to North America believed the preservation of the German language to be necessary for their survival as a church. This was particularly true of the Mennonites from Russia, where they had become accustomed to including instruction in the Bible and in the German language under the term *religion.* One of the primary reasons for the establishing of their own schools was, in fact, this need to preserve *both* the faith and the language. A minute of a conference meeting in Kansas in 1879 showed how inseparable the two appeared, when it stated that, "A fundamental religious instruction must be given in the German language in order that in the future our congregations may find resources prepared to maintain religion."[2] As late as 1960, the following words appeared in the Mennonite paper *Der Bote:*

> What will happen if we lose the German language? Our spiritual position will decline. In our churches quarreling and fighting develop and lead to splits. So it has been and so it will happen again. New churches will have to be built. . . . What, then, shall we do? The German language is our mother tongue, the inheritance from our fathers which we are obliged to pass on to our children. . . . We have the important assignment of transmitting to our children the inheritance of our fathers, which is our mother..tongue. . . .[3]

In spite of this concern and protest, the language transition from German to English was in full progress among the churches in Canada in the 1960's, though slowed here and there by the presence of the immigrants from Europe and South America after World War II. The transition had been completed much earlier and without causing serious problems among the Swiss Mennonite groups in the United States, except the Old Order Amish. English gained the ascendancy late in the 1920's among the immigrants who had come from Russia in the 1870's. The Amish continued to use a mixture of High German and Pennsylvania Dutch in their worship services and Pennsylvania Dutch almost exclusively in their homes. With the change to the English language came an increasing desire to see other than ethnic Mennonite names on church registers, and new experiments in evangelism and church extension were common. Membership in the church was coming to be more in terms of a voluntary decision, as in early Anabaptism, rather than as a birthright, but American evangelism may have been more responsible for this than the influence of Anabaptism. The German language continued to be promoted as a cultural asset and as the international Mennonite "Latin" or universal language, but it was no longer seen as inseparable from the historic faith of the fathers.

### Nonresistance

The wars of America naturally also involved the Mennonites in one way or another. In the United States this included particularly the War of Independence (1775-83) and the Civil War (1861-65), as well as World Wars I (1914-18) and II (1939-45) in which Canada was also involved. A study of Mennonite experiences during these years of conflict becomes an interesting and revealing commentary on their attitudes and sense of values as a people. Though no special privileges, such as the Mennonites enjoyed in Russia for a time, prevailed in North America, few of them emigrated but some suffered and a few died for their faith.

During the War of Independence the Colonial Assembly was most cordial in its treatment of Mennonites and Quakers, warning zealots against violating the rights of the conscience of others, while at the same time encouraging nonresistant people to ". . . cheerfully assist in proportion to their abilities . . ." those who were suffering from the war. The same year, on July 18, 1775, the Continental Congress passed the following resolution:

As there are some people who from religious principles can not bear arms in any case, this Congress intend no violence to their consciences, but earnestly, recommend it to them to *Contribute Liberally,* in this time of universal calamity, to the relief of their distressed brethren in the several colonies, and to do all other services to their oppressed country which they can, consistently with their religious principles. [5]

Beginning in November, 1775, a special fee was imposed on those not in the military services. In addition to this all people had to pay a war tax, but many Mennonites refused and it was consequently collected by confiscating their goods. Some Mennonites believed strongly that Jesus would have paid the tax, and a schism came to the church over this issue.

The Mennonites were also often accused of being Tories or Loyalists, and some did leave for Ontario in order to remain true to the British crown. Their motivation, however, was usually not political but stemmed from their being asked to renounce the British government to which they had given their pledge of obedience, which they did not wish to break. Some, perhaps, may have felt more comfortable under a monarchy than under a democratic form of government, but most of them soon were giving full obedience to the new American government.

During the Civil War (1861-65) a system of hiring substitutes was available to the Mennonites both in the Union (North) and in the Confederacy (South). Most Quakers and some Mennonites objected to hiring others to do what they would not do themselves, but the majority of the Mennonites were content with the arrangement. Some opportunity for hospital service was also provided in the

North, but very few took advantage of it. Because of a decline in the teaching of nonresistance in the churches, Mennonite young men were poorly prepared for the war and its demands, and "to judge from the records, many men from Mennonite and Amish homes must have entered the ranks of the Union Armies."[6] Most of these were likely not church members, since they normally joined only just before marriage at that time. In the South the Mennonites had a rather difficult time since they were not only nonresistant but also opposed to slavery. Some fled to the free northern states; others hid in the mountains of Virginia. Some were drafted under protest and decided among themselves, together with other peace church men, that they would not shoot. This became enough of a problem for General T. F. (Stonewall) Jackson to say:

There lives a people in the Valley of Virginia, that are not hard to bring to the army. While there they are obedient to their officers. Nor is it difficult to have them take aim, but it is impossible to get them to take correct aim. I, therefore, think it better to leave them at their homes that they may produce supplies for the army.[7]

Some served as teamsters and cooks for the army. Many suffered hardship, as did the Mennonite communities of Virginia, where many of the battles of the war were fought. It was a very difficult time for the church, and there were many failings, but the church itself never sanctioned participation in the military either in the Union or in the Confederacy.

World War I found the church better prepared and more creative in thinking through the issues involved. Conscientious objectors were legally exempt from military service, but they were subject to the draft and being taken to military camps. There some of the men were abused, and a few died of injuries inflicted on them by antagonistic officers and enlisted men. Misunderstandings also occurred in the home communities; some church buildings were painted yellow, and several ministers were tarred and feathered and abused in other ways. One was hanged from a telephone pole by a mob but rescued before he died. But the war forced the Mennonites to clarify their stand on several issues, including noncombatant service and the purchase of war bonds, both of which were rejected. In place of the bonds a new zeal for relief ministries gripped the Mennonite churches, which led to real sacrifices on the part of many. In 1920, two years after the war, the Mennonite Central Committee was formed to serve as its relief agency. During the war most of the eligible Mennonite men were assigned to significant farm projects, which marked the beginning of the full-scale alternative service program of World War II.

As World War II approached, leaders of the peace churches (Mennonites, Brethren, and Friends) approached the United States government with the plea that no law establishing universal military training be adopted, but if it was that provision be made for those conscientiously opposed to all forms of military service. The Selective Training and Service Act of 1940 granted this request, assigning conscientious objectors to work of national importance under civilian direction. This led to the setting up of Civilian Public Service (CPS) camps where such men did work in soil conservation, dam building, and other projects. A similar program was provided by the Canadian government. The cost to the churches of supporting the CPS camps in the United States amounted to over three million dollars. Overseas relief ministries were proposed for draft age men, some actually leaving for the Far East, but they were recalled while on board ship because of new government regulations and returned to service in the United States, including also Puerto Rico. Eventually many men volunteered to serve as attendants in mental hospitals, where they gave distinguished service and helped to bring about a revolution in the treatment of the mentally ill. The regional psychiatric centers established by the Mennonite churches since World War II were a direct outgrowth of this earlier involvement.

By the end of World War II in 1945, the Mennonite churches were more than ever convinced that the doctrine of love and non-resistance meant for them a continuing relief and service ministry around the world. These continuing services included emergency food, clothing, and medical aid, as well as agricultural development programs, work in the field of education, and a host of other areas of human need. By the 1960's it was almost taken for granted that all dedicated young people would include voluntary service of some kind in their life plans. In 1965, a total of 300 workers were serving abroad under the Mennonite Central Committee in thirty-six countries, while an additional 481 workers were serving in twenty-six locations in the United States and Canada. To these were added over five hundred persons annually, who entered voluntary service directly under their conferences for shorter or longer periods, in areas of racial tension, poverty, and other places of human need in North America. Since the military draft continued in the United States, 6,888 Mennonite young men did their alternative service in hospitals and other self-supporting I-W programs during the ten-year period from 1952 to 1962. Others chose to work overseas in the peace (Pax) and

Teachers Abroad Programs (TAP) of the Mennonite Central Committee.

These ministries were made possible by parallel developments in the life of the churches, including a new sense of social responsibility, more inter-Mennonite cooperation than ever before, and increasing economic abundance. Mennonites had become a rather well-to-do middle-class people, subject to all the temptations which great economic prosperity could bring, but many were deeply conscious of the terrible needs of the world and were giving of themselves and their possessions joyfully and sacrificially. Their involvement with the problems of mankind inevitably brought them new problems. Should a nonresistant people pay taxes for war? Did discipleship mean participating actively in the racial revolution of the 1960's? How should Christians witness to government against war and selfish foreign policy? What might be the Christian answer to the economic and spiritual challenges of communism? What about world hunger and overpopulation? As the Mennonite churches in North America opened their lives to the needs of the world, many became troubled in conscience and searched deeper for the meaning and relevance of their faith, but there were also those who were content to enjoy for themselves the unmerited blessings of God.

## Church Life

We have seen in earlier chapters how the Mennonites who came to North America through several centuries brought with them a tradition of religious and social nonconformity. This meant that they were prepared to be different from their Christian neighbors in their understanding of the faith and from Christian and non-Christian neighbors alike in their way of life. Their rejection of war and violence, for example, made them different from most other people in North America. They differed in their understanding of the church and how it should be organized. They were very much concerned that their profession of faith in Jesus Christ should be seen in all their actions. Some emphasized their nonconformity by adhering to distinctive styles of dress which continued to be used from one generation to another, regardless of the prevailing fashions.

For about one hundred fifty years the Mennonites remained largely insulated from other churches by a strong sense of loyalty to their heritage and by their use of the German language, which was part of their tradition. In the 1840's, a change began which is still going on and which brought a kind of crisis upon them. It came about through increasing contact with other churches and the consequent influence upon Mennonite life and thought. If they refused to admit such influences, they might preserve the faith, but they would surely lose their young people, they felt. If, on the other hand, they allowed outside influences to overrule, they would lose their heritage. The story of Mennonite integration into North American church life is the story of this conflict between the old and the new, the familiar and the unfamiliar, prejudice and forbearance, gain and loss.

*Sunday schools:* The Sunday-school movement began in England in 1780, quickly caught men's imagination, and in six years was found in Virginia, from where the schools spread rapidly through the whole settled area of America. Most denominations adopted the Sunday school, and the American Sunday School Union was formed in 1824 to coordinate the work and prepare class materials. For a long time the Mennonites did not adopt Sunday schools, though they lived among Baptists, Methodists, and others who took them for granted. Sunday schools were simply not a part of the Anabaptist-Mennonite heritage and were regarded with considerable disdain and suspicion, particularly since they seemed to bring with them other aggressive methods of evangelism—Bible and tract societies, temperance societies, mission societies, and other institutions, including young people's work.

By the 1840's, however, Mennonite children and young people began attending these non-Mennonite Sunday schools and young people's activities, sometimes with, more often without, the consent of parents and ministers. The reason was simply that there was nothing in the Mennonite churches which met the needs of the young in the way these new "inventions" did. Unfortunately the young people were often drawn away permanently from the Mennonite churches—"Through this avenue many thousands of lives were diverted to other denominations from the Mennonite Church which needed them so badly."[8] The only answer was for the Mennonites to have Sunday schools themselves.

Four early Mennonite attempts at establishing a Sunday school deserve mention, though none have continued to the present. The first was established in Waterloo County, Ontario, in 1840, in the Wanner and Bechtel—now Preston—meetinghouses. The second, not a purely Mennonite venture although conducted at the Mennonite Church, began in Berlin (Kitchener), Ontario, in 1841. The third was begun by Bishop Nicholas Johnson in Fayette County, Pennsylvania, in 1842, and the fourth was begun in Vineland, Ontario, by Jacob Gross and Dilman Moyer a few years later.

Soon after his ordination in 1842, John H. Oberholtzer began afternoon children's Bible classes. Later he began to use the European Mennonite catechisms for these classes, which by 1857 had come to be a regular part of the West Swamp church life. Another Sunday school was begun in the Amish Mennonite congregation at West Liberty, Ohio, in May, 1863. The man responsible for it was David Plank, minister of the church. He broached the idea in 1863, and with the consent of Bishop Jacob C. Kenagy as well as of the whole congregation, a Sunday school was begun during the summer months. It was designed to teach children the Bible and teaching materials were purchased for this purpose. This is the oldest continuing Sunday school in the (Old) Mennonite Church. This one was followed by many others. By 1875 they were to be found in every state and province that had Mennonite congregations. This was true even of the newly arrived Russian Mennonites in Kansas; before the end of 1874, a Sunday school had been organized in the Brudertal church near Hillsboro through (Old) Mennonite influence.

Most of these early schools met on Sunday afternoon only during the summer months. Gradually, however, "evergreen" or all-year-round Sunday schools were introduced. To begin with, they were only for children, since adults received their instruction in the sermon and young people in the catechism class. Among the first to include adults were the new General Conference churches of the immigrants to Kansas. Only gradually did the practice of family participation gain widespread acceptance.

Opposition to the Sunday schools did not disappear overnight among the Mennonites. A strong protest movement, for example, developed in Virginia. The Sunday school, it was said, was merely copying other denominations, it was not under the control of the church, and it encouraged "Sunday Christianism." This protest succeeded in closing down the schools in Virginia until 1882. Complaints voiced elsewhere concerned the use of non-Mennonite materials and teachers and the accompanying social aspects such as Sunday-school picnics. In some Mennonite communities these were referred to as pagan feasts. It was also objected that the children were not under the eyes of their elders and that they became proud because they acquired more Bible knowledge than their elders had. Moreover, it was asserted, the Sunday school would lead children from true belief and introduce the spirit of criticism of the Bible. N. B. Grubb, a noted General Conference pastor and leader, reported parents telling him they "would rather see their children play cards or even buried than have them go to Sunday school." Others feared that the Sunday school would lead to loss of the German language, and when the schools came anyway, some used them primarily as a German school for a time.

Though the Sunday school had been the direct cause of schism in some congregations, it was difficult in the 1960's to imagine a Mennonite church without it. Numerous congregations, in fact, owed their origin to a Sunday school which had been established there earlier. Mennonite publishing boards put forth great effort to produce good material for pupils and teachers. Many Sunday schools carried on significant service and witness projects in their communities. What originally appeared as a threat had, in fact, become a major avenue of church growth and teaching.

*Other schools:* Attention has been drawn earlier to the school systems of the respective conferences in connection with the discussion of their history and development. All, without exception, were concerned for the education of their children and willing to make sacrifices for it, not least among the Amish. There were many church-operated elementary schools in the pioneer era, but most Mennonites welcomed the coming of tax-supported state schools. Some Mennonite groups, however, and some Amish have continued to maintain their own elementary schools. In 1964, there were 208 Mennonite- and Amish-controlled elementary schools, with an enrollment of just under 10,000 pupils, but it was becoming increasingly difficult and expensive to operate them. Also, as Mennonites became more active in community and school activities around them, they found it difficult to justify separate elementary schools.

Secondary schools, on the other hand, increased after 1940, there being some twenty under Mennonite control in Canada and the United States in 1964. Most of the Mennonite colleges, of which there were six four-year and two junior colleges in 1964, likewise began as academies, not including the two Bible colleges founded in Winnipeg in 1944 and 1947. Most of them also were first founded to train Mennonite young people for work in the church and were closely related to the mission concern of the conferences. Gradually their purposes were broadened to include a liberal education in all that is best in the heritage of mankind, to do this in a Christian framework, and to provide this opportunity for non-Mennonites also. Four seminaries served as graduate schools for theological education, two of them working together as the Associated Mennonite Biblical Seminaries in Elkhart-Goshen, Indiana.

Much of the history of Mennonite education centers around key men who gave themselves to the realization of a great vision, often at considerable personal sacrifice and even misunderstanding. Among these might be listed H. H. Ewert of Gretna, David Toews of Rosthern, A. H. Unruh of Winnipeg, Noah Oyer and Harold S. Bender of Goshen, C. Henry Smith of Bluffton, C. J. van der Smissen of Wadsworth, C. H. Wedel of Newton, and P. C. Hiebert of Hillsboro. There were many others who brought a great love and unique gifts to their calling, but none more than Christopher Dock (d. 1771), the "dean" of North American Mennonite teachers. His *School Management* was among the first treatises on pedagogy published in America; his death at the teacher's desk, while kneeling in prayer for his students, has inspired many of his successors to greater faithfulness.

*Revivalism:* Another major influence of the North American environment on Mennonite church life, in addition to the Sunday school, was the revival method of recruiting members and stirring those already in the church. While revivalism as a specific method for bringing about a religious experience is now common practice in many Mennonite congregations, Mennonites were as opposed to it initially as they were to the Sunday school, and many continued to the present day to see it as alien to their heritage.

Most of the early Anabaptists of the sixteenth century stressed the importance of the new birth, usually identifying conversion with regeneration. Menno Simons wrote a major treatise on the new birth, in which he states:

We must be born from above, must be changed and renewed in our hearts, transplanted from the unrighteous and evil nature of Adam, into the true and good nature of Christ, or we can never be saved by any means, whether human or divine. [10]

His colleague Dirk Philips wrote, "Here the kingdom of God is absolutely denied to all who are not born again of God, and who are not created by Him anew after the inner man in His image. . . ." [11] In its first articles the Schleitheim Confession of 1527 states that,

Baptism shall be given to all those who have learned repentance and amendment of life, and who truly believe that their sins are taken away by Christ, and to all those who walk in the resurrection of Jesus Christ . . . and to all those who with this significance request it . . . for themselves. [12]

Since membership in the church required a radical break with their past, the Anabaptists knew nothing other than a free, voluntary decision on the part of each individual. Because of the pressure of persecution, such decisions were most often made through personal encounter or in small groups, rather than in large, open meetings attended by unbelievers. The situation of the person who grew up in a Mennonite home and church in succeeding generations was, of course, different from that of these pioneers in early sixteenth century and brought the problem of traditionalism with it. Was the child of Mennonite parents to be considered a Mennonite, or not? It was this situation to which revivalism brought an answer.

As a technique, revivalism was completely American, though George Whitefield of England was one of its early promoters in the New World. It began in 1720 with the work of Theodor Freling-huysen, a Dutch Reformed minister in the colonies, and led to the Great Awakening of mid-eighteenth century under the preaching of Jonathan Edwards, Gilbert Tennent, and others. The second Great Awakening swept through the colonies soon after independence, but had run its course by 1820. These movements did much to give American Christianity its present character, with a strong emphasis on individual decision and a personal code of ethics. The movements also led to many divisions and, therefore, new denominations on the American scene. In the nineteenth century revivalism was carried on by two great evangelists, Charles Finney (d. 1875) and Dwight L. Moody (d. 1899), and in the twentieth century by Billy Sunday (d. 1935) and Billy Graham, together with a large host of other evangelists.

Mennonites seem to have come in contact with revival meetings first in Virginia in the 1760's toward the end of the Great Awakening. A Baptist evangelist preached in the Mill Creek Mennonite Church in Page County and brought about renewal. The result, however, was that one of the ministers and some members joined with the Baptists to form a new church which came to be known as the Mennonist Baptist Church. Further influence came through Martin Boehm, bishop of the Pequea Mennonite congregation in Lancaster County, who began to preach in revivalistic, i.e., emotional and very personal manner following his conversion in 1758. He became active in the Great Awakening evangelism after 1761 and was excommunicated for this by the Mennonite Church in 1777. Together with Philip W. Otterbein he founded the United Brethren Church, which later merged to become the Evangelical United Brethren Church, and took a number of Mennonites with him.

These experiences were at least partly responsible for Men-

303

nonite hostility toward revivalism, and it was not until one hundred years later that revival meetings began to be accepted among them. In the 1770's revival meetings were referred to as "the work of Satan" by the Virginia Mennonites, which is not surprising after the tumult it had brought them. In the nineteenth century Solomon Eby had experiences similar to Martin Boehm, likewise preaching and praying in an emotional manner and being expelled for it by the Mennonite Church in Ontario before 1874. Numerous Mennonites, however, were being won to other churches through revival meetings.

These developments over many years prepared the churches for the work of John F. Funk and John S. Coffman. Funk had come under the direct personal influence of Moody in Chicago and had blended evangelical fervor with his quiet Mennonite dignity and sincerity. In 1872 he and Daniel Brenneman held the first revival meetings in the Mennonite Church which did not lead to schism or expulsion. This was in Masontown, Pennsylvania. It was the love, tact, and patience of Coffman, however, which really made evangelistic meetings acceptable in the (Old) Mennonite Church. His first meetings were held in Michigan in 1881. After this, because of his success, he was much in demand. Against considerable opposition he held meetings in Virginia in 1888, which led to forty-five conversions, and in 1891-92 in Ontario, where over three hundred were converted under his preaching.

Except for the Mennonite Brethren, which had a strongly evangelistic character from the beginning, the Mennonites who emigrated from Russia in the 1870's and the 1920's were much slower in adopting revival technique. Only in the 1950's did General Conference Mennonites in western Canada seriously begin to reckon with evangelistic meetings as a significant part of the church's effort to win its own young people to Christ. In the mass culture of the 1960's many saw it as too impersonal and mechanical to be used effectively; others accepted it as helpful in communities at large but unsuitable for use in the typically small, local Mennonite congregation. Some pointed to the misuse of revivalism at the hands of irresponsible evangelists as characteristic of all revival meetings. Such excesses were indeed to be deplored, even as the stirring of formerly tradition-bound Mennonites was to be welcomed. Its effectiveness in winning persons who were not ethnically related to the Mennonites still remained to be demonstrated.

*Unity*: There was a wholesome growth of intergroup goodwill and understanding among the Mennonites of North America since World War I, and particularly since World War II. Among the inter-Mennonite ventures may be mentioned the establishment of the Mennonite Central Committee in 1920, the Association of Mennonite and Affiliated Colleges in 1944, the Mennonite Research Fellowship in 1946, the Association of Mennonite Hospitals and Homes in 1951, the Association of Mennonite Aid Societies in 1955, and the Associated Mennonite Biblical Seminaries in 1956. Much joint work was also being carried on by Mennonite publishers, seen for example in the preparation of the four-volume *Mennonite Encyclopedia,* 1955-59. North American Mennonites were also taking an active part in the Mennonite World Conference activities discussed in Chapter 19. In 1963 this led to an all-Mennonite ministers' conference in Chicago, and to plans for its continuation. Few mergers were occurring among the Mennonites, however. As a whole Mennonites believed that cooperation and spiritual unity were to be preferred to organizational consolidation which might threaten the freedom of any one group. Most of the groups were ready to cooperate just as much as possible for the sake of more effective witness and service, as the organization of a Committee of Mission Board Secretaries (COMBS) in 1959, to deal with mission problems and issues, demonstrated.

With the adoption of North American methods of church work and witness, Mennonites had also come into increasing contact with other denominations, as was seen earlier. Early in the twentieth century this led the General Conference Mennonite Church to join the Federal Council of Churches of Christ in America, whose stated purpose was "to manifest the essential oneness of the Christian churches of America in Jesus Christ as their divine Lord and Saviour." But the Mennonites became very uneasy in this fellowship during World War I because of the militarism of much of American Protestantism, and in 1917 the General Conference withdrew from the Council. This relationship was not reestablished later. Cooperation with other Protestants continued, however, especially in the missionary enterprise, through agencies like Church World Service, and the education and stewardship boards of the National Council of Churches of Christ (NCC). Canadian Mennonites worked closely at many points with the Canadian Council of Churches. A number of Mennonite conferences were sending observers to the sessions of the NCC, as well as the National Association of Evangelicals (NAE). The Mennonite Brethren and the Evangelical Mennonite Church had been full members of the NAE since its formation in 1944, while the Evangelical

Mennonite Brethren joined since then. In addition to these direct contacts at board and conference levels, Mennonites were becoming increasingly involved with other Christians in local communities over questions of peace, social justice, and other pressing issues of their time. At times these relationships seemed to indicate that the Mennonites had become an integral, and sometimes indistinguishable, part of the North American environment, but there were also signs that their witness was springing from a recovery of deep Biblical and historical roots which they were in a unique position to use.

*Notes*

1. Leland D. Harder, "The Quest for Equilibrium in an Established Sect: A Study of Social Change in the General Conference Mennonite Church." A PhD dissertation, Northwestern University, 1962, p. 253.
2. *Ibid.*, p. 310.
3. Quoted in *Ibid.*, p. 113 from *Der Bote*, December 20, 1960, p. 3.
4. *Ibid.*, p. 313.
5. Wilbur J. Bender, "Pacifism Among the Mennonites, Amish Mennonites and Schwenkfelders of Pennsylvania to 1783," *Mennonite Quarterly Review*, I (October, 1927), p. 23.
6. Quoted in Guy F. Hershberger, *War, Peace, and Nonresistance* (1946), p. 101.
7. *Ibid.*, pp. 107-8.
8. J. C. Wenger, *The Church Nurtures Faith* (1963), p. 27.
9. Silas Hertzler, "Early Mennonite Sunday Schools," *Mennonite Quarterly Review*, II (July, 1928), pp. 205-6.
10. *The Complete Writings of Menno Simons*, edited by J. C. Wenger (1956), p. 92.
11. *Enchiridion*, p. 376.
12. J. C. Wenger, "The Schleitheim Confession of Faith," *Mennonite Quarterly Review*, XIX (October, 1945), p. 248.

## FOR FURTHER READING:

*The Mennonite Encyclopedia*, 4 vols.

*Christian Living* (October, 1959), pp. 3-6; (September, 1961), 22-24; (June, 1965), pp. 17-45.

*Mennonite Life* 3 (October, 1948), pp. 18-31; 4 (July, 1949), pp. 24-36; 6 (January, 1951), pp. 16-27; 10 (January, 1955), pp. 45-48; 11 (April, 1956), pp. 61-64; 11 (July, 1956), pp. 104-27; 12 (April, 1957), pp. 19-27; 13 (October, 1958), pp. 169-86; 17 (January, 1962); 17 (July, 1962), pp. 101-25; 19 (January, 1964); pp. 186-87.

Melvin Gingerich, *Service for Peace*, Akron, Pennsylvania: Mennonite Central Committee, 1949.

Guy F. Hershberger, *The Mennonite Church in the Second World War*. Scottdale: Mennonite Publishing House, 1951.

Robert Friedmann, *Mennonite Piety Through the Centuries*. Goshen College, Indiana: Mennonite Historical Society, 1949.

J. C. Wenger, *They Met God*. Scottdale: Herald Press, 1964.

John H. Yoder, *The Ecumenical Movement and the Faithful Church*. Focal pamphlet No. 3. Scottdale: Herald Press, 1958.

# Chapter 21

## *THE CONTINUING VISION*

IN THE PRECEDING CHAPTERS the history of the Anabaptists and the Mennonites has been told from earliest beginnings to the present time. It is a history of obedience and disobedience, of human strength and weakness, and of the grace of God. It is human history, in which by faith we see the hand of God.

Having studied this history, it is in order to ask questions about its meaning for the individual, the church, and the world today. Does the Anabaptist-Mennonite faith have a contribution to make to our own day which would not be made without it and, if so, what is it? If it has vital significance for people today, why is it that the Mennonites have remained a small denomination of just under half a million members in the world? Have Mennonites kept the faith of their fathers, or recaptured it and, if so, how is it being expressed? Is the Mennonite faith more at home in rural agricultural communities, or can it survive and perhaps even flourish in the growing urban centers of society?

Rather than attempting to answer these and other concerns by projecting what might actually happen in the future, it may be more helpful to return once more to the Anabaptists, with whom we are now familiar, to see how they fitted into their time and served the people of their day. In so doing we may see more clearly the issues and possibilities facing the Mennonites in the second half of the twentieth century. Let us do this by seeing the Anabaptists both as others saw them and as they saw themselves as individuals and as a people, placing these images into the context of our contemporary life to see if they belong and how they might be applied. Times have changed, but in doing this we should be alert to (a) the unchanging nature of the good news of Jesus Christ, (b) the sinfulness of human nature, which has not changed with increased knowledge, and (c) the continuing tension between the church as the people of God and the world as the city of man.

### Revolutionaries

In turning to the sixteenth century we are struck by the extremely harsh names with which the Anabaptists were identified by some of their contemporaries, who honestly considered them to be tools of the devil. Surely such hatred must have shriveled the souls of those who felt it and closed their eyes to new truth. For the most part, however, these were persons in authority in Catholic or Protestant churches, or in the state. The common people were not unfriendly to the Anabaptists, unless they were aroused by the authorities. The hatred of officials was, in fact, poured out upon the Anabaptists precisely because they were so popular with the people.

When we search for the reasons for this popularity, we soon discover that the clean living and simple faith of the Anabaptists met a deep longing in the hearts of the people who were fed up with the corruption of the church and the oppression of the state. In redefining the nature of the church to consist of believers only, the Anabaptists were also redefining the nature of the state, since church and state were one society which all were expected to enter through infant baptism. As heretics they were thus also considered to be revolutionaries, people intent on undermining the state. The charge of sedition, of being revolutionaries, is very common in the records of the court hearings available to us.

There were other reasons for this charge in addition to their rejection of infant baptism. They refused to swear an oath of any kind, including the required oath of loyalty to the state; they would not serve as soldiers and generally believed a Christian should not be in government; because of persecution they frequently met at unusual times and places, giving the further impression of secrecy and subversion. Besides this they were extremely zealous promoters of their cause, ignoring all risks for the sake of spreading their faith. Felix Manz was the first of many who died because they would not promise to keep quiet about their faith. When they were caught and tortured and burned, they died as victors, not as victims of a cruel age, confident to the end that their cause would ultimately

308

triumph. All of these signs convinced the authorities that they were dealing with dangerous revolutionaries for whom the only answer was death.

There was a final major reason for calling the Anabaptists revolutionaries. Revolution meant violence to the authorities; the tragic events of the Peasant's Revolt under the leadership of Thomas Müntzer (Chapter 1) and the equally tragic Münster episode a few years later (Chapter 6) convinced them that all Anabaptists were revolutionary at heart. Even the most peaceful, they said, were no more than wolves in sheep's clothing waiting for the right moment to overthrow all government and order; "For although Müntzer is thrown down, yet his spirit is not; it lives even yet, indeed rules in many corners--especially in the Anabaptist sect which was planted by Müntzer in this part of the land--and it has been impossible up to now to root it out." [1]

This interpretation of Anabaptism as being related to revolutionary violence of Müntzer and Münster was accepted by many scholars almost to the present time. Because of this others spent much time and effort in research to show that the Anabaptists actually had very little to do with these movements, and that they cannot be understood as anything but a peaceful movement seeking as disciples to follow the example of their Master. This legitimate goal of showing the peaceful, nonrevolutionary nature of Anabaptism has been reached, but in the process the radical nature of the first generation of the movement has been obscured. They have emerged as unfortunate victims who were born before the world was ready for them, as quiet and timid people who wanted only to be left alone. But this is not a faithful reading of the sources and was not the image most of the early Anabaptists had of themselves. They did not want pity; they were out to change the lives and destinies of people at any cost. In a way they were indeed revolutionaries, and history has shown that they did succeed in changing the church and even society at numerous points.

It is clear that the Anabaptists were peaceful to the point of nonresistance. Instead of violence their method of revolution was love, witness, and faithful discipleship; but this method was already so revolutionary that it threatened the foundation of church and state enough for the authorities to execute all the Anabaptists they could find as a measure of self-defense. The Anabaptists did not have a revolutionary program for society; their message was a call to repentance and faith and obedience, but they knew that those

309

who responded would need to make a radical break with the old church and with society in a way similar to the response of those who followed Jesus during His ministry on earth. With the Apostle Paul they were announcing a new order (II Corinthians 5:17) and like him, were accused of turning the world upside down (Acts 17:6). It was revolutionary to propose the complete separation of church and state as they did, together with freedom of religion, and a church composed of adults who would freely decide whether to join it or not. In talking thus about the church they were, in effect, saying that the existing church was no church at all. All of this seemed decidedly revolutionary, though the Anabaptists insisted it was simply what the Bible had taught from the beginning.

In the history of mankind the nonviolent revolutions promoted by people like the Anabaptists have usually been more effective and have changed the course of society more permanently than violent political or other revolutions. We think of the deep changes over the centuries in the history of ideas, of science and its Copernican Revolution, of the Industrial Revolution and the revolutionary developments in contemporary technology. Revolution in itself is not a bad word but has come to be so interpreted because of its association with violence and because it brings many rapid changes which threaten the established order of things. It is for this reason that the social and economic revolutions going on in Africa and Asia in our day are feared, though they constitute no more and no less than the movement of people in a hurry to catch up with lost time. The Civil Rights movement in the United States is a further illustration.

To accept the label of *revolutionaries* for the sixteenth-century Anabaptists, therefore, means to associate with them a great vision and courageous witness in the face of severe resistance from church and state. It means a willingness to pay the highest price anyone can pay, life itself, to see the vision realized. Normally people resist change today as much as they did 400 years ago. They still confuse the church with their cultural environment and are still unable to distinguish between church and world. Society will go to great lengths to defend itself against those who threaten the established order of things. It is much easier and safer to conform. Whether the heirs of the Anabaptists can in their turn be revolutionaries in the highest sense of the word also, speaking and acting where it counts, depends on the extent of their recovery of the Biblical witness in our day as the Anabaptists did long ago.

Related to the charge of being revolutionaries was the interpretation of the Anabaptists as socialists or even communists. It was believed that they came from the lower classes of society, and that all of them practiced community of goods, a system which they hoped to impose on everyone eventually. Court hearings and inquisitions in torture chambers often centered around this issue, showing how afraid the privileged classes were of losing their wealth and status. There have also been attempts by modern socialists to identify the Anabaptists as pioneers of economic and social equality.

Actually neither of the two charges was true. Research has shown that Anabaptism did not arise among the poor and disinherited and friendless primarily but counted among its members persons from all classes of society--laborers, nobles, priests, artisans, fishermen, theologians, and others. It is also well known that only a small number of Anabaptists--the Hutterites--practiced complete community of goods, and that none of them ever believed it could or should be practiced among any except believers who agreed to do so voluntarily. But they did teach that the Christian has no moral right to a selfish enjoyment of goods while others suffer want. While being severely tortured one Anabaptist said:

. . . And as to community of goods, no one is forced among us to put his property in a common treasury and we have no intention of making it common by force. But he who possesses and then sees his brother or sister in need, he is duty bound in love and without constraint to help and to succor. [2]

But they refused to believe him as they refused to believe the others, and suspected him of communism. Under further torture they told him, ". . . though you say that this community of goods is meant for you and your people only, yet your heart and ambition are far different, in actuality to have the goods of all men in common." [3]

As with the former charge of being violent revolutionaries, so here the charge of communism against them was false, but underlying it was a deep insight into the nature of Anabaptism nevertheless-- that Christians must not attach themselves to things of this world, using them only as instruments in the service of God for the welfare of others. Their persecutors were puzzled and suspicious of Anabaptist indifference to material possessions, an attitude which struck them as unnatural and demonic. In a time when the majority of the people of the world are poor and suffer malnutrition, and when an underlying factor in many revolutions of our day is a struggle between those who have and those who do not have possessions, it goes without saying that the Anabaptist concern for sharing with the less fortunate is a vital part of Christian obedience. Modern Mennonites have a good record of service and relief ministries around the world, but even that is no more than a fraction of what they could do if the Anabaptist sense of responsibility for their neighbor around the world really gripped them as a people. With the Anabaptists this sense of responsibility arose out of their great joy over what God had done for them in Jesus Christ. To help the needy physically as well as spiritually was an integral part of the good news of salvation.

### Salvation by Works Christians

The Anabaptists were also often accused of trying to earn their own salvation instead of relying on the free grace of God because they stressed the importance of obedience and moral purity. Luther and the other reformers also wanted clean living and church discipline, but they wanted even more to have everyone in the church in order to be saved. To them the church was like the ark of Noah, a place of refuge and salvation, while the Anabaptists saw the calling of the church to be a city set on a hill as an example for all men to see. To the former grace was first and last, and while good works would hopefully grow out of faith, it was grace that really mattered. To the Anabaptists faith without works was dead, meaning that the way a person lived showed how and what he believed.

In time it came to where anyone living a pure, clean life was suspected of being an Anabaptist. It was reported at the trial of Hans Jeger, for example, that ". . . because he does not swear and because he leads an unoffensive life, therefore men suspect him of Anabaptism. . . . He has for a long time passed for such, because he did not swear, nor quarrel, nor did other such-like things." [4] Some even considered good works a hindrance to salvation and pointed to the disciplined life of the Anabaptists as a further sign of the work of the devil. So Bullinger wrote about good works that "This is an old trick of the devil, with which he has in all churches, from the days of the Apostle Paul, sought to catch his fish." So synonymous did good works become with Anabaptism that historians have frequently been tempted to identify as Anabaptist any movement which stressed moral uprightness in any period of history. [5]

It must have been a wicked age if anyone who lived a clean moral life was suspected of being a heretic, an Anabaptist, because of it. For them, however, it was not work-righteousness, but holiness brought about through faith, by the power of the Holy Spirit. The first article of the Schleitheim Confession of 1527 speaks of the candidate for baptism as one who "desires to walk in the resurrection of Jesus Christ." Menno Simons wrote much about the relationship between grace and good works, including the following:

> The regenerate, therefore, lead a penitent and new life, for they are renewed in Christ and have received a new heart and Spirit. . . . And they live no longer after the old corrupted nature of the first earthly Adam, but after the new upright nature of the new and heavenly Adam, Christ Jesus. . . . Their poor weak life they daily renew more and more, and that after the image of Him who created them. Their minds are like the mind of Christ: they gladly walk as He walked; they crucify and tame their flesh with all its evil lusts. . . . They put on Christ and manifest His Spirit, nature, and power in all their conduct. . . . [6]

This emphasis on obedience has been described by the word *discipleship*. The Anabaptists were convinced that Christians need not lightly resign themselves to the necessity of sinning; sin could be overcome by the grace of God. Thus their refusal to baptize infants was not because they believed that little children were not sinners. They were optimistic about the possibilities of man and assured of the salvation of infants because of the power of God as they knew Him in Jesus Christ. It has been suggested that they were able to achieve holiness in living because (i) they insisted on conversion and personal commitment of every member of the church, (ii) they worshiped in small groups where everyone knew each other and could admonish and help each other, (iii) they had high standards for the Christian life, (iv) they practiced church discipline, and (v) they were able to keep themselves separated from the evil influences of society around them. [7]

If the Anabaptist vision and witness is to continue among the Mennonites, this description of the church and discipleship might well serve as a model for today. Words are easily spoken, but often mean little. People need to see the love of God in order to believe. Christ was the Word of God made flesh, setting the pattern for His disciples to follow with His help. If the Mennonite faith can produce such disciples, then it has an urgent and continuing calling indeed.

### Bible Christians of the Reformation

In recent times two images of Anabaptism have emerged which may help us in understanding them. The first of these is that they were the Bible Christians of the Reformation. In 1931 Walther Koehler (d. 1948), the well-known church historian of Heidelberg, wrote that "The Anabaptists are the Bible Christians of Reformation history . . . seeking to restore the Early Church of Jerusalem as a holy people, strictly separated from the world."[8] Before him an Old Catholic historian C. A. Cornelius had called them *eine Kirche der Radikalen Bibelleser*--a church radically committed to the reading of the Bible. More recently it has been said that the rediscovery of the Bible was *the* great and all-inclusive contribution of the Anabaptists, as seen in their attitude to the Scriptures:

> Thus, the inspiration, infallibility, unity, and authority of the Bible was fervently affirmed. Yet, they maintained the basic distinction between the old and new covenants; and they did this without denying the inspiration of the Old Testament. . . .[9]

There is no doubt that Anabaptism arose because there were those who believed that the Scriptures meant what they said, and ought to be obeyed. Many of the early Anabaptist leaders had received an excellent university education and had come under the influence of humanism. One of the major contributions of humanism to the Reformation, including the Anabaptists, was its stress upon the importance of studying the sources. Its slogan *ad fontes* (to the sources) led to a new interest in and recovery of the Scriptures, which in turn led to the Reformation. All of the major reformers had been deeply influenced by humanist Biblical studies in their earlier years, but where they insisted that only a trained minister could really interpret Scripture, the Anabaptists believed with Menno Simons that "The Word is plain and needs no interpretation." Not that they understood it all, but they were troubled at how the learned were able to twist Scripture to suit their own purposes. So they became convinced that what was needed was not more knowledge but more obedience.

It was from the Scriptures that they also received their model of what the church should be like. Instead of a reformation they wanted *restitution*--to restore the church as described in the Bible. The church had fallen by becoming a state church under Constantine in the fourth century and could be restored only by returning to a point before the fall. It was with the fall, they believed, that infant baptism, militarism, clericalism, and all the un-Christlike characteristics had come into the church. The true church, according to Menno Simons, should have (i) pure doctrine, (ii) Scriptural use of the Lord's Supper and baptism, (iii) obedience to the

Word, (iv) love, (v) a willingness to witness, and (vi) a willingness to suffer. This desire to restore the New Testament church has sometimes been called *primitivism,* meaning a return to the first or primary model.

It is this faithfulness to the Scriptures, seeking to apply its message to the needs of our time, which makes the church more than just another organization set up by people to serve their own interests. Often the Scriptures are used by the Holy Spirit to bring under judgment the things men do and fail to do. Because of this no great renewal has ever occurred in the history of the church without a recovery of the Scriptures and a willingness to listen to what God is saying through them. The Bible is not God; it points to God and His saving work in the lives of men. Mennonites are not the only ones who love the Bible and seek to follow its teaching, but most Christians still do not read it as seriously as the Anabaptists did who believed it meant what it said about love, peace, swearing of oaths, and other emphases which are contrary to human nature, and therefore, unpopular in any society. But if, as the Anabaptists believed, God is in control of the destinies of men and nations, then those who know and do His will with the help of the Scriptures also serve the best interests of men as they serve God. The calling to be Bible Christians of the twentieth century in the full sense of the term as the Anabaptists understood it is a major challenge and holds great promise. Whether the Mennonites can indeed become this more fully, and witness to its power, remains to be seen.

### People Ahead of Their Time

The second image which has emerged in recent years has been that the Anabaptists were far ahead of their time, advocating principles which it was to take further centuries to make acceptable, and some principles which still seem to be unacceptable to society. One of the men saying this was the German sociologist and historian Ernst Troeltsch (d. 1923), who ended his discussion of Anabaptism with the words, "The whole·movement was an early premature triumph of the sectarian principles of the Free Churches." Among those who agreed with this view was the Quaker Rufus Jones, who wrote:

And yet, as has happened many times before and since, with movements that have been showered with scorn and opprobrium, the conquered and defeated became in the end the conqueror . . . when nearly every one of the constructive principles of the Anabaptists got written into the Constitution of the United States, or got expressed in some important branch of American Christianity. [10]

By the "sectarian principles of the Free Churches" Troeltsch meant what Jones also implied, the separation of church and state, freedom of religion, and voluntary church membership. In contrast to these principles, much of the history of Europe has been characterized by a power struggle between church and state, and the domination of one or the other; church membership has not been voluntary, and consequently there has been little freedom of religion. The Anabaptist vision of a church composed only of believers, and free from interference by the state, was completely opposed to the idea of a state or people's church which included everyone from birth to death.

While these tributes are indeed encouraging, it is doubtful whether the Anabaptists deserve all the credit. Historian Roland H. Bainton has suggested that the principles of the voluntary church, the separation of church and state, and religious liberty came into North American life and thought more through the Puritans and the influence of the French Revolution than through the Anabaptists, though the latter were the first to hold them in the western world. Bainton does not deny the influence of Anabaptism in these areas, but limits it. [11]

Though these three principles are now generally accepted in the western world, they are often perverted or not put into practice. Freedom of religion, for example, has frequently come to mean freedom *from* religion or the right to make decisions about faith without asking anyone about it; "what I believe is my business." In many churches practicing adult baptism, and including many Mennonite congregations, young people do not really make a free and voluntary decision to be baptized and join the church; they do this because they are "old enough," or because their friends do, or because their parents did and want them to do so also, or because they belong to a certain social class in society and conform to its demands. Similarly it is becoming difficult to keep the demands of the church separate from the demands of the state— in business, in paying taxes, in time of war—even though the courts are constantly alert to these problems.

A great and exciting contribution can be made to church and society by Christians who seriously believe these principles to be true, and work to put them into practice. To believe in separation of church and state then means, for example, to witness prophetically to government in word and deed; to believe in freedom of religion then means to love those who believe differently and those who do not believe, while at the same time witnessing to them about the power of God in one's own life; to believe in voluntary church membership at the local level and be done with traditionalism. Innumerable other implications arise from serious belief in the truth and importance of these three principles. Will Mennonites today recapture the initiative of the Anabaptists in these areas? There are some signs of hope.

## What Shall We Do with It?

Now that we have considered some of the possibilities of recapturing in a new way the vision of the Anabaptists of the sixteenth century, what shall we do with it? There seem to be at least five choices before us, in addition to a variety of combinations of several of them:

*First,* we can choose to do nothing with it if we are Mennonites. Since a Mennonite has traditionally been defined as one who is born into a Mennonite family, there is really nothing those who are so born can or ought to do about it. Being a traditional Mennonite has become quite respectable by now—Mennonites have the reputation of being good farmers and honest businessmen. If difficult questions are asked about the faith, we can always quote a text, or say that this is what our church teaches, without really knowing much about it ourselves. If non-ethnic Mennonites join the church occasionally, they simply confirm what we have known all along—that we have been right for over four hundred years and that our faith is too demanding for most people to accept!

*Second,* we have the choice of rejecting the claims of this history upon us as meaningless and irrelevant to our day and age. While the accounts of faith and martyrdom inspire us, these are all history. As a faith Mennonitism is then considered quaint and unrealistic, hopelessly outdated in a time which talks of cybernetics and the death of God. But since it takes a good deal of courage to announce publicly that one is rejecting the faith, and raises a lot of fuss, a simpler way is to limit and finally avoid participation in the life of the church and drift away little by little.

*Third,* we can acknowledge the great contribution of the Anabaptist-Mennonite tradition to church and society, but also feel that the time has come to let Mennonitism die—either by changing the name to something more acceptable in our culture, or by becoming nondenominational Christians, or by merging with other Christians as part of the ecumenical movement among the churches. Such choices might be motivated by a feeling of sacrifice, or inferiority, or simply frustration with the organized church and a desire to get rid of all the traditionalism by starting over. If such a new beginning is made in small groups, discipline could become possible, and one might hope to prevent the old hardening of the arteries from repeating itself.

*Fourth,* in frustration over the sad state of the church as we may know it, we can select some period of the past, either in Anabaptist or earlier history, as the *Golden Age* and spend our time talking about how wonderful it would be if everyone would catch that vision of the church. All the while, however, we would continue to be conscious of the humanness of people even in the church of Christ, and we would recall the impossibility of turning back the pages of history to reproduce the past. Positively, the holding up of such a model for the church to imitate would remind Christians of their high calling in Christ; negatively, it could become an excuse for not becoming involved in the life and work of the church.

*Fifth,* we can choose the Anabaptist-Mennonite heritage as the faith which seems to us to be a most faithful interpretation of the Biblical message and by making it truly our own, testify to its truth and power in word and deed. The glory and obedience of the fathers then becomes our history also, as does their stumbling and disobedience. In studying them we learn to understand ourselves better and become more able to discern where we are going, both as individuals and as a church. Instead of seeking to start all over with the church we begin where we are. By accepting our past we become free to change, adapt, and relate in new ways to the needs of our time without being bound by traditionalism on the one hand, or by the emotional effects of rejecting the heritage. This choice means we then have nothing to defend--neither ourselves nor the church, nor a rejection of the church nor even the Gospel; we have then only to testify to the power of Jesus Christ in the past and in our own living experience.

*Notes*

1. Justus Menius, *Von dem Geist der Wiederteuffer* (1544), quoted in Franklin H. Littell, *The Anabaptist View of the Church.* Second edition. Boston: Starr King Press, 1958, p. 145. Reprinted as *The Sectarian Origins of Protestantism.* New York: The Macmillan Co.
2. *Quellen* II, p. 238, quoted in Leonard Verduin, *The Reformers and Their Stepchildren.* Grand Rapids: Wm. B. Eerdmans Publishing Co., 1964, p. 235. Used by permission.
3. *Ibid.* Used by permission.
4. *Ibid.,* pp. 108-9. Used by permission.
5. For example the work of Albrecht Ritschl (d. 1889) on Pietism, Ludwig Keller (d. 1915) on old evangelical brotherhoods, and the recent work by Leonard Verduin, *The Reformers and Their Stepchildren.*
6. Menno Simons, *Complete Works* (1956), quoted in Harold S. Bender, "Walking in the Resurrection," *Mennonite Quarterly Review,* XXXV (April, 1961), p. 100.
7. *Ibid.,* pp. 108-9.
8. *Die Religion in Geschichte und Gegenwart* (1931), 5:1916-17.
9. Donovan E. Smucker, "The Theological Triumph of the Early Anabaptist-Mennonites," *Mennonite Quarterly Review,* XIX (January, 1945), p. 10.
10. *Mysticism and Democracy in the English Commonwealth.* Cambridge: Harvard University Press, 1932, pp. 32, 33.
11. "The Anabaptist Contribution to History," in *The Recovery of the Anabaptist Vision,* Guy F. Hershberger, ed. Herald Press, 1957, pp. 317-26.

*FOR FURTHER READING:*

The Mennonite Encyclopedia, 4 vols.

*Christian Living* (January, 1955), pp. 14, 15; (February, 1955), pp. 8, 9; (May, 1955), pp. 6, 7; (November, 1956), pp. 6, 7; (June, 1964), pp. 26-28.

*Mennonite Life* 6 (October, 1951), pp. 21-38; 9 (April, 1954), pp. 83-90; 10 (October, 1955), pp. 147-49; 14 (October, 1959), pp. 160-63; 17 (April, 1962); 19 (January, 1964), pp. 36-39; 19 (April, 1964); 19 (July, 1964); 20 (April, 1965).

*Studies in Church Discipline.* Newton: Mennonite Publication Office, 1958.

C. J. Dyck, *They Gave Themselves.* Newton: Faith and Life Press, 1964.

LeRoy Kennel, *Mennonites: Who and Why.* Scottdale: Mennonite Publishing House, 1963.

# Index